Indian Voices

Indian Voices

Listening to Native Americans

ALISON OWINGS

RUTGERS UNIVERSITY PRESS
NEW BRUNSWICK, NEW JERSEY, AND LONDON

Library of Congress Cataloging-in-Publication Data

Owings, Alison.
Indian voices : listening to Native Americans / Alison Owings.
    p. cm.
Includes bibliographical references and index.
ISBN 978–0–8135–4965–1 (hardcover : alk. paper)
    1. Indians of North America—Ethnic identity.   2. Indians of North America—Social
conditions.   3. Indians of North America—Cultural assimilation.   4. Indians,
Treatment of—North America.   5. Indians of North America—Biography.   I. Title.
E98.E85O85   2011
970.004'97—dc22

                                                                            2010028683

A British Cataloging-in-Publication record for this book is available from the British
Library.

Visit our Web site: http://rutgerspress.rutgers.edu

Manufactured in the United States of America

For those who talked and trusted
And again, for Jonathan

"It's a lot to grasp."

—*Louise Erdrich on the subject of*
contemporary Native American life

Contents

Preface

Let me start with my own ignorance.

While driving in rural Arizona for the first time, a road sign shocked me so much I did not know whether to brake, turn around, or look for a toll booth.

As I recall, the sign read, "You are Entering the Navajo Nation."

I am? I thought. Nobody is stopping me? I'm allowed? Ever since childhood I had felt American to my core, almost primevally American, but for the first time within these United States I felt intrusive. After stopping to look at my map and realizing that to turn back was unwise, I drove on into, then eventually out of, the Navajo Nation.

Later, taking stock of my ignorance, I tried to equate it with innocence. As a non-Native New Jersey schoolchild far from known Native influences, my education on the subject was cursory: Pocahontas was heroic, a scout could walk down a trail silently, and Indians used every part of a buffalo. (Not always, I later learned.)

From schoolgirlhood to the Navajo Reservation sign, I was all but Native-less in consciousness, but for only a few things I can point to. One is an eighth-grade report I unearthed titled Whiteman (spelled out with rifles and bullets) vs. Indian (spelled out with bows and arrows). In one corner of the cover, a smiling Indian stands by an intact teepee (as we spelled it); beside him is a frowning Pilgrim, his home burned to the ground. "Before," I labeled that. In the opposite corner I had drawn a coonskin-hatted Davy Crockett–type man smiling by his intact cabin, while a frowning Indian stands beside a smoldering teepee. "After." The text (which my teacher critiqued as "factually accurate and written in an easy style that I trust is yours") included this passage about Whiteman vs. Indian wars. "The Indians, seemingly inferior, really had the best excuses. For why shouldn't they?" On the last page, my pictorial summary went from "This is the land the Great Spirit gave us before the palefaces came," to "We take the trail of tears as the white man pushes west," and concluded, "Working at the arts of our fathers, we keep alive our Indian memories." Americans love happy endings.

In my education effluvia I also found a long-forgotten report I wrote as a college sophomore for an economics class. "The Economic Situation of the Contemporary American Indian." As embarrassing as my (then) contention that reservations should be terminated was realizing that I had entirely forgotten several basic historical facts I had so carefully typed upon Eaton's Corrasable Bond. The work ("represents thought," critiqued the professor) was written in prose properly labeled sophomoric. "What they [American Indians] have given us is immeasurable and what we have done in return has little ethical justification." What good are such spurts of documentable and empathetic interest about Native Americana, however, if neither remained in my memory?

Then came a pair of events that galvanized Native America and at the very least startled non-Native America enough to stay in our collective memory: the 1969 takeover by Native activists of Alcatraz Island in San Francisco Bay and the 1973 confrontation at Wounded Knee on the Pine Ridge Reservation in South Dakota. When each ended, though, so did much non-Native attention, including, yet again, mine.

Then came Arizona. It was the site of one of many research road trips I was making around the country for a book about American classism as revealed through waitressing. This trip resembled others (lots of driving, lots of voluble waitresses), except for the inadvertent detour through the Navajo Nation. Not only did I feel ignorant but abashed. It so happened that I was on my way to find a waitress of the Tohono O'odham Nation in southern Arizona to interview. Obviously, I knew nothing of Native America, but I did know that when most people picture "waitress," they do not picture a Native American. At least I could skew that stereotype.

Then, during a stopover in Tucson, a staff member at a museum warned me that "those people" (the Tohono O'odham) will never talk to an outsider. Hmm, "those people." Another stereotype beckoned. Within hours, during the post-lunch lull at a reservation café in Sells, a Tohono O'odham waitress was talking candidly to me about her work and recounting extremely personal information. Later, as I put together her story (omitting at her request and my regret much of that personal information, and giving her a pseudonym), I romanticized her a bit. Her bearing alone dazzled me.

In writing about her, I remembered various Native people going about their business at the café and along the streets of Sells. I remembered visiting a shop whose proprietor had gone to Stanford University, where she studied under a professor I knew. I remembered driving around the reservation to get a feel for it and seeing a lone tourist taking pictures of a woman making tortillas, and the tortilla maker looking annoyed. I remembered watching Tohono O'odham employees at the tribal casino outside Tucson and being struck by their laughter amid a grim-seeming clientele. My limited views into their everyday lives made me wonder about their views from the inside out. What did they see? What did other Native people see?

Once the waitress book was finished, I began reading widely and wildly about Native Americans. My goal was not only to slay my ignorance but to find out—every writer's concern—if someone had written "my" book, however inchoate it was? The reading loomed endlessly. Native scholar Donald Fixico confirmed that some 40,000 volumes exist about Native Americans. Thanks to him, to various librarians, and to assiduous Web searching, I concluded that of the 40,000 volumes, none involves a wide array of Native people across America discussing their lives today.

That settled, I continued reading, talked with and met a number of Native people through friends and various endeavors, and realized this project was the most complex I had ever undertaken. Even belatedly starting a card file threw me. How should I arrange the names and business cards of contacts? Kirk Francis, tribal chief of the Penobscot Nation. Under F or P? Or M for Maine? Deanne Meetze, administrative analyst, Morongo Band of Mission Indians. Under Meetze or with three other Morongo cards? What about Ed Ironcloud and Kevin Killer? (The Lakota got "the cool names," I heard

Sherman Alexie say with mock jealousy.) Should Ed be filed under I for Ironcloud, L for Lakota, P for Pine Ridge? For Kevin, K? O for Oglala Lakota College, which was on his card. S for South Dakota? Or both under I for INDN's List, which sponsored the conference where I met them?

Organizing books was even harder. After buying dozens and dozens, new and old, it was imperative to arrange them, but how? My solution is imperfect. One section goes alphabetically by tribe, starting with *Apache Reservation, Apache Voices,* and *Women of the Apache.* Another section contains more or less sociological histories, another arty coffee table–type volumes I must store sideways and therefore overlook when scanning titles. Novels go together. So do biographies and oral histories. Finally, there is a section of often-consulted overviews, including Fergus M. Bordewich's *Killing the White Man's Indian,* Vine DeLoria Jr.'s *Custer Died for Your Sins,* Peter Nabokov's *Native American Testimony,* Jake Page's *In the Hands of the Great Spirit,* and a book I had to buy, Devon Abbott Mihesuah's *So You Want to Write about American Indians?*

Early in the reading, my ignorance increasingly appalled me. It is painful to give examples, but I know I was, and am, not alone. The phrase that struck me from several books was "boarding schools," as in many Native children going to. Wow, I thought, with visions of Andover, Choate, and other fancy places. A lot of families must have been better off than I realized.

"You're kidding!" a young Native man recently exclaimed when I confessed this.

I wish I were, but no. I knew nothing about the practice, from the mid-1800s to the first decades of the twentieth century, of taking tens of thousands of Native children from their families to military-type boarding schools, sometimes thousands of miles away, and for years, to be "civilized," meaning, for starters, to be stripped of their hair, their clothes, their beliefs, their language, and their culture, including, when possible, their prayers. Some children, urged by their families, went voluntarily, perhaps because before World War II many U.S. public schools would not enroll Native children.[1] Most children, though, went under duress.

I learned it was army officer Richard Henry Pratt, founder of the infamous Native boarding school in Carlisle, Pennsylvania, who coined the infamous dictum "Kill the Indian, but Save the Man."[2] What a motto for a homesick child to live under. Even if Pratt and others were well-meaning, instances and varieties of abuse are still the stuff of family sagas. Photographs of boarding school cemeteries do not lessen the sense of misery. Then, imagine "civilized" graduates going home to families whose language they no longer spoke. I knew nothing of this.

Nor did I know much about governmental acts and policies meant to aid assimilation—or, as such acts also are called, cultural genocide. I had not even heard of (or, ahem, remembered) the despised Dawes Act of 1887 (also known as the General Allotment Act) that decimated Native lands and that resonates among Native people today as if it happened yesterday. There was so much I did not know. I did not know that many non-Natives live on reservations, nor that a majority of Native people live off reservations. I did not know that in traditional Native societies, homosexuals were accepted and sometimes honored for their differences. I did not know that Native American men seldom go bald. I did not know that many Native people spend an inordinate amount of time driving, mostly to visit one another. And, I had no idea that Native Americans are known—among one another—for their great sense of humor.

Was my ignorance a part of living an "all-American" Eurocentric life? If my relative, Jason M. Case, had not been a drummer boy with the 8th Regiment of the Connecticut Volunteers, would I have known less, cared less, read less, about slavery and the Civil War? If he had been a Cheyenne, would I at least have known about the Dawes Act?

With many questions unanswered, the biggest was this: Would people whose lives were changed irrevocably by the likes of my people, talk to me? I set out, nervous for being nervy. The old joke did not help. How many people are in an Indian family? Five. Two parents, two children, and an anthropologist.

By now, I also knew that Native people were celebrated for their strong oral traditions. Anglo stranger trots up, microphone in hand, to conduct, more or less, an oral history? Was it coals to Newcastle or a coal smote in the eye?

Both nervy and naïve, and as polite as I knew how to be (which proved no match for Native courtesy), I wended my way across the country in trips both exhausting and exhilarating. My sole criteria were that each interviewee identify as a Native person and speak candidly. Those who responded to my quest and questions did so with varying mixtures of frankness, suspicion, patience, generosity, hospitality, and, usually, humor.

In seeking the widest variety of people I could find, I happened upon several commonalities. Most interviewees had emotional ties to specific areas of land. A majority of interviewees were all too familiar with alcoholism. Almost all I met happened to have jobs relating to tribal life. Since the interviews, the situations of a number of interviewees have changed, especially regarding jobs. In most cases, I did not update the information but presented each account as true at the time we met.

As I neared the book's end, too many years after I began, a final organizational challenge arose: how to arrange the chapters. Staring at my study walls covered in Indian-iana, including maps, a solution hit me. The chapters would unfold east to west, the direction in which the settlers/conquerors/invaders had moved. This plan, too, was imperfect. The English, French, and Spanish took different routes at different times. Also, an interviewee might come from one place, work in another, and consider home yet another. Nonetheless, more or less east to west it is, from a Passamaquoddy blueberry harvester in Maine to a Hawai'ian chanter on Kauai. The last inclusion may be controversial but will be explained. And a little aloha is always a nice farewell.

Although every interviewee knew more about past and present Native life than I ever could, it became apparent, mostly during informal conversations, that Native people in one part of the country often knew little about those in another. The wildly popular dugout canoe event in the northwest? News to tribal members in the northeast. The existence of the Lumbees of North Carolina? The practices of the Haudenosaunee in New York? News to tribal members in the southwest. In lieu of the legendary "moccasin telegraph," I felt privileged to convey such tidings.

Meanwhile, the more my ignorance faded, the more I was aware of the alarming evidence of ignorance among other non-Natives. Numerous examples came down to the shock that Native Americans are part of contemporary society.

At some point, I also became aware that fellow non-Natives (or nons, as I sometimes think of us) were, if ignorant about Native life, also timid and self-conscious about possible encounters with Native people. The clue question, asked as if a mistake hovers, is, "What do you call them?" (How many books include a note about whether the author has opted to use Native American or American Indian?) My answer: as an outsider of perhaps overly delicate tendencies, I virtually always write or say Native American. Sure, I know that Native Americans generally refer to each other as Indians. But I'm not one. I also learned, through Donald Fixico of Arizona State University, that "American Indians is also a tough phrase, but is an effort on the part of Indians to claim ownership to the word 'Indian' and make it theirs." Surely this is the impulse behind newer cooler versions, like Indianz and NDNs. Bureaucracy may have the final locution; a Lakota friend reports that the federal government has introduced the phrase "Native American Indian."

Other questions from fellow nons implied anxiety. "What would I say to . . . ?" "Do they mind if . . . ?" Some tiptoeing may be a screen for guilt. A staff member at the Museum of the American Indian told me that the guides, all Native people, sometimes are tearfully embraced by visitors who weep about "what my people did to your people." Tip: Do not do that.

Such awkwardness may indicate that most Americans have never knowingly met a Native American. The gap is felt both ways.

———

Over dinner at a Vietnamese-American-run Greek-American restaurant in a largely Spanish-speaking section of Albuquerque, a Native American woman with the glorious name Randella Bluehouse shook her head and sighed. "We're invisible."

This was not the first time Randella had told me these exact words, nor the first time they gave me a start. She is young, raven-haired, a bit plump, and beautiful. How could Randella Bluehouse be invisible? Furthermore, she is a member of the Navajo Nation, which in terms of reservation size and population is the biggest in this country. How could it be invisible?

By then, I knew she meant a wider invisibility, one within everyday American awareness. Where are Native Americans in terms of television shows/political clout/advertisements/films/news coverage/pop culture/ finance/business/sports and more? Usually they are missing in inaction.

Randella also meant something more personal: the invisibility of Native Americans such as herself amid other United States of America Americans. Her latest experience occurred in Washington, D.C., where she attended a conference on aging, in relation to her work with tribal elders. The only Native person there as far as she knew, she and another young woman struck up a conversation. At some point, Randella mentioned she is a Native American.

The young woman was struck silent. Finally, she said, "Oh, like a unicorn!"

Randella, who generously considered the response amusing, got the message. She was invisible, a fantasy until proven real.

In past fantasies, Native Americans were thrillingly warlike or inspiringly peace loving (take your pick). Plus, they were so colorful with all their Indian stuff. Is there a stronger graphic image than a (modern spelling) tipi? And how about those feathers? Consider in contrast the imagery-challenged nons who first invaded American shores. Colorfully clad Pilgrims? Hardly. Through the centuries, other nons heading west might have been so overwhelmed by the collective visual splendor of Native life that there was no mental retreat. Pipes, wampum, canoes, headdresses, beaded moccasins, baskets, pottery, totem poles—the icons are endless. Purveyors of popped culture followed, leaving indelible pictures, many false. (False sounds, too. Where *did* that 1–2-3, 1–2-3 Hollywood drum beat come from? No drum circle I ever heard.)

In comparison to the original stylish trappings, today's Native progeny mostly live in regular homes like other Americans and dress like them. They do not wear feathers daily, not on casual Fridays, anyway. They therefore may be difficult to spot. Yet they are here. Native Americans comprise a little under 2 percent of the population in this country, almost five million people. One percent is a considerable drop from 100 percent and is more than some people, including those who hunted them as sport, wished. But they are among us. Just, sometimes, invisible.

If a Native person goes into a store on or near a reservation, chances are she or he is assumed to be Native. What if that store is in a city, suburb, or town that has not been home to a Native community for a hundred years or more? Without a signifier—perhaps black braids, a hefty turquoise bracelet,

some dream catcher earrings, or a baseball cap spelling out Native Pride—
the customer may be considered other. Mexican? Possibly Asian? Someone
from Europe or the Middle East? A hodgepodge melted-pot American of no
evident lineage?

Until my visit to the Tohono O'odham Nation, I had not knowingly met
any Native Americans either. I had expected similarities (the optimist's
amulet) and was startled by differences. One example? Conversational etiquette. Native Americans, or those I met who live outside urban centers,
wait for the other person to finish speaking. They pause before responding.
They never interrupt. They stop talking if you interrupt. In their silence, you
prattle on, shaming yourself.

There were other, deeper differences, too, as you will notice in the following pages. Yet no matter the differences, I wanted to say to my fellow
non-Natives, they're just people. Individual people. Okay, more polite
than not, and certainly affected by their history in ways that non-Native
Americans are not. But we have much in common. We are all Americans of
the twenty-first century. If nothing else, I hope this book serves to help us
become better acquainted.

As for that long-ago abrupt confrontation with my ignorance in Arizona,
I think of it when people ask, What made you decide to write this book?
Short answer: to help stem ignorance such as mine.

Minutes after I reread these lines, I checked my e-mail. There was a message from a new tribal tourism department about a series of videos it made
to promote trips around its reservation, trips to "demystify" its people.

Exactly.

Introduction

A cartoon reprinted in the book *Do All Indians Live in Tipis?* shows Christopher Columbus arriving on an island, and a bright-eyed Native man and woman looking at him.[1] The man says, "We've thought and thought, but we're at a loss about what to call ourselves. Any ideas?"

A perhaps apocryphal account that could also be funny, or not, reports that when Columbus and his men first made western landfall, the local people bowed their heads, brought gifts, and otherwise behaved in a manner they thought proper to guests. Columbus and company regarded the behavior as evidence of submission.

What about famous land sales, including that of Manhattan for twenty-four dollars? Because Natives generally considered private ownership of land ludicrous, some scholars doubt actual sales were intended, that such transactions may have been closer to granting permission for farming and hunting.

Misunderstandings have not abated. How many non-Native Americans today believe that Native people (*a*) pay no taxes, (*b*) are all rich because of casinos, and (*c*) live in tipis?

When one thinks of the Europeans who first came to these shores, their progeny in the next centuries, and the other numerous newcomers, and what they all helped the United States of America become, some phrases stand out. "Rugged individualism," "entrepreneurial spirit," "every man for himself," "nation of immigrants," "Manifest Destiny," "youth culture," "nuclear families," "westward expansion," "We're number one!"

Native American cultures, from my experiences and readings, bring other phrases to mind, none explicit enough for quotation marks: Consensus, lack of interest in material goods, staying close to ancestral graves, honoring elders, communal life with extended families, environmental attention, humans as creatures superior to none.

Could there have been a more pronounced culture clash? No. One worse for indigenous inhabitants? No.

To summarize five hundred years of history, the newcomers not only took over an immense territory that was not theirs but tried to change the people already here. The people already here never tried to change the newcomers. Help them, yes. Attempt to coexist with them, yes. Attempt to fathom them, yes. (Why did these overly dressed people blow their noses on embroidered hankies, then place the hankies in a pocket as if saving a precious object?) But change them? No. Change was on the agenda of the interlopers.

To the zeal of change add misunderstanding, greed, condescension, righteousness, pity, racism, compassion, and of course, ignorance. The result for indigenous people has been one disastrous governmental and nongovernmental move after another. We all know the phrase "broken treaties." Most of us also have heard of horrors so legendary that they are cited as titles. The Trail of Tears, the Long Walk.

Less publicly known governmental policies entailed other devastations. As the boarding school era (described in the preface) was getting under way, the U.S. Congress delivered the second punch in the form of the 1887 Dawes Act. The most generous interpretation is that the act was intended to encourage recalcitrant tribal people to become (nuclear) family farmers for their own good. The federal government—whoosh!—took control of reservation territory, broke it into allotments, assigned some to Natives to farm (whether or not the land was arable, whether or not the people wanted to farm), and sold much "surplus" land to waiting-in-the-wings homesteaders. That is a main reason reservations today include non-Native people and a tangle of legal, financial, and emotional issues.

How about the Indian Reorganization Act of 1934? The IRA did stop the hated practice of allotments, although not its damage. The IRA also provided money to cash-strapped tribes. One of its most enduring effects, however, is also its most controversial. The IRA encouraged, or coerced, many tribes to abandon their various traditional forms of government and elect tribal councils instead. These councils exist today, with mixed results.

One more governmental disaster? Following World War II and the participation in it of many Native soldiers, from the celebrated code talkers to infantrymen in both theaters, some elected officials in Washington thought those stubborn Native people still were not getting with the program. It was time for "termination."

Let us set the scene. Native Americans had tried to hold together a semblance of traditional life after centuries of formal and informal policies that proved disastrous to them. There were few jobs on increasingly destitute reservations, those fractions of land mass that once fostered self-sufficiency. But rather than help build an infrastructure, encourage tribal enterprises, or fulfill the financial obligations of treaties, the federal government suggested terminating tribes by stopping agreed-upon payments. Now, despite having lost much of their land, not to mention other aspects of their lives, Native people faced losing their remaining touchstone: their tribal nation, however reduced in size it was. Termination meant terminating reservations and terminating federal treaty obligations to the people on the reservations. (The U.S. State Department tallies the number of Indian–U.S. treaties at 374.)

The reasoning, as far I can make out, sprang from a mixture of paternalism, fear (this was the Cold War era, and reservations seemed awfully communistic), fiscal conservatism, land greed, and the conviction by many, although not a reluctant President Dwight Eisenhower, that termination would motivate those last recalcitrant Natives to hop into the fabled melting pot—for their own good.

Congressional hearings in 1953 led to back-and-forth plans (to terminate which tribes now, later, never?) and to terrible consequences for some tribes, until the termination policy itself was terminated in the early 1960s. The twin of termination was relocation, the push to move people from reservations to cities. You'll hear from relocatees.

There were more insults along the way. In 1884, the Supreme Court held in *Elk v. Wilkins* that Indians were not citizens, so they were denied access to the Court of Claims to try to recover stolen land. Voting in federal elections was denied Native people until 1924. Not until a lawsuit in 1947 were Native Americans in New Mexico and Arizona allowed to vote in state elections. Native people in Maine were not allowed to vote in federal elections until 1954. Donna Loring, former Penobscot representative to the Maine legislature, told me, "As far as Maine was concerned, Maine tribes belonged to the state of Maine. Maine, just like the Southern states kept the African Americans from voting, used the same rationale." Her relatives, too, met to figure how to do away with poll taxes. Only in 1967 were Maine's Native populations allowed to vote in state elections. 1967!

Meanwhile, countless calamities were occurring across the country: the unsanctioned building of dams; the pollution of water, land, and people, some by the mining of various minerals from uranium to coal; the robbing of graves; the adoption of Native children by non-Native families; the bribing, plying, or supplying increasingly unhappy and displaced people with alcohol. The list, as they say, goes on.

If the intention of some actions is debatable, the results are not. Apart from creature comforts (and at such cost), if there is anything beneficial that Native America received from non-Native America, I do not know what it was.

———

As a group, Native Americans were considered inferior in countless ways. Suffragist Estelle Reel, superintendent of "Indian schools," was quoted in a 1900 newspaper as describing "the Indian child" this way. "The very structure of his bones and muscles will not permit so wide a variety of manual movements as are customary among Caucasian children, and his very instincts and modes of thought are adjusted to this imperfect manual development."[2] Does one laugh or weep?

The wonder is that through the centuries, outward rebellion by Native people has been so minor against such stupidity, and against injustice. The wonder is that their stance toward non-Native America has been so accommodating. Readings of Native history are replete with examples of their forbearance and friendliness (up to a point), examples that to me far exceed the measure granted by newcomers, including the U.S. Cavalry. The toll of Native losses—of land, mobility, independence, culture, way of life—seems to have been directed inward, not outward, as the term "historical trauma" found its countless recipients. Then came the activism instigated by Indian fishing rights protests in the mid-1960s and the protests at Alcatraz and Wounded Knee, arguably changing much of Native America's sense of itself. Red Power! was, or is, the phrase.

Where is Native America now? If we picture a fulcrum, one side may carry despair and discord, problems relating to unemployment, ill health, alcoholism, gangs, drug addiction, and suicide. Have the wretched policies of the past and the loss of continuity, self-sufficiency, and self-esteem damaged people to the point of no return? Many statistics are grim. One among many: Native Americans experience violent crimes at more than twice the rate for the country as a whole.[3]

The fulcrum has another side, though. There we see hopefulness and engagement, as activism's progeny (and the money from gamblers) takes on tribal construction projects, language immersion programs, restoration of habitats, and the living of productive, sober, and healthy lives. Laura Harris (Comanche), executive director of Americans for Indian Opportunity, exclaimed, "What's going on among Indians now is probably the greatest social movement that's ever taken place in the U.S. It's a Renaissance."

Which side of the wavering fulcrum will dominate? The individuals in the following pages represent only themselves, but their lives and thoughts may offer clues. They may, in more ways than one, also offer guidance.

Indian Voices

CHAPTER 1

A Man of the Dawn

DARRELL NEWELL (PASSAMAQUODDY)

On the first day of the Passamaquoddy blueberry harvest, Darrell Newell slept until two A.M. or so, tossed and turned for an hour, then gave up on sleep. He left the Northeastern Blueberry Company's ranch-style house in Columbia Falls he uses at harvest time, walked down the driveway into Northeastern's warehouse, and got to work.

Around seven A.M., he was consulting his clipboard and assigning the last drivers and loaders their areas. The men nodded and left. Darrell went into the adjoining office, spoke with two women working there, including his eldest daughter, Nakia, got some paperwork, and climbed into Northeastern's pickup to head to the blueberry barrens himself. A walkie-talkie, seldom mute, hung on the dashboard. A feather hung from the rearview mirror. A ZZ Top CD peeked from a door pocket.

As manager of the Passamaquoddy-owned Northeastern Blueberry Company, Darrell is in charge of the tribe's biggest annual event. That meant organizing the harvest's every aspect, from getting the barrens and the five sleeping camps operation-ready, to hiring eight hundred or so blueberry gatherers, loaders, and drivers. That meant overseeing everything. "I try to orchestrate the flow of things," is how he put it, in a soft slow baritone, his demeanor reminiscent of old Jimmy Stewart movie roles. He seemed completely unhurried and calm.

"It appears that I'm stressed," he offered, as he shifted gears and steered west on Route 1. "I am, only because so many things are happening at one time, but it kind of plays itself out. Whatever will happen will happen. Each season is different, similar but different."

Darrell is an arresting figure—a tall, slim, dark, craggy, mustachioed man of forty-nine, in T-shirt, jeans, rubber-soled moccasins, a ponytail almost to his waist, his arms adorned with tattoos. His wife Pam, who shares the house at harvest time, along with other family members, said, to help me locate him amid the warehouse hubbub, "He's gorgeous." He did not act as if he would agree.

While we rode, I peppered him with questions he answered with increasing amusement, skewering one cliché after another. Was there some ceremonial beginning to the harvest, such as a prayer in the barrens when the sun came up? Nope, the first day of each season involves just work. Someone of significance picking the first berry? He shook his head. How about a last-day harvest ceremony?

"No formal ceremony," he said, beginning to smile.

People get out every day and pick?

"Yep, pretty much." The correct term, I learned, is rake, but Darrell was too polite to correct a near stranger about terminology.

How about harvest taboos? Like in some tribes pregnant women not being allowed to sit in a drum circle and play the drum?

"Taboos?" He laughed a little, as if trying not to. "I don't think we have anything like that. Women rake alongside of men. Kids, too. I mean, we have to go by the law. The Department of Labor requires that a child be twelve years old before they can work. Before the law came into play, families would come and little children would be raking to help with the family needs and with school clothes. As a boy I raked some. I wouldn't make a living at it. I'm not that good. You need to a good back, certainly, but it takes about every muscle in your body to do the work. Pretty labor-intensive."

After several miles on sparsely trafficked Route 1, he signaled, turned onto a side road away from the ocean and the last scent of it, then onto unmarked dirt roads. Finally, the pickup reached the hilly terrain where shin-high bushes bore berries an intensified color of the cloudless sky, and where hundreds of people working or walking uphill and down brought to mind painted tableaus of harvests centuries ago.

Up-close observation verified Darrell's unromantic assessment; the work is labor-intensive. Raking requires semi-stooping to ground level, swinging the rake—a kind of squared-off dustpan with long protrusions extending from the bottom side—in an arc into the low bushes, like a bird of prey swooping down on a mouse, then lifting up again, the prize held. Some rakers were as graceful as infielders snagging a ball and swirling to make a double play. Some were more dogged than graceful, hacking at the bushes to fill their rake. The most adroit rakers, as a final flourish, shimmied the rake's contents into the air, letting leaves and twigs blow away, the ageless method of separating wheat from chaff, rice from hull, before recatching the berries and depositing them in a sturdy plastic box.

Darrell, nodding at some rakers and returning a wave to others, recalled another federal law, one requiring Northeastern to build a dining room for the crews. It did so at considerable expense, but as the Passamaquoddies knew, rakers prefer to eat in the company-built wooden cabins with their extended families or friends. As if to prove his point, in one raker camp late that afternoon, a young woman wearing oven mitts carried a bowl of baked potatoes from the camp kitchen to her cabin. The Labor Department–mandated dining hall, where no dining takes place, has become a base for tents.

Puncturing another cliché, Darrell said the harvest does not begin on any celestially significant day. "I determine when it starts and basically it's persuaded by how ripe the crop is. Like we guessed August sixth, and this year we were on target." The harvest does not end on any day of significance, either. "Ten heavy days and then it lingers for another week or so."

The biggest cliché buster: the blueberries are not organic.

"These tracks," Darrell said, pointing from inside the pickup, "are where our sprayer goes for chemicals. We used to aerial spray. Then the local environmentalists started to pressure the two noticeable large growers, Cherryfield Foods and Wyman's. They were in the media back and forth, debating about drift from aerial spray and lawsuits. Our board decided to be proactive and not to be exposed to the media. So we decided to begin to ground spray."

"Our board encourages us to devote a portion of our acreage to organic, but it's not practical. You get a higher price for the product, but it costs more to grow it. Even though you see a lot of weeds here," he indicated with his chin, "if we were organic, there would be more weeds than berries."

"I'm just spoiled and trained to be a commercial grower as opposed to organic. I'm having difficulty getting enough hand-weeders to take care of our nineteen acres of cranberries, let alone a thousand acres of blueberries, or eighteen hundred, if we wanted to do it all." Blueberries can be harvested only every two years, he explained, pointing out fields of immature berries. Therefore, the annual harvest takes place on about half of the tribe's acreage. As to what happens to the berries once the drivers haul them to the processing plant, Darrell paid little attention. He believed some ended up in blueberry cake mixes. My vision of Authentic Passamaquoddy Organic Blueberry Granola was over.

Like many Native people, Darrell was used to fencing with clichés from non-Natives. Some neighbors in drought years suggested he pray for rain. "My attempt at humor is to reply, 'Well, that would be cheating, so I don't do that.'"

He did not joke about the harvest. "We pretty much take what Mother Nature gives us. We try to help her along with what tools we have to have a good crop, but basically she tells us what's going to happen. We're constantly dependent on weather. She's been good to us this year. We're anticipating an above-average to noticeably above-average crop. Our average crop is about 3.2 million pounds. I think we'll be shaving 4 million pounds if everything goes right."

"What makes us unique," he said, "is we're exclusively manual harvest." And yes, a harvest this large is unique in being tribal. "Our primary labor force are the Micmacs from Canada and Nova Scotia and New Brunswick, but the Maine tribes are also noticeably involved." Most are Passamaquoddy, but there are Penobscot and Maliseet rakers as well.

Many families make the trip, with tribal reunions of sorts occurring every year. "It's more culturally motivated than economical or business motivated." Still, the money—each filled box got a raker $2.50—is especially appreciated where work is scarce. The unemployment rate was about 50 percent on the two Passamaquoddy reservations, Indian Township and Pleasant Point.

The Passamaquoddies, like other Maine tribes, are called "people of the dawn," but geographically they may have the best claim, located as they are in the northeasternmost part of the state. The blueberry acreage, a good day's drive south and east from the reservations, became theirs as a result of the famous Maine Indian Claims Settlement of 1980. That came about after a U.S. Court of Appeals ruled that several tribes were legitimate claimants to 60 percent of the entire state. The ruling sent alarms throughout nontribal Maine. Negotiations quickly followed. A $81.5 million settlement was divided among three tribes.

The largest, the Penobscots, are using some of their money to deal with a horrific environment challenge. "We are river people," tribal chief Kirk Francis told me. Yet the sacred Penobscot River that flows within and around the reservation and once sustained the tribe with fish, game, and clean water, and is lovely to look at and boat upon, is so polluted by dioxin from upriver paper mills that it is not safe even for swimming. People have dioxin scars from trying. Unlikely to win battles with better-funded polluters, the Penobscots are concentrating on other income avenues, including bingo games and wind power.

The Passamaquoddies, at the urging and intervention of a non-Native lawyer, in 1981 spent $2 million of their settlement money on the blueberry land. That might not sound like much, Darrell said, but would have been impossible before the settlement.

Today, as he drove the pickup carefully from barren to barren, raking area to raking area, camp to camp, he stopped frequently to collect or pass out paperwork, and once to deliver a late-arriving teenaged raker. At many stops, Darrell handed out checks to people who had prepared the land for the harvest. Crew supervisors, for example, had twined the barrens into strips four or so feet wide, so raking crews literally could stay in line.

All exchanges were as polite as they were understated; there was nothing of the boss man about Darrell Newell.

Sometimes, when he climbed out of the pickup for whatever reason, he bent to pluck a few berries himself. Yes, a nontribal member is allowed to eat them, Darrell said, trying to hide a smile. Once, to demonstrate technique, he swung a rake a few times through a berry bush, his arc signaling grace and experience. But nope, he is not really good at it, his shrug implied.

Throughout the day and the barrens, the mood among the rakers seemed convivial. "It's a pleasant experience more than stressful." At times, in and out of the truck and on and off the walkie-talkie, Darrell solved logistical problems, inquired about crew members, and visited briefly with people he saw once a year. Often the chat, on the two-way or in person, was in Passamaquoddy, Darrell's first language.

Most crews were comprised of people from the same family. Not all were Native. One was made up of Spanish-speaking men; another included Anglo locals. Each crew had been carefully assigned the same amount of land, including hilly areas and flatter fields. There was some joking about crews being sent to the hilly areas first, "rough ground," Darrell called it, so flatter fields would be a reward later. Rakers who started in flat areas tended to be less enthusiastic when they reached the hills.

Darrell did tell one crew supervisor that he thought an area looked carelessly raked. She agreed and told him she planned to have the crew rerake. Overall, he seemed pleased. "The harvest supervisors seem to be doing their job in asking the rakers to rake clean. I think we're all kind of complacent," he said back in the pickup. His "theme" this year is for everyone to do better work, including himself. "Let's not come here and talk about this being a cultural traditional event. Let's hold it sacred. Let's do a good job, not just utter the words and go out and butcher the land. A lot of years, you can walk through the strips and see 20, 40 percent of the berries laying on the ground because they knocked them off to get through it. This year I'm encouraging the people to be leisurely. I mean, everybody's working hard, but to take their time and try to get all the berries and not just 60 percent." There is good reason to get all the berries; claims that their antioxidant properties reverse the aging process have been good for business.

Maximizing workers was as much a concern as maximizing berries. "I hire on thirty, thirty-five loaders, and we'll begin to see shrinkage right away. It's not work for everybody." Hefting hundreds of filled berry boxes, about two feet square, onto trucks hour after hour is arduous. Labor "shrinkage" usually starts within three days. This year, Darrell is especially ready. "I have six loaders for each truck, where I usually have four." A driver may help load, "but he has more responsibilities too, moving his truck and making sure his load is secure, all of that. A good crew will interact."

Darrell pulled the pickup off a dirt road overlooking a wide landscape of barrens, rakers, water stations, portable toilets, rakers' cars, trucks, and picnic coolers, to have lunch behind the wheel. With the pause, the conversation veered back decades.

———

He grew up on the northernmost of the two reservations, Indian Township. Nuns at the reservation missionary grammar school did not allow Passamaquoddy children to speak their language, he said, holding up weathered hands. "I got the knuckles to prove it, 'cause they hit us with the ruler." Another school souvenir is a piece of graphite inside the ball of his right thumb. "A nun had a handful of sharp pencils and I was all excited to get one. She didn't do it on purpose. I was raising my hand to get one and it accidentally stuck in there." After pointing out the residue, he unwrapped the sandwich Pam had packed for him and offered half.

All in all, school was "okay." The nuns often tied lessons to religion, he said. "I was cooperative, I was submissive, and all of that."

In a joking way, he started talking about identity. "I've been American Indian for almost fifty years," he said, allowing a small grin, then added he knows the term Native American has become "popular and politically correct." The grin continued. "I'm politically correct, too; I use Native American."

Because I had spent several days in and around the Penobscot reservation with Donna Loring, a Penobscot tribal representative active in getting the insulting and beyond politically incorrect word "squaw" removed from Maine place-names, I asked Darrell what he thought of the word. His grin disappeared. "Oh, no no. No, I don't do that," he said with atypical vehemence. "The word comes from *squ'smoos*, which is a reference to a female dog."

In a book about her legislature experiences, including the battle over the name changes, Donna traced the origins of "squaw" to the word *otsikwaw*, "which referred to a female body part."[1] Another book less delicately translated the word as "vagina."[2] If the linguistic origins are debatable,[3] context is not. The Algonquian languages intended no insult, it is agreed, but the English word "squaw"—as heard or misheard by trappers centuries ago— has become synonymous with the worst one can call a woman. Loring, and Maine's other tribal representative, Donald Soctomah (Passamaquoddy), persisted in their battle. Despite much opposition that included this-is-our-local-tradition and a-change-will-hurt-business arguments, they won. In 2000, the Offensive Names Bill passed, banning the word "squaw" from state sites. Private enterprises, such as Big Squaw Mountain Resort, kept it.

Darrell was unswayed by pro-"squaw" arguments. "My view is that if it's offensive to someone, then it's reasonable we challenge it and make issue about it."

After lunch and a brief visit with a Micmac crew leader friend, a school principal who opened a treatment facility solely for youths addicted to inhaling solvents, Darrell restarted the pickup and got moving. Over the walkie-talkie, he elaborated on something he had mentioned earlier; all Native people are assimilated, but to different degrees. "Being assimilated doesn't make us less of who we are." Native identity "becomes blurred and kind of foggy, but it's still very much intact." When someone like him, who has grown up in poverty on a reservation meets someone who has grown up in the city, "It's interesting how it plays itself out, the dynamics of different levels of assimilation. That's been interesting to me, anyway."

"I grew up with my grandparents," he said quietly. "Kind of like what we're doing for Ryan now." Ryan, the child of Darrell's second daughter, was born with addictions so pervasive, it took eight months for him to be clean, Pam told me. The boy is now lively, curious, chubby and—thanks in large measure to Pam's efforts, said Darrell—is off all medications meant to control hyperactivity. He is not easily sated. While in the truck with Darrell and me for a few hours, he seemed unable to let two seconds go by without a question or request for food. Darrell and Pam were models of loving patience. Taking care of Ryan "kind of has come full circle for me," Darrell said. The circle began when his own mother gave him up.

The subject arrived circuitously, as he described his marriage several years ago to Pam, a Passamaquoddy as effervescent as Darrell is quiet. They had been friends as children, both said, and best friends as adults. Their marriage to one another is the second for both.

Pam was involved with the harvest, too, cooking, relaying messages to Darrell on the two-way, keeping a close eye on the many activities in and around the house. To young male rakers who camped out in the yard, she announced if she so much as heard a soda can pop, she would assume it was beer and kick them out. And if anyone made a move on the raker girls staying in the house . . . When not cooking or commanding, Pam relaxed by watching *The Price Is Right* or whatever videos would not frighten Ryan. One evening, an extended Newell family group, including the toddlers of Darrell's daughter Nakia and her husband Matt (he worked a security detail during the harvest to prevent boxes of berries from being stolen), watched *Sponge Bob Square Pants.* They scoffed about objections by conservative groups that Bob is gay. "Give me a break," hooted one mother.

The wedding to Pam, Darrell said, the pickup bouncing along barrens roads, took place in a friend's backyard within the Passamaquoddy reservation of Pleasant Point. After the friend's daughter, a justice of the peace, "did the legal formalities," an elder pipe carrier conducted what Darrell called "the ceremony." He paused. "It was nice." Pam had taken charge of the wedding attire. "She knew a Mohawk friend, and she arranged for her to make me a buckskin shirt. It was too cold for a loincloth," he said, looking impish, "so I wore jeans. Moccasins. She wore a matching buckskin dress. It was memorable. Yep."

Did he cry? I felt compelled to ask. Aw, shucks, said his face. "Did I?" He almost chuckled. "I think so. Shed tears, anyway. I wasn't sobbing or anything." Not like Pam. "Oh yeah, she was sobbing. She was a mess." He chuckled for real.

"We had a feast. And a cake. It was $200 or more. It was beautiful, I just didn't expect to pay that much for a cake." The feast was held at the reservation's grade school cafeteria, the only place big enough for the occasion. There was "a mixture of folks. I didn't take a count. But my mom was there, so it was special that way."

With that, the subject opened. She had some problems, I understand, I said.

"Chemical dependency," he said evenly, eyes straight ahead. "She was a single parent. Basically the problem was alcoholism. It all makes sense here," he said, pointing to his head with his right hand, steering with his left, and staring at the road, "but it doesn't make sense here," pointing to his heart.

I asked if he and she had talked about it.

"Oh, yeah. She's been sober a long time, and she's been dealing with that problem for a long time, so we've had an opportunity to chat about it." He cleared his throat.

And, asked reluctantly, his father?

"I never knew who he was," he said, eyes still on the road. "My mom's explanation is that alcoholism had such a great play in it, she really doesn't know herself for sure."

At this point a barrage of calls started. "700 to Grace?" came one. Grace works in the Northeastern Blueberry's office adjoining the warehouse.

"It's kind of embarrassing to share that with you," Darrell said, "but I'm kind of used to sharing the truth."

Darrell waited until Grace and the caller worked out a problem involving the man's needing more rakes. "10–4, *miigwetch*," he said. *Miigwetch*? It means "thank you" in Ojibwe.

"I mean," Darrell was saying, "if I were more uncomfortable, I wouldn't share it with you."

Temporarily distracted by the thought of Ojibwes being in Maine, I returned my mind to the question of who Darrell's father might be. Your mother has an idea?

"Yeah. She's given me a couple of names and I've gone out of my way to . . . we've done DNA testing." He paused. "Well, the two people that we narrowed it down to didn't come through, DNA-wise."

The walkie-talkie crackled again with a message for someone else.

"I approached this one gentleman after my mom and I talked and she gave me the name. I asked if he'd do a DNA test and see. He said, 'Sure, I'll do it.' Of course, there was the anxiety leading up to it. I almost didn't ask. The embarrassment and all the uncertainty." The man was cooperative, Darrell added, clearing his throat again. "He said, 'If it comes out positive, I'll take you fishing.'"

Darrell seemed relieved to let the story out, then paused. "We never went fishing."

The second man on the list had died. "I approached his children and the ex-wife. We DNA tested his ex-wife and their mutual children. Isolated his DNA by that process, and then tried to match it with mine. It didn't match."

Darrell knows he looks like his mother, so there was little point trying to find a resemblance among local men. Rather than go through any more anguish, he stopped searching. "What interests me is my loyalty to the people that raised me. That *those* were my parents. They cared. They loved me unconditionally. That's why I'm so spoiled now." Another grin. He seemed especially relieved to be off the subject of his birth father's identity.

His mom and dad, as he called his grandparents, Darrell clearly cherished. "My dad was a hard worker. He used to work on the river drives when they transported logs down rivers to get them from the forest to the processing lumber mills. They'd have logs in the river tied together, and I remember him running across those logs. Impressive! They were good people. Basically, that's what I grew up with. Strong Native people. There were probably a hundred people, in Indian Township, what they call The Strip. Nobody locked their doors. Nobody knocked *on* the doors. You'd just go to somebody's house and walk in. If you knocked on the door, you'd hear people inside say, 'Oh gee, that must be a white person.' Kind of an annoying kind of thing."

Darrell looked tempted to apologize.

He talked more about his birth mother, saying he loves her, but "there's just no content to it. There's not a lot of bonding." She had other children, three girls. "She abandoned me and gave me to a family, and she tried to raise my older sister and my two younger sisters. That's what's kind of complicated to understand for me. So right from go, I felt like there's something wrong with me. There's moments when I still feel that way, but generally I feel okay. I didn't expect you to get *this* personal," he said, his voice lower.

About then, he stopped the truck to drop off and collect more paperwork. From seemingly out of nowhere, a young man walked up to his open window, smiled, and put his hand on Darrell's arm resting on the window frame. Both nodded. Neither spoke. The moment felt charged with significance. After a few seconds, the young man nodded again and walked off.

Darrell explained. He once went to a sweat in Canada put on by an Ojibwe. ("*Miigwetch!*") "Every day the Ojibwe and his helpers would come and they'd take us from our lodges and gather us up and put us in the sweat. The Ojibwe put on a pretty hot sweat." Community members offered food and beverages, but Darrell and others were fasting and took none. "He"—a slant of his head indicating the man walking away—"was one of the people that would come visit. After a few days of fasting you get kind of tired. One time we were having a sweat and it was almost burning. This young man here, he came into the sweat and he laid on top of me and protected me from being burnt. It was kind of nice. I can't remember his name, but that's my memory of him whenever I see him."

The fast lasted four days and four nights.

Darrell said he had not been on a vision quest, a common reason in some tribes to go for so long without food or water. "I wasn't fasting for anything in particular. I was just trying to strengthen my understanding of things."

———

As a boy, Darrell lived in homes modest at best. "The one I grew up in until my dad died, when I was ten, was a two-room house he built. We had a kitchen, dining room, living room area, and we had another room for sleeping quarters. When my dad died, my mom decided to sell it. We moved into another house which was smaller, a one-room tarpaper shack. Smaller than the camps we have here now." They were dependent on the Indian agent for food. Darrell remembered one staple in particular. "Salt pork goes a long ways. My mom would fry up salt pork and make gravy out of it. She would fry bread in the frying pan and that would be our meal. I still crave for a meal like that every now and then."

The family's sole heating source was a wood stove. In the twenty-first century, the Passamaquoddies were among recipients of free heating oil from Venezuelan President Hugo Chavez. A Northeastern Blueberry Company employee told me he does "not care much for Chavez," but free oil "was very beneficial to our people."

Despite deprivations, Darrell's grandparents did not complain. "I think more common was a positive outlook, that 'This is the way it is, but it's okay.' " During winters especially, Darrell learned "old ways," including the tradition of storytelling. "I told this story to Ryan about a bear who wakes up in the springtime and he's hungry. He's out foraging, so he comes across this blueberry field and he starts gathering up the blueberries, and he eats and he eats and he eats." After a while, "he finds this tree and he goes behind the tree and does his thing, and he realizes he doesn't have anything to wipe with. About this same time a white rabbit comes up. He grabs the rabbit and he wipes his butt with it. That's how the white rabbit became to be a brown rabbit." Ryan repeated the story in school during show and tell, Darrell said, shaking his head and looking pleased.

He looked even more pleased talking about a 1984 Jaguar. "When I got married to Pam a few years ago, I said, 'Pam, if you ever see me buy a Jaguar, dig me a hole because I'm ready to go.' " Darrell's story involved driving by a car repair place and seeing an old Jaguar in the yard. "It looked like junk, but it caught my eye. It was an '84 XJ6 Jaguar. I'm partial to that year and model." He went on about a rude and/or surly mechanic, an offer of $1,500 rejected, then accepted, and getting a tattoo, 84XJ6, to celebrate his ownership. He pointed it out on his left arm. Then he pointed out his others. "This one here," also on his left arm, "way back when I was a teenager, I chiseled my initials on with a needle and thread: DJN. In recent years I wanted to cover it up." He had feathers tattooed over it. He also covered up a tattoo of his first wife's initials. A newer tattoo was a braid of sweet grass circling high on his upper left arm. Ouch! Yeah, he said, "it way hurt." Another tattoo says "Pam." "She has all kinds of tattoos." He grinned. "She has one behind here, on the back of her neck. She says it says 'Darrell,' but it's Chinese lettering and it could say 'poop' for all I know."

Speaking of Pam, I said, she told me that as a child in the 1960s and 1970s, she and other Natives were not allowed to shop in certain stores.

"Oh yeah. That would be in Princeton," a town outside the Indian Township reservation. "I remember my dad taking me to the barber shop. Of course we'd wait like everybody else, but if a white person would have come in and get a haircut, we'd have to go at the end of the line. There would be a common understanding, if a white person came in, they would be next and the Indian would have to sit and wait." He paused for comic timing. "That's not how we got long hair, but I think that contributed to it."

In Darrell's opinion, Maine has "wannabe racists. I don't think they're as generational and well established and outright racist like the South. They're more, 'Look at the South. Look how racist they are. I want to be like that.' They try to be, but they really aren't." He added, "If it weren't for blacks, Indians probably never would have made the progress we've made in terms of civil rights. It's the black folks that did it for us."

———

At thirteen, Darrell made his first trip outside his known world, riding a bus to Harrisburg, Pennsylvania, to visit a suburban couple he had "been pen-paling with" through the Save the Children Federation. "They were very nice people," treating him like a beloved only child. "I'm not sure which spouse was not able to have children, but as a couple they were not able to." Although he felt out of place, "the people were so kind and focused on my presence, everything that felt awkward felt okay because of the way they received me and took care of me while I was there."

This child was not saved, though. "I took a bad turn shortly after that." Darrell became a drug addict. Getting high "was the most important thing in my life. Nothing or nobody was more important than that. In the beginning, it was a magic potion. I wasn't shy and introverted anymore. I was outgoing and kind of the life of the party. That's what kept me going back and that's what got me addicted. It took me ruining my life and the lives of the people closest to me. That didn't stop me until I hit a bottom and another bottom and another bottom." He paused. "Things have changed since I've been away from active addiction."

Meanwhile, he had children. "I fathered my daughter Nakia when I was fifteen. By the time I was seventeen I had fathered three children—my other daughter Ella and my son Joe [both pseudonyms]. I have six grandchildren. One of them is our son now, Ryan." His first wife was the mother of Nakia and Joe. Another woman gave birth to Ella.

He is not in touch with his children "in a regular way or a frequent way. Even my daughter Nakia [who lives on Indian Township too], coming here is the most interaction that we have. Occasionally we get together for dinner or something, but it's not like a regular, frequent, family get-together kind of thing. Ella and I are kind of estranged, or at least awkward. And my son, he's active too with his illness, so that kind of keeps me away." Joe was recently in jail, allegedly for trafficking prescription pills. "The person that bought from him was wired. I don't know a lot about it, but that's what I understand."

Darrell visited him in jail and later telephoned, but the relationship is difficult. "We're not estranged, it's just I make every effort to stay away from active addiction for my own survival."

In the 1970s, when Darrell was younger than his son is now, he joined the army. "I had a young family, and there was not a whole lot of job opportunity at the time. That's basically why I joined. I was stationed in Fort Carson, Colorado, near Colorado Springs. We lived there in town. My ex-wife managed an apartment building. I was a field artillery surveyor, and I was also on a funeral detail, which was interesting to me."

That experience, helping to bury veterans, led to Darrell's involvement in helping to bury the unidentified remains of Native Americans. "I mean, this is important to me," he said, gesturing to the barrens of berries. "I have to work, I have to provide for my family, and I enjoy it. I'm a husband, I'm a dad, I'm all those important things, but I think the most valuable spiritual thing I do is bringing back the bones of our old ones and putting them back in their proper place." He seemed frustrated that remains from an archeological dig in Blue Hill, Maine, not far from Mount Desert Island, were being held by Harvard University's Peabody Museum of Archeology and Ethnology. "They hold sacred burial belongings and human remains that date back 65,000 years." Argument seemed difficult. "We don't have an archaeological background. They're the educated people, so it's real difficult to be at odds with them and be effective. Their position is that [the remains] are not culturally affiliated to Passamaquoddy or any present-day living tribe, so technically they're culturally unidentifiable." Darrell just wants to rebury the bones and funerary items—all of them. (For more on the subject, called repatriation, see chap. 6.)

Darrell's excursions into "the dominant society," as Native people some-times call it, have been mixed. "There was a period of time I kind of tried to fit in and tried to be somebody I wasn't, trying to live up to other people's expectations. To have a nine-to-five job. I still recognized that I was an Indian. I just made a lot of effort trying to fit into a white world."

In his late thirties, a time that he implied coincided with "coming to," he began college at the Machias campus of the University of Maine, about fifty miles from his home. "Every mile that passed, I could feel the distance from my home reservation to the university." He evaded the question of who encouraged him to go. "I have friends that have college education. I think it was pretty much self-motivated."

At Machias, Darrell began studying business administration. Tribal leaders took notice, as did the Northeastern Blueberry Company. "The manager of the company and the president, they approached me to come and work for them. They thought I'd be a good candidate." Darrell helped learn the ropes of Northeastern under the company's first manager, Francis Nicholas. In 2001, when Nicholas retired, Darrell was promoted. A plaque honoring Nicholas, "in recognition of his lifelong contributions to family and community, tribe and country," hangs on the outside of the warehouse facing Route 1.

Working for a tribally owned blueberry business proved less difficult than did moving to a part of the state unfriendly to tribal people. "When I came to work here eighteen years ago, my former boss drove me around to show me the geographical area of our land. We'd drive around and meet vehicles and I'd be waving, and then waving, and then waving again, every time we'd meet somebody. Finally he just took my hand"—Darrell grabbed mine and slammed it down on the seat—"and he said, 'Don't wave to them. They don't want you waving to them.'"

"I'd go to town. I'd go into a store and I'd greet somebody and say hello and they would have almost a rage in their facial character. They were offended I would make contact. That I would say hello to *them*. That's how open the racism was back then here."

Darrell flipped on his turn signal as he turned back toward the ware-house. "Now we're established. Now they know when they come here, we're here."

Established? At my accommodations, the Blueberry Patch Motel down the highway, I had picked up an elaborate program trumpeting the upcoming church-sponsored Machias Wild Blueberry Festival. Machias, about ten miles east of the Northeastern complex, is not only a university town but the site of the processing plant where Northeastern's trucks take their blueberries. I looked at every page—color photos of past festivals, a schedule about the Blueberry Musical, a staggering list of other events, including a banner contest, a blueberry pie-eating contest. There was news about the festival's crafts, including a blueberry quilt. There was a schedule for worship services. There was not a word about the Passamaquoddy harvest, nor about the Northeastern Blueberry Company, nor about the history of the area, such as which people were here, eating blueberries, first.

My outrage about the omissions, which I vented to Darrell as he drove, met with maddening rationality. "Well, one thing is, we're not a retailer. We're a farm. I think we're kind of humble that way. I mean, it would be nice if there was a Native presence to the festival, but it may be because we're kind of reserved and we're not pushing that. Maybe Native folks ought to be recognized or something." I steamed in silence. "They know we're here." Then he pointed out that the tribe does not advertise its berries or advertise for labor. "Maybe that's what makes us a bit invisible."

While the pickup approached the warehouse, he became contemplative about the time when Europeans first arrived on the land of the people of the dawn. "My view is that we're kind of welcoming. Obviously we didn't fight with the people that came. We must have somehow welcomed them and tried to coexist. I mean, they had guns. They would have killed all of us off. There must have been a voluntary cooperation on our part. I think the Passamaquoddy in particular are humble people. Some of our people try to use the word 'nation,' Passamaquoddy nation. I don't think that's appropriate. We're a tribe."

At the Passamaquoddy blueberry harvest, the first day lasted well into the first night, as trucks made their way to and from Machias. Weeks after the last day, I called the office. The total yield, I was told, had been 3.9 million pounds. Or, "shaving 4 million pounds," as Darrell Newell had predicted.

CHAPTER 2

"Indians 101"

ELIZABETH LOHAH HOMER (OSAGE)

In her sparkling office at Homer Law, a few steps off Dupont Circle in Washington, D.C., Elizabeth Lohah Homer was having her standard lunch of "roast beast" sandwich, as she calls it, Diet Coke, and a small bag of Utz potato chips. Resplendent in a black-and-pink-pinstriped power suit that perfectly complemented her black hair and pink fingernails, Elizabeth, an attractive and hearty woman with a dimple in her chin and a voice that carries, was talking between bites and sips about myths—not myths that figure in tribal creation stories, but myths that non-Natives believe about Natives.

As she talked, she looked increasingly exasperated.

A common myth: only tribal members live on reservations. "The impression is that tribes are somehow divorced from the rest of the country. Most reservations today, like my own, the Osage Reservation, are populated with people from all different races, creeds, colors, and religions." Few if any reservations, she added, do *not* include nontribal members.

A more harmful myth: Native Americans do not pay taxes. "The fact of the matter is, Indians *do* pay taxes like everybody else, but there are some limited exceptions." In Elizabeth's opinion, the tax issue "is among the most poorly understood by nontribal members, and has caused no end of grief for tribal peoples over the years, particularly when it comes to politics."

A particularly harmful myth: Native people get government handouts. Again, wrong. "This is one of the most entrenched misconceptions, ideas, myths . . . call it what you want, it's absolutely, completely wrong. Indians

do not get 'free money from the government just because they're Indians.'"
Yes, tribal governments receive federal subsidies for such matters as fire and
police protection, she said, after a sip of Diet Coke, "but these types of federal subsidies are provided to state and local governments as well." A tribal
member may get federal welfare aid, too, like any other citizen. The "free
money" myth began, she believes, when the U.S. Treasury, after collecting
payments and royalties from lands that tribes leased out, usually for the
development of oil, gas, minerals, or timber, sent checks for the payments
and royalties to tribal members. Once the checks were seen in town, perhaps
by a bank teller, the myth began. "No matter how many times you put out
the information—you write it down, you clarify it, you testify before the
Hill, you do videos—it seems to be one of those intransigent myths that
people can't get over. Myths like these make it very difficult for tribes to
work on certain kinds of legislation or deal with policy makers. You always
have to start at the very beginning."

That she does, over and over. Among Native Americans, the endless
introductory lessons, usually to people of power, influence, and ignorance,
are known ironically as "Indians 101."[1]

"I've taught 'Indians 101' courses many, many times. I can't tell you how
many." She added, wiping pink lips, she continues to teach the courses
because tribes face so many difficulties "based upon stereotypes and ignorance. Ignorance and stereotypes, it kind of goes hand in hand."

"We're either stoic and noble or tragically flawed, you know? I get so tired
of that." Like many other Native people, she loved the television series
Northern Exposure for showing "a complex, diverse, varied world. An
incredibly fascinating and interesting one filled with all kinds of different
personalities—people with different interests, thoughts, ideas, and ways of
doing things." She went on, almost imploringly, "The real world, the way it
really is for tribal people, is infinitely more interesting and complex than I
think most people in this society appreciate. I enjoyed *Northern Exposure*
because here would be all the Natives sitting around in Levis and a cowboy
shirt, talking about nuclear power and geoglobal politics. That's really how
it is. Tribal people are intelligent. They're part of the twenty-first century.
You're not trapped in some nineteenth-century doomsday scenario. It's a

survival story, it's uplifting, triumph of the human spirit, all of that," she said, waving pink nails.

To get the story across, Elizabeth teaches "Indians 101" "with infinite patience. No question is too dumb to answer for the ten thousandth time, you know? I remind myself of what Will Rogers said. 'We're all ignorant, just about different things.'" Elizabeth often quotes fellow Oklahoman and Cherokee Nation member Will Rogers.

"My favorite dumb question, or the dumb question I love to hate the most? It's some twist on this"—she leaned forward, feigning a perplexed look— "'How much Indian are ya, anyway?'" She all but sputtered. "I can't even tell you how annoying that question is. It's like having one's entire identity questioned. 'Do you want me to give you my whole lineage here or what?' Gawd, I want to say, think about what you're asking somebody. If I say to you, 'I'm Osage,' and you say, 'Well, how much Osage are you? Are you just part Osage or are you full Osage or what kind of Indian are you?' I find it deeply offensive."

Elizabeth has a trove of "pithy little" responses, although admitted she never uses them. "When people say things like, 'Well, you don't *look* Indian,'" she is tempted to respond, "Well, you don't *look* rude, either."

She fumed anew. "It's really inappropriate."

She recalled conducting a training session for Pentagon officials, "'Indians 101' at a very high level," she called it. "The presentation by the person who spoke before me concerned Indian service in the military and how Indians had such a distinguished record of service, how so many Congressional Medal of Honor winners are Indian. He recounted all of these interesting facts and statistics. He spoke about how the code talkers helped win the war in the Pacific and explained that there were code talkers in Europe too; he clarified that in addition to the well-known Navajo code talkers, there were Comanche code talkers and Lakota code talkers. After he finished, it was my turn to talk. Before I was even warmed up, one of the participants confronted me—I could see that he was genuinely struggling to put together what he had been hearing. He asks me in a somewhat brusque tone, 'If the government of the United States is so terrible to Indians, why do Indians serve in the military, join the army, serve more than any other group of people in the country?' I said to him, 'Because this is our country. You defend your country.' The room went stone silent for a split second, then they all went . . . uhh!"

Elizabeth mimed a big gasp, before her dark eyes filled. "It touched me. I felt like they really got it, that somehow I had helped make a difference, that in some way I helped create a moment of understanding." She recovered her composure as she crumpled up her lunch trash. "When you can help people understand what the situation is, what the tribes are about, then you can go on and have infinite patience, because" once in a while "somebody who didn't get it, gets it."

"Getting it" is more challenging when her talk involves Native-run casinos. It often does; the client base of Homer Law, which Elizabeth founded in 2003, is casino tribes.

The subject is controversial not only among non-Natives but among Native people, if to a far lesser degree. Some Native people question, for example, tribes giving up any cherished sovereignty to enter into gaming compacts with state governments. Some question how tribal leadership determines who benefits from casino proceeds—that is, who is enrolled as a tribal member, who is not enrolled, and, most controversially, who is "disenrolled."

If Native Americans have a gamut of knotty questions about the gambling business, gambling per se is less of an issue, perhaps because it is traditional. Many Native cultures gambled, not necessarily with money. The impulse behind gambling games was to socialize, or spread the wealth, or give a winner the illusion of riches amid scarcity, not to become a millionaire by risking the rent. As for Native people becoming economically self-sufficient by making money from non-Native gamblers? No issue at all.

Elizabeth's focus was on the bigger picture. "The tribes don't have a property tax base, because Indian lands are not taxable—not by the feds, not by the states, not by the tribes. Gaming revenues basically serve as a substitute for the lack of a property tax base. They buy the fire trucks and the ambulances and emergency vehicles, and they pay for the police officers and the sanitation and water systems and all of those kinds of things governments have to take care of." Our lunchtime conversation had ended and resumed over dinner at a restaurant a few blocks away. Elizabeth talked between bites of a steak.

"People in American society expect there's going to be a policeman when you call one. That when you need an ambulance, an ambulance will come for you. That when you pick up the phone, there's going to be telephone service. Or you're going to have electricity. Those are the kinds of things that can't be taken for granted in all of Indian Country, even today. Most people in this society have no appreciation of that. And they have no appreciation of the fact that tribes have to engage in other economic activities to pay the costs for those governmental services. That's what the gaming is all about. Everyone thinks the Indians are off getting rich. People need to understand, there is a real distinction between commercial gaming and tribal government gaming. Tribal government gaming is essentially a 100 percent tax, because it goes for governmental programs and services that tribes deliver." Owners of Las Vegas and Atlantic City casinos can spend their profits however they want. Tribal casinos must return profits to the tribe.

"Gaming produces for some tribes—not all tribes, but for a good number—the kinds of revenues that are enabling them to address a lot of social and economic needs. Take health clinics. There are some tribes located where members would have to drive two hours to get health services. Imagine having a heart attack and you're looking at a two-hour drive? Now many tribes are able to put [in] clinics and have defibrillators right in the community. A lot of people in our society take the availability of health care for granted, but for tribal communities, quality health care within a reasonable proximity has long been unavailable. That's changing, and gaming dollars are helping make that change.

"The other thing that's changing too are the kinds of programs tribes can offer. Language preservation is a very high priority for a great many tribes. A lot of people in the early days of tribal gaming used to think, 'Gaming's going to ruin tribes, it's going to change the culture.' But the fact is, gaming revenues have enabled tribes to preserve and perpetuate their culture by funding cultural and language programs and establishing museums and libraries. They fund writers and researchers, often their own tribal members, to record tribal history and conduct language projects. There was never any funding for that."

Some tribes use casino profits to invest in other businesses, like technology. Such investments are increasingly popular, especially among skeptics who consider casinos "the buffalo of today."

Some tribes also distribute casino returns to tribal members in the form of per capitas, or per caps. The edgy Rez Dogs clothing line features a T-shirt reading "Got per cap?" But per caps also yield great debate. A wealthy tribe might issue per caps of thousands of dollars a month, with the result that the sober and the inebriated, the drug counselor and the meth addict, have a lot of cash. A tribal government of lesser means might issue per caps of a hundred dollars a month, helping make daily life easier for people on small fixed incomes. According to Elizabeth, the majority of tribal governments do not distribute per caps but use the money for the collective tribal welfare.

As for non-Native opposition to Native casinos, she thinks it is part of "an old struggle that has characterized the relationship between tribes and states from the beginning. Who gets to call the shots? The law, under the Constitution of the United States, is [that] on Indian lands the tribes call the shots, not the state." She pursed her lips. "A lot of times people think these are new issues, but they are the same old issues that have run like a thread through American history. The tension between local communities and local levels of government and state governments versus tribal governments and tribal rights and tribal powers and tribal authorities."

Another myth involves casino size. They entail "this vast diversity," she said, "all the way from a few gaming machines in a double-wide trailer at this extreme," she gestured, arms apart, "to the Mashantucket Pequots' Foxwoods, which is the largest casino in the entire world. That is your range in Indian country." Most are at the double-wide end of the scale, she said, and fewer than a quarter of them make a profit. Elizabeth herself gambles very little. "I'm always afraid I might win and then everyone will say, 'How did that lawyer win?' Mostly, my tribal clients are tribal gaming regulatory agencies, so it would be highly inappropriate for me to gamble at their gaming facilities. I've tried to keep my inhibitions relatively high." What does she play when she plays? "Maybe blackjack, or I might try some of the new machines that have the little bonus games in them I think are cute."

She is used to another lament: that prosperous casino tribes do not share more of their profits. "Generally, you'll find that tribes are very generous with their gaming revenues. They fund really remarkable and extraordinary things, not limited only to tribal community initiatives, but projects in their local communities, local charities, schools, and an infinite variety of other events and activities," including disaster relief. One major project tribes anted up for was the Smithsonian's National Museum of the American Indian in Washington, D.C.

Tribes take great umbrage, as does Elizabeth, whenever congressional policy makers propose forcing tribes to share their proceeds with other tribes. "It's like, wait a minute," she said, leaning forward and frowning. "Are you going tell the state of Nevada it has to take its revenues and give them to Utah? Would that be asked of any other governmental entity in this country?" She called the idea "inappropriate," and sat back.

Elizabeth was happier talking about how Indian gaming has changed some attitudes "within surrounding non-Indian communities once bitterly opposed to tribal gaming. The sense was, 'It's going to wreck us, organized crime is going to be here.' There's this long list of horribles. 'Everyone's going to be addicted to gambling and people will be losing their houses.' Then, the tribe builds the gaming operation. Suddenly there are all of these jobs and economic opportunities. Tribal gaming operations actually provide pretty decent salaries. A lot of tribes offer benefits no other employers in their areas offer, like retirement plans, health insurance." Furthermore, she added, casinos lead to more work for area plumbers, electricians, and florists, among others.

"Sure, gambling has been associated with certain negative social consequences, but you're not seeing a huge outcry from local communities, because [gambling addiction] is a concern that tribes are sensitive to. There are programs to address these kinds of things."

All in all, "you go to a community that ten years ago was adamantly opposed to gaming and talk to the local community about legislation intended to 'do something about this Indian gaming,' and they're like, 'Leave our Indians alone!'"

What about off-reservation casinos? "It's the political hot button for sure," she said, then pulled from her store of "Indians 101" a striking perspective.

Sometimes the impetus for Indian casinos in East Coast cities, for example, does not come from tribes. "Mayors, city councils, or others will contact the tribe that once lived there and say, 'Are you guys interested in coming and opening a gaming operation here?' The people opposed to this call it 'reservation shopping' and they blame the Indians for it. 'Oh, these Indians, they're overreaching and trying to expand their gaming empires.' Let's face it. In the last twenty years, a lot of states have made permanent reductions in their tax base. That was the politically expedient thing to do at the time and it's a very difficult thing to undo." A re-welcomed tribe, however, might bring in a casino that would increase revenues without increasing taxes. Elizabeth did not have to spell out the irony. Descendants of people who live on land they forced the Indians to leave, look to descendants of those Indians to return and generate cash. Hey, welcome home!

On-reservation casinos alone give her plenty of work. "Tribal governments are now major employers. There are increasingly complex tax issues tribes have to face. To say that tribal governments operate in a substantially more complex legal environment is an understatement."

There are tribal lawyers and then there are tribal lobbyists. Elizabeth bristled when asked about the fallout from the scandal involving lobbyist Jack Abramoff, who made enormous amounts of money from tribes he misrepresented. The scandal prompted a congressional overhaul of federal lobbying laws in 2007. "I never met the man," Elizabeth wrote when I asked her about him, "but I do know that his unlawful and unethical conduct in relation to his tribal clients has given everyone who lobbies a bad name."

"It's especially harmful to tribal interests," she added. Not only is there "a special political relationship between tribal governments and the United States deeply rooted in the Constitution and laws of our nation," but any restrictions on that relationship make it harder for tribes to communicate with the federal government. A related problem, of course, is that federal government employees generally need substantial doses of communication. (Read: "Indians 101.")

———

Among the tribal governments Elizabeth represents is her own; she is general counsel for the Osage Nation Gaming Commission. At last count, the

Osages had seven casinos within the reservation in northeastern Oklahoma, from Tulsa to Bartlesville to Ponca City to Hominy and Pawhuska, the Osage political capital.

What are the odds of an Osage girl from Hominy heading a law firm in Washington that specializes in the fractious and complex field of Indian casino law?

Pretty good.

For one thing, the town with the curious name (Hominy is an Anglicized version of an Osage word, not a corn product, although the school news-paper was *The Grits*) was a stable community, with a population of roughly one-half Native, one-quarter African American, one-quarter white. Children attended integrated schools and cheered the high school football team, called to this day the Hominy Bucks. The pep squad, though, is no longer the Squaws.

Before the advent of good roads to Tulsa and an even closer Wal-Mart, Hominy's Main Street thrived. It still looks well functioning, with restau-rants, an art gallery, and more. There are literally signs to preserve the Osage language; an octagonal red stop sign reads, in smaller letters, *o-tee-do*. A mile or so outside Main Street stands Elizabeth's childhood home, with chunky wooden and brick porch pillars, a big garage, and a view of fawn-colored wheat fields, fallow and blanketed with snow when I visited. Her school bus stopped down the hill.

Elizabeth, the middle child between her two brothers, blossomed in Hominy Elementary school, which she attended in the 1960s. Career school-teachers with master's degrees ("How frequent is *that* in public schools nowadays?" she wondered aloud) "were very kind to me." She recalled her fourth-grade teacher, a Mrs. Adams, bringing in books from her own library to lend Elizabeth. "I was reading the classic American authors, like Longfellow, Thoreau, and—my gosh, my favorite author of all time. 'By the sea, the beautiful Annabelle Lee'—Edgar Allan Poe."

"I know I got extra attention from some of my teachers" in part because they had taught her parents. "While I think I could have had a stronger back-ground in math and science than we had in Hominy, I don't think you could have possibly found better teachers for English. Reading, vocabulary, writing,

American literature. I attribute my academic success to those strict, brilliant school teachers who quite literally dedicated their lives to the children of Hominy. I wouldn't be where I am without them."

Elizabeth did less well trying to emulate Osage dancer Maria Tallchief, a prima ballerina of the New York City Ballet during the 1950s and early 1960s. The name Tallchief could be based on an accurate description; observers from Thomas Jefferson to Lewis and Clark, among others, described Osage men being often well over six feet tall. "Gigantic," wrote Jefferson.

Maria Tallchief studied with Bronislava Nijinska, joined the famed Ballet Russe de Monte Carlo, danced for and then married choreographer George Balanchine, and with her ballerina sister Marjorie started the Chicago City Ballet. In Osage, the fame of the Tallchief sisters was inescapable. "Like all little Osage girls of my age, [I] went to ballet school. We all wanted to be famous ballerinas someday," Elizabeth laughed, then sighed dramatically. "I often wonder whether Maria and Marjorie Tallchief know how some of us chubby, uncoordinated little Osage girls really weren't so crazy about having them as role models. I kid," she added. "They were so beautiful and so talented. They were very much a big influence. I did take years of ballet lessons, all of us did, because we knew that little Osage girls could someday grow up and be prima ballerinas if they worked hard enough." In a later e-mail, Elizabeth wrote that she had studied under Moscelyne Larkin, "another Oklahoma tribal ballerina (Shawnee/Peoria), who danced with the Ballet Russe. It wasn't meant to be, however. It turns out that I possessed an excruciating lack of talent in the arena of dance."

Amid what seemed like an untarnished childhood was one shadow. It was an epoch in Osage history—mostly unknown to this day outside Native America—so horrible that Elizabeth cannot remember learning about it. "It just seems I've always known." It was the Osage Reign of Terror.

As she explained, the Osage bought their reservation from the Cherokee Nation in the 1860s, paying with money received from the United States for giving up aboriginal lands. Having reservation land was, of course, no guarantee of keeping it. In 1906, the federal government focused on clearing the way for white settlement in Oklahoma, including on the Osage Reservation.

Osage leaders, however, worked out a rare beneficial negotiation. By a unique act of Congress, the Osage Nation kept title to the reservation's subsurface. That meant mineral rights—tin, gold, whatever. A roll was prepared with the name of all tribal members. Each was entitled to a "head-right," an equal share in the proceeds of any minerals that might be discovered. Upon death, the "headright" went to the next of kin.

The Osage Reservation proved to have one of the largest deposits of oil in the United States. By the 1920s, the Osages were considered the wealthiest group of people on the planet per capita. Some became famous for lifestyles marked by chauffeur-driven luxury automobiles, notable jewelry, and mansions with crystal chandeliers. One Hominy resident told me his grand-father saw Osages hitching a pair of horses to the front of a new car, putting it in neutral, and going for a ride. The ostentatious gusher life did not go unnoticed. An "unsavory, criminal element," in Elizabeth's words, came a'courting. In every description I have read, these were white men familiar with the Osage inheritance law.

They married Osage women, then murdered them. They also murdered their wives' family members. Maria Tallchief herself wrote in her autobio-graphy of female relatives who were killed, including one poisoned just after her wedding.[2]

The young Bureau of Investigation (which became the FBI) stepped in. Eventually, it solved some cases, focusing on several men.[3] The suspicion remains, though, that many other Osage deaths during this period were murders. The estimated number of victims varies from twenty-four, when the FBI investigation began, to "hundreds and hundreds" according to one FBI official.[4] The shudder among Osages has not ceased.

As a child, "God yes, I knew about it," Elizabeth said. "Who wouldn't? To my knowledge, none of my family members were victims of murder at that time, but that doesn't mean any of us escaped the horror of it, even genera-tions after the fact. It was truly a reign of terror and it happened to our people. That's why the laws are such as they are. Non-Osage spouses can't inherit one's Osage property." Any money or property "goes back to your nearest Osage next of kin or ultimately maybe back to the Osage Nation." The federal law is "on the books today."

Elizabeth is part of a family tradition that helped put federal law on the books.

———

"My family's been coming to Washington for a long time," she said with a smile. "Many, many, many years. More than a hundred years for sure." Photographs of predecessors line her office walls. "One of the things that I wanted to do when I opened Homer Law is have my work environment reflect my background. These old pictures and the pictures from home, my paintings in the foyer—it's all related to my background as an Osage. Service to community is a principle deeply instilled in me." She pointed. "The top picture, the man on the right, is my great grandfather O-loh-hah-walla. He served as chief during the last constitutionally elected Osage tribal government before the Osage Allotment Act in 1906. He was quite an outspoken fellow and conceptually opposed allotment as an effort to divide and undermine the Nation as a whole." She pointed to her grandfather Henry Lohah, her Aunt Hazel, and her father, Charles Henry Lohah, all of whom were among family members with business in Washington.

"I guess I followed much the same path to D.C. as my father." Charles Lohah became a lawyer after much family urging and, she said laughing, after watching some Oklahoma lawyers. "How hard can that be?" he asked himself. Eventually he became an Osage County judge, then went to Washington to "advance Indian policy." The Lohah family joined him when Elizabeth was a teenager. "I went to high school in suburban Maryland for two years. I did my undergraduate degree at the University of Colorado and went to law school at the University of New Mexico. It doesn't matter where I am, home is always home. A lot of people say, 'Well, you don't live on the reservation.' The fact of the matter is, Osages have always gone off and come back and gone off." She added, "I actually claim the entire southwestern United States, from the Mississippi River all the way to the Pacific. Because I grew up in Oklahoma, was educated in Colorado, got my law degree in New Mexico, and married into Arizona."

Her dashing husband, Pete Homer, is Mohave, "a member of the Colorado River Indian tribes." They tease one another about differences in their tribal backgrounds, she said, refusing to give an example, but each has "great admiration" for the other's tribe. "A lot of people don't know anything about Mohaves, which is too bad." Among the uninformed was a librarian at the school their daughter, Ashley, attended in northern Virginia. (The Homers have an older son, Courtney, who, to Elizabeth's delight, has made her a grandmother.) During November—Native American Heritage Month—students were assigned to write a report on a tribe of their choice. Ashley, about nine, chose the Mohaves. When she asked the school librarian for help, he told her there was no such tribe. The Homers intervened.

The tour of Elizabeth's office walls moved on to photographs of Osage roundhouses of the Native American Church. Most are "in very bad repair right now and we may be losing them." One is on property belonging to Elizabeth's relatives. Because I knew a little about the church's history—that the NAC started in Oklahoma and was illegal for a time because it uses peyote as a sacrament, but that passage of the Native American Religious Freedoms Acts in the 1990s made the church legal again—I asked if she were a member.

"I never discuss any kind of religious affiliations," she answered firmly. She then drew attention to a photograph of a water drum used in church ceremonies.

Elizabeth preferred talking about law. She went to law school to prepare for a career in "Indian economic development" but got sidetracked after spending a required semester in the Albuquerque district attorney's office, prosecuting DUIs and other perps. "I loved the work. It was fun. It was interesting. Working for a DA's office, you feel very much a part of your community." In criminal law, "there aren't a lot of gray areas. Someone either committed the crime or didn't. You either have good evidence or you don't. There's not a lot of agonizing over rights and wrongs." She liked it so much that she "ended up going off on a frolic and being a prosecutor for almost a decade."

In midfrolic, she moved to Washington to join the Justice Department's criminal division under Attorney General Janet Reno. The assignment was "to pull together a department-wide initiative to increase the prosecution of child sex crimes on Indian reservations." In addition to the crimes themselves there were, and are, complicated jurisdictional issues. Reno, she said, allowed the Justice Department divisions to change the way "Indian cases are handled in the U.S. attorney's offices across the country. Lo and behold, U.S. attorney's offices were very responsive. A lot of really good work got done in terms of the prosecution of not only child offenses, but other major crimes."

From Justice, Elizabeth was courted to join the Interior Department, which includes the Bureau of Indian Affairs, or BIA, to work on Native issues. She said, looking pleased, "I headed up this cool little policy shop. It was called the Office of American Indian Trust." The challenge was to help federal policy makers understand Indian law and policy. (Read: "Indians 101.")

"I felt like I was a translator. I said, 'I know everyone spoke English, but a lot of times they weren't talking the same language.' Here's a great example. I won't name names, because you don't want to criticize either the agency or the tribe, because they worked it out." The example involved an (unnamed) agency that in the 1930s conducted an experiment resulting in the defoliation of a watershed on an (unnamed) western Indian reservation in an (unnamed) mountain community. The reason for the defoliation—cutting down cottonwood trees and junipers that grew alongside the community's stream—was to see if it would increase the downstream flow of water to an (unnamed) desert city. "A very large desert city." To measure the flow, the agency installed gauges in the stream. Over time, the gauges got more sophisticated and became part of the national warning system to predict flash floods.

Years passed. "Some of the children who grew up playing in those cottonwood trees, [became] elected officials." They also became angry. "Not one drop of additional water was produced by cutting down those magnificent, ancient trees, in which countless generations of children played, or the bushes along the watershed. What actually happens is terrible erosion, as the land along the bank is washed downriver increasingly over time. The erosion became so bad that people's cornfields were being washed away. Then there's the silting up of big, important dams producing hydroelectric power downstream. It's really a bad thing to defoliate the watersheds. Very bad idea. Understandably, there were some hard feelings about this."

Feelings got harder. The tribe's environmental department, which was trying to restore the watershed, needed data maintained by the (unnamed) agency, much of which came from the gauges. The (unnamed) agency denied the first request and ignored later ones.

"At some point, the tribe discovered the agency had let its lease payments for the gauges lapse. A letter was sent to the head of the federal agency saying, essentially, 'You get these stream flow gauges off our reservation by such-and-such a date or you can pick them up on the highway outside the reservation line on such-and-such day.'"

The ultimatum worked.

"That's when the agency asked my office to get involved. To its credit, the agency was equally disapproving of the manner in which the tribe had been treated." Elizabeth resolved the conflict with a single field visit and a couple of follow-up calls. "The tribe didn't take the stream flow gauges out. The agency provided the public information the tribe wanted. Once they started talking, it was simple to resolve. My office simply facilitated the dialogue."

Despite the "happy ending," as she called it, the conflict pointed to a major problem tribes face in the federal bureaucracy: turnover. "That's part of the Indian experience, too. You finally get where you've got a decent relationship with the agency, then somebody retires or they get transferred and it all starts all over again."

How? With "Indians 101," an encore presentation.

"One of the things I've come to accept is that we'll always have to start with 1492, every time there's someone new to educate. Whether it's the Congress, a new administration or agency head, or the press, you have to start at 1492. Then you have to talk about the Constitution and about the existence of Indian tribes as political entities. You must recite article 1, section 8, of the United States Constitution. You have to move step by step through American history. Yes, Indians are citizens, but they've only been citizens and allowed full voting rights since 1924. By the time you've skimmed the surface, they're kind of glazed over because you've had to spend so much time setting the legal and political context to get to whatever it is you're discussing. You lose people sometimes. Does that mean that you don't do it? No. It just means you have to make another run at it."

In 1999, just before the Clinton administration became the Bush administration, Elizabeth decided to leave her cool little policy shop. She was appointed vice chairman of the National Indian Gaming Commission for a three-year term. The work included "a number of rule-makings" that were "intended to strengthen the overall regulatory framework for tribal gaming." As her Web site (www.HomerLaw.com) states, she is "a proponent of collaborative rulemaking." Working things out as a group, as any student of Native life knows, is a Native tradition.

From Justice, to Interior, to the Gaming Commission, and Homer Law, Elizabeth's commute barely changed. Washington, D.C., "is such a center of power with regard to Indian affairs, because it is the Congress that sets Indian law and policy and the administration that effectuates it. Historically, tribal governments have had to interact with the Interior Department, but today virtually all of the federal agencies have some nexus with tribal governments. There is also the National Gaming Commission and the Indian Health Service. Washington is a natural place for politically active tribal people to devote some amount of time. Some of us just stick around a little longer."

As if to prove her point, Elizabeth took me to a bustling reception—fancy hors d'oeuvres, standard soft drinks—that the National Museum of the American Indian held to kick off the annual convention of the National Congress of American Indians. The NCAI, founded in 1944 in response to the disastrous federal policies to "terminate" tribes, is based in Washington too. Name tags pointed out Native stars. EchoHawk! Fire Thunder! Elizabeth, flashing a brilliant smile, seemed to know everybody.

———

Much of Indian law comes down to land and trust—legal trust. To Elizabeth Lohah Homer, the basic connection between the United States government and Native lands is simple. The same way an individual sets up a trust for a family member, so does the federal government have Indian lands—some sixty-six million acres—in trust. "The United States holds title to the land. But the rights, the private property interest, belongs to the tribe or tribal members. They are the beneficiary of the trust"—including land and the land's resources.

It was another day, and she was getting rewarmed up. "To put it as simply as possible, the United States has certain duties and responsibilities to tribes and tribal members." Federal controls over tribal properties have "relaxed significantly" over the past decades, as laws gave tribal governments and individuals more say. But "certain transactions are still subject to the approval of the Interior Secretary. And the Bureau [of Indian Affairs] continues to collect and distribute proceeds, in most cases." As examples, she listed a range of transactions from "simple grazing leases" to "major natural resources development such as timber, fisheries" and "the extraction of minerals, oil, and gas production."

Basically, the U.S. government, with its enormous interest in Indian land, has a legal obligation to perform trust functions properly. "The Osage reservation, for example, produces oil and gas. Companies will bid for leases on particular tracts of lands, and they will develop those resources. Once [the resources] are in production, the royalty that the tribe is owed for those minerals is paid to BIA." The BIA deposits the money, whether from oil and gas or whatever, in the Treasury. The money, as specified in numerous treaties, is then distributed to tribal members. That was the plan. But the BIA and its parent company, the Department of the Interior, failed so spectacularly they were at the heart of a massive class action lawsuit. Native people simply call it Cobell.

In 1996, Elouise Cobell, treasurer of the Blackfeet Nation in Montana, sued the secretary of the interior for mishandling trust responsibilities from 1887 on. The year 1887 was the date of the Dawes Act, which cut up reservation land in return for ever-decreasing income to individual owners. Cobell's tally for the money owed to some 500,000 individuals came to $46 billion. Billion! At one point, her lawsuit led to a court-ordered shutdown of Interior Department computer systems to prevent data from being destroyed.[5]

"Think of it like this," said Elizabeth. "Your bank calls you up and says, 'You know all that money in your trust account your parents set up for you fifty years ago? We've lost the paperwork and can't tell you how much of the money on deposit in our bank belongs to you. We're probably not going to be able to find it either, but don't worry, all of the money is still here.' Now, what is a reasonable person going to do? Say, 'Gee, thanks for letting me know? No hard feelings, we don't really need that money?' I seriously don't think so." The amount of money must be significant. "Indian Country" is "rich in resources. That's the fuel that built the economy of this country."

Musing, she wondered if the amount of money owed could be figured with economic modeling. "We know how much of X kind of timber one acre of land on X reservation can produce, because we know the silviculture. We know the life cycle of the tree and how fast the trees grow. If you have 10,000 acres, you can project how much timber could be produced over a 150-year period." And so on. "You do the math and arrive at some projections."In December 2009, thirteen years after Cobell started, Cobell settled, without Elizabeth's economic modeling. The tab was a little over $3.4 billion. About a third would be put in an accounting/trust administration fund for individuals affected by the mismanagement, with each individual receiving an initial $1,000 check. About two-thirds, in a trust land consolidation fund, would buy back cut-up pieces of land and return them, merged, for tribal use. As one of many unenthusiastic Native people put it, "Using our money to buy back our land."

Still, Cobell was settled. Two primary factors seemed the key. One, President Barack Obama, leading the third administration facing the lawsuit, was committed to finding a solution.[6] Two, Eloise Cobell was affected by the aging of those whom she wanted to help. She called the settlement "a bittersweet victory, at best." More obstacles lay ahead though. The U.S. House of Representatives twice passed the appropriate funding, but not until November 2010 did the Senate do so.

Elizabeth thought Cobell could have settled much more quickly, if—a major if—the federal government admitted error, then moved on to work out details. "Our judicial system is adversarial in nature. There's going to be a winner and there's going to be a loser, in most cases. Nothing drives parties further apart more than litigation. Usually there is a way to work things through to a reasonable resolution." Elizabeth Lohah Homer long has preferred the reasonable approach.

———

A few months later, we met again, at the Pechanga Resort and Casino. The self-described largest Indian casino in California rises from the desert east of San Diego. In summer especially, one staggers inside for relief from heat so intense, the feeling is like a hundred hair dryers aimed at every inch of one's body. The interior reprieve of cool is soon forgotten, however, as other assaults are delivered to the senses, particularly hearing. On the ground floor, home base for low rollers, the noise from electronic bells, clinks, whooshes, and indescribable upper-register emotings drown out most human conversation. At the same time, countless colored lights blink from every angle, including those from literally thousands of slot and video machines that stand in rows, beckoning like an army of robotic Loreleis.

Many customers looked subdued, if purposeful. Women pressed through the aisles on the highest of heels, an old man rolled by in a wheelchair equipped with an oxygen tank, some patrons, hunkering on a stool in front of one slot machine, managed with outstretched arms to commandeer three. The endless low rollers and the flusher ones upstairs were bringing Pechanga, owned by the once near destitute Pechanga Band of Luiseño Indians, hundreds of millions of dollars a year.

It is a safe bet, most gamblers are unaware that Pechanga and other large Indian casinos also offer adjoining but calmer worlds, where the divide between Creator and mammon is vast, and serious conferences address Native issues. This is the case in Pechanga.

Only steps away from the casino clangor, past the hotel registration desk and through a few turns of hallways, one comes to standard-issue ballrooms and meeting rooms with not-so-standard-issue names: Eagle's View, Turtle, Mountain Lion, Red-tail Hawk. In these rooms one August, when temperatures outside were hellish and room rates lowered, some hundred Native members of Women Empowering Women of Indian Nations, or WEWIN, gathered to attend talks such as "Lobbying and Federal Advocacy."[7]

One of the liveliest sessions with the least lively title—"Intergovernmental Relations: How to Work Effectively with State, Local, Federal, and Tribal Governments"—took place in Coyote Room. There, Elizabeth Lohah Homer, one of the two speakers, made the occasion a time of laughter laced with outrage, as she recounted various ways (off the record, unfortunately) she confronted power on behalf of tribal clients and won. One hint in preparing strategy: get to know the official's staff, rather than the official.

Throughout the session, Elizabeth looked entirely at home. She was talking about law, she was doing so within an enterprise she knows well, and her audience was composed of other Native women. Nobody needed "Indians 101."

A Trio of Lumbees

PAMELA BROOKS SWEENEY, CURT LOCKLEAR, AND MARY ANN CUMMINGS JACOBS

What is the largest tribe east of the Mississippi, the largest least-known tribe in the country, and the largest tribe the United States government does not recognize?

The Lumbees.

"A ballpark figure" puts the population at around 56,000, says Dr. Stanley Knick, who heads the Native American Resource Center at the University of North Carolina at Pembroke. The commercial and social hub of Lumbee country, Pembroke lies about two hours inland from North Carolina's southernmost coast and is surrounded by expanses of flat farmland. Beyond that are swamps, treasured in part for having kept centuries of marauding Europeans, and European Americans, away. Through the swamps meanders the Lumbee River, officially the Lumber River. This is Robeson County, which to Lumbees is a sacred phrase.

My visit—set in motion years ago by a suggestion from Kentucky's Campbellsville University librarian John Burch—began at a Saturday morning rendezvous in the Pembroke McDonald's parking lot with the new head of Native American studies at UNC-Pembroke, Prof. Mary Ann Jacobs, herself Lumbee. She soon steered me to the Baptist Student Union, where for $15 I rented the office couch for the night. There were no hotels in Pembroke. Next, she drove me to a soccer field, her daughter among the girls running hard, where she introduced me to another Lumbee soccer mother, Pam Sweeney, who grinned a greeting under a Great Smoky Mountains

souvenir hat. By the end of practice, Mary Ann and Pam had recited how they are related, talk that prompted an older woman on the soccer field sidelines to point to the sky and say, "We have the same Father." Pam also had agreed to an interview and had invited me to stay at her home the following nights. The combination of Native American and Southern hospitality must leave few strangers in the rain.

With time on my own that afternoon, I visited the lightly attended thirty-seventh Lumbee Fall Powwow. It was immediately clear this was not a major cultural event, unlike the Lumbees' annual homecoming, which lasts a week. The powwow booths sold such folksy (not notably Native) items as "britches washcloths," homemade pickles, and sandwiches comprised of two slabs of fatback in cornbread. Among many T-shirts for sale was a Lumbee edition featuring the question "Who are Your People?" To figure that membership is a consuming Lumbee pastime, and the T-shirt listed twenty or so of the most common Lumbee names. They include Brooks (Pam's maiden name), Cummings (Mary Ann's maiden name), and Jacobs (Mary Ann's married name). Another common name, encountered virtually everywhere, is Locklear. It takes up six pages in the local phone book.

In the powwow's center area, dancers moved to drums and songs as they do throughout the country, but their regalia resembled that of Plains Indians. The image returned when, at Mary Ann's recommendation, I read a provocative essay by Seneca scholar Barbara Alice Mann, who scoffs at a pan-Indian powwow look she calls "Lakota Lite."[1] Yet who is to say what makes a person Native? In comparison with the Lumbees' full-throated embrace of, say, Christianity, the Lumbee powwow seemed more like a polite nod to hazy ancestry. And what an ancestry.

PAMELA BROOKS SWEENEY

"This is the home place. This land. That's where I was born. Have always known we were Indian. The only thing it meant to me back then, it was I was not white. I was not white. We went to a church where it was all Indian. Didn't have a lot of interactions with white people other than if they were in school, like your schoolteacher. Did we do a lot of powwow things growing

up as children, lot of *Indian* so-called?" asked Pamela Brooks Sweeney, making air quotes around Indian. "No. We didn't. Just knew that we were Lumbees."

Pam Sweeney is an almost-always-in-motion forty-year-old devoted daughter, sister, wife, mother, working woman, and children's choir director at Berea Baptist Church, an imposing building across the street from the UNC-Pembroke campus. She made time to talk in her big brick house on a block-long street in the countryside, a street shared by several relatives in their own big brick houses. In one lived her parents and an unmarried sister; in two others lived her other sister and a brother with their families. The Sweeneys' contains Pam, her husband John, who works at a factory that makes train brakes, and their children: John Phillip, twelve, and Paige, ten. It is packed with consumer goods, from her exercise equipment to a grand piano, which she and her children play. An enormous garage, site of John's many hobbies, opens onto a kitchen so well outfitted (a device keeps bananas from touching the counter) and well stocked that the family might be able to survive months without leaving. Throughout the sparkling clean house, whose floors John had just waxed, is tangible evidence of Christianity: a crèche on the piano, biblical-passage magnets on the refrigerator. Pam's extensive paperback collection, which she invited me to browse or borrow, is, with the exception of volumes by romance writer Nora Roberts, what might be called Christian Easy Reading. Such genres as Amish romances (e.g., *When the Soul Mends*, by Cindy Woodsmall) are arrayed next to other female Christian-oriented authors. The jacket copy for Terri Blackstock's *Shadow of Doubt* read, "Either her client's Christian faith is a sham, or she's the victim of a deadly frame-up."

Pam helps run the Brooks family's two nursing businesses, one for "assisted living," one for home care. Her workday outfit is scrubs, but this afternoon she wore the stylish track suit she had on during soccer practice. Pam looked both relaxed and animated while sitting on a plush couch in the family TV/movie room. "Sitting" is not entirely accurate. In addition to air quotes, Pam's other habitual speech add-on, when emphasizing a point or indicating that something was meant in jest, was to lean forward and touch the leg or arm of whomever she was talking to. She also jumped up frequently to retrieve photos from the elaborate bookshelf and cabinet her father had built into a side of the room. On top of the cabinet were three large Indian baskets "from somewhere in the southwest." They constituted almost the only physical indication of "Indianness" in the house.

Pam's family has lived in Robeson County as far back as anyone can remember. "We went to school here, we went to church here. Our friends and family were here. I can remember Mom or Dad's segregation stories, where 'We had to use this bathroom' or 'We had to use this water fountain because we were not white.' By the time we came along, that didn't exist. I didn't have bad feelings about or negative feelings that I was Indian, because we just kind of worked in our circle."

The phrase "segregation stories" brought me up short. Until then I did not know that people delegated to use "colored" drinking fountains and the like included not only individuals whose ancestors were brought to this country against their will, but those who were here first.[2] In her sunny side of the street way, Pam added, her parents were so poor, "They probably didn't even have a lot of opportunities to attend things that would put them in a segregation [situation], like going to the movies." They certainly could afford movies and more now. "Daddy" Brooks, as Pam refers to her father, became a successful contractor.

Pam's career path began when she was a child. Her "mom's mother" moved in with the family after having a stroke. "We had to give her a bath, you had to help her get up at night to go to the bathroom." After high school, "I said, 'I'm going to be a nurse because this is what I do. I take care of Grandma.'" Pam also helped her uncle, a pharmacist. "From junior high on, we worked at the pharmacy. You couldn't do that these days, even help fill prescriptions."

Because UNC-Pembroke had no nursing program, Pam set her sights on UNC-Greensboro. Her parents lived paycheck to paycheck ("The biggest traveling we did was to the beach for a day") and could not help financially, nor could the tribe, so Pam applied to the Indian Health Service. It came through with a monthly stipend for all four years of college. In exchange, she had to work a "two-year payback." The IHS is connected only to federally recognized tribes, so there was no IHS facility in Lumbee country.

Pam did her payback at an IHS hospital in Lawton, Oklahoma. Most patients were Kiowa and Comanche. Yes, they had heard of Lumbees, she said, laughing high, tap on leg, "because we invade everywhere." Lawton was an eye-opener. "If you had your card from whatever tribe, it was accepted. You came in and saw the doctor. You didn't have to pay for anything. That was different for me. It was kind of like some things are a down side, because people would come and hang out at the hospital. They didn't worrrrk," she said, drawing out the word.

As for college life in Greensboro—virtually her first time outside the Lumbee world—Pam was "the only Indian on our floor. They paired me with somebody from New York. She was a black girl, but her skin was whiter than I was. She was an albino black." Nobody on the floor fussed about such differences, she recalled, possibly because everyone had a bigger commonality of being freshmen. "We were new, not make any waves." She and her former roommate Dawn still send one another Christmas cards. "I was darker than she was and she was black. And I'm Indian and I look white and she looked white."

Thus did the subject of color arise.

"Do we look like the typical Indian? No. Versus what you see on TV. The long flowing hair, the nice dark-toned olive skin. No. See, everybody in my family is this color," she pointed to her pinkish arm. I managed to interject that her son is considerably darker. "You can see the difference between him and Paige, can't you?" Pam jumped up to find a photo. "Especially in this picture. This is when they were sweet," she trailed off for a second. They both seemed sweet to me, John Phillip serious and engaged, Paige winsome and curious. "See how olive he is? And see how pale she is?"

Of her part Irish American and Italian American husband, whom Pam met through his sister, also a nurse, Pam said, "He's red. I mean, his skin tone is just red." She found another photo. "These are my dad's brothers and sisters. This is my dad. See, he's kind of light. This is his brother that was born right under him. He has a dark complexion. This is the one that's a doctor." She segued into stepsiblings and further mixtures. "Uncle Martin had six children with his first wife and [after] those six children, he married a white lady. Very fair skin. They have four that are very white, light complexion, and two very dark children." She went on about a sister "white like me" whose husband is very dark, as is one of their children. If people saw them together, "they would probably think that was not her child, that kind of thing."

She smiled. "If you ask my mom, 'What are you?' she always says, 'I tell them I'm a little bit of everything.' Because there's white descendants down her line. Has to be. And down my dad's line. Not necessarily intermarrying." She clapped her hands. "Sometimes off to the side!"

Then there is hair, which Pam expounded on. Paige's is wavy and brown; John Phillip's is black, wiry, and short. Pam joked earlier that there's "good hair and bad hair," and she keeps John Phillip's "cut to the good." Of her own reddish brown hair, Pam said, looking not thrilled, "I have currrrrrly curly curly hair." Her father has hair similar to John Phillip's, but gray. As for Pam's friendly and spunky mother, who answered my "Nice to meet you," with "What's left of me," she wore a wig, her hair gone: chemo. She died only months later.

———

Where had the "little bit of everything" come from? One possible place is a fabled island off the North Carolina coast. Said Pam without inflection, "They say we're descended from the Lost Colony."

The theory, well known in Lumbee lore, centers on the group of settlers sent by Sir Walter Raleigh to live on Roanoke Island in 1587 under the direction of Governor John White. After returning to England for more supplies, White came back to Roanoke in 1590, the Spanish Armada of 1588 having disrupted his schedule, and found no trace of the settlers, only carved letters spelling out C.R.O. and Croatoan. He thought the "lost" settlers were safely inland with tribal people, attest the authors of *The Only Land I Know: A History of the Lumbee Indians.* Did some of the once lost end up in Robeson County? Partial evidence, posits the pro–Lost Colony Lumbee faction, is that 43 percent of Lost Colony names, including Locklear, are found among today's Lumbee names.[3]

Lost Colonists or no, there may have been fewer European ancestors than thought. Barbara Alice Mann writes, "Several Southeastern groups . . . were, at contact, white-skinned people." To back up her claim, she offers seven footnoted citations, from 1610 on.[4] Her assertion is both provocative and logical; if other continents had indigenous people of different hues, why not North America? Could light skin color thought to be European in origin be Native? What of the reddish hair supposedly typical of North Carolina's natives centuries ago, hair that by description looks like Pam Sweeney's?

The Lost Colony lore itself is backed up to some extent by family stories, says the Resource Center's Dr. Knick, who is not Lumbee but has lived in Robeson County for decades. "There is at least the oral tradition in some families of a connection to the Roanoke colony, and to the Indians who are affiliated with it, which would have been coastal Algonquians." The Algonquian language, along with eastern Siouan and Iroquoian, were the three major tribal language stocks in what became the Carolinas. It is not known what language Lumbees spoke, but they speak it no more.

One might say that what got "lost" centuries ago was not a colony but a culture, or manifestations of one, including whatever religion was practiced before Christianity took hold, whatever dances were danced before today's amalgam showed up, and whatever language was used before Lumbee tongues wrapped themselves around English, or what today is called Lumbee English.

The dialect is one by which, the boast goes, any Lumbee in the world can recognize and understand another. The corollary is that virtually no non-Lumbee can understand much. The dialect has at least three elements: specific words for certain things, like *ellick*, which is coffee with sugar; various verb formations in sentences such as "He be took it" or "I'm been home"; and a taffy-like accent I inadequately describe as Southern plus. Add all three, plus other linguistic elements and speed, and there is Lumbee. (My few conversations with "purer" Lumbee speakers put me in mind of times I used high German to interview Bavarians. In Munich then, as in Pembroke now, we tried, but the gap was great.)

Lumbees like Pam Brooks Sweeney can tamp down the local locution and render a standard y'all North Carolina accent. Her speaking style also included a tendency to stop one sentence and start another while repeating parts of the first, almost like a round. A long story involving off-campus college roommates and the "cohesiveness" of her people ended with, "If you would hear anything, it wouldn't be against Indians. It would probably be against blacks."

With that, we came to the most volatile race card in the Lumbee equation, African American ancestry. The general belief about Lumbee heritage is that there is a triple gene pool, comprised of possibly many Native groups, blacks, and whites. The genetic trio is not without consequence. One young Lumbee man told me that when he attended UNC-Charlotte, he was called "high yellow." After graduation, he hurried home, where he needed to "pass" only as Lumbee.

It seemed evident, from reading Lumbee histories about escaped slaves being adopted into the tribe, from hearing references to some Lumbees owning slaves, from looking at old photographs, and from looking at some faces of Lumbees going about their business today, an African connection exists. There was, historically, also an African *dis*connection.

In 1835, a time when abolitionists had gained power and stature, and slaves had become increasingly rebellious, or were feared to be, the nervous North Carolina General Assembly rewrote the state constitution. It further segregated whites and blacks and put Native Americans into a third category, "free persons of color." The category was no boon; the new constitution also took away a number of Natives' rights, such as voting.

The effect on North Carolina Indian communities was twofold: they were even more unfavorably inclined toward the white establishment, and their bonds with one another strengthened. Left to increasingly segregated lives, various North Carolina Natives built their own churches and schools. It is debatable whether such efforts were undertaken to maintain tribal identity or to separate themselves from the even more oppressed African American population, or both. But separate themselves they did. Then came the Civil War. Many Lumbees were conscripted into Confederate labor gangs but escaped back to the swamps, where they aided runaway slaves and Union soldiers who escaped prisoner of war camps.

The first nineteenth-century cataclysm in the region predated the rewritten constitution and the war, however. It began in 1830, when the U.S. Congress, encouraged and directed by President Andrew Jackson and

prompted by Georgians eager for Cherokee land, passed the hideous legislation to "remove" eastern Indians "voluntarily" to west of the Mississippi.
There had been much opposition from congressional Republicans, petition-
gathering northern women, and the affected tribal Nations themselves. But
the government-mandated exodus, the infamous Trail of Tears, was law.
There followed a ruling by the Supreme Court and an eloquent majority
opinion written by Supreme Court Chief Justice John Marshall (in *Worcester
v. Georgia*) against the legislation, but nothing helped. Jackson famously
defied the Court. Constant harassment from white land-grabbers, aided by
Southern legislatures that were making life miserable for tribal members,
plus a major schism within the pivotal Cherokee leadership—to leave or try
to stay—contributed to Natives being forced a third of the way across the
country, often on foot, to Oklahoma.[5]

The best-known refugees were the Cherokee, for whom the direction
west symbolized death, presciently so. According to a missionary who
accompanied them, about a quarter of the population, 4,000 people, died.
The Cherokees were not the only ones displaced. "By the end of the nineteenth century, over sixty tribes, mostly from the East, had been exiled to
Oklahoma," report scholars Theda Perdue and Michael D. Green.[6]

During this sorry chapter in American history, the Lumbees lay low. It
was not a time to push for a treaty with the federal government. It was a time
to hide in the swamps. Lumbees avoided the federal government for their
own survival. Consequently, however, their descendants have no treaty to
help prove they are legitimate.

While the Lumbees took cover in their swamp homeland, some Cherokees
took cover in their mountain homeland, with government permission. Their
descendants, the Eastern Band of Cherokee, are the sole federally recognized
tribe in North Carolina.[7] They also constitute the primary opposition to the
Lumbees' political goal of being granted federal recognition.

If the Lumbees did receive federal recognition, presumably they would
receive federal monies for such needs as housing and health care, which
might reduce funds assigned to Eastern Cherokees. Publicly, the Cherokees
maintain that they do not oppose Lumbee recognition, but I know no
Lumbee who believes this. The Cherokees say they merely want the Lumbees

to go through the proper recognition procedures. The Lumbees argue that they have tried, are trying, and will keep trying, no matter how many obstacles are put up.

In the 1930s, some relatives of today's Lumbees were so determined to get federal recognition that they went through the humiliating and bizarre process of being examined—teeth, nose, skull, and so forth—by Harvard anthropologist Dr. Carl C. Seltzer to prove their "Indianness." He actually concluded that two children from the same parents could be differentiated— one as Indian, the other not.[8]

The ongoing Cherokee blockade has not led to touchy-feely relations between the two tribes, yet there is neighborly activity. Pam and her family vacationed "in Cherokee," as she called it. "To me, it's just like another place in the state of North Carolina. Except it's mainly Indian populated. Do I have anything against Cherokees? No."

The reverse, she said, is not true. When she looked for an Indian Health Service facility to do her two-year payback, "the closest place you could go, east of the Mississippi, is Cherokee. The likelihood of Lumbees going to Cherokee to work are nil." She said she knows of no Lumbee ever getting a job at the Cherokee IHS.

"I don't think the Cherokees kind of like us. That's the impression we've always gotten. They don't consider us to be true Indians. Because the Lumbees here are from all color extremes. You have blond Lumbees, you have, you know," she waved the air.

Among the arguments by Cherokees and others against Lumbees' attempts to gain federal recognition is that their tribe's name has changed. It is now the Lumbee Indians of Robeson County, but over the years the name was changed at least four times, not necessarily with Lumbee consent. An early version was the Croatan Indians.

Another argument against recognition is that the Lumbees would put up a casino, as the Cherokees have. The Baptist- and Methodist-centric Lumbees scoff. "We don't even have bingo!"

Dr. Knick, speaking near a display of artwork at the Native American Resource Center, described the conundrum this way. "There are a number of misperceptions about Lumbees, having to do with the absence of a traditional language, having to do with an amalgamated history, as opposed to a single track of history." He went on, "We can see in the colonial period remnants of tribes coming into this area from various sources and joining up with the preexistent groups who were here. There's a very rich archeological record. We know there were people here in pre-contact times [at least 14,000 years ago] and up through the mid-1700s." There were also "post-epidemic remnant groups." After listing several influences, he said, "It makes for a very complex history. I think that has contributed greatly to the resistance for recognition."

As another scholar wrote, "Lumbees challenge almost every preconception of what Indians should be."[9]

Then there is quantity. "I think it would be easier for Lumbees to get recognized if there were 600 of them, than if there are 56,000 of them," said Dr. Knick. "That's just a fact."[10] Another fact is the African American connection. Could racism be keeping Lumbees from their goal? That has nothing to do with objections, say Cherokees and their allies, nothing at all.

———

Late Sunday afternoon, after days of talking and visiting with the Sweeneys, and a piano recital by both children, Paige and her father John accompanied me to the last day of the powwow. Attendance had not picked up. I snapped a photo of Paige posing with Miss Lumbee. That evening, to thank the family for their hospitality, I treated them to dinner at a restaurant of their choice: Ruby Tuesday's in nearby Lumberton, which has less of a Lumbee presence. It was and is considered "white." It also served liquor. I ordered a beer. When the waitress brought it, Paige's eyes grew ever wider and more horrified. "I thought you were a *nice* person," she said and hid my offending beverage with her menu.

The Sweeney future looked secure.

CURT LOCKLEAR

"Mr. Curt" may be the most popular eighty-four-year-old in Robeson County, "a jewel," in the view of Dr. Knick. About four decades ago, Curt

Locklear started Pembroke Hardware (now True Value Hardware, but nobody I met called it that). He still worked there, coming in virtually every day to preside—or "hold court," some said affectionately—at an old desk smack dab in the middle of the hangar-like inventory-filled store. The business's success, said community members, was due to Mr. Curt's way, from the beginning, of treating each customer with respect.

Like many Lumbees his age, Curt Locklear grew up scrambling to eke out a living from the earth. Generations of Lumbees, although not he, were sharecroppers. Farm work was replaced with manufacturing, until NAFTA came along and, by one estimate, Robeson County lost 9,000 jobs.

"I grew up very, very poor. 'Course, everybody grew up poor back then. I stayed in the back woods with my grandmother and my granddaddy." Mr. Curt is a tall man with a creased face, a thatch of straight gray hair, a little trouble hearing, and a gentle matter-of-factness. We began talking in the main part of the store, but within a minute, that notion ended. An elderly man came by as if to say hello and joke about their ages. "I'm as old as the hills," said Mr. Curt. "I'm the oldest deacon at that church now," said the other. He added miserably, "I thought I had to speak to you," and imparted the news, or what I could make out from Lumbee dialect, "the boy killed in the motorcycle" was his twenty-seven-year-old grandson. "He never smoked a cigarette, never drunk a beer," he said, as Mr. Curt listened. "He just loved fast vehicles." Prayers were promised.

When the man left, Mr. Curt suggested we move to the break room. It had several vending machines, in which health-conscious Mr. Curt puts no money, and a long table, which we shared with a few women. They were eating a fast-food supper, at which he looked askance, before their shift began. One announced, "We're the clean-up ladies," and pronounced Mr. Curt "sweet." He winced.

Almost the first thing he talked about was identity. "Everybody was the same thing. You didn't have a mixed-up crowd like you got now." He clarified, "There's more this crossing. Black marry white, white marry black, Native American and so forth. See, back in those days, Indians weren't allowed to marry a white. If they married a white person, they were run out of the county. Or vice versa. I never shall forget the woman that first married a white man and stayed in the county." He remembered a Lumbee man who trained to be a teacher, married a white woman, and was forced to leave, ending up teaching in his wife's home state of South Carolina where, so I gathered, his identity was not known.

Mr. Curt would return to race and racism but now spoke with great affection about farming. "Some would call it tough, but really I enjoyed it. I was robust. I felt like work. And I worked like the dickens. I plowed, I did things that was to be done on the farm. Grow about three or four acres of tobacco and five, six acres of cotton and corn." He had one sibling, a brother. "Both of us loved the work." Their grandparents had some land. "It was a little farm, but they owned it. I doubt it would have took care of us, but we got out and worked on other people's farms. We put in tobacco one day a week for ourselves and the rest of the time for other people. My mother'd get that money." Days started around dawn. "In the summertime, like five, five thirty. That's not early. We went to bed right time. It was nice. We didn't have many people back then in the community."

Curt Locklear met his wife, Catherine Locklear, when both were students at what was then called Pembroke State College. "The college was so small, every time we'd have something, everybody'd get together. It was simple. I went to college and one day she came along and that was it. I got married and haven't thought about a thing but marriage since then. I never knew what doing wrong was. I've been married almost sixty-two years. I worked so hard I forgot about the mean things."

The couple began having children, nine in all. "Nine would be terrible today. But back when I had them, shoot." He rhapsodized a bit more about hogs, cows, and a vegetable garden. "Oh, we were planting collards, cabbage, turnips, potatoes. We had about eight or ten things we grew in the garden. Most of that was put up in the summer to use in the winter. 'Course we had a winter garden, too. And we had ham meat, all kind of meat. Tell you what. I had better meals then than I have now. I had a Southern meal every day, three times a day."

There were, though, issues both deeper and wider. In a 1973 interview, the late Lumbee historian and poet Lew Barton asked him about an inferiority complex affecting "our people."

Mr. Curt eventually turned the question back on him. "I mean being completely honest with yourself. When did you start thinking that you was good as white man? Have you always thought you was good as a white man?"

After Barton admitted, "No, not really," Mr. Curt laughed and said he hadn't either.

In the interview, Barton recalled going to a local movie theater that hired an "Indian boy" who "knew the Indians from the white people" and whose job it was to separate who went upstairs to the segregated balcony, one side for blacks, one side for Indians, and who was allowed downstairs. "When a boy wanted to show off a little bit and sit downstairs with his girlfriend, he might tip this little Indian boy, and he'd let him go." Mr. Curt said he never tried that. "I saw where those superior people were sitting. I knew that wasn't for me, Lew. I headed on upstairs, where I's supposed to go."[11]

When World War II got under way, Curt Locklear became part of the army's 260th Combat Engineers. Again, racism caused strange confusions. Some North Carolina draft boards tried to put Natives in "colored" units, but there was resistance. Most North Carolina Natives, including Mr. Curt, ended up in white units.[12] He was sent to Europe. "I didn't get frightened to death at anything back then. I was young. I was sort of wanting some action." In his telling, he did not get a lot. He began in England, then was sent to France after the Normandy invasion, then to Germany, then Austria. He did not liberate any concentrate camps. "Somehow I missed them, which is all right." (The week after my visit to Pembroke, another Lumbee veteran was scheduled to speak about his World War II experiences, including liberating Wöbbelin concentration camp in northern Germany.)

While in the army, Curt Locklear was introduced to liquor and cigarettes. He drank "a little. In the army, who didn't?" Cigarettes had a different consequence. "If I hadn't stopped [eight years earlier], I wouldn't be living. I was beginning to have lung problems. Never smoked a cigarette until I went in the army. The Camel, I went nuts over it."

Throughout his army years, he met only one Native: a Lumbee. "I got hurt in Salzburg, Austria, and was sent back to 134th General Hospital in Rheims, France. And lo and behold Earl Lowry [Lowry is also a well-known Lumbee name] was the commanding officer. He was a local fellow, and he loved to get local news. He invited me down to his quarters, had oranges and apples."

Private Locklear never doubted where he would live after the war. "I left the cotton patch picking cotton when I went in, and came straight back to it. Couldn't move me. No way. All my family's been that way."

He was, though, a different man, as revealed in the 1973 interview with Lew Barton.

Locklear: "When we left here and went in the army, we simply didn't think about this stuff anymore. We were equal with everyone else. . . . But then, just as soon as I come back to Robeson County [after three years in the army] and sit down on a chair in Maxton [in Robeson County] after nine days of being discharged, because I'd forgotten a little about the situation, and was refused to have my hair cut, I started to thinking about it again then."

Barton: "They let you know you were back home, quick."

———

Curt Locklear finished college in Pembroke, taught high school chemistry for eight years, "dropped out," as he put it, to go into the insurance business, taught again, then entered the hardware business after another man went out of business. "It wasn't a thing that was planned. We wouldn't plan a thing like that back in my day. You had nothing to plan it *with*."

All Mr. Curt had was a "small amount of merchandise. But it was a start. Weren't nobody else had nothing no bigger than I had, hardly. It was all on a credit." To get the business going, he borrowed $22,000. "Whoa, gracious alive. I told my mother that. She said, 'I didn't think I raised two crazy young'uns.' But I paid that off like it was nothing. And the next one. And the next. I kept borrowing money." He kept working, as his business and family grew, but segregation kept gnawing at him. This incident took place in the early 1950s.

"I went to Lumberton with my girls. Cute little girls. Pretty dress on. Made out of a cotton sack or something, but it was pretty. Starched and everything. Did a little shopping. They wanted some water." His expression said it all: no fountains for his girls. "I had to take them to a spigot to get them some water. Now, that burned me a little. Not much. And they got their water and we came home."

One observer recalled a Robeson County courthouse that in 1967 had three drinking fountains with faded signs over them reading WHITE, NEGRO, INDIAN.[13]

"Lumberton was baaaaad bad. They ain't no more of that now in Lumberton. I mean, it's there in the mind. But it's not in the actions, it's not in the actions. The civil rights movement helped that, you know, with the black and everything."

What he did not mention and I learned about only later was his involvement in a famous Robeson County rout. In 1958, the Ku Klux Klan, upset about a Lumbee woman dating a white man and a Native family moving into a white neighborhood, burned crosses in both their yards. Then they scheduled a big rally in Maxton—the town where Mr. Curt was denied a haircut. A capsule version of the story, which made national news, is that several hundred Indians, among them weapons-carrying World War II Lumbee veterans like Curt Locklear, showed up that night. Insults led to shots being fired; tumult ensued, the Klansmen scattered. "I shot up in the air a few times just to make a racket," he told an interviewer.

By the end of the night, the Lumbees also had a souvenir: a KKK banner.[14] Publicity about the action helped spread the new tribal name, the Lumbee Indians of Robeson County. It replaced an especially unpopular one, the Cherokee Indians of Robeson County.

In Mr. Curt's opinion, racial attitudes started improving within a few years of the KKK rout. "I could see the change come about, just feel it in the air." Yet he did not think that discrimination against Native people touched him much, partly because he was working so hard and partly because he "didn't get mad at anybody." He added, "You probably get some Indians that had a different experience than I've had. Mine has been okay, because I didn't let little things bother me. Far as what a white man had and this and that? He just had it. I was going to work around it. Because Indians got a bad deal. Some of them couldn't do no better. There were Indians worked the white man's farm, and the white man took it all at the end of the year."

He has a reputation in the store, I mentioned, of being fair to everybody. Nothing to do with discrimination, he said. "I was sort of born like that. I couldn't see it no other way." He also has a reputation of extending credit, lots of credit. "I got a customer right now that owes me a $127,000." He did not look worried. "These people that owes me this money, very few of them's going to get me. Because I know what I'm doing and most of them are people that I know. It works out pretty good."

He seemed more concerned about a family problem. "We're loaded with drugs in this area. I got five sons, I got one that's on drugs. People tell me how lucky I am." Lucky because only one child is on drugs. "He's the baby. He's forty-four years old. He went to Chapel Hill, was there for two years and made superrrrrb grades. Then all of a sudden he got with a gang and that was it. Smartest one I had." (In an off-the-record interview, a Lumbee man said crack cocaine and alcohol have had "a devastating effect" on every Lumbee family he knows. He wondered out loud, why do "Indians have such a high addiction rate. Maybe it's our personalities. Most people think we're stoic, but we're not. We're very social.")

As Mr. Curt indicated, my glimpses of prosperous and healthy Lumbees showed only part of the picture. Dr. Knick helped confirm reality. "The unemployment rate of the Indian community is the highest of the three major races in Robeson County." That rate is "twice the state average. Then there's data like accidental death, alcohol-related death, homicide, and suicide. Robeson County has higher rates than virtually anybody in the state. Higher rates than some of the big cities. Those two facts should give you an idea of the enormity of the differences among Lumbees."

"There's a term around here," added Dr. Knick. "You hear some people talk about brickhouse Indians and sand road Indians. There are a whole lot of Indians living back up the sand roads that don't participate in that brick-house Indian life very much."

The Lumbee tribal council, I learned, was working to improve the lives of people living in substandard conditions, such as broken-down trailer homes. So was the Lumbee Regional Development Agency, formed in 1968. There was debate about whether the two were at odds or complementary. I say at odds. Their separate Web sites did not even mention the other entity.

Mr. Curt said he was not interested in tribal politics, other than donating money when he was asked. He had enough going on with the business. "I'd starve retired." He was happy to go home after work, maybe listen to music.

He liked the kind "you kick up your heels at" as well as "this long-haired music." He also liked hearing music in church, and for fifty-nine years has attended Berea Baptist, where Pam Sweeney conducts the children's choir. "She's a good girl."

His assessment of the future was positive. "We'll all be together one day. I've thought a lot on it. What the white has, the Indian has, and so forth. They'll all be together. We didn't have a doctor in the community. We got so many of them now, you shake a stick and a bunch of them fall out. Got so many lawyers, same thing. Of all the professions that you can name, we got 'em, right here in Pembroke."

During the 1973 interview, Mr. Curt put a version of progress more poignantly. "We've come a long way that we shouldn't had to come in the first place."

Mary Ann Cummings Jacobs

Prof. Mary Ann Jacobs stood before her classroom of fourteen juniors and seniors at UNC-Pembroke and wrestled with her PowerPoint presentation. "See how technology dependent I am now? Awful. If this thing doesn't come on . . ." When it did, her lesson in Native American populations got under way. The class was aimed at future social workers who were not Native— most of these students were not—but who might work in a Native community. They needed what she called "culturally appropriate techniques."

Today's lesson centered on responding to "two-spirit" people, that is, Native gays. An older woman in the class made a face. Mary Ann immediately addressed her. "It may be more than you're ready to talk about, but you need to be able to talk about these sorts of issues with your clients. They're going to be wanting to have this opportunity to be themselves with you, okay?"

Today's lesson included YouTube videos about Native gay experiences. One involved a man weeping as he told of an antigay marriage gesture from a tribal elder. Another featured comedian Charlie Ballard. "It's hard being Native American and gay. I worry about dating white men. Not because of getting HIV, but getting smallpox," he said, to laughs from his audience on screen and the Pembroke classroom. "White boys are cute, but don't cough on me." He ended, "My Indian name is Dances with Men."

Mary Ann, a substantial woman with long brown hair, dark eyes, and olive skin, who could be taken for Italian or Middle Eastern, addressed the students with authority and encouragement, alternating empathy with questions and musings. Homosexuality is so honored among some tribes, she said, that when a lesbian friend of hers visits her home reservation, women hand her their babies to hold, for good luck. It seems that among the Lumbees, though, it is okay for a homosexual man to be out of the closet, as long as he is not too far out, but not okay for a lesbian. Anybody want to comment? One woman said in essence, it's not just sex; men can do lots of things women can't.

By the end of the period, the overall lesson seemed to have taken; even within a minority within a minority, there is sexism.

Afterward, in a conference room near the classroom, Mary Ann was as frank about her own life as she had been about her lesson. When "young and foolish," she made two major wrong decisions. The first was to attend college at UNC-Chapel Hill. "My dad said, 'You're not going anywhere!'" He wanted Mary Ann, the youngest of eight children, to stay home and attend Pembroke. Her mother agreed. Mary Ann left anyway. "Chapel Hill is not a good place for undergraduate work. Even then, when I went in the '80s, you rarely saw a professor. You were almost always taught by a graduate student." She did like "meeting all sorts of different people" who were not related to her. In fact, although many students were from North Carolina, they did not know Lumbees existed. "But there were other Lumbees there and *we* knew we existed."

She realizes the Lumbee situation is unusual. "Early intermarriage with European and black populations" resulted in "the racial differences that make us appear to disappear." Then came "the legal disappearance of Native people" after the Trail of Tears. "We weren't legally supposed to be here. North Carolina was literally unmaking Indian people and making 'free persons of color.' That's how we became mulattos and octoroons and all these other things. [Officially] we were never Indians after the removal. But who was going to bother to come down here in this swamp and take us out?

That saved us." Despite certain differences, she feels a commonality with "eastern Indian people, all up and down the United States."

Mary Ann's second major youthful decision was to marry Russell Jacobs, also Lumbee. The couple moved to San Clemente in southern California, where Russell, a chemist, had found work. She did not. "I went to the Indian Center in Orange County and I spoke to an idiot, who basically told me, 'Why don't you just take a secretarial position somewhere?'" By then, Mary Ann had a master's degree in education, focusing on school counseling. "I was very homesick. It was awful. I would come home, by myself, usually for two weeks at a time." When a grandmother died, Mary Ann's first child was three months old. Rather than expose her baby to such a long plane trip, she did not attend the funeral.

Eventually Mary Ann got a job directing the American Indian Studies program at Cal State Long Beach. "That's when I decided, I'm a professor now, I better go get a PhD," she said, laughing. A PhD in what, was the problem. Definitely not education. "There were so many Indians with a PhD in education you could shake a stick at them." Definitely not American Indian studies. "There were very few jobs for academics in American Indian studies, unless someone died."

She decided to get her PhD in counseling. Convinced that "if I was going to be a woman and a minority, I better have a good degree or nobody's going to hire me," she applied only to top-rated schools. The University of Chicago came through. Off she went, toting baby Marcus, followed by Russell, who again got work as a chemist. Mary Ann's dissertation, which centered on "foster parenting, kinship care, adoption," took years longer than anticipated. "I was there nine years. Between work [at the Children and Family Research Center] and my kids [now numbering two, her daughter born a few years after her son]." Stresses on the marriage could be inferred. To celebrate the acceptance of her dissertation, "My girlfriends took me out, at a local bowling alley on campus."

Mary Ann's path back home followed a detour to San Diego, where the family moved after she accepted a teaching job at San Diego State. When a Lumbee friend told Mary Ann years later that UNC-Pembroke was looking for a new chair of Native American studies, she was not interested. After experiences at Cal State Long Beach, "Indian Studies did not have a warm place in my heart. Then I thought, it'd probably be a good idea. And Russell said he would be so much happier if we moved to North Carolina." Figuring it was a long shot, she applied.

"I'm a social worker. I don't think they're going to want to hire me as a chair," despite her having taken many classes in Indian Studies. She literally was a native daughter, though. After some hesitation, apparently on both sides, she got the job. She remained wary. " 'I'm going to meet all the same people from high school.' It hasn't been like that at all. Mostly because people have grown up. The people who were awful to me in high school are not anymore. They've become decent folks." Her laugh exploded. "I was kind of the shy bookworm person, didn't have many boyfriends, anybody all that special to me. Except Russell. And that didn't happen till after high school." Another surprise Pembroke offered was "how good things are here. In terms of the growth in the town. The university. The sophistication of my colleagues." Well, almost all.

Mary Ann Jacobs knows she is on the high side of sociology. "The poverty rate in Robeson County, it's always been there. I guess the 1950s would have been a kind of a flat period, where you would have found most people in the same economic status or very close. Now you're seeing a big wide gap in economic development between people who are what I would consider wealthy . . . and those who are at poverty level and under. Most of the people who are under that poverty level are folks who are single moms with children, like you would see everywhere." Complicating the situation was that so many good jobs are gone, along with hope. Mary Ann spoke sadly "of the high dropout rate we have here in Robeson County." A related painful fact is tribal illiteracy. When her parents attend senior citizens groups and VFW meetings with former classmates and co-workers, "they're constantly shocked at how many people don't read."

Despite community concerns and a number of personal ones, after decades of being away Mary Ann seems glad to be back. She is, after all, near her very large family. "It was great, because everybody was really happy and excited for me to come home."

One evening, Mary Ann took me to a reunion of her Cummings side. About 120 people of all ages—more than I saw at the powwow—had shown up at one relative's comfortable spread-out home. They had eaten heartily, as empty casseroles indicated. Children chased one another in the warm evening air while adults talked, several trying to figure their precise kinship.

Early the next morning, tired but ravenous, for we had arrived at the reunion late, I headed to McDonald's, where a newfangled coffee machine prompted me to order a latte. With it came a lesson in Lumbee entrepreneurship. The manager, Mickey Locklear read his badge, walked to my table to ask how the latte was, explaining they are still learning the machine. I admitted the drink was awfully sweet. Although the idea of coffee without sugar startled him, he insisted on making a new latte on the house.

Around 9:15, Mary Ann, Russell, and children Marcus and Flora picked me up for what turned out to be a full day of religion, one almost undone by a wardrobe crisis. Mary Ann, concerned I had not packed a skirt, finally allowed that my black pants and a blouse would pass muster. The Jacobs van sped, late again, to the sprawling Mount Airy Baptist Church, "Where the Word is faithfully preached and the Holy Spirit is genuinely encountered," said the bulletin. After splitting off through various hallways for age-appropriate Sunday school classes, we three adults arrived at a packed class taught by Alton Hagans, a portly, balding man. The lesson, printed in the Southern Baptist Convention's Bible study guide, *Life Words*, centered on the travails of Paul. Hagans said, "Most of us Christians, we get bogged down, get discouraged when we leave God out of it. Paul talks to these Romans right here, about what happens when we try to do without the Holy Spirit. You know what we do? We usually mess up." There was assent to that, and his asides. "I believe farming is a little bit better now than it was fifty years ago" when "we pulled cotton by hand." Things are better with the Holy Spirit, too, was the message.

After Sunday school, another warren of hallways led to the church sanctuary, a huge bright room of gently curving pews. Over the minutes, about 900 worshippers filled it. Yes, Mary Ann whispered back, almost all were Lumbee. They were conservatively and properly dressed, every woman but one in a skirt. (Dr. Knick later told me, with apparent admonishment, that churches are "self-selecting." Despite 900 well-dressed Lumbees at Mount Airy, many "sand road" people lack the clothing, confidence, or wherewithal to attend such a church.)

The bulletin's listing of "welcoming and recognition, birthday and anniversary, worship through giving, hymns, children's sermon, prayer of thanks and concerns" did not do justice to the building energy and emotion. Amid requests to "pray for Miss Stella, Miss Joanne," a piano started the notes to "Amazing Grace," bringing hundreds of people forward to be blessed. At other Native gatherings, when prayers are offered, the most frequently invoked word is Creator. At Mount Airy, the word is Jesus.

The Rev. Steve A. Strickland, from my distant vantage point a tannish attractive man, gave a sermon that lasted forty minutes. He spoke of Job. He felt for Job. "This man has gone through some stuff I don't even like to think about. I could have me a good old cry just thinking about those things." Toward sermon's end, Rev. Strickland shouted, whispered, and shouted again, about being upset with God himself, then understanding, like Job, "the best is yet to come." As he wound up, past a few "Amens" and "Yessirs" from the congregation, the choir began singing "Sweet Hour of Prayer."

When calm returned, Rev. Strickland announced that Family Fun Day, having been postponed from Saturday because of rain, would be today, no small thanks to his wife and others. He suggested everyone change their clothes and come back to enjoy the festivities and food. Please, allow senior citizens to eat inside. Senior citizens? I thought again of Native gatherings, where the word would be "elders."

Within an hour, at the expansive Family Fun Day grounds, Mary Ann introduced the now casually dressed Rev. Strickland, who looked and acted as if he had gone through the week-long emotional detox I was certain he needed after reliving Job. His fit physique, and that of most other Lumbees there, was striking. Yes, some Lumbee bodies exceeded their frame, and the picnic fare was standard Southern fried, plus soft drinks and minus alcohol, but the obesity in other Native communities was not apparent. Lumbees— that is, these Lumbees—looked to be in good health.

Family Fun Day included a flatbed truck on which individuals of many ages sang gospel songs, mostly a cappella, while hundreds of celebrants ate, walked, laughed, or indulged in the Lumbee pastime. "We're related by marriage to David . . ." "Oh, her sister's Rena . . ."

Alton Hagans showed up, too, and after we were introduced began waxing proud about his people. "We don't sell land, we buy land," he announced, then went on about extensive church property the Lumbees invested in and leased out. He and Mary Ann talked about Lumbees trained as teachers at UNC-Pembroke, which began as an all-Indian school, then became an Indian teachers college before its current incarnation as part of the UNC network, thus going from a school built solely for Native people to a school where Natives are now a minority. "The only job [Lumbee teachers] could get was in an Indian community," she said. This has led to a sense "throughout Native North Carolina that all teachers are Lumbees." They laughed about that.

When I asked Hagens if he thinks Lumbees are better off without a reservation, he said he thinks so, then launched into a story about "probably fifty of us from up around here" going to a reservation "out west"—he said he could not recall exactly where—to build a church. "When we got there, these people were having church under a big tent. It was full of holes. We jump in and built that church and they just sat back and watched us. All they done the whole time. They didn't work." He remembered Gallup, New Mexico, a town infamous for alcoholism, especially among Native people. "People were riding up and down the streets hollerin,' drunks everywhere." He raised his voice over the singing. "I tell you what, those people were much farther behind than we are. Economically, educationally, spiritually." Hagans put me in mind of what another Lumbee told me, "There are two things that man cannot strip from you, and that's your salvation and your education."

A lanky older jeans-clad fellow on the flatbed said he was going to sing "The Old Man Is Dead," about being lost in the darkness and needing to look for light on the inside. "I'm as nervous as I can be, so pray for me."

———

If a group of strangers were to walk or drive around Pembroke, they might not realize they are anywhere near Native Americans. The Lumbee Guaranty Bank, formed by a group of Lumbees who had been denied loans at white-owned banks,[15] gives little clue. UNC-Pembroke advertises itself as Home of the Braves, but that might be just another disputed sports mascot. (It was, in fact.) As for Eaglefeather Arts and Crafts and the Lumbee tribal offices, neither is especially prominent, nor likely to turn heads. The group of strangers might overhear a dialect that baffles them and might wonder about the genetic heritage of people they see. It is unlikely, though, that they would sense the intricate linguistic and cultural history around them or the extensive kinship systems keeping the community together. The group of strangers may never even know Lumbees exist, nor who they are. But Lumbees, they know.

CHAPTER 4

Elders of the Haudenosaunee

DARWIN HILL (TONAWANDA SENECA) AND GERALDINE GREEN (CATTARAUGUS SENECA)

The two-row wampum belt, created four hundred years ago to straighten things out with Dutch traders, explains a lot.

The pattern, made by stringing together shell beads, consists of five rows. The top, bottom, and middle rows are white, the other two purple. The white rows represent the river of life. The purple rows represent two vessels floating on the white. In one purple row travel people of the Iroquois Confederacy in their canoes. In the other row travel Europeans in their ships. That the rows do not touch is significant. The meaning is, we know you have arrived, Europeans, and are not going away. To respect one another and live in peace, we agree to coexist, separately.

The message from that one wampum belt has led to a remarkable and largely unknown situation in today's United States,[1] one exemplified by Darwin Hill and Geraldine Green. In a way, the belt led me to them.

One warm, moist, crickety summer evening during Field Day (actually, Field Weekend), celebrations on Tonawanda Seneca territory northeast of Buffalo, Janine Huff, a clan mother, was relaxing on the porch of the old wooden frame house she shares with her father, Stuart Jamieson, and her son, Ira. Among the porch sitters was her sister, LuAnn Jamieson, and several other relatives. Stuart, an amiable and attractive man of eighty-two, chief of Tonawanda's Hawk clan, was good naturedly resting on his laurels; that day he had scored the winning goal in a lacrosse game. Ira, a hefty incoming Syracuse University freshman and aspiring writer, was practicing lacrosse moves on the lawn. As people chatted, joked, and ate a bowl of chilled cherries Janine had provided, a van of rollicking teenagers drove slowly by. They were hanging out doors, shouting and waving. The porch group waved back.

"Welcome to the rez," said LuAnn, smiling. (Like other Tonawanda Seneca, she rejects the word "reservation," but "rez," of course, is affectionate insider slang.) She added that that kind of driving probably would not be allowed in towns outside Tonawanda Seneca, prompting Janine to explain Two-Row wampum.

Hundreds of years before such messages were necessary, ancestors of the porch sitters and van riders established a network of interdependence known as the Iroquois or—as its citizens call it—Haudenosaunee Confederacy. (Having mispronounced Haudenosaunee for years in my mind until hearing it, I still struggle: haw-dehna-SHAU-nee.) The word is translated as People of the Longhouse. Longhouses were, and are, buildings for ceremonies. This being upstate New York, the longhouses reflect upstate New York architecture: white clapboard and pitched roofs. From the exterior, they differ from local houses mostly by being, in a word, long.

Haudenosaunee nations once stretched more or less from the Mohawks, in what is now northeastern New York and Canada, then swooped in a gentle U shape to western New York and northeastern Ohio, home of the Senecas, who were known, among other titles, as Keepers of the Western Door. Although the nations no longer comprise an uninterrupted sovereign swath, a map offers a sense of gems on a necklace, with the center brooch remaining the confederacy's geographic, ceremonial, and cultural hub, the faith-keeping nation of the Onondaga. In today's geography, it is off Route 81, five miles south of Syracuse.

My path to the Haudenosaunee,[2] involving years of persistence (or stubbornness), and attempts to overcome the reputation that white journalists get everything wrong, led to a western doorkeeper of sorts, LuAnn Jamieson. Her many efforts to get her people healthier include leading six A.M. cardio classes at the 1930s WPA-built Tonawanda Community Center, aided by Richard Simmons's *Sweatin' to the Oldies*. Yes, she likes the popular "Rez-Robics" video, to see brown people exercising, but Simmons works better for her class. Tonawanda health has a way to go; only at the

countdown for a Field Day 5K footrace did runners crush out their cigarettes. LuAnn, a lovely middle-aged woman with enviable runner's legs, also
instituted a Tonawanda "Greatest Loser" competition that releases as many
laughs as pounds. "Don't weigh me until my hair dries!" cried one participant. "Wait," said another, "Let me take off my watch." The biggest non-
loser—one week, LuAnn's sister Janine—must wear a plush moose hat for a
day and endure endless kidding.

On the subject of her people, LuAnn did not joke. "Our story is more than
about casinos and taxes and smoke shops. Our people are very rich. Not in the
material sense, but in the cultural and spiritual sense, because we have and we
pursue this connection with all living things. That's what we see we've been put
here for. We assume that as our responsibility as longhouse people. Nobody
talks about *that* part. Nobody sees that part as the value to our people's presence here. Our whole union of nations comes from the concept of peace."

Two elders I met through LuAnn worked constantly for the "union of
nations," whose millennium-old government has as little as possible to do
with that upstart, the United States of America.

DARWIN HILL

Field Day was nothing if not noisy. People cooked with clatter, children yelled,
the occasional motorcyclist drove up, shouts rose from games. Many young
mothers, some lithe, some chubby, steered strollers past baby admirers. Non-
Natives showed up too. Everyone was welcome. Through the clamor and
diversions, Darwin Hill, in T-shirt, shorts, and small round sunglasses, his
gray hair in a long ponytail, sat at a picnic bench and endeavored to make his
soft voice heard. He is a slight man, with a twinkly smile, a courteous and
deliberative manner, and an understated sense of humor. He was named for
the city in Australia, he deadpanned. He was seventy or seventy-one, depending on conflicting records. Home births in 1939 or 1938 were not always
concerned with such facts as dates. He prefers 1939: makes him a year younger.

For the first time, the August celebration and homecoming included
bocce ball, a friendly nod to nearby Italian American communities. Darwin
has wondered if his love for Italian food might be a sign he is part Italian.

Amid the day's merriment was one solemn moment. A man who makes wampum belt replicas presented an enormous one of the Hiawatha belt to Tonawanda's chiefs and subchiefs. The Hiawatha belt represents the original five nations. A tree in the middle stands for the Onondaga Nation. Two connected boxes on either side represent the Mohawks, Oneida, Cayuga, and Seneca. Among those in the receiving line for the gift were the Hawk clan's chief, Stuart Jamieson, and subchief, Darwin Hill.

"Subchiefs really don't hold a title," Darwin said. "They're just a helper for their chief." His modesty was consistent. He shied from the designation "elder," feeling it had more to do with knowledge than with age.

After the presentation, the fun, games (horseshoes, lacrosse, and bocce), and shopping resumed. At some twenty stands rimming the grassy field, one could buy beaded jewelry, modern Native-themed clothing, raffle tickets to various prizes, and an array of food from the beloved unhealthy (there was a fry bread contest) to the rediscovered nutritious (fruit smoothies!). Darwin's wife Janet bent tradition by offering chocolate-dipped strawberries. She sold out.

All financial proceeds from Field Day went to support Tonawanda's longhouse.

What supports the Tonawanda Seneca Nation itself? Not the federal government, nor state government, nor county government. The Tonawanda Seneca Nation—all but unique in this country—refuses any government aid. It receives no government grants, whether from the Bureau of Indian Affairs or Health and Human Services, including Head Start. It asks for no stimulus money, no nothing. Darwin is not even enrolled in Medicare. He does get Social Security, having paid into it. Individuals can apply for what they may need, such as food stamps, but as a tribal nation Tonawanda applies for nothing. It would accept a federal grant if it were recognized as a treaty obligation, Darwin allowed, but that was not expected.

Tonawanda is as independent as it can be.

"We've never looked at our community as being something where we had to have services like they do in almost every municipality or other forms of government," said Darwin. There is no tribal police force, just one marshal. If somebody saw somebody breaking into a house or hurting another, the procedure would be similar to that of, say, Buffalo. "Many people, probably the higher percentage, would automatically call the county sheriff. But while they're doing that, they will also call either the marshal or one of the chiefs." Would Darwin as a subchief be called? "Oh yes. The county dispatcher, which actually works with the county sheriffs and the New York State police, they have all our phone numbers. They go right down the list."

Tribal relationships are "generally" fine with responders, such as police officers. "I mean, they're part of a community just like *we* are." Tonawanda tribal members serve, for example, as volunteer firemen in the region. (Tonawanda tribal members Darwin and Janet Hill are also enthusiastic supporters of the Buffalo Bills, for whom they have season tickets.)

There are problems, despite meetings, with law enforcement higher-ups who feel they have the jurisdiction to come on Tonawanda Seneca land uninvited. "That's where the disagreement comes in." In Darwin's view, the situation is like New York State Police not going to Pennsylvania to enforce the law, the FBI not going to Canada.

But could the Tonawanda marshal arrest an outsider who was assaulting someone on the reservation? "Well, those are always the questions. Somebody's always making a new law on that. Which doesn't resolve anything." For one thing, "we don't have the facilities to imprison anybody either." The marshal typically hands over miscreants to county authorities. "It's kind of a mutual or shared enforcement issue." Despite positive discussions with the local U.S. attorney, Darwin said he thought jurisdictional situations may not be cleared up for generations.

A related issue is taxes. The basic situation here is the same as on most reservations. If Tonawanda tribal members have jobs off Tonawanda territory, as most do, they pay income taxes like anyone else. If they buy anything outside Tonawanda, they pay sales taxes like anyone else. If they own property outside Tonawanda, they pay property taxes like anyone else. If they live on the Tonawanda Nation, they do not pay property taxes. It follows that the Tonawanda Seneca Nation has no tax base whatsoever.

The Nation's sole source of income, from one tribal enterprise on Tonawanda, is a percentage of profits from cigarette sales. That would not be called a tribal tax? "Oh no. No," said Darwin with unusual firmness. "We even stay clear of using that word." The cigarettes, bought by armloads of cartons, are sold in so-called smoke shops. The shops' popularity among smokers, but not among sellers of cigarettes in neighboring communities or tax-seeking governments, is that the cigarettes are cheaper because—despite a "never-ending saga," in Darwin Hill's words, to change the laws—they are not taxed. They are not taxed because places such as Tonawanda consider themselves, by treaties, to be sovereign independent nations.

Cigarette sales therefore comprise all the monies that support the minuscule Tonawanda government, whose few employees (all nonsmokers) include Darwin Hill. He is officially the clerk, a job that originally meant recording meetings. "It kind of grew from there and kept on growing, I guess." He now is essentially the tribal administrator. Between his subchief duties, for which he receives no pay, as per tradition, and his administrative work, he puts in about fifty hours a week, he estimates.

As a tribal employee, he pays no taxes on his salary but does pay taxes on nontribal income, such as investments. He files with the IRS every year, in part to show losses on his mutual funds to offset any potential profit, if, he chuckled, a profit ever comes. The complicated tax situation throughout tribal nations, he conceded, is generally a "mess."

Tonawanda's separation from other governments extends to voting. "I would say the very, very high majority of the traditional people do not participate in voting. We feel it's not even *our* form of government to participate in. State elections, local elections, or even voting for president and so forth." As far as he knew, a lot of Tonawanda's "church people," he called them, do vote.

Asked if people thought it would not have mattered whether Senator John McCain or Senator Barack Obama won the presidential race, he frowned. "It's hard for me to answer those kind of questions, because even though I've lived in both worlds, I still don't follow that form of government closely. I don't understand it, other than the way I learned when I was in school." He added, "A lot of people thought it was probably a positive thing with the election of a black president, thinking that maybe it'll change some policy as far as how the federal government deals with Indian issues."

What about the census? "We kick 'em out of here! They're persistent. We do make it known to the Census Bureau that we don't participate in the census." The Haudenosaunee Confederacy wrote "a very clear statement" explaining its position.

"We're not actually *part* of that whole system they say is to count you, so you can see what your representation is. We say they don't represent us in Congress, and all these other things they say go along with that census. It's to tell how much money each area gets. We don't use that money anyway. We have all of our reasons, which we state. They partially acknowledge it but, again, say their duty is to count everybody. They'll come up with some kind of figure we know isn't tallied from a door-to-door perspective." He sighed. "We get through it."

What led to such formal separation? The answer is simply—or not so simply—tradition.

"The original governments of the Confederacy, the Haudenosaunee," said Darwin with patience hinting at repetition, "were formed, some say, over a thousand years ago."[3]

"The leaders are chiefs, selected by clan mothers. Generally it's one chief for each clan and a subchief for each clan." Together they make up a council of chiefs. He added, with some asperity, "At Tonawanda, it's the only governing body." His voice barely carried over children's yells. "What we have, actually, is what we've always had and we've never seen a reason to change it. It's always served us well."

In the Tonawanda council, the chiefs are male. "If people grow up in our system, understand our system, they know that this cannot be a woman." Some "forms," he said, tried to mix an elective system with the chief system and have female chiefs, "but in our system it cannot be female. They have to be men. The women actually have other roles. [They] select the chiefs. They have their roles, we have our roles, and they complement each other." He went on, "We have eight clans and eight clan chiefs. They're not equally distributed." Not all eight clans have a title. The Snipe clan currently "has three of the titles. The Turtle clan has two of the titles. That means three other clans don't have a title. It still works out in the end."

Intricacies of the clan system seem both fascinating and endless. "I'm a subchief for the Hawk clan. I'm actually borrowed for that position, because I am in a different clan myself"—Beaver. When clans were established, "it was said there were certain traits those people have," such as beavers. "We're always told that we're like industrious people. We dig in and get things done, things people think of as beavers anyway." According to LuAnn, this is Darwin's reputation. Her father also was born into the Beaver clan but borrowed into the Hawk clan. The subject turned to his stunning lacrosse goal.

The original meaning of lacrosse, said Darwin, is nothing like what takes place during competitions, such as those on Field Day. "Lacrosse was a gift to our people from the Creator, to be played for his enjoyment and also as a medicine game for healing. It's evolved into quite a different thing, but the origins and the way it's still used in our communities is for men only." They play it on behalf of a person who needs healing. Any information beyond that, said Darwin, is private.

Two Haudenosaunee nations have the same council of chiefs system as Tonawanda: Onondaga and Tuscarora. The others split off to go with the elected tribal council system the U.S. government more or less foisted upon Native communities as an improvement to earlier policies.[4] Those "others" include a separate Seneca Nation of Indians, whose Web site lists three reservations, all south of Buffalo: Allegany, Cattaraugus, and Oil Springs.[5]

The split formed "essentially two Seneca nations," of "separate peoples, even though we're intermingled by a lot of marriage, a lot of other relationships. We still have our relationship between our longhouse and the longhouses on the other Seneca reservations." People do not leave one system for another, said Darwin, but "more or less work within your own system."

Tonawanda has faced internal dissent. In the 1990s, five tribal members, business-motivated, in his opinion, tried to do away with the council of chiefs. Finally, the council "banished" them as members. "We consider them to be not there." Three still live on Tonawanda, however. Darwin avoids them. "We're not the punisher. The punisher is in the next life."

Even absent such dissent, all of Tonawanda's population does not think alike. "I always describe our population as half traditional, half maybe not traditional. In other words, they're followers of a Christian religion." Or, half the people at Tonawanda go to longhouse, half to church. He did not bring up religious discord between the two halves, but LuAnn did, saying Christians on Tonawanda try to convert tribal members, with one minister even using funerals to proselytize. Some Christians in her own family mock her. "My cousins say, 'Why don't you just wear feathers and buckskin?'" It is not easy to maintain, in the present, what some consider the past.

Darwin does, assiduously. His commitment to the Tonawanda Seneca Nation emerged after two long detours. As a child, he was sent to a boarding school, although not the infamous type meant to "civilize" Native children by stripping them of their culture. His was meant for children from "broken families and things like that." A county organization had stepped in after his father left. "Myself, my next younger brother, and my next younger sister, we were taken away." As to why his father left, Darwin said he never asked. He remembered going fishing with him, and called the family "close," yet the leaving remained a mystery. "I knew him in later years before he passed on, but we never talked about things that happened." Darwin was equally reticent with his mother. "My mother and I were close, in our later years, but I never asked what happened in those times. I just knew we went through them."

The place the three Hill children were sent was "kind of like" an orphanage, near Buffalo. "They had their own school system within that. When I first went there, because I had never gone to school, I was like eight or nine years old, in kindergarten." His family, furthermore, had mostly spoken Seneca at home. "I went into an environment where only English was spoken and only English was allowed to be spoken." The school consisted of two rooms, kindergarten and grades one to three in one room, grades four through six in another. Fortunately for Darwin, "Everybody was grouped together. Nobody knew who was in what grade." He more or less adjusted, he said, and rebelled only moderately, running away with his brother, but returning when hungry.

Not once did Darwin go home, nor did his mother visit. "We were completely apart for all those years." He received no letters either. "It's almost like we were in a separate world. There was actually no contact, no relationship, with people here or my family. I guess it might be amazing to people, but that's just what we did. I think we survived. We did okay."

When he was about fourteen, he and his brother were moved to Batavia, about twenty miles away, and stayed with a non-Indian foster family, as they had during some previous school years. There they finished high school and then "came back to the reservation." Does he recall first seeing his mother again? He paused. "No, I really don't. It's almost like all of a sudden we were back together."

Darwin's other detour was the air force, which he joined as a teenager and stayed in until retirement, working as a mechanic, engineer, and electronics technician. He liked "flying, seeing the world." After five years in the service, he married Janet, whom he had met on Tonawanda during a visit. She accompanied him almost everywhere he was stationed—air force bases in Alaska, Washington, Arizona, Kansas, and Florida. The Hills always planned to return to Tonawanda. "When I had sixteen years, I put in for a job that was in Syracuse so I could be close to here." The offered job was as a recruiter. "It's the worst job I ever had," he said with a little laugh. "But I put up with it for four years." The problem, in effect, was personality. "Back then, it wasn't as easy for me to talk openly with people I didn't know. Now I can do it easy."

In 1979, as recruiting days dwindled and retirement approached, Darwin started letting his hair grow. "Sometimes I got reminded that my hair was too long. 'I know it, because I'm getting out.'"

During our Field Day talk, as well as in several follow-up phone interviews, his message was consistent; his military career was over. "I'm certainly not ashamed and I don't regret it, but it's not anything I use nowadays."

"This"—he gestured to the people and land around him—"has been my life for the last thirty years. Entirely." It is "a seven-day-a-week responsibility we have here. Besides having a great family. I only had one son, but now I have nine grandchildren!" Since then, the Hills also have a great grandchild.

"I have not ever encouraged my son or any of my family to join the service. In fact, I worked to have them be exempt from that, because of our positions about being drafted and so forth." A major reason he opposed the draft for Native people harkened to early agreements with the Europeans. "We will not fight them, we will not fight *with* them. Those were part of our discussions in the early days of forming the Constitution. The Confederacy position . . . even prior to a draft" predated the American Revolution. "We had agreements during those times that we would never have to serve in any of the military branches, because we were not a part of that."

Confederacy position did not trump Selective Service law, however. "The draft still affected Indian people here, as well as all over. Almost 100 percent I'm aware of that were eligible for the draft, did get drafted during those years, prior to the draft ending."

When Darwin Hill returned to Tonawanda as a civilian, he took the clerk job that has lasted longer than his time in the air force. His ceremonial duties started later. He first was approached about being a subchief some twenty years ago, when another clan, needing someone to fill a subchief position, asked Darwin if he would consider taking it. On the advice of his mother, he declined. Her reasoning involved a then unsettled situation within his own Beaver clan.

"This time, when the Hawk clan leaders asked me about it, I took it back to several of the women in my clan, because my mother wasn't here anymore. They said they would think about it and talk about it. They came back to me about a week or maybe less, and said if I wanted to take that, they would allow me to."

Asked what made him want to take the position, he laughed. It is not a matter of wanting, he said. It has to do with agreeing to take on a responsibility.

Darwin Hill became Hawk subchief in 2004. Or as he put it, "I believe our condolence ceremony was five years ago." The age-old, or at least Haudenosaunee-old, ceremony takes place after a chief dies. Precise protocol is required. All nations are notified of the death by one or more "brother nations," not the nation whose clan chief died. For the Tonawanda, brother nations of Oneida, Cayuga, and Tuscarora are specifically designated to notify the others. Representatives from all the nations then come to the longhouse of the nation whose clan chief died and conduct the ceremony. "You don't do a condolence ceremony for yourself." After the dead chief is mourned, it is time to approve the man whom the clan mothers selected as the new chief. "One of the last stages is that they're stood up and identified. You 'see their faces.' That's what the words are. Show the *face* of this person. If anyone else sees a reason not to allow their title to be held, they can say so. Otherwise they're essentially all approving them."

The condolence ceremony lasts "pretty much all day. It starts in the morning and will end up four, five, six o'clock in the afternoon." Social dancing follows, that is, Native social dancing, with people attired in tribal regalia. "Some [dances] are for men only. Some are for women only. Some are both." The circle has been completed again.

The council of chiefs and subchiefs tries to meet at least once a week, always in the longhouse. They start as they have for centuries. "We do the opening thanksgiving address. That kind of kicks off our process."

In versions I have read, the thanksgiving address is a beautiful homage to the Creator for everything the speaker wants to include, from insects to wind to pebbles to five-fingered beings, who decidedly do not count more than other creations, and on. And on. Is it true it can last several minutes or several hours? "Exactly. Depending on the speakers, the circumstances. There could be a lot of variables."

In Tonawanda, the address is delivered in Seneca, even though one or two chiefs, Darwin thought, do not speak the language fluently. Nor can he. He still understands Seneca and can say some words, but following his years away, "I never regained the ability to speak."

After thanksgiving, council work begins. "Typically, at a discussion of any of the issues at a formal council meeting, they still ask me, or my chief will ask me, or the council together will ask me, my opinion. It's hard to say if one particular thing or one particular area or even one particular issue is the most challenging. As a whole, we're challenged just to keep everything intact," he said, raising his voice a little over sounds of an enthusiastic child. "We're involved with things for all of our people within the reservation, day to day activities, much like any local government. But on another scale we're involved with things that involve our leadership, with New York State, right to the governor and the federal government."

Involvement with the federal government is as limited as possible. "There are times we do need to talk with them [New York senators and congresspersons] and have them understand who we are and why we need to work with them or have them work with us on certain issues. We don't typically work a lot in that direction, going to Congress. We almost never do that, unless there's a particular thing that looks like it's dangerous to us."

One example: a number of years ago, a bill was submitted to both houses of Congress that would ratify all unratified treaties and land claims going back to the 1700s, "so they could make all these transactions legitimate." The attempt, said Darwin, was to make Indians land claims illegitimate. "It was kind of a rough job from some congressional people. We did go down there and explain to a lot of individual Congress people that would listen to us the reasons why they should *not* try to pass a bill like that. We had all of our reasons lined up, and of course the bill got defeated," thanks also to legal scholars who testified that the bill was unconstitutional.

The delegation brought their wampum, as their ancestors did. "The ones we use in the longhouse are the real ones, but these other ones we take and use to show people and explain what they are, are typically replicas."

What about pushing one's case through the long-standing National Congress of American Indians, the NCAI? "We're not part of that." Such entities are lobbying organizations, he said, and the Haudenosaunee do not like to lobby, nor do they like go-betweens. "We do not see how an organization can represent us in any other forum." He remembered, unhappily, when "some organizations kind of put themselves out there as representing all the Indians in North America. That kind of thing happened. It was actually an old AIM [American Indian Movement] trick."

No matter the group, no matter its intent, the answer is no. "'You cannot represent us. You cannot speak for us.'"

Although the Haudenosaunee spurn virtually all U.S. organizations, they are, as an independent nation, very much involved with the United Nations. Darwin recalled meetings as far back as the 1970s to develop a UN declaration regarding Native peoples throughout the world. In 2007 the United Nations Declaration on the Rights of Indigenous Peoples finally passed. It read in part, "Indigenous peoples and individuals have the right not to be subject to forced assimilation or destruction of their culture."[6] Darwin hoped that over time it "will lead to what is called 'customary international law.'"

"We were at the United Nations in New York when they adopted it, the actual roll call day. The disappointing part is that four countries in the world voted against it. They were four countries that have major populations of Native peoples. Those were New Zealand, Australia, and in this hemisphere,

Canada and the United States. We knew it was going to happen that way. We worked hard with all those four countries, unfortunately not successfully."

The defeat did not dent Haudenosaunee resolve. In 2010, Darwin and others were scheduled to meet with State Department lawyers to explain their view of the declaration's validity. Meanwhile, there was the hemisphere to work on. "We're doing a similar project in the OAS, the Organization of American States." That entails trips to South America. For such journeys, Darwin uses his tribal passport.

He has had one since the 1970s and has used it in Europe, as well as in Costa Rica, Bolivia, and West Africa. He had a U.S. passport too, which made traveling with his family easier, but let it expire. In the past, there was easy passage for Native people back and forth to Canada, tribal relations having predated the border, but now travel is more difficult everywhere. The issue became an international incident in July 2010, when the Iroquois lacrosse team, whose members held Iroquois passports and did not want U.S. ones (or Canadian ones for the Canadian-based players), was denied permission to travel to a lacrosse tournament in England. After intervention by Secretary of State Hillary Clinton, the United States agreed to at least a one-time honoring of the Haudenosaunee passports, but Great Britain refused. The players whose ancestors invented the game had to stay home. Meanwhile, the Haudenosaunee Confederacy is working with a firm to update its passport as an electronic ID.

Before going abroad with his Haudenosaunee passport, Darwin gets a visa from each country he will visit. It is "generally not a problem" to reenter the United States. JFK Airport in New York, home, after all, of the Confederacy, was fine. In Miami he was held up for hours. Haudenosaunee was not listed among the countries with which the United States has relationships. And Darwin Hill does not consider himself a citizen of the United States.

———

In terms of population, about 2,000, and land mass, about 7,000 acres, Tonawanda is similar to a few nearby territories, or reservations. Compared to spiffily maintained surrounding towns, it is visibly poorer. "The most obvious [difference] would be housing conditions," said Darwin. "But I think it gets back to where we were sixty or seventy years ago, when I was a kid. We didn't know we were poor." He has no regrets that Tonawanda, unlike other Seneca nations, has no casinos, nor the governmental bureaucracy necessary for them. "I kind of liken it to a shiny car theory. Somebody's got a nice shiny car in their driveway, they must be making a lot of money. But maybe they're not. And what does it *mean* to the people?"

The Tonawanda Seneca have other riches, including being part of one of the oldest governing bodies in the world.

The Confederacy legendarily began when brutal intertribal fighting among the nations was brought to an end by a heroic peacemaker, a person whose name the Haudenosaunee utter only at specific moments within ceremonies. Otherwise, he is referred to as The Peacemaker, written with proper capitalization. (Mention of his name in anyother way is considered so offensive, I have been asked not to write it. A mystery series by Thomas Perry, starring Seneca Tonawanda detective Jane Whitefield, uses The Peacekeeper's name for her fictitious hometown, which may be why the series has not caught on among Haudenosaunee readers. Darwin had never heard of it.)

A major debate about the Haudenosaunee Confederacy is its legacy. Did it influence the founding fathers of the United States, including Benjamin Franklin, who negotiated with the Haudenosaunee? Is the U.S. Constitution based on Haudenosaunee tenets? In *Iroquois Diplomacy on the Early American Frontier*, Timothy J. Shannon, who curiously never uses the word Haudenosaunee, calls such assertions a myth. "The misguided notion that the Iroquois somehow served as midwives to the birth of the United States has come into full flower within the last generation or so," he wrote, and claimed their much more valid legacy was diplomacy. "To the Iroquois, relations with others—whether kin or outsiders—were … a perpetual give-and-take aimed at sustaining peace and prosperity."[7]

Darwin, of course, knew of the debate. Perhaps as a sign of his own diplomacy, he came down in the middle. "The history we know of points very much toward [connections between] our leaders and the early American leaders, where they were learning some of these processes we had, and then actually adopted some of those."

The most important Haudenosaunee legacy may be that its common themes, like "consent of the governed" and "consensus as a social ideal,"[8] are to people such as Darwin Hill worth working for every day.

———

With sounds of Field Day in the background, my head and body filled with hospitality, helpfulness, and one piece of fry bread, I began the complicated drive from Tonawanda Seneca territory to the Cattaraugus Reservation, about an hour south. I soon got lost. Pulling up to a family-style restaurant closing after brunch, I asked for directions. Several related employees offered suggestions by the earful. Then one asked, where was I driving from? The Tonawanda Seneca Nation, I said. The entire dining room, in mid-cleanup, went quiet. What, the apparent paterfamilias finally asked, a chill to his voice, would you be doing there? I thought of something LuAnn said to me on the phone years before, something so unnerving, I had written it down. "Some people don't think we're human beings."

To the silent dining room, I explained my purpose, and drove off.

GERALDINE GREEN

"How many legs does a fly have?" she asked out of the blue. "That came up on my test in school. There was a fly sitting on my desk so I counted the legs. I was one of the two that got it right." The answer is six. "I didn't have to remove the legs, either. I just watched him walking across my desk." Geri Green crinkled her lined brown face into a grin of part mischief, part impudence.

We had met earlier over lunch at LuAnn Jamieson's house on the Cattaraugus Reservation. The house, like the converted-storage-shed home she maintains in Tonawanda next to Janine and family, was studded with photographs and Native-themed ware from sheets to dishes, like Mikasa's "Indian Feast" featuring a rising sun. As we prepared for Geraldine Green's arrival, setting a table on the back deck for a feast of bison burgers (LuAnn got the ingredients in a Buffalo supermarket, thus buying buffalo in Buffalo), it was clear the guest was a person of respect.

The respect was threefold. At eighty years of age, Geri, as she was called, was an elder in a culture that values elders. She also was one of the few remaining fluent speakers of Seneca. Finally, she employed that knowledge as handmaiden to her enormous obligation, Keeper of the Four Ceremonies,[9] a position requiring extensive knowledge about the intricacies of the Seneca belief system. In ceremonies that last up to ten days, the Keeper knows who should do and say what.

Geri also used Seneca in daily conversation. "It *is* a language. We *do* talk," she once said, with one of her looks.

By appearance alone, an outsider might have no idea of her esteem. As she entered LuAnn's house with her clan sister Janine, she hardly presented herself as a solemn repository of rites. Short, on the plump side, missing her front top teeth, to LuAnn "not a quality that we even perceive or notice," within minutes she made everyone laugh with a story about buying slacks at a great sale, only to realize later they were maternity slacks. Geri Green definitely disarmed people.

In the following days, we met at her house, either on her small front porch amid sounds of birdsong and treebreeze or in her packed-to-the-gills living room amid a surround of mementoes. The house, which sits on the Cattaraugus Reservation about a mile or so from LuAnn's, was built in 1941, mostly by Geri's father. She proudly spoke of the square beams he ordered, "the beams that's holding the house."

It was home base for any emergencies. She had a treadle sewing machine, her own well, kerosene lamps, "oodles of candles," a clothesline, and much food, including a staple of dried corn, some in bags, some in a jumbo tin labeled pretzels. She also had whatever her garden yielded. A neighbor's son tilled the plot, about ten by twenty feet, on the other side of her unpaved driveway. During a short tour, she said she was not growing much. Some corn, pole beans, cucumbers. "There's supposed to be butternut squash somewhere . . ." She often made a sandwich of a thinly sliced cucumber and tomato, both from the garden. "I have a tendency toward getting all that flaxseed bread. I'm a weird one. I watch what I eat." She liked her poached eggs plain. "They always ask me, 'Yuck! How can you eat it like that? With no salt, no pepper.' That's just the way the chicken made it."

My attempts to glean medicinal garden lore—which LuAnn told me was one of Geri's many areas of knowledge—went nowhere. Considering a patch of Queen Anne's Lace, Geri said she once shaped some into a Christmas tree. This clover? "You make a tea out of it," she commented. Do you dry it first? "You can dry it if you want." She was more interested in the corn, which she roasted, made into soup, and put up in jars. Growing up, she ate "veggies." Also, "We had our own pigs." And 1,200 chickens. "There's a lot of money in the babies."

In a plastic tub on her porch grew some leafy plants about five inches high. They were a type of tobacco, she said. At some point, she picked the leaves, let them wilt two days, "then I stick them in the oven and put it on 200. When the oven goes off, I leave it out until it cools down and the leaves are dry." The tobacco was used for ceremonies inside the Cattaraugus long-house. "They burn it as they're talking, making a speech." The tobacco could be smoked "if you want to, but I don't smoke."

A few feet off the porch, she pointed, a lopsided shrub was home to a small bird. "He refuses to move. He's there in the morning, shakes himself out"—she did a shimmying imitation—"looks all around. He either snuggles back in his nest and stays a little while longer or takes off right away. This evening he'll be back again." She had been trimming the bush when she saw the nest, and stopped. For Geraldine Green, a lopsided shrub was preferable to messing with nature. She did not approve of people who did, or of those who acted as if they were the only living things around.

"A lot of people don't believe we're here. Do you know there was nothing mentioned in history books or anything when I was in school? It's that bad. Out of sight, out of mind, kind of deal there. See, what they have trouble with, is that we're 'discovery.' They didn't discover anything. We were here already. And we were doing fine until they got here. They didn't start building stockades or anything to keep undesirables out until after the whites came. Because they liked to come and invade." She was on a Geri roll.

"Trees were trees, not bushes like you see now. That's what we consider those trees there," she said, indicating what seemed until that moment a forest along the road. "We had big trees before they came. Whatever they see, they cut down, and they want to use it for something. Usually not for a very good reason. They're taking sand and processing it in some factory and getting crude oil from it. Raise whole acres and acres of corn and they make that into fuel. Pretty soon there's not going to be anything to eat. They're going to have used it up. That's why I've got those few corn coming up, so we can have fresh seeds."

She brought up the subject twice, angrily. "We honor the green [just ripened] corn, because that's really your staple if you think about it. It's the staple of the world. Look what they're doing with it. They're turning it into oil. How are you going to eat, drink, oil? How many miles you going to get out of that?"

Making food into fuel was unthinkable to this woman, born only months before the Great Depression began. "A few ounces the wrong side of five pounds," she described herself. "I was a little tiny thing. Then I blew up." Not that far up. "My grandfather used to carry me to the corner to go to school, because I was too small. Especially during winter. I could run under this table, go out the other side."

Geraldine entered the world under circumstances she asked remain private and was raised mostly by foster parents, a Seneca man and woman she referred to fondly as her father and mother, pointing out their photographs. She, they, and eventual siblings from various marriages, all spoke Seneca. "When I went to school, when I was six years old, I didn't know my name. I didn't know anything in English." (To my ear, Geri's English, although fluent and colloquial, was punctuated by usages—mostly omitted in these pages—indicating that for her the language remained somewhat foreign.)

The school was on the reservation. Asked what it was like to learn English, she replied, "Well, you had to learn something, because if you didn't, you were up a creek. Without a paddle." She made a face. "The teacher didn't talk anything else. I had to make allowances for her."

Geri managed to avoid the local Thomas Indian School, a boarding school infamous for punishing children who spoke Seneca.[10] The combination of her age and diligence ("I got busy and learned so I wouldn't have to go.") kept her safe. She knew the school's reputation. "They weren't very happy, the children. They couldn't understand why they were being slapped for speaking their own language. It wouldn't be so bad if we slapped the teacher too, when she spoke her language." The grin did not last long. "But you know and I know it don't work like that."

Some Seneca children attended a Quaker school on a neighboring reservation. Not Geri. "That's where they supposedly learned how to set the table. I already knew how," from one of many jobs she had taken since the age of ten. "This is hard times, back them days. Anything you could work and bring in a little money to help out the pot, that was good. When I worked on the farm, I learned how to cook a lot for little money. What you can do to change it and make it more palatable. It's more healthy and stuff like that. That's what I was interested in. Then that lady would teach me how she wants her table set. Her husband must have head up some kind of a farmers group and they would get company in from other countries and they would serve lunch. She wanted it set certain way and she would show me. I could never understand why I had to haul so much silverware when one was plenty. Like one fork. It wasn't my place to question it, but I always thought that was a waste. Could be doing something else besides that."

"When I got bigger, I got so the horses were my friends. All I had to do was talk to them and they did what I wanted. The farmer could never figure out what it was with me and the horses." Geri spoke to the horses in Seneca. "'Course, I didn't tell the man that. Well, he never asked me. If he asked me, I would have told him. But I'm not going to volunteer any information." The impish smile was wide. Her relationships with white people were "good, no problems," she said, adding with one of her looks, "as long as you knew what they wanted."

In 1953, Geri married a Seneca man who "worked in cabinet making. It was good money. They made these fancy stairways in new homes, like curved stairways." She was not an eager bride and could not remember her wedding date. "October 22. 23? One of the two. You know how you get license and it's only good for so long and then it expires? We let one expire." Asked if either had cold feet, she answered promptly. "Me. I liked the way I was. I didn't like anybody telling me what I can do and can't do. But I guess in the long run I was more strict than he was." She paused. Her husband, whom she never named, liked things "one way or no way at all. Not my way necessarily," she sighed, "but you're supposed to do it."

At Geri's instigation, the Greens took a trip to Washington, D.C. "I had a lot of stuff to look up in the archives." She was trying to find out "How they looked at us, what they actually knew about us." The "they" meant "who was writing stories or whatever about us. About the Iroquois and all the different Nations. What they really didn't have a handle on is the government. They didn't know how we could get all those six nations together, to cooperate and agree. [The original Haudenosaunee nations numbered five, but now the Tuscarora is included, for six.] They really didn't understand that. I thought, that's *their* problem."

Her digging revealed that "they knew there was something, but they didn't know exactly what it was, what glue it is, that holds us together. They don't understand the rules and regulations. I was looking to get some kind of explanation on finding out how they can so misunderstand us. What their problem is. They can't get along now."

In her opinion, the keys to the Haudenosaunee are "cooperation" and "the voice of the people," both of which U.S. politicians lacked. "They think they can do what they want. But they're only working for those people who have elected them." She went on, chastising "the Democrats and the Republicans [who] can't sit together and agree to have a meeting in Albany." She had a proposal. "Since they're not producing anything, they shouldn't get paid."

Geraldine Green certainly knew about producing. Decades earlier, she was a crackerjack employee of Remington Rand in Buffalo. "I worked in a duplicating department. I was able to run the machines within the department. I was able to break them down and put them back together. They called that fixing it. Maybe it is fixed after I got done with it. It's just that you clean it, but I didn't tell them that," she said, one eyebrow raised. She worked for the company eleven years. "Then they moved to Michigan. They asked me if I would go with them for six months to help set up over there. I [told] my husband what they wanted me to do" and explained what it would entail. He told her to go ahead but "didn't realize the depth of the commitment, he didn't take me seriously," she said, until she was gone. The Michigan assignment proved challenging. "There's a *lot* of problems I came up against, but I was able to handle them. Like working with the [Printers' Union]. That's a bucket and a half, of whatever you want to call it."

In animated detail, she described her work, about reduction and enlarge-
ment procedures, about the addressograph, and more. As far as she knew,
she was the only Native employee.

"I came back about every third week and visited a couple days," always to
this house in Cattaraugus where her parents lived. "My mother said, 'Is it all
right if we tell him [her husband] to come for dinner when you're home?' I
says, 'Oh, sure. That would be great.'" Why did she visit her parents, rather
than her husband at their apartment in Buffalo? "He didn't say anything
about me visiting him. I had to be invited first." She tilted her head. "That's
the way I am. It works best that way. *I'm* the boss."

After the Michigan assignment ended, her relationship with her husband
was "much better. Talked to me about plans."

She herself "came apart," however. The list of physical maladies was
awful, beginning with waking up bloody, being rushed to the hospital and
having an emergency hysterectomy. "That was the end of *that* noise." After
recuperating, she had to have an appendectomy, then have her gall bladder
removed, then got a hernia. "That's how I spent like three years before I
could go back to work." Remington Rand was waiting, with a job in the city
of Tonawanda, New York.

She accepted, but the bus trip made her late every morning. "That doesn't
look good for your record, no matter where you went." Geri quit to take a
job two blocks away at a nursing home. She "barely got minimum" wage,
despite the responsibilities. "You have lives that depend on you." Most
patients had been released from the hospital. "They can't do anything more
for them. That's when you get them." She never forgot "a little old lady"
whose only relative was a sister in Italy. Too sick to join her when alive, "it
wasn't until after she died before she got sent back to Italy. I never ran across
anything like that. To dwindle down to that."

Although Geraldine Green never had children ("The line stops here," she
said at one point), there was no dwindling in her world. From the Seneca
community to the Haudenosaunee Confederacy, "We're all related." As for
children, "I've got a lot of kids, but not where I would say they were mine.
These little kids, they all talk to me, they know who I am, and they listen to
what I have to say. Sometimes I'll be sitting there minding my own business

and here's a little one that comes and stands at my knees, sticks the thumb in her mouth and sucks on it and leans back into me. She looks up and she'll say, 'Thank you.' She walks away and goes back to her own mother. She draws the energy from me. That's what the one lady said they were doing. 'That's why you feel so tired, because they're taking all your energy.'"

Much of Geri Green's energy also went to maintaining millennium-tested protocol. Unlike Tonawanda, Cattaraugus has a modern tribal council as well as the traditional council of chiefs. She clearly preferred the latter. "In the longhouse, I can go to Onondaga or to Tonawanda and present my case. But I have to speak in my language." In the Cattaraugus longhouse, "if you got to speak English, you go into the cookhouse and talk there. When you finish and you agree, they elect somebody to announce to the people in the longhouse in our language." But the language is languishing.

In 1986, she went to "a Grand Council [of chiefs] in Onondaga. Beautiful up there. I was hard pressed to locate two of them and they both didn't speak Indian. They didn't understand it. I had to recite what I wanted. They told me they don't understand my language. 'Uh, excuse me?'" They assured her a gathering of chiefs would meet and consider her request. She assured them in return, she laughed in the telling, that she would sleep in the doorway while waiting for the answer.

The issue involved tradition versus modernity. "The gas company came in and made a deal with the [Seneca] Nation that they were going to put in gas storage wells. A thousand feet from the storage well was going to be all theirs. Well, that doesn't cut nothing for me." The distance would have included the Cattaraugus longhouse, in which fires are traditionally burned. "They put out my fire in my longhouse! The president signing that agreement, he literally put out *my* fire. I wanted that rescinded. I. Wanted. That. Rescinded." Her protest and fervor worked. "I won the case."

A Cattaraugus tribal member who had hoped to marry his white bride in the longhouse got Geri equally upset. "That's when I put my foot down. *No* white person gets married in my longhouse." The groom was "supposed to know better than that." Of all things, to marry someone in the longhouse who not only was a white woman, but "a *blonde*. I never saw an Indian that was blonde." The impending wedding raised in Geri no age-old Iroquois diplomacy and negotiation techniques whatsoever. "There's a lot of big spaces out there where you can go and get married. Go to Nevada. You can get married at every street corner." She still looked angry. "I suppose he thought he could get away with it, but it just couldn't be. It's bad enough there's so few of the younger people are interested in it, I don't think it should be jeopardized. There should be more . . ." She paused until she found the English word. "Respect."

The bride had met her match in Geri. "When she first came here, I heard she was Dakota." The background became ever more uncertain. "I heard she had been to the Mohawk country trying to be recognized as a Mohawk. She mentioned Florida, the what-do-you-call-them? Seminoles. I thought, 'You can't tell me she [is] Seminole. Not with her blonde . . . They're all black kinky hair, those I have met, that live in the swamps."

The wedding took place, but at the entrance to a tent set up outside the longhouse. Geri attended. A sudden rainstorm punctuated the ceremony. "It rained right on them as the man was talking to them. I said, 'Okay, I'm done here. I did right.'" She left.

Geri was no less candid with Hillary Clinton during a remarkable meeting in 1998. The First Lady wanted to know how Native women affected women's suffrage. "The ladies who started the suffrage fashioned their ways according to the Native women. They have so much going for them, Native women," said Green. She was not alone in her assessment. In the book *1491*, Charles S. Mann called the Haudenosaunee system a "feminist dream," for such reasons as women being able to choose and depose male leaders. He wrote, "Under this regime women were so much better off than their counterparts in Europe that nineteenth-century U.S. feminists like Lucretia Mott, Elizabeth Cady Stanton, and Matilda Joslyn Gage, all of whom lived in Haudenosaunee country, drew inspiration from their lot."[11]

Said Geri Green, "Whites, the other ladies that came [to what became the United States], they didn't have that. Ladies who got the babies. Period. That was their function. Even the kids, after she had them, they weren't really hers. She didn't have anything to say about their upbringing. It was the man that made all the decisions. Here, in *our* society, it's the woman that has all that."

Hillary Clinton's request to meet Native women elders came during preparations for her visit to the Iroquois Cultural Center of Ganondagon near Rochester. "I got the call like the night before and I had to get myself ready, make sure I had gas in the car. I didn't know how to dress for that. Some of the ladies were dressed in their what do you call it? Regalia? Whatever it is. I don't. It becomes my clothes when I buy it. That's my regalia," she said with a big laugh. Today, her regalia was a loose long-sleeved T-shirt and looser trousers.

There were about seven women at the meeting, no entourage, no reporters, said Geri, just Hillary Clinton and the Native women. "That was right around the time her troubles with her husband and that Lewinsky. She says, 'What would you do with a husband like that?' We all looked at one another. We just laughed. We decided to go around the table and give our views. We had a real candid talk."

Geri thought the question was meant seriously, because Native women knew how "the white ladies" feel. "They didn't count for anything. Their opinions were not asked for. We think that they're here, living the life, why shouldn't they have a say in it? We also told her this is the reason why some things are turning out the way they are. The women don't have the say."

"I said that if one of the chiefs did what her husband was doing, there would be problems. She says, 'What kind of problems?' 'Just leave him there. He's made it very clear that he doesn't need her.'" Geri meant that in the Haudenosaunee system, such a man would not remain a leader, because the women would intervene. "Knock him right out." If an Iroquois husband had an affair, "nobody else will touch him with a ten-foot pole," said Geri. "There are guys like that, that will go and get a woman pregnant, have a child, and then go on and get another. After a while that guy is bad news. He's not even welcome back to his own people." If it were someone power-ful still living at home? Like Bill Clinton, having an affair while married? "You have to make a choice. He has to leave his position. In other words, impeachment. Because he is not a very good example."

At the meeting, "she was talking, she was okay. One on one, like you and I are talking. She said she realized she had a problem." Her appearance, said Geri, was "sad." At least she looked sad until Geri blurted out her advice.

"'It's up to you if you want to cut it out. You can take that both ways.' The ladies started *laughing*. 'Sure, cut it out!'"

Hillary Clinton "was the first one to laugh. That's when I first thought of what I said. I wouldn't rescind it. It was there."[12]

After becoming New York senator, according to several people I spoke with, Clinton initiated another meeting with Haudenosaunee women. They showed up, but she did not, sending a stand-in. One person who went told me she was insulted. Geri was sick so did not go.

Geraldine Green did not vote for Hillary Clinton for the same reason Darwin Hill did not. "I don't vote. The reason why I do not vote is because I don't want them to come and tell me what I can do. We have our own ways. Unless they can live in my shoes for about a couple years, then they have earned the right to tell me what I can do." (Like Darwin, Geri, although she was immersed in Haudenosaunee life, had many contemporary interests. Two she mentioned with enthusiasm were the Hubble space telescope photographs and the singer Andrea Bocelli.)

Did she ever think what would have happened without European "contact"? She paused, then pounced. "They ran out of space or what? Now they're running out of space here. That's why you have bears in your back-yard. They're not doing anything wrong. It's us that are in their space. Put them somewhere where there's a forest. Don't kill them off." Her message to the Europeans continued. "You had a spot over there. Why didn't you stay?" When people do not stay "where they're supposed to be, that's why this world is so topsy-turvy." She looked grim. "They're not set. They're not in one place. That's why it isn't unusual to meet people who have lived in different countries. They're trying to find their place in this world. They don't find it. They keep on wandering. Go from country to country, continent to continent."

What if Native people had not helped the first Europeans? Now she looked almost angry. "They said we were savages and all that. If we were, they wouldn't have succeeded in having that village [Jamestown] down there. We would have killed them off as they approached the shores. Besides that, they sent us all crooks. They emptied their jails and sent them over here. What does that say for them?" Some came for religious freedom, I worked in. "What religion were they practicing in the jails?" she retorted. "Now it's our turn to empty our jails and send them over there."

To Geri, a related problem was that "with these casinos and everything," non-Native men "go after the ladies" of Seneca, get married, and live with them on the reservation. And non-Native women "come in and they marry the men. There's a lot of that." She looked troubled. "That is not working out the way it's supposed to, I don't think. Not from what I see. Because the feeling doesn't go all the way down deep, like they're supposed to feel about your family. It's just a dead zone."

She believed people like her who grew up with a Seneca mother and father are becoming scarce. "You're going to have to go far before you find anything like that, pretty soon. I'm trying to get them to teach the kids, they are the reason those clans are there. Cooperation between those clans [is] survival. If they don't know about them, how can they survive?"

"My people [Seneca], they got a lot of guts to stay right here. Knowing the conditions we are in. In my eyes, it's not really stable." She herself "can live like this and still be okay," but others "turn to alcohol, drugs, and whatever else there is." The thought brought her to struggles in other countries, including the fight against apartheid in South Africa. "They called *us* savages," she repeated, with a bitter laugh.

Everyone, in Geri Green's opinion, should "get back to the old ways, the old values. That has carried for many, many years. I don't see why it wouldn't now." After a deep breath, she added, "the big business thing is something else that's standing in our way, because they're out for themselves. They're sure not for the people. It's for their own pocket," she said, all but spitting out the *k* and the *t*.

The "old ways" certainly include the Seneca language, one of Geri's heartfelt specialties. It makes English seem like child's play. For "hello," the common greeting is *nya:weh sgëno,*' which translates to "I am grateful for your well-being." Seneca, furthermore, has thousands of pronouns. Thousands! A man is "he," she said, but "he does a lot of things. He doesn't just sit there as a lump. The word tells you what he's doing, what he's capable of doing. That's all it is, really." Her explanation of English–Seneca language differences was earthy. "We're backward. I always say ass backward.

What's in the front of your sentence, mine goes in the back." She pointed to a book, *The Seneca Verb: Labeling the Ancient Voice*, which she used for private students, as well as for helping teachers at the Cattaraugus Community Center. They call to ask about such matters as words with multiple meanings. Seneca "is difficult to learn," Geri acknowledged, adding, "but once you learn it, you can pick up on the other five languages."

Her commitment to keeping her heritage going seemed preordained by the importance of her clan, Turtle. "A *snapping* turtle," she smiled. A turtle "holds up the tree of peace and all the clans are in the tree. We have a big responsibility. Because if we have to do something and there aren't any birds present, go to a turtle." Missing the point about birds, I asked more about turtles. "You help out all the other clans, but there's just so much we can do. For a long time there were no snipes. We had to cover that with turtle, whose father is a snipe, or a mother. That's why I say a turtle with feather sticking out off his shell. Then you hold them up, but not many people want to." She continued affably, as if her audience of one were not lost beyond words. "Then keeping track of the names. Why does that bird have an animal name? There's nobody I can ask. They're all gone. That's what happened to me. I looked all around, sitting in the longhouse. It falls here," she said, pointing to herself. That, anyone could understand.

Her evident dismay caused another Seneca elder much amusement. He was "sitting down there on the men's side [of the longhouse] and I could feel him shaking and laughing. He knows what happened, that I discovered myself sitting there by myself, that there's no place I can go to confer." She paused. "He's gone now too. He's the Cayuga's chief. He was."

Geri's reference to "keeping track of the names," it transpired, meant knowing the names and their translations for hundreds of people in Cattaraugus's eight clans. "I'm supposed to be just keeping watch over the Turtles, but I'm watching all eight."

With hesitation—how much more could I ask without comprehending the answer?—I brought up another responsibility. You are Keeper of the Four Ceremonies, I hazarded. "That's what it says," she shrugged, as if the title were lost in translation, and then spoke of a nine-day-long winter ceremony celebrating the new year, a ceremony preceded by weeks of meetings.

Like Darwin, Geri also was involved in Haudenosaunee condolence ceremonies. "The first day we meet, they tell us how many faces we're going to be missing. They have left us. We meet back ten days after that. That stands for the ten days after they die. Well, we have ten days to collect the information they had pertaining to these ceremonies and we symbolically put it into the ceremonies." She talked of different people having different duties, of working information into the ceremonies "so that nothing is lost. That's how we keep all these words together. There's nothing written down."[13]

Geri's knowledge was also called on whenever a Seneca who died somewhere else wanted to be buried back home. "I have to do coaching on long distance," in Seneca, about protocol. "At the hospital when the person passes, there's a certain speech. And when you take them to the undertaker or whoever. Then if you take them home, there's a speech." When the body is taken from the home, another speech. "When you get to the longhouse, there's another speech. Then the big one. Then by the gravesite services."

Wisely, the Cattaraugus community asked her to record such speeches, "because we're getting few fluent speakers." She did so for funeral speeches and "the ten-day feast," she called it. "It's all in Indian. Now I'm translating it and recording it in English."

After such exertions, Geri "regroups" in her garden. "That's where you can work out your frustrations, too. That's like making bread. After a ceremony, I'll come home and I'll make yeast bread. 'Take *that*.' Pound the heck out of the bread. Best bread after a ceremony."

Speaking of frustrations, why did she think there was so little knowledge among people in the west, both Native and non-Native, about Native people east of the Mississippi? She sat up a bit taller. "They were told that we were dead. We were all done away with." Her voice took on a teasing tone. "Sorry to disappoint you. We're very much alive. Did you ever hear about somebody hiding in plain sight? Well, here we are."

Almost three months to the day later, Geraldine Green died. She had been hospitalized with an aneurism. Later, failing, she was brought back to her house with the little tobacco leaves growing on the front porch. LuAnn wrote me, "The community and those close to her worked diligently to bring her home so she would have every last ounce of spiritual care, with a great hope that some miracle of healing and health would keep her with us. But, if it was truly her time, she would spend her last days with her people. All kept vigil by her side until her very last breath."

People from throughout the Haudenosaunee Confederacy attended her large funeral.

———

"There are four of everything," Geri Green stated. "Like four different colors of people. Like flowers. Plants, like chicory. There's blue, white, yellow, and pink. And the squirrels. How many different color squirrels do you have?" Answer: gray, brown, black, and white. "You're privileged if you see a white squirrel." She did, once. "Down 438, driving along. There it was, sitting in the middle of the road when I went around the curve! Just long enough for me to see him."

CHAPTER 5

City Kid

ANSEL DEON (LAKOTA/NAVAJO)

One brisk Chicago morning, twenty-seven-year-old Ansel Deon set about his job within the tribal hall of the American Indian Center, or AIC. Around and above him, cultures clashed. Banners comprised of tribal flags hung from a high ornate molded plaster ceiling. A mural of three Native women extended over a Corinthian pilaster. A grand stage filled one side of the room, opposite it a soft-drink machine. Ansel, barely looking up, made his way down a row of folding tables. Reaching into a tattered cardboard box, he selected two small balls of different-colored yarn and positioned them next to a slim, round stick. He then rummaged in a plastic box containing colored feathers, chose one, and added it to the yarn and stick.

After making eight such place settings at each table, leaving one place empty, he moved to the next table and repeated his task, unknotting or rewinding yarn as necessary. There will be forty-two grade school kids this morning, he said, and no, he does not need any help. But thank you.

It was November, Native American Heritage Month, or, as Ansel referred to it privately, "Rent-an-Indian Month." As cultural coordinator of the AIC, one of his jobs is to help non-Natives understand what a Native person is. He knew he would be the first Native most of the schoolchildren would have knowingly met, that he is, in effect, the rented Indian.

For reasons he revealed later, he wore everyday clothes: a baggy short-sleeved polo shirt, baggier jeans, tennis shoes, and a backward baseball cap with a Rez Dogs logo. From time to time, he removed it to flip back a glossy forelock of black hair. Apart from the cap, and turquoise stud earrings, Ansel did not advertise his heritage, but did not hide it either.

There was little hiding Ansel. He is maybe six feet, two inches, and wide. The 200-pound mark must be a distant memory. When second graders, humming with barely suppressed excitement, arrived from Chicago's Belding Elementary School, Ansel's was a commanding presence.

"I would greatly appreciate it," he announced with his usual courteous phraseology, "if everyone would put their coats and lunches on the tables there"—he pointed to a space under the mural of the Native women. He asked the children to sit at the table settings, and teachers and chaperones to sit at the empty places. The children, a world medley with name tags of Khan and Velkov and Rodriguez (Belding's Web site calls the student body a "mini–United Nations"), followed Ansel's instructions in near silence. They seemed nervous until his deep-set brown eyes lightened. He had them shout "Hello!" then asked, did they like the bus ride over? "YES!" When he was a kid, he always liked it when his school bus went over bumps, did they? "YES!"

The group was his. Ansel launched into an introductory talk he would repeat almost word-for-word to second graders from Chicago's Lozano Elementary the next day. In years past, he traveled to the schools to make presentations, but teachers recently requested that the children go to the center instead. Overall, there have been fewer visits than usual. Ansel confided that this November is "a subpar Rent-an-Indian Month."

You could not tell it in his delivery. "To give you guys a brief introduction to what I am," he said, making his fingers into air quotes, "I am a full-blooded 'Native American,' or 'American Indian,' or 'First People,' or 'First Nation,' or 'aboriginal,' or 'indigenous person.' You have all of those things working to one person. I belong to two different tribes. I am an enrolled member of the Oglala Lakota, or Oglala Sioux, tribe from Pine Ridge, South Dakota, and I'm also a Navajo, or Dinéh, from Farmington, New Mexico."

"I am born and raised here in Chicago. I spent twenty-seven wonderful years, and then again twenty-seven not-so-wonderful years. Now that's just me growing up. As you kids know, sometimes we have those real high points and sometimes we have those low points." He confided none, instead delivering some heavy-hitting context.

"The American Indian Center was founded back in 1953. The reason is at that time the government forced a lot of Native Americans off their reservations, forced them to move here to Chicago, Los Angeles, New York, Minneapolis. It was a way to 'civilize' the Indians." Air quotes isolated "civilize."

The second graders were attentive. "When the government relocated the Indians, they promised them many things, like money, housing, food, jobs and clothing, if they relocated to a city. Once the Indians got to the cities, the promises weren't kept. This is the reason the American Indian Center was founded. It was a way to give those Indians a place to stay for a while."

The government's plan (see my Introduction) was to "terminate" the reservations and encourage people still on them to "relocate" to cities and fend for themselves. For many Native people who made the move, the journey from a collective, if financially impoverished, life in an often rural area to a city life where individualism was prized was so difficult, many were soon adrift. They were less relocated than dislocated.

Into the breach emerged urban Indian Centers, including Chicago's—among the oldest in the country. Because termination and relocation are no longer official federal policies, the remaining centers are part relics and part social and cultural touchstones. They themselves are located, of course, on what had been Indian land in the first place.

Chicago's AIC began in a rented space on LaSalle Street. Then, thanks in part to the American Friends Service Committee, the current building on West Wilson was purchased from an order of Masons. The neoclassical/pan-tribal disjuncture became clear; the AIC had been a Masonic temple.

Ansel's face lit up. "How many here have heard about the new National Museum of the American Indian in Washington, D.C.?" It lets people know "Indians are alive today," he said, adding that Chicago's Native American community was the only urban Native American community to have an opening exhibit at the museum. He seemed tempted to say more, but held up a yarn-and-feather-bedecked stick.

"This is what we call a talking stick." He handed one to each table. The children touched it carefully, passing it around. "In our culture, we have stories of how different things have come to the people. Creation stories, origin stories. The story behind the talking stick is about a young man. He was a part of a tribe. They would gather and have meetings, called council meetings. It's sort of like the government nowadays," he said, but instead of "a secretary of defense, secretary of state," there was "a head warrior, a head farmer." The trouble was, "everyone would talk at one time. No one got a chance to listen to one person. This young man decided he wanted to help his people out. He prayed to the Creator, God."

Ansel's story continued, the young man found a stick, attached pieces of animal hide, fur, and a feather, and took it to the next tribal meeting, where he shouted over the usual chaos for everyone to pay attention. " 'Whoever has this talking stick is the only one that can talk. Everyone must be quiet and listen. Once this person's done talking, he'll pass it on to the next person, and that person is the only one that can talk.' That meeting became very successful."

The children seemed itching to get going.

"This is a step-by-step project," Ansel cautioned them. "No one is going to jump ahead of anyone. Once we are done with one step, I'm going to ask you guys to put your sticks on the table. Some of the steps are going to be kind of tricky, so I'd like you guys to pay attention. Also, chaperones, teachers, if you can help me out, I would greatly appreciate it, too."

Ansel then demonstrated how to hold a piece of yarn over the edge of the stick, wrapping it. "Take the beginning of the yarn—don't let the ball roll off the table. If the ball unravels, you're going to have to ravel the ball back." A couple children, however, began trading their yarn balls. "I did not spend an hour out here for you to trade colors, okay? All this is color-coordinated." For close to an hour, he walked among the tables, overseeing the work. "Take your time, all right? There is no prize for first place. Your prize is you get to sit there until the last person is done." Sitting was not enough for all. The chubby Rodriquez boy began making tentative kicks at the slender Velkov girl opposite him. She pulled her legs away.

Ansel's next instruction involved wrapping the whole stick with yarn. "A couple pointers for you guys, if you want them." He demonstrated a swiveling technique. "If you layer it, your stick will look ugly. You don't want an ugly stick, do you? No." Finally the children got to use their feather. "Do not tuck the feather in. You are tying it."

Near project's end, when Ansel announced the children could keep their talking sticks, several all but jumped out of their chairs with excitement.

Now came context. "A lot of people, like teenagers, the age that you guys are going to be getting to, feel, 'My parents don't understand me.' How are they going to if you do not tell them? How are they going to know about a bully in your school that's picking on you every single day? This is a great way to break that ice, to talk to your parents. You can do it once a month, once a week, once a year. This is the only way these talking sticks are supposed to be used. Understand me?"

After getting the response he wanted, Ansel said if teachers saw any child using a stick for poking or playing, he hereby gave them permission to take it away and decide if and when it should be given back.

Ansel then led the children to bleachers he had hauled to the other side of the room, and had them stretch. This was to undo any hand cramps from making talking sticks and to "wake them up a little more so they'll get more information," he later explained. After they sat again, he looked at them intently.

"Once your teachers told you, you were going to come here to the American Indian Center, how many of you expected to see an old man with long hair, probably braided, with a big headdress, wearing a leather outfit and saying, 'How, kids!' How many expected to see that? Be truthful."

A few hands rose, slowly.

"For those who have raised their hand and the ones that haven't, are you disappointed in seeing me the way I am right now?"

No child moved.

"The reason I ask is, this is who we are, okay? We're ordinary people. We wear ordinary clothing. We are not the people you see in cartoons, you see in movies, you see on TV, what you might read about or what people might say about us. We are not these people. Indians, we go to school, we go to work. You might have an Indian teacher in your school. You might have an Indian principal. You might know an Indian cop, Indian judge, Indian lawyer. This is who we are. And that's how we want to be. Okay?"

Receiving enough nods to satisfy himself, Ansel picked up his hand drum, began beating it, then stopped. What does the beat remind them of? A child responded immediately: a heartbeat. Ansel praised him. One place you hear drums, he continued, is at a powwow. He asked who knows what a powwow is, told everyone they had really good guesses, then answered the question himself.

"It's a celebration where some of us Indians, we sing and we dance. We also make new friends and renew old friendships. A powwow is made up of four circles. The very first circle you'll see at a powwow is the drum. It represents a heartbeat. The heartbeat of the powwow, the heartbeat of Mother Earth, also the heartbeat of her children, which is all of us in this room and outside this room. Without this heartbeat, there will be no powwow."

Women gave men a drum, he said, so they could create a heartbeat too. Male drummers (second circle) sit in a circle around the drum to protect it from bad energy. Women (third circle) stand behind them, dancing and making sure the men keep the rhythm. If they don't, a woman might haul a man off by his car. The children especially enjoyed this idea.

The fourth circle is the spectators. "If you ever get a chance to go to a powwow and you feel you're not a part of the powwow, you are."

Holding his hand drum aloft, he said he was going to sing a song whose title they were to guess. He asked them not to stomp their feet or clap their hands, because that sometimes throws him off. With that, he closed his eyes and launched into a shouted number, whose first sounds made a number of children clasp their hands to their mouths and giggle wide-eyed before calming down.

After the song, greeted by some breathy "Whoa's!" amid the applause, many guessed correctly: the song was "Twinkle, Twinkle Little Star."

Ansel turned his attention to the rest of his exhibit, first recounting an origin story of a woman's jingle dress. He held one up, pointing out that the jingles, or cones, on the fabric are made of twisted lids from chewing tobacco cans. Further information may have been difficult for second graders to comprehend, such as that the woman who invented the dress had smallpox, "the disease that was introduced to the Indians right around when America was trying to establish itself," that it was "the first chemical or germ warfare of this whole world," that the woman got smallpox from infected blankets distributed by the U.S. cavalry.[1] She prayed for her people, dreamed of the dress, had it made, and the smallpox moved on. (In another version of the story, the sick woman's grandfather told her after a vision quest to make the dress. She did, danced in it, and the sound of the jingles called upon healing spirits, which made her well.)

Ansel held up pieces of his dance regalia. "We do not call any of these outfits 'costumes.' The definition of a costume is when you put it on, you pretend to be something you're not. When we put these outfits on, we're not pretending to be Indian. We already are Indian. So please do not call them costumes. You can either call them outfits, dance regalia, or regalia."

One by one, he pointed out the symbolism and use of each article he wears as a traditional dancer. "Cool," whispered the children. This eagle feather fan, he showed them, moves prayers up to the Creator. Native people consider it selfish to pray for oneself. One should pray only for others.

Most children seemed enthralled and respectful throughout. Once, however, a boy made a muffled stereotypical war whoop. Ansel, without acknowledging he heard it, varied his talk. "You guys don't want to be made fun of, right? We don't want to be made fun of either. Like going like this: 'Woo woo woo woo woo,'" he said, putting his hand to his mouth and making soft woo woos. "From here on out, I hope you guys don't make that noise. If anybody you know makes it, please stop them and let them know Indians don't do that. If they ask, 'Who are you to tell me?' say, 'An Indian taught me to not do that.'"

When the session ended, the children left the bleachers in as orderly a fashion as they arrived, then dashed to their packed lunches. A male chaperone shook his head as he stood and said, in Spanish-accented English, that he was amazed how much he had learned. Ansel sauntered to the soft-drink machine, bought a Pepsi, and sat on a table near the group, watching, waiting. This is the time children come over with private concerns.

In the two days I observed, nobody whispered the secret he is most used to hearing: the child is Native American. That secret is the reason Ansel stays close to the tables during the talking stick project. "They stop me and tell me, and I talk to them a little. That way everyone else is still minding their project and not listening to our conversation."

The "secret" is also why he mentions Indian teachers and Indian judges in his talks, but never says there may be an Indian child among them. "I know how it feels to be the only Native in the school."

———

Ansel seemed reluctant to elaborate. Indeed, wordy as he was in his presentations, he was all but silent otherwise. Cyndee Fox-Starr, the center's elders coordinator—who was preparing a massive Thanksgiving turkey dinner in the AIC kitchen while I sliced celery for it—said he hardly speaks in board meetings. (Of Odawa/Omaha background herself, she recalled her daughter coming home from her Chicago elementary school and asking, "Mom, what does it mean to 'run around like wild Indians'?")

Cyndee is one of many people at the center who has known Ansel since he was a baby. She said he was a quiet child too, like his mother.

Lorraine Deon, from the Navajo Reservation, was among the Natives relocated to Chicago in the 1960s. So was Edsel Deon, a Lakota Sioux relocated from Pine Ridge. The two, Ansel told me, got together "pretty much how any other moms and dads met back in the day. They went to the bar. Later on came my sister and then my brother. That's all they wanted. Then a mistake happened and I was born. I always tease them that I was a mistake, but they still love me the same."

If his brother had been in charge, Ansel joked, he would have been named John Wayne. "But my dad's name is Edsel, like the old car, and wanted something that sounded like it." Ansel's brother was already Edsel Jr. "Deon is my grandma's on my dad's side last name. My grandfather's name is Catches. Catches is actually short for Catches the Enemy. When my grandmother died, my dad honored her by changing to her last name."

"My dad wanted all his sons and daughters to enroll in the Sioux tribe. My mom, based upon her teachings, did what the male figure in the household wanted," even though, he acknowledged, children of a Navajo woman traditionally are raised as Navajo. Loyal son Ansel did his best to explain the contradiction. "In a way, she was still the dominant figure by letting him have us go to his way." His mother, who taught the Navajo language at Chicago's Native American Educational Services College (NACE), maintained some Navajo culture in her children's lives. She called Ansel "yash," he said, "which means 'son' in Navajo."

As a child in the poor to modest Chicago neighborhood of Uptown, he often ran in and out of the center. He also had a mischievous streak, lying to playmates that mothers wanted them home. When he was young, his parents adopted twin Indian boys, Kyle and Lyle. "The family at the time didn't want to put them in a foster home, because they would have been split up."

Initially, the Deon family seemed to do well. "My dad, he worked for People's Gas. He would fix meters." The family became homeowners too. Ansel's chores included "the regular take the garbage out, sweep." There was one major problem.

"Everything I remember, whether it was in the household or out of the household, still affects me. It's something not all kids should go through." The "it" turned out to be his father's drinking. "I know other families out there or other children . . . I'm not saying mine was the worst."

"I didn't really speak up to him until about I was like nineteen," he said softly. Not "like challenge him fighting, but just challenge him." As if to soften even that admission, he said he and his father had to separate "to actually appreciate" one another. "I miss him." The home years were difficult for his older siblings too, "but they saw it up to a specific age and then they end up leaving the household. Me, I stuck around. So I got more of the visual." He did not elaborate. His parents divorced.

Ansel has visited their homelands, going to Pine Ridge with his father several times and once to the Navajo Reservation with his mother. Neither place pulled the city kid. "The rez is like a small town with nothing to do." His mother visits the Navajo Reservation nearly every year. Struggling to sound matter-of-fact, he called her "probably the best mom in the world." He and she and a niece shared an apartment a fifteen-minute drive from the center.

What about problems, implied in his presentations, regarding school? The early years were all right, he said. He had the "luxury" of his older brother and sister being a few grades ahead of him. By high school, though, they were gone. He had "incidents." Such as? "Just name calling," he explained in an e-mail. "Whether it was from students or teachers. Boys would do the heavy calling. Girls did the same, but less." What names?

"Students have called me Geronimo, Sitting Bull, Crazy Horse, Chief, Squaw, and others. Teachers really did not call me anything, but one teacher did say something that I did not agree with. He said, 'How do Indians get visions? By smoking weed.' "

Ansel felt "stereotyped every single day" and "isolated from everyone" because of being "the only Indian in the school." What was a bullied urban Indian on his own to do? Casting about for a symbol, Ansel got himself a Cleveland Indians cap, the one with the leering "Chief Wahoo" mascot.

"Then one day my [older] brother came into town, and he saw me wear it. 'Why are you wearing that hat?' 'I want people to know that I'm Indian, because this is how people know that Indians are.' He goes, 'So you're telling me that you're a cartoon. That you have a cheesy smile at everyone. You have a big nose. You have a feather growing out of your hair. Are you that?' I looked at him and I go, 'No, I'm not.' 'Then why are you wearing it?' "

It was a defining moment for Ansel. "I still had the hat, but what I did, I altered it. Got a black pen, blackened in the teeth a little so it looked kind of messed up. I would wear it around. People would ask, 'What happened to your hat?' I'm like, 'I sort of had a change. I don't want to be a stereotype. I'm wearing this because I'm protesting it now.' "

Some background Ansel may not have known: In 1897, Louis Francis Sockalexis, a Penobscot from Maine, played baseball for a team named the Cleveland Spiders. Heckled with war whoops and so on when he went to bat for the first time, he hit a home run, and closed out the season with a .338 average. Sockalexis died in 1913. Two years later, the Spiders, whose fans had grown to adore Sockalexis, renamed themselves the Cleveland Indians.

There is debate whether the name change was a tribute to Sockalexis or a marketing ploy. No such debate attends "Chief Wahoo."

The loudest mascot uproar when Ansel and I met was not about "Chief Wahoo" but "Chief Illiniwek," the eighty-year-old symbol and mascot at the Urbana campus of the University of Illinois. "Once people find out you're Indian, that's the first question they'll ask. 'What do you think about Chief Illiniwek?' "

The "Chief," generally a white male student in feathered and buckskin regalia bought from a destitute Native man (the Lakota would like it returned), pranced about during college games, leading cheers, until 2007. It was retired not because of increased sensitivity by the school's administration, students, or alumni, or because Native people despised it, but because the National Collegiate Athletic Association (NCAA) ruled that Urbana was prohibited from hosting postseason NCAA tournaments unless the mascot was removed. "Chief Illiniwek" had a grand send-off at a University of Illinois basketball game.

Ansel rolled his eyes at the pro–Chief Illiniwek argument, that use of the mascot is a form of honor and respect. "It's hard to comprehend the fact you're honoring and respecting us, but won't listen to what we have to say."

He sighed. "Whenever I do presentations, from the last two or three years now, it's been always a question, the mascot debate. Sometimes my frustration comes out because some people just don't get it." He feels like telling them, "Concentrate on knowing the people." He is grateful not to be the first Native American faced with stereotypes. "Knowing that people before me have dealt with it and succeeded, of not getting into a fight or not getting frustrated, I take that and I use that."

After Ansel graduated from Sullivan High School, he enrolled at a Chicago trade school, ITT Tech. "I was studying to be an electronic engineer, so I would have been making switchboards. I wanted to use my hands. That's what I was good at. I felt since my math skills were up there and my science skills were up there, why wouldn't I try out electronic engineering?" He did, but dropped out, for reasons he did not discuss, and lived for a while with his father and twin brothers, taking care of the boys when they got out of school each afternoon. "I pretty much raised them for five years." He sacrificed himself for them, is how he put it. "My sister and my brother went out and made their lives. I didn't have that luxury of someone being there for me."

In his midtwenties, Ansel stopped by his old play area, the Indian Center. "The executive director at the time, she would run these school visits. Then one day she found out I was a singer and I had a hand drum, so she said, 'Come on in, and while they're doing a project I want you to sing for them.' I came in, did my little thing. Then I said, 'Do you need anything else?' 'If you want to, you can come back tomorrow and answer phones.'"

After about a month, Ansel was put on the payroll, and later became part of the school tour program.

"When I first started doing presentations and everything, I was just a dancer and singer. Then the speaker for our group got tired of speaking. He goes, 'Ansel, next performance, you're going to speak.'" Initially, Ansel protested. "I wanted to be an electronic engineer. But when this opportunity came to me, like anybody that's been given the ball, would you run with that ball or would you fumble it?"

His first forays at the microphone were uneven. "Even though we're supposed to be professionals, we're Indians, so we like to kid around a lot." Soon, though, he was making trips far from his preferred and known Uptown base—Chicago Cubs territory, he pointed out, not White Sox. "I go to Carson Pirie Scott [department store], which is on Michigan Avenue. I went there to do a presentation for their employees. I went to the Boeing building, which is right by the Chicago River, downtown, and did a presentation for them. Sears Tower. I've been in John Hancock to do a radio station interview."

At first, Ansel did not take well to what he called stupid questions. "I gave them a response like, 'What the hell?'" He has been asked, "Do you hunt animals?" Answer: no. When asked at one kindergarten, "Did you guys ride a horse here?" Ansel's partner replied no, they had ridden a Dodge Ram. Ansel laughed at the memory.

"A lot of white adults do sometimes ask stereotypical questions. The colored adults, whether you're black, Hispanic, or anything like that, don't ask those questions as much. They either won't ask those questions or they want to get to know you or understand you." He said students reflected the adults; whites asked more stereotype-based questions, nonwhites, fewer.

In years of making presentations, Ansel himself changed. "Now I feel there are no stupid questions, because someone who is an outsider doesn't really know these questions are stupid." At least they want to learn, he told himself. He developed a technique too. "I turn it around a little. Not to degrade the other person, but to have them look at themselves." At one school presentation, "one of the students asked me, 'Can you be Indian with short hair?' I looked at him for a second, I looked at everyone else, and I said,

'Am I Indian?' He goes, 'Yeah.' 'I have short hair, right?' 'Yeah.' 'Well, there you go.'"

As he spoke, Ansel took off his cap and again smoothed back his forelock. "Then I gave him my story of why I had short hair. Because my sister passed away." Ansel spoke flatly. "She was a real good person. She danced here. Whenever she danced, she always had a smile. Can't go anywhere without anyone knowing her. My sister sort of put me where I am now. Without her wanting to get into the powwow culture dancing-wise, I probably wouldn't be singing, I probably wouldn't be dancing."

Her name was Tamra. "She was a princess in the community." In high school, Tamra had a heart attack or stroke. "Her heart wasn't right. She had a problem with the beats." Eventually she moved to New Mexico, married, and had a daughter. "She actually married an EMT [emergency medical technician]." He monitored her condition, which did not improve, while she waited to be put on a priority list for a heart transplant. One day, while driving with her husband, "she felt something wrong." He rushed her to a hospital. "They were trying to bring her back and nothing was possible. That's pretty much how she died. The day she passed was the day we found out that she got on the list."

Tamra was twenty-seven, Ansel's age now. The ritual of cutting hair after a death is "a way to sort of forget, but then again not forget. It's a way of letting that person go. The hair is your line. When you cut it, that means someone passed away in your line." Now, years later, he was regrowing his hair.

With his mother, Ansel took over the care of Tamra's daughter. It was unclear why Tamra's father did not. The girl's name is Winona. "It's Sioux for first born. I look after her and try to give her the things my sister would have." To Winona, now thirteen, Ansel has become a loving, stern uncle. "She knows if she wants a boyfriend, they have to be okay by me." He said he sees his sister's face in hers.

The other woman in Ansel's life was his girlfriend of two years, whom he first mentioned in regard to an issue that can sear Native communities: degree of "blood." "Myself, I have a girlfriend who is mixed. She does have some black features, but she's tired of people judging her because she's black." She is "Creole, she's Italian, and she's Blackfoot. Right now she graduated from U of I in Champaign Urbana, got her bachelor's degree, and she's going after her master's in public health," he added with evident pride. The "blood" topic troubled Ansel. "It's really hurting our people." He was uncomfortable anyone could decide "who's Indian and who's not," yet believed "we need to control it a little." He wrote in an e-mail, "I know I should be with someone who is full blood to keep the 'Indian' alive, but with my experiences most 'Indian' girls did not want to be with me."

After debating the issue, he emerged on the side of happiness with his girlfriend. "There will be individuals who will have negative things to say. I'm not going to put them down. I'm not going to hate them for that. If there was something wrong, my mom would say something and she truly hasn't said anything about the race factor, if you may. My dad, he might have something to say, but he still won't say it to me, yet."

"Everyone is happy in the community, because they haven't seen me around with anyone, holding hands, stuff like that." He took his girlfriend to a high point in his life, the opening of the National Museum of the American Indian in September 2004. "It was a great way to sort of celebrate our year of, you know, being together."

The subject of the opening renewed the enthusiasm he had shown the schoolchildren. He raised a caramel-colored arm and pinched it. " 'Hey, you're just like me!' Being there and seeing . . . thousands of people, Indian people. It's part of history. Not too many people can be like, 'I went to Washington, D.C., for the opening of the National Museum of American Indian.' Who can also say, 'I'm one of the co-creators for the exhibit too?' " He went on, "Seeing how many people were walking around, looking at arts and crafts displays, or selling of jewelry, or the radio station was there, or presentations, or singing and dancing." Ansel seemed transported.

He was also enthusiastic, if guardedly, about an entrepreneurial idea. While visiting his brother, stationed with the navy in San Diego, the two started talking about brands of Native clothing that had cheeky or sarcastic slogans. "I didn't feel that pride." The Deon brothers decided that "we need to come up with something that is for everyone. Not just for Natives, but it's a Native perspective." For their own line, Ansel created a brand name: Tribal Funk. A logo eluded him until a friend painted a tipi with three feathers on

Ansel's hand drum. "When I first got it from him, I was struck. That's my logo! If you look at the feathers, they sort of have an urban street tagging . . . you know, graffiti?" Now he has the name, the logo, and ideas. What he lacks is funding. "I have to get the other people to help me to raise the money. The logo specifically, I haven't trademarked it yet. That's a thousand dollars right there."

Finances concerned Ansel not only in regard to Tribal Funk but the AIC. The nonprofit is not flush with funds but by mandate serves everyone, Native and non-Native. "So long as you live within the zip code 60640, you will get services here." Donations to the center include goods of questionable value. While preparing Thanksgiving dinner, Cyndee Fox-Starr surveyed donated boxes of powdered gravy mix before deciding to make her own. In another room was a mountain of old computers. "We have someone here who pretty much fixes computers, so he can go in to see what can be used or what can't be used," said Ansel, gesturing. "Some of them we use and some of them will be thrown away." The center sells them for about $25. "It's like with the food pantry downstairs and the clothing." As he spoke, an array of people hauled used clothes out of the building to a nearby bus stop.

Ansel's concerns about the financial health of the American Indian Center were well founded. Two months after our last talk, he was among four employees temporarily laid off. Two grants had not come through.

He was fretting too about personal matters. He missed his father, whom he last saw in Pine Ridge some two years ago. There, he observed a sun dance. The arduous days-long ceremony involves fasting, hoped-for visions, and for men, piercing of the participant's flesh. To get an idea of what is involved, he suggested I watch the 1970 movie (mostly derided by Native people) *A Man Called Horse*. Ansel was not ready for the sun dance himself. "Where I'm at right now is sort of new. Being away from my dad is another perspective of life for me. I haven't really been away from him for this long of a period. Do I need to call him, you know?"

Because of his father's past behavior, Ansel sometimes worries about his own, as does his mother. "I'm sort of caught in a bind. I never do raise my hand or anything." He paused. "She calls me on it every once in a while. 'You're acting like him.'" He looked pained.

"Her personality," he said, pausing again, "is the dominant figure in the household. So she does have her moments also. Like any mother would have," he added.

Ansel's immediate future did not seem to include a family of his own. He almost smiled. "My mom is always like, 'When are you guys going to have a kid?'" She has a grandson and granddaughter from Edsel Jr. and a granddaughter from Tamra, but. . . . Ansel's head ducked into his shoulders. "I'm the baby of the family. 'We're waiting for you.'"

Waiting might be in order. "Wednesdays I always have drum practice, so those days are already set. Monday nights I watch my favorite TV show. I watch wrestling on Monday nights always. You leave me alone on that day; you leave me alone on Wednesday. Any other days, I can fit you in."

On some of those other days, he goes out with friends. He portrayed himself as a person of temperate habits, a nonsmoker, except in prayer ceremonies, and a moderate drinker. "I started drinking really when I was eighteen, but it wasn't an everyday type of thing. It was more on and off. When I got twenty-one I drank again, but something in my mind was saying, don't do it. I was on and off again. I really stopped drinking two or three years ago. If I do go out, I usually drink a Long Island [iced tea]"—a strong cocktail, he agreed. "But I'm a big guy and it takes like three drinks to actually hit me." He usually cuts himself off at two, he said.

Ansel's girth did not reflect a healthy life, his financial future was uncertain, and certain relationships were unresolved, but his greatest concern seemed to be the challenges he faced as a Rented Indian.

"Whenever I speak, it does in some way touch someone, and it gives me something, that I'm making a difference." He looked somber. "A lot of people don't see Indians anymore, so when they first hear you're an Indian, all the stereotypical points of views come out," and all are negative. "Here Indian students have the highest dropout rate. There's many factors into that. Being called names, being stereotyped. Then again, getting in the wrong crowd or not giving a damn about your education. Any other community feels that same way, that education's not going to help them out in the long run. We're no different. But we are, you know, original people here."

"A lot of presentations I do, I get frustrated. But then I realize the frustration in my voice and I want to turn that around. I don't want to come off as a frustrated Indian, 'Boo hoo Indians.' I want to come off as someone who is passionate about his culture and someone who wants to do something for [it]," he said, finishing his Pepsi. "Being here in Chicago, I've dealt with all those things. I want people to deal with that also, from their own perspective of their life and culture. That's why I always say to whoever, 'Know who you are. Know where you come from. It will help you on your way of life.' I wanted to be an electronic engineer. But when I got in this, my pride came out even more. I want to use that as an example, to find out who you are. 'You can be a part of mainstream society. But just know who you are.'"

CHAPTER 6

The Drum Keeper

ROSEMARY BERENS (OJIBWE)

"When I was really little, I used to walk on this dirt road to my cousin's house and look up a long, sloping hill. It was just a big field all full of grass and trails going across. There'd be clouds going by and looked like they were at the top of the horizon. I used to think, if I go up there, I'll fall off, because that's the edge of the earth. I'll never be able to get back on. That's what I thought the world was, the village I lived in and the people I lived with."

In ways, Rose Tennant Berens never ranged far from the northern Minnesota Bois Forte Reservation that encompassed her childhood. She is a member of the Bois Forte band of Ojibwe, sometimes known as Chippewa, and inherited the region's accent, her *o*'s in words such as *go* or *throw* seeming to come from a well.

Rose stands about five feet, three inches, looks petite despite the flannels and Polartec she favors, and at fifty-six has unlined dark skin and a turned-up nose. When she twists her long brown hair into a knot above her bangs, she is somehow as adorable as a child. Her lineage includes part French from her Ojibwe mother and part Scots-Irish from her Ojibwe father. She lives with her third husband, Mike Berens, a rugged white man who acts besotted with her. When they met, at a local bar, where she was celebrating her sister's birthday, he did not believe in anything religious, but "evolved," as Rose put it. "I took the time to explain things to him. First time we went hunting and got an animal . . . I always carry a little plastic thing with water. I offered water and tobacco, then had to explain to him why I was doing that"—the water is to quench the thirst of the animal's spirit, the tobacco is to thank the

Creator—"and what I said, and translated. He said, 'It all makes so much sense, the way you do things.'" Mike is now a pipe carrier in the Bois Forte band, an honor reflecting his respect for Ojibwe ways. "He's not discriminated against because he's not Native. I don't even know if people know that he's not."

The marriage is the third for him too; both say three's a charm. On weekends, they care for their sled dogs, hunt, fish, make wine from strawberries or rhubarb, go to powwows, or, depending on the season, ride snowmobiles or Harley-Davidsons. Their wedding rings are tattoos based on the Harley shield. His says "Rose," hers, "Mike." This was Mike's idea, after Rose feared losing the diamond ring he offered to buy.

Rose needs her diversions. As manager of the Bois Forte Heritage Center and Cultural Museum, a round modern building ("Everything is round with us") set within an embrace of birch trees, one of her major responsibilities is the daunting work called repatriation.

The word "repatriation," as part of the acronym NAGPRA, generally draws blank looks from non-Natives I have queried and emotions close to tears from Natives. NAGPRA, the 1990 Native American Graves Protection and Repatriation Act,[1] requires U.S. museums to send tribes a list of objects that might be from that tribe, and gives tribes the impetus and clout to reclaim—to repatriate—them.

"It's not as easy as it sounds." Rose made the grand understatement one weekend afternoon in the staff meeting room. Repatriation is "a really long process, and it can take two or three years, even longer, to get stuff back." When I visited, she was negotiating with the Denver Museum of Nature and Science for nineteen items—she pushed her granny glasses down her nose and consulted her notes—including "birch bark scrolls, two rattles, a fawn-skin bag. The fawn-skin is something they will keep their *midewinin* medicines in." According to an Ojibwe-English dictionary Rose consulted, *midewinin* means "grand medicine." The phrase indicated the translation's limits.

Negotiations get stuck in cultural divides. "When we first went to Denver, one of the items they had was a net for catching fish. It was made by one of the band members who was still alive. Her name was Ruth Sauk. They had a net and eight sinkers." The Denver staff resisted its return, suggesting instead a loan of several sinkers. "I said, 'No. You don't understand. Eight is a very important number for us. You would never set a net and use five sinkers or three sinkers. You would always use eight sinkers. If you didn't, the fish in the lake, they have spirits, too, and might become angry because you're not doing things right. You may never get any fish.' We truly believe that."

Denver could not argue but did not budge.

To bridge anticipated divides with Harvard University's Peabody Museum, Rose helped write a grant to pay for Peabody staff members to visit Bois Forte. "We felt if they could come here and see our museum and how we exhibit things . . . I guess you'd call it cultural sensitivity. The way we work with items and how we feel about them more so. We took them up to Nett Lake." Located within one of three areas that comprise Bois Forte (pronounced Boys Fort) Reservation, Nett Lake contains the world's largest connected wild rice beds. In the midst of the lake is a wooded protrusion, Spirit Island. "We actually took them to the island and talked to them about the land, the rice, the lake, so they would get an overall picture of who the Bois Forte people are." She described the visitors as "very respectful."

Small wonder. The access granted the visitors was extraordinary. Nett Lake is generally off limits to nontribal members, its waters and rice crop carefully guarded. No motor boats allowed, of course, canoes only; also no urinating allowed in the vicinity, no lead bullets allowed in nearby hunting. Tribal members harvest the rice by the traditional technique called shattering—hitting the stalks in a way to make kernels fall into the canoe. Shattering is economically inefficient and environmentally sound. Many kernels fall back into the water, hook onto the muck at the bottom, and germinate.

More proscribed than going onto Nett Lake is going to Spirit Island, which contains sacred petroglyphs. Frankly, I was envious. Even Rose was not able to gain permission for me to be in a canoe on Nett Lake, much less go to Spirit Island. Instead, she and I strolled the Nett Lake shore, mostly in silence. She talked about Spirit Island, then chided herself for almost pointing. You point with your lower lip, she demonstrated, not your finger; a pointed finger could cause the wind to come up. That is not good at ricing time, which was now, midautumn. Before we left the shore, she placed a few tobacco flakes on a stone as a prayer of thanks and was pleased to see another person had done the same on a log. "One of the men I know who's a spiritual advisor says if an Indian person tries to pray without using tobacco, it's like trying to talk to someone on the phone without dialing." Even "a couple of grains" opens up the lines, as does tobacco smoke. "The smoke rises and carries your prayers to the Creator."

The Harvard visitors' answer to repatriating items from the Peabody was yes.

Back at the Bois Forte Heritage Center's meeting room, as coffee percolated—Folger's has cornered the market on every reservation I ever visited—Rose read from the Peabody list. "Two pair of moccasins. A birch bark box. Quillwork boxes. Soapstone pipe inlaid with lead and catlinite.[2] A pipe bowl of black pipestone. It was a woman's pipe. A buckskin pouch with beadwork strap."

"A lot of the things like moccasins are considered utilitarian, so we're having a real hard time getting things like that back. There's different categories you can repatriate. Spiritual items, items of cultural patrimony, funerary objects—associated and unassociated funerary objects—like something buried with a body or buried later next to it." Utilitarian objects are not such a category. "But for us as Native Americans, everything we use is sacred because of the process we use to go out and get these things. A birchbark basket, for instance, that is used every day to hold your sewing items? You have to go out into the woods, you put down tobacco at the base of a birch tree. Then you pray in your own way and say, 'We are not taking your skin for no reason. We are doing this for something that we need. Thank you for what you're going to be giving us.' Then you take off the bark and go home and make your basket. That whole process is very sacred. Museums don't recognize that."

Case in point—the Heard Museum in Phoenix. A Bois Forte delegation led by Rose went to look at fourteen items listed as being from the tribe. "One was a cradleboard. Our word for that is a *dikinaagan*. The cradleboard was made by one of our elder's mothers. She recognized it. 'My mom made that!' We can't get that back because that's considered a utilitarian object. In order to make that cradleboard, the wood used is offered tobacco and prayed for. The beads on the material are *manidoominens*—they're little spirits. The whole cradleboard is a very spiritual object." The Heard was unmoved. Not only was the cradleboard deemed utilitarian, it did not belong to the tribe collectively. "You can't repatriate something that belongs to a single person."

One reason so many precious objects went so far, said Rose, was that museums reflected widespread expectations that Natives would soon be extinct. " 'Collect everything you can get your hands on. Then bring it back so we will have a collection that a hundred years from now, when there are no more Native Americans, we can show how these people lived.' " Collecting, she said, coincided with the increased distribution of alcohol.

She pictured Native people drinking, running out of liquor money, "and all of a sudden here comes this man who is offering them a hundred dollars for a cradleboard. It's something you normally wouldn't sell, you'd pass on from generation to generation." Rose knows families who never drank but were in financial need when collectors with "slick tongues" came by. Bois Forte items are in Germany, England, and "all across the country," including a museum in Tower, four miles away. It possessed a Bois Forte drum. One of Rose's co-workers "is a lineal descendant from the people who kept that drum" and wanted to repatriate it. Rose and her curator, a non-Native Quaker man, both authorized NAGPRA representatives, started the process. "It's *not* an item owned by one person. It belongs to the whole tribe. I called the gentleman who is the director of that little museum. He said, 'You do realize that the historical society paid for this drum.' I said, 'There is no language anywhere in the NAGPRA law that says anything about us compensating you for something you bought. I am requesting you send this back.' He said, 'Why do I have to do that?' I said, 'Do you know anything about NAGPRA?' He said, 'Very little.' I said, 'Then you need to get on a computer and pull up the NAGPRA page and read about the laws. You receive federal money. You are bound by law to send me an inventory.' "

At the time of my visit, he had not done so. Within months, Rose had the drum.

Bois Forte also lost items to its Indian agent stationed there in 1914. "By hook or crook, he accumulated a lot of things. He dug up some graves. He got people drunk. He did all kinds of stuff. Then he went down to Ottawa, and he sold all this stuff to [a museum]. It's all documented. But we can't get it back." The scope of NAGPRA, of course, stops at the border. In lieu of repatriating the items, Rose and others visited them.

"We went down there as a delegation from Bois Forte to have some ceremonies. We took a spiritual person with us. When I went in there, boy, did I have a hard time. I started sobbing. This horrible, horrible lonely feeling." She paused. We were now in her car, returning from Nett Lake to the Heritage Center, her mind at the museum. "They have a huge storage area, and it's filled with actually millions of artifacts from all over the world. They have kayaks from Alaska made out of sealskin. They've got masks from the East Coast. Tons of things. A lot are very, very spiritual items. When I walked into that room, it was like walking into a void where there wasn't quite enough air. I got this funny feeling in my throat, almost like it was closing up. I kept walking along with everyone else, and went to the area where they had the Bois Forte stuff. The man we took with us as a spiritual advisor took out his pipe and started to pray. I started to cry. I cried the whole damn time he was praying," she said, then laughed. "I felt so embarrassed and I couldn't stop. I've had that kind of problem every time I go to a museum. I'm not quite sure what I need to do to fix it. I don't even know how to explain it. It's like I'm feeling like they feel. They've been away from home for a hundred years and they're locked away in an area where they aren't able to see their relatives."

Such excursions exhaust Rose. "All the energy is sucked out of me. When I come home I'm really tired for three or four days, sometimes a week." She continues anyway. "I pretty much force myself, because I think it's real important the director of the museum go and they see that person coming there." Excursions necessitating airplanes are the worst. Rose has a fear of flying so acute, she vomited on the tarmac. A doctor prescribes something to calm her.

Even more emotionally draining is trying to repatriate museums' collections of Native bones, which of course are almost impossible to identify. Rose was pondering an idea. Maybe Bois Forte could bring bones back from various area museums and rebury them at an agreed-upon place, witnessed by representatives from all Minnesota tribes. "We don't know who they belong to. They might be my relatives, they might be from Mille Lacs or Grand Portage." She added, "They shouldn't be sitting in a museum somewhere in a box. I certainly wouldn't want my bones floating around. I think my spirit would be very, very uneasy."

Occasionally, human remains are uncovered on Bois Forte during construction projects. The workers know to call Rose at any hour. She will open the center's storage room and make arrangements to have the bones reburied at a special site. "We do it with the utmost respect. We use a lot of sage, a lot of tobacco. No one is allowed to go in and look at them." Any items found with the bones are reburied, too. "If they buried that person with a pipe, they thought that pipe would never be seen by human eyes again, and that's the way it should be."

There is no funeral. "There's already been a ceremony when that person was originally buried." Instead, a "spiritual person fluent in Ojibwe" is brought in "who will talk to the spirit of that person and tell that spirit why they're here, that we're not doing this in any derogatory means whatsoever, we're trying to do what is right. As Indian people, we're trying to do what is right."

———

Many repatriated items are displayed at the Bois Forte Cultural Museum, but others are too sacred to be shown. "We have repatriated some stuff from the American Museum of Natural History. They're all *midewinin* items, so we can't put them on exhibit. We have them in our storage area. What we're planning to do is to set up a meeting with *midewinin* people, spiritual people, and some elders and find out what they want us to do." The answer may be to put them "out in the woods on the land they originated from."

Propriety about keeping sacred objects from view is evident also in the underground storage vaults of Chicago's Field Museum. Although rows of breathtakingly beautiful baskets, pottery, and other works line seemingly miles of shelves, visible to anyone fortunate enough to be granted access, white curtains shield some items from outsiders' eyes. Anthropologist and repatriation specialist Helen Robbins, my conduit to Rose, said Native people on research or repatriation quests sometimes break down when a curtain is lifted and an object revealed.

With the exception of museum employees such as Helen Robbins, Rose is often frustrated in her dealings. She shook her head. "Their way of thinking is so different than our way of thinking. The language they use is so different. That's why it's important for us to go out with a delegation of elders, spiritual advisors, and tribal members. We spend two or three days there and talk to them and try to make them understand how we feel about our traditions and our cultures." She half smiled. "Some people, when you're talking to them, you can see it go over the top of their head and their eyes kind of glaze over. They don't have a clue what you're talking about. There's other people that as you're speaking, you can see in their eyes and in the way they start moving their body, they understand. Something clicks. That's really nice for us."

She well knew the museums' argument that repatriation quests will empty display cases of Native American collections. She strongly disagrees. "They have things they don't know who they belong to. They send out notices to all these tribes. The tribes don't know who they belong to either. If they sent us something and said, 'It comes from somewhere in Minnesota, Michigan, or Wisconsin,' which is a huge area, we would look at maybe moccasins and say, 'That kind of looks like Bois Forte.' We take it to the elders. The elders might say, 'No, those are not Bois Forte.' So we write back. 'These are not Bois Forte.' We don't want anything that does not belong to us. Every other tribe is like that too. That's a big taboo." Rose also argued that tribes would gladly lend works back to museums for exhibits.

Once a museum does relinquish objects, another step of homecoming begins. "There's a special way things need to be packed. Some items need to be wrapped in red felt with little pieces of cedar. Others are wrapped in green felt, depending on what the item is and what the spiritual advisor instructs us to do." Rose was horrified when I asked if objects are shipped back by plane. "If there's more items than you can carry, we would never get on a plane and have them put in the cargo hold. We'd drive to wherever it was to pick them up and personally bring them back. It has to do with the deep respect for the items. If you had a really, really old grandma, maybe you never knew about her before and all of a sudden you found out about her, you wouldn't call up whoever she was staying with and say, 'Okay, put that old woman on a plane and send her back here.' It's a thing we don't even consider."

Similar images came up often. Drawers in the center's storage area are kept open a little, glass display cases in the museum have air holes—all to let grandma breathe.

More such breaths were to come. Rose was thrilled about a recent call from a man in Bowling Green, Kentucky, whose father, while a doctor on the reservation, acquired forty-two Bois Forte song scrolls—accounts on birch bark of songs and stories "we don't know anymore." Some were more than two hundred years old. The doctor gave them to his son, who wanted to return them. "We're still in awe." The collection is "probably *midewinin*," she said. "We will not be able to use them to put on display, but they're very, very important tools for us."

If repatriated items are not sacred, Rose uses them for education. She sure would like Ruth Sauk's fishing net back. "No one makes nets anymore, because nobody knows how. That's part of our culture that is lost." If she had the net, she could find someone who could figure how it was made and "reteach our young people. We just need one who can take what we all know and carry that on to the next generation."

But does the next generation want to know? "The problem all reservations are having is that the young people are not interested in the traditions and the cultures. They would rather be out driving around with their friends or playing Gameboy or watching some sport thing on television." Despite such distractions, she hoped Bois Forte parents conveyed to their children "the most important thing there is to teach them, which is respect. You respect your elders, you respect your parents, your teachers. You respect yourself, which is very, very important. You respect the land and the trees. You learn that everything is alive. If you can teach a young person that, even if they do go off and play Gameboy and don't learn the language, if they learn about the respect, that might change their attitude about a lot of things."

Language lessons are offered at the Bois Forte center, but people are hardly clamoring to attend. "The thought of spending three hours a night, three nights a week, sitting in a classroom learning Ojibwe language does not appeal to them. They are modern Indians." A flyer at the center announcing language classes ended with "If there is no interest or participation there will be no further classes."

The fragility of the language link pointed to the fragility of the cultural link. Rose pictured that after Ojibwe children came home from far-off boarding schools, "they didn't really have anything to go home to." Linguistically and culturally estranged from their families, they married each other or non-Natives. "When they had their children, they taught their children what they had learned, which was the European lifestyle."

"There's approximately two and a half generations of Native Americans all across the United States, Canada, Hawaii, Alaska, that don't know anything about themselves. They are nothing more than brown-skinned Europeans." She added, "We don't know who we are anymore."

———

The former Rose Tennant, whether working in her hi-tech and semi-cluttered office, or giving a tour of the center's museum, which includes a mural depicting the five-hundred-year-long journey of the Ojibwe people to a place where "food grows in water," or walking along Nett Lake, where food does grow in water, seemed sometimes stunned to have the job she does.

An only child until she was thirteen, she "climbed trees and shot guns and had slingshots and fished and did pretty much anything I wanted," including following her paternal grandmother around. Among other things, she taught Rose how to boil prickly nettle, strip its leaves, and pull and rub the stalk into a rope. "The nettle fiber people," her grandmother told her, gave Nett Lake its name. Rose also learned, when harvesting raspberries, to leave some for the bees, so they won't bite. "I spent quite a bit of time with her out in the woods. Before we were allowed to pick anything, we always had to put down tobacco. She told me once, 'This land we live on is a garden. This belongs to *gitchi-mani-do*, the Creator. Anything we pick, we're picking out of his garden. So you need to put tobacco down to say, Thank you for the gift.'" (Could such behavior demonstrate a greater contrast with the 2010 oil spill in the Gulf of Mexico? Rose e-mailed, as the oil gushed: "It is just another of man's catastrophic disasters and his inability to forecast or resolve this type of tragedy. He's going to kill the planet, you know.") Another important lesson was, after cooking a meal, do not eat until you offer food to the Creator. Rose still obeys. "The first walleye I bring out in my net, I take home, immediately fry one up and do that offering. When I get a deer in the fall, I do that with my meat. I do that with my moose." She puts a bite of whatever it is on a piece of birch bark and places it in a clean hard-to-reach spot. "You don't want dogs peeing on it."

Like other Ojibwe children, she learned how to harvest and parch wild rice. If the parched grain's hairy-tailed husk, called a rice beard, flew into someone's eye while being tossed in the air to separate grain from husk, the pain could be excruciating. Her grandmother was prepared. She would have paddled across Nett Lake to find pitcher plants filled with liquid and collected the contents of each flower into a glass vial. "When anybody got a rice beard in their eye, she'd use an eyedropper and put a couple of the drops in their eye" and cover it. By the next morning the rice beard was gone, the eye unharmed.

Her grandmother imparted behavioral lessons too. As a girl, Rose once shoplifted sunglasses and a comb, not understanding that was wrong. "She marched me back up" to the shopkeeper to return them, then imparted a warning. Anything more Rose steals will be carried on her back when she dies. In the afterlife, she will come to a huge meadow, where her ancestors will be happy to see her, but will ask where the items on her back came from and will turn away. "I've never stolen anything in my life."

In her childhood, Rose and friends also collected firewood for "old ladies" at their sugaring camp. "To pay us, they'd give us tin cups with maple sap that had been boiled down, kind of between sap and sugar." The children would find a spot of fresh snow and carefully pour their reward, perhaps writing a name, before it turned hard.

Rose's childhood might have been an idyll were it not for her parents. Her father was an alcoholic. A long story involved his parents separating when he was a boy, his roaming from relative to relative doing chores, at night curling up with a blanket by the stove—like a puppy, said one uncle. He was sent to an Indian boarding school in Flandreau, South Dakota. "My dad had blond hair and blue eyes, so you can imagine how hard that was, when everyone else is almost a full-blooded Indian." At twelve, he took off—way off. "He *walked* all the way to Nett Lake, Minnesota, in the wintertime," a distance of over four hundred miles. He told Rose he survived by going up to farmhouses, knocking on the back door, and offering to do any work— shovel out manure, chop and haul wood—in exchange for a meal, usually soup and bread, and permission to sleep in the barn. Mornings, he would milk the family's cows if any, receive breakfast, and be on his way.

Once home at Nett Lake, where few paying jobs existed, he chopped wood for three days for a man who rewarded him with a single bullet, which he loaded into a borrowed rifle. With ammunition so precious, he became an expert marksman. "He would go out into the woods and hunt and get a deer and would gut it and field dress it, quarter it, haul it into the village and give it away." The practice assured him some meals. "He had a real hard life. All of these years I've had to try inside myself to find an excuse for him, why he was the way he was."

Mostly, he was doting and loving, teaching Rose seemingly everything he knew, including fishing. He and other tribal members chose their catch carefully. "They only took the [sturgeon] males, because the females don't spawn until they're twenty years old and only spawn once every five years." He once asked her to shoot a partridge, which she did, then had her look at it closely. " 'Whatever you shoot, you have to eat and have to realize you are killing something.' It made me very, very aware of life and death."

When Rose's father drank, though, he beat her mother. She left him several times, taking Rose with her to her mother's, or to Minneapolis, or once to a resort near Canada, where she worked as a cook and bartender. Each time, the abject husband followed, pledged reform, and Rose's mother returned. "I said, 'Why do you keep going back?' She said, 'Because I love him.' I said, 'How can you love someone who gives you a black eye or a fat lip?' She said, 'He doesn't really mean to do that. He's not like that when he's sober.' "

That was true, Rose acknowledged. She fondly recalled the family's winter bathing routine, her father filling milk cans with water from the village pump, her mother heating the water in a tub on the stove, her parents lifting the heated water to the floor. "I would take a bath first, because I was the littlest, then my mom would take a bath because she was the woman. My dad would take a bath last because he was a man and he was the dirtiest." In the summer, the family bathed in the lake. Rose's aunt heated water for dishwashing the same way, then threw the dishwater and rinse water off the back porch. "In the wintertime, after she did that for six weeks or so, there was this big gray blob of ice. When we couldn't go skating on the lake, we'd go skate on that dirty dishwater."

Throughout Rose's childhood, her father's fury never touched her. Then she turned thirteen.

An excruciating story began with her waiting, before her ten P.M. curfew, for the school bus that would return the basketball team, including her "kissing boyfriend," from an away game. "My dad's pickup pulled up. He rolled down the window and said, 'Get in the truck.' I went around and got in. I turned to look at him. I got a fist right in the face. My nose started to bleed, my glasses fell off. I jumped out of the truck, went running, and I slipped and fell." He caught her, slapped her again, she got away again, fell again, he grabbed her by her hair and dragged her back to the truck. "When we got to my house, my mom took one look at me and said, 'What the hell have you done to that girl?' He said, 'She should have been home.'" Rose ran into her bedroom, sobbing, her face bloody, her lips split. Her mother ran in after her, her father started "raging through the door," but her mother slammed it and held it closed.

After he beat Rose a second time, she planned her days to avoid him, running to relatives for safety. "My grandma used to get really, really mad at my dad" but "tried not to interfere too much."

Rose faced other challenges from her mother, whom photos depict as tall, slim, dark-skinned, and beautiful. Whereas her father spoke Ojibwe and followed some Ojibwe traditions, her mother did neither. "My mother was raised a very strict Catholic. Didn't know any Ojibwe language. She didn't know anything about traditions, she didn't *want* to know about traditions." After Rose's grandmother braided her hair, her mother would unbraid it. "Her mother had been sent to a boarding school, and one of the things [they taught] Native American children was to be ashamed of who they were.

When you asked her, 'What nationality are you?' she'd say, 'I'm mostly French.' She did have French in her, but it was French Canadian. All French Canadians are, are Indians." Rose smiled.

Her mother continually encouraged Rose to adopt Roman Catholicism, but at fourteen, during a Sunday mass, Rose finally rebelled. "I wasn't born with a horrible sin. There's nothing wrong with my spirit. I got up and I walked out."

The family dynamics grew so difficult, Rose quit school at sixteen and eloped to Chicago with "a Finn named Dave." He was a Vietnam veteran her father "hated." Then, for reasons she never knew, after the newlyweds returned, "my dad was completely different. He accepted Dave and almost went back to the way he was when I was younger." When Dave was at work and Rose was home alone, pregnant with the first of her two now adult children, her father took her hunting and fishing, like old times. A pregnant woman hunting or fishing was probably a tribal taboo, she added. Her grandmother would have had a fit.

Throughout the years at her grandmother's side, collecting her knowledge and beliefs, Rose never thought they might translate into an occupation. Nothing else had. "I tried to sell Kirby vacuum cleaners, I went to college for a while, I was a waitress in town where my mom worked, and was a bartender there, and a short-order cook. I worked as an admin assistant for the Native American Indian Studies program at Mesabi Technical College," in Minnesota.

After a divorce from Dave and from her second husband, a Bois Forte band member, Rose took stock, unhappily. "I was forty-two years old. I didn't have any kind of training. The only thing I knew was traditional stuff."

Enter Bois Forte's Fortune Bay Resort Casino, which opened in 1986. An acquaintance urged her to apply as a hostess. "The thought of getting a job at a casino scared the hell out of me." Rose's then "very, very shy" personality was not based on a sense of discrimination. "Sometimes you meet people and they just don't care for you. I never think, oh, they don't like me because I'm an Indian."

To summarize many subsequent career steps, night owl Rose was hired, proved her friends wrong by showing up at 6:30 in the morning, and became possibly the most assiduous employee the casino ever hired. "I didn't know a soul in there," so when people signed in, "I'd look at their name and I'd look at their face. That's how I got to know who everybody was." She later forced herself to apply for guest services manager. "I was as honest as I could possibly be. Told them I had never, ever had that type of position before, but they could look at my record. I never missed work, I was never sick, I worked overtime, I took people's shifts, I knew everybody." Rose got the job, ran herself ragged, and resumed the smoking habit she had quit. "I would come in, in the morning, do my job, then someone would call in [sick] in the afternoon, so I'd fill in their shift. Then someone would call in at midnight and I'd have to do a midnight shift."

Much of the problem was high turnover, furthered by a tribal member who handed her a folder with the name of the person he wanted her to hire. "I was very ignorant about what I could and couldn't do, so I would hire these people and they wouldn't show up for work." Finally, a relative took her aside. "He said, 'What the hell do you think they hired you as a manager for?'" The next time the man with the folder came by, Rose said no. Instead, she hired "this mousy little girl," an Ojibwe who reminded Rose of her former self. "I was real patient with her. She had never even turned on a computer." Rose smiled. "She's still there today. She blossomed. Well, I did, too."

One of Rose's innovations was to ask all employees to pick the shift they wanted, then hired others to work the person's days off, rather than have everyone fill in. The turnover rate plummeted. "I learned more from that job than I could have going to any management school. I learned how to manage people. I learned how to get along with them and make them want to be at work." Bois Forte's gamble was paying off.

———

The Fortune Bay Resort Casino sits on a grassy rise amid low forested hills a couple hours' drive north of Duluth, up Route 53 past signs for White Face River, Pale Face River, and turnoffs to Embarrass and Hibbing, famous as Bob Dylan's birthplace. The resort hotel is a handsome log cabin–type building with two wings, one containing the small- to medium-sized casino, one containing guest rooms. The entrance, past plantings of petunias, bore a notice that firearms must be checked at the front desk. A group of boisterous young golfers signed in ahead of me. "Last name, Good, first name L-o-o-k-i-n-g," one told the wanly smiling female clerk. The next day, a guest in the lobby abruptly left his armchair, rushed outside, and shouted into his cell phone that the reason for the bad connection is "We're in the middle of nowhere."

Some tribal members criticize the casino—up a road and around a corner from the Heritage Center—for attracting Ojibwe gamblers. Rose is not among the critics. The casino has enabled Bois Forte to fund numerous projects, including the Heritage Center itself. In fact, the main reason the band built the center was the prospect of repatriating Bois Forte items.

When she first heard of the idea, Rose was all for it. "If you can get some-one else to understand who you are and where you came from and what you're all about, they'll be less likely to be prejudiced against you." As the casino's guest services manager, she had no intention of working at the center herself. Then something happened.

"I'm very spiritual and I'm very traditional. I am a drum keeper for one of the drums in our village. I'm also a pipe carrier. I'm the seventh genera-tion of women to carry this pipe. And I was given the gift of this drum through a dream." Rose spoke at length about the dream, about long-haired men pounding a drum that had lacing below and fur on the sides. She described going to a powwow with her second husband at Mount McKay in Thunder Bay, Ontario, looking up from cooking breakfast on a camp stove to see the dreamed-of drum on a mountain ledge, of others being awestruck as they, too, saw the drum.

The tale continued, of a man who was there later asking her to go to his home in Grand Portage, because he was making the drum for her. Rose obeyed. At the man's home, he showed her the moose hide he had prepared on a drum frame, told her he was going to do a long ceremony and she better go to the bathroom first. When she returned, "he proceeded to start talking in Anishinaabe, our language, for four hours straight. When he was done, he took a little bitty vial and dipped his thumb on it, and he went all the way around the top rim of that drum, the outside edge, and dipped his thumb in that again and he went right like this," she demonstrated, "on my forehead, right at the center, and he said, 'Now you are connected. What she feels you will feel. What you feel she will feel.'"

He told Rose that in the four hours, "'I took you and the drum to the outermost parts of the universe and introduced you to everything and everyone out there. I took you to the very core of the earth and introduced you to everyone and everything there. I took you all over the earth, from one end to the other and introduced you to all the peoples and all the animals and all the trees and everything that grows in the garden. Now when you travel around, everybody will know you.'"

Later, Rose and others drove a van through the snow back to Mount McKay and took the drum out. She placed tobacco, and the men sang a song on the drum. Her job is to keep the drum, not play it. "That's how I came to be a drum keeper."

When not used, the drum rests on a blanket, leaning on an east-facing wall of her home. The staffs that hold the drum are kept separate, or the drum will expect to be pounded, Rose said, just like pipes and stems are kept separate when not in use, or the pipe will expect to be smoked. "We do try to do things properly."

When Rose asked tribal leaders why she was chosen to be a drum keeper, she was told its spirit was in the mountain and needed to come out, that thunderbirds flew around and sent out dreams, including the one she received. All that "coincides with the job that I have now" as the first director of the Bois Forte Heritage Center and Cultural Museum.

As with her other jobs, she was reluctant to apply, and as with them, she was hired immediately.

Apart from her work in repatriation, Rose—leading a four-person staff—oversees the center itself. Its exhibits are so well designed that in 2008 the national "Official Best of . . ." organization named it the best cultural site in Minnesota.[3] It includes a museum about Bois Forte life, from its creation story to the present, a reconstructed traditional dwelling, a gift shop where one can buy local items, including maple syrup, wild rice, and the now ubiquitous pan-Indian dream catchers, believed to have begun in this part of the world. There is also an electrified map showing former and current Ojibwe lands, which have shrunk greatly over the years. Bois Forte is comprised of three separate areas—Nett Lake, Deer Creek, and Vermilion (which includes the casino and the cultural center and museum)—established at different times during the second half of the nineteenth century.

At the museum's entrance, near a montage representing every Bois Forte family, are photographs of the band's military veterans. "Bois Forte is very proud of the fact that we are one of the bands that per capita have had more people enter the armed forces than anywhere else in the United States," Rose said, pausing during a fact-heavy tour she must have given many times. One band member was in Iraq and two have returned, she said, adding that she assiduously avoids taking sides on any issue that could be construed as political, including war. "I'm almost like a ghost, I suppose." She added, "I'm for all the people."

Rose has sometimes been asked to pray for someone or something, as she was by a mother of a young soldier. "She said, 'Nathaniel is going to be shipped out to Iraq.' She offered me some tobacco and said, 'I know that you're a pipe carrier and I'm asking you to pray for him while he's there.' Whenever I would smoke my pipe, I would think good thoughts of him and hope he would be well. He did come home, not necessarily because I prayed for him, but probably because a lot of people prayed for him."

Rose's tour of the center included mention of the horrors many tribes share: land taken, annuities such as food promised in exchange, but that food sometimes being spoiled, or left a great distance away from where the people lived, and, finally, following one deprivation after another, people more or less giving up their past.

"You can't go live like a woodland Indian anymore. It's practically impossible. A lot of the land, even on the reservations, is being developed. Those of us who are traditional, we live in two worlds. It's a very difficult lifestyle, because you have to live in the European world and go to work every day and make money so you can survive. On the other hand, you have to try to use tobacco, you have to try to pray on a daily basis, you have to try to go to powwows and to do things your grandparents taught you. I've been living like this for many, many years, and I've gotten somewhat used to it, but it's still really hard."

While at her office, she might get a call from the tribal council saying they are putting up a new building and need her to go get her drum and bring it to a ceremony for the plants and animals that will be disturbed. "I have to stop everything I'm doing at my job and switch over into the traditional mode."

Rose's embrace of tradition also had a most unexpected consequence. "One summer they had a powwow up at Nett Lake. I took the drum up there, and I put on my jingle dress. Just before the powwow started, my mom came in. I waved to her and she sat down. She was getting pretty old already. I went out and sat in the middle and smoked my pipe and did all the things I had to do, and we had a small ceremony. Then I got up [to] sit with her for a minute. She had the strangest look. She had had a couple of heart attacks, and I thought maybe she was getting sick. I took her hand and said, 'Are you all right?' 'No.' 'What's the matter? Is your heart bothering you?' She said, 'No. You know what? I need to ask you to forgive me. All of these years when I hounded you and hounded you to go to church. I saw you there today and this is where you belong. This is what you were meant to be doing.'"

CHAPTER 7

"How's everybody doing tonight?"

MARCUS FREJO, AKA QUESE IMC
(PAWNEE/SEMINOLE)

Along Route 51 in northern Oklahoma's Pawnee tribal territory, forests rolled by and snow fell lightly as disparate questions wafted. How had the Pawnees, who originally lived hundreds of miles to the north, survived past winters? When would the cell-phone dead zone end? Which of two available radio stations was preferable? Choice A: golden oldie country. Choice B: even older Deuteronomy. Neither seemed likely to play Native son Marcus Frejo, the rapper Quese IMC.

He has performed live for Pawnee audiences near here, as well as for audiences from New York to North Dakota, Florida to Hawaii, and at a November event called a Thankstaking. One December evening, Quese (rhymes with peace) and two of his bros, as he introduced them, drove up from Los Angeles to perform in Oakland, California, at the Intertribal Friendship House's Roots of Resistance holiday market and artist showcase.

The showcase included at least nine performers. Notwithstanding the riveting Sista Hailstorm and lavishly feathered Aztec dancers, Quese was the most compelling. Stylish too. He wore a baseball cap featuring a big M, signifying Milwaukee Brewers once, Marcus now. His forelock was blue, the rest of his hair a thin black braid. From his earlobes swung mother-of-pearl circles. A smooth-faced thirty-two, he was compact and energetic.

"How's everybody doing tonight?" A faint rah-rah from the room of about fifty people. "No, how's everybody *doing* tonight?" Cheers erupted and never died. "All my people from the Bay Area, make a round of applause for yourselves for being here! A night of culture. How many people come from a culture?" Huh?

Having warmed up the crowd, Quese asked them to put down any cameras and recorders while he sang "some old, old Pawnee songs." In his light baritone, he rendered lovely prayer-like melodies. Then, cameras popping, he went full on hip-hop, dancing about the small space, fleet of foot, mike in hand, arm in air, getting the crowd to stand up, move in, shout out. A performer who earlier had recited a doleful poem, hand drum punctuating beats of sorrow, slumped nearby, as if re-defeated.

Quese's energy also came through off stage, whether over spicy lemongrass soup at a Thai restaurant next door to Friendship House or at various sites in Los Angeles. So did his sense of ceremony. At the small cottage in Boyle Heights in East L.A. that he shares with one of his sisters, he said I could photograph everything—recording equipment in the corner, friends' paintings—except for a shelf of sacred items, including a hank of partially burned sage. When he gets in his car, a purple '69 Beetle with a gas leak and stubborn window, he strokes a safety-pinned eagle feather hanging from the rearview mirror before taking off.

Quese had moved to Los Angeles "to try it out and see what happens." And? "It's been good. I've been productive. I've accomplished a lot of goals. I know there's a lot more that I could accomplish, but it's a matter of staying focused, you know?" The challenge was evident. As we cruised Los Angeles, its skyline that day the color of dryer lint, a police helicopter thwacked above and patrol cars blocked off street after street. A standoff, it seemed. A tailored couple, Central Casting perfect, strode toward the action, slim briefcases by slim hips. "Negotiators," Quese guessed, trying to reach his landlord by cell phone to find out if he knew "What's going down?" We never found out.

Quese grew up in the quiet Oklahoma City suburb of Moore, his parents having moved there for nearby jobs, he figured. His father worked for the Indian Health Service, his mother for the Federal Aviation Administration as an inventory management specialist. Quese's first childhood home, on curving South Victoria Drive, which a friend drove me by, has a gently arched roof and groomed lawn. My image of a cheerful childhood was way

off. "I was amongst white people. There was something about them I just
didn't like. I remember that as far back as three years old. They say kids can
sense things. Even back then, I sensed they were different. Almost like they
weren't right. I'm not saying that white people aren't right. There's all kinds
of people, no matter what race they come from, that aren't right, even our
own people." He added, "I had friends that were white, but the ones around
me, they seemed dirty."

We were now sitting outside an L.A. coffee shop. Quese's forelock today
was yellow-green. He wore a hoodie designed by his bro Votan that read
"Warrior" and included a portrait of Crow warrior Plenty Coups. Quese had
put down his hazelnut latte and, rare for him, was not checking his cell
phone. "When I'd be walking to school, maybe like in kindergarten, as the
white ladies from down the street would drive by, they'd put their hand up
by their eyes like this," he held one hand flat against the side of his face. It
happened "all the time. Imagine what that does to a kid at three, four, five
years old." He told nobody. "How do you talk about that? I didn't know
what prejudice was back then. It was just a thing that made me feel a certain
way." Some remembered revenge made him almost smile. "In the morning
before the bus would pick me up, I'd go and I'd start lighting all the white
people's trash cans on fire, and run."

The neighborhood white ladies "made me not like white people even more.
I would say it in school. If the teachers got on to me, I'd yell back at them. 'You
don't like me because I'm Indian.' That's as far as I can remember."

The teachers' behavior may have led to another consequence. "I remember growing up always having white teachers, so I got conditioned to believe
only a white person could teach me. Whenever I finally got an Indian teacher
in college, I thought, I don't think they can teach me correctly. That's the
power of conditioning."

The son of a Seminole mother and a Pawnee and Mexican father, Quese's
roots come from two displaced peoples. The Seminoles of Florida fought
bitterly and long against removal to Oklahoma, until 1842, when President
John Tyler decided the last swamp holdouts would never be vanquished,
and, in a rare victory for Native resistance, finally withdrew American
troops.[1] The majority of Seminoles, however, were forced into "Indian

Territory," present-day Oklahoma, under military escort, with hundreds dying along the way. "My great great grandma *walked* to Oklahoma," said Quese. As a consequence of the unwanted split, today's Seminole Nation of Oklahoma is comprised of descendants of people made to leave, the Seminole tribe of Florida descendants of people who managed to stay.

The Pawnee Nation of Oklahoma had been a Plains tribe, largely in Nebraska. Its people were known as village-dwelling farmers before the arrival of horses encouraged Pawnees to be buffalo hunters too. Part of the Pawnees' fate was location. They were squarely in the path of westward migration, and consequently devastated by smallpox and cholera.

As a child in Moore, one of Marcus/Quese's positive influences was an older brother. "Brian Frejo, also known as Shock B. He's like my DJ like when I perform. He got into music in 1984. I was six years old. He'd go to the east side in Oklahoma City, where the black people live, and he'd go buy records. He got a turntable, and I'd just listen to music. I remember when I was even younger, maybe in '82, hearing a lot of music at one of my aunts' house, which was like Chaka Khan and stuff like that? Music kind of always reminded me of something. It was so new and so fresh to my mind. I would say in '84 is when I actually heard hip-hop music for the first time. From my brother being a DJ. I was just captivated by it, you know?"

He reeled off childhood favorites. "Whodini, Run-DMC, Schoolly D, Black (male)," who seems to have vanished. "It's too bad because he was one of the first hip-hop shows I ever saw, when I was like nine or ten. He gave me a high-five, a hip-hop hand shake, when I was watching him perform." Quese also liked "A Tribe Called Quest, Eric B. & Rakim, Biz Markie, you know, all the old school hip-hop." They were Quese's introduction to "mainstream, modern-day music, non-Native music." Native music, on the other hand, "was always around us. That's what I remember growing up, hearing Indian music, songs, seeing dances, going to powwows, going to ceremonies."

In mid-memories, he remembered tradition. "I'll introduce myself, where I come from. My name is Marcus Frejo. Little Eagle. I'm Pawnee and Seminole. From my Pawnee side I come from the Skidi band, which is the Wolf band, and on my Seminole side I come from the Nokuse clan, which is the Bear clan." He listed ancestors one by one, then added, "My great grandpa was from a place called Silao, Guanajuato. Don't know much about that side."

Quese was the last and "wildest" of his parents' five children, the only one who made his mother sick in pregnancy, a "Tasmanian devil" as a boy. Another older brother, Connie, chose a military career. Quese and he disagree about U.S. policy, "But he's a veteran. You respect your veterans. Especially in Indian country. It's what we're known for. All these Indian people always fought for our land. Regardless if the fight is unjust, which pretty much 99 percent of all U.S. wars are unjust, fought in an unjust way, there we are, right there, fighting with them. What can you do? You know, this is our land."

Quese has two sisters, Happy and Lucky, whom their mother named after friends. Lucky and her family live in Oklahoma. Happy, also a musician, recently moved into Quese's cottage. He gave her his bed; he sleeps on the couch. He was glad to do it, he said without elaboration. It was Happy who gave him his performing name Quese, which, he said, stems from Pawnee words. IMC is "just IMC. Like, I emcee." He was considering changing the last name on his birth certificate to Little Eagle, from a great grandfather on his father's side.

Quese's work, admired by Native and non-Native people of different ages, is message-centered. "These things I have to say, they're for everybody. Before my music caught on, I was just writing music I felt good about talking about. I *love* the music I make. It didn't really matter if anybody else liked it. Back then, in the mid- to late '90s, people didn't understand my music. I didn't really care. The music I talked about was about cultural awareness, which means being aware of your culture, being aware of where you come from. Empowerment. Meaning be proud of who you are as Indian people. I have a message I've always had."

"People get it now. Now you have people talking about these things all over, which I think is awesome. It's not just *my* message. There's many out there who have a way, and our ways are all similar." In 2009, contenders in the Native American Music Awards' category Rap Hip-Hop included Quese's *Bluelight* CD. The winner was a Yakama group, Rezhogs. "We're not the only ones, you know? But I'm glad we're the only ones doing it how *we* do it."

From Quese's song "Hero," on his *Bluelight* CD: "Ever wondered how time flies / young with bright eyes / care-free to the world's life and lies / that gave me my lows and my highs / my prize / was to survive in times / when hope dies."

Later comes the melodious hook. "One day you're a hero / everybody wants to know your name / the next day you're a clown / the next day they want to tear you down."

"Hero," said Quese, is "a story about the life of any young person going to school and being an outcast or being talked about or being made fun of, pushed around." He said only "little parts" were based on his experiences. "Most of it was stories I know about." He had allies in school, "random friends here and there, some black, some Mexican." As the song story continues, the narrator is about to shoot his tormentors, when a girl bumps him, drops her books, and apologizes. As he picks up her books, "just then the bullies pass / they kick you in your ass / you fall down and they start to laugh / she's shocked / you fallen / demons calling / guns cocked / she stands in your defense and says 'fuck you jock' / she picks you up, the most beautiful thing you ever saw / when she walked over to that jock and socked him in the jaw." (His mom, he said, wishes there were less cursing in his work.)

The song ends "that day his life could begin / and nobody's life would end," thanks to the smile of a "down ass cihuatl." Cihuatl? Quese said it means "girl" in the Aztec language, Nahuatl.

He often introduces Native language into his work. "Turahe!" he shouted to the Oakland audience. "Turahe!" they cried back. The Pawnee expression means "It's good," he later explained, "but English can't really translate our words."

One song, beautifully eerie, begins with an old recording of an elder speaking Pawnee. From the background comes a drum, which segues into a hip-hop beat and Quese's verses.

Fluent neither in Seminole or Pawnee, which has only a few fluent speakers remaining, Quese said he is learning both. Like many children whose families come from different tribes, he grew up speaking English.

When Quese was six, his parents divorced. "My mom left him. After that, he quit drinking. I would say it was a good thing. They never got back together or anything like that, but—you know." He semi-shrugged. "Sometimes that's what alcohol does. Breaks up families, especially in Indian country. But it's what you make out of it."

And there was big brother Brian. "He was one of the first Native DJs to DJ on an FM radio station, played hip-hop music. He was like really famous in Oklahoma City. All the non-Natives—white, black, Asian, Mexican—all knew him. He was a really high regarded DJ. I saw that growing up, then I saw that he was cool. He also didn't drink, he didn't smoke, he didn't do drugs. That was one of the big reasons why I never drank, smoke or did drugs."

Cool trumped temptation, but temptation was there. "Oh yeah! All the time. Back in the day, a lot of my friends would ask me if I wanted to drink or smoke weed or do drugs and stuff. But, honestly, I always felt there was these things with me, these ancestor spirits, telling me, 'Don't do it.' It helped me. It guided me. I remember that as a young kid. I always just said no."

It helped too, Quese was athletic. "I played basketball ever since I was like six. Now I don't play that much, but I like to get out there and play every chance I get. Shoot around, play pickup games." He likes college basketball, especially the "Oklahoma Sooners, when they're worth watching."

"Basketball's a part of Indian culture, you know. It's really huge." No question there. "The Indians invented it." Question there.

What about the man credited with putting the game together in the late nineteenth century for pent-up Massachusetts students during long winters? "James Naismith got the idea of basketball from Native American games that we played. It comes from our people. They say he invented it, but he didn't." Basketball is "an old ceremonial Indian game."

My search for any corroboration included contacting a Native longtime basketball coach and a scholar of Native history. Neither heard of anyone but Naismith inventing the game. In a tense exchange of e-mails, Quese wrote, "It's right there along with the blues coming from native american ceremonial songs, and lacrosse being invented by natives. It was never documented or written by white folks so its not fact according to them." See my Iroquois chapter about lacrosse, I wrote him. A later e-mail from him was more tempered and ended, in regard to basketball, "That's just what

I was told a long time ago by some elders. If I'm wrong then my elders are wrong." He concluded with :)

Quese also disputed other matters, such as data that Los Angeles has one of the country's largest populations of "urban Indians." The 2000 Census put the number at 53,092.[2] "I don't see 'em. Where? Where are they exactly? There's a small community though, of Natives."

He preferred talking about Native participation, or lack of it, in sports. He said he left Oklahoma because of hardships he experienced in high school athletics for being Native American.

"You rarely ever see Native Americans in NCAA sports. Why? Because colleges don't invest their time or don't give the chance to Native American athletes. Why? Because they follow the stereotype that 'Oh, they're going to drop out. Oh, they're going to come off the rez and they're going to feel homesick and they're gonna just ditch the school and leave.' They're 'high-risk,' you know? 'They have a lack of people skills or social skills or they can't exist off the reservation.' I've had friends, great athletes, who got overlooked by NCAA schools. Their school records in athletics were far more better than kids getting scholarships. That's why, because they have that mentality. That mentality goes back to 'Oh, dumb Indian.' 'They're just dumb Indians.' That's what they called us. We're like dogs. We're still fighting that today.

"If people looked at us as educated people, as great athletes that could actually be an asset to these NCAA teams, things would change and a sense of empowerment and pride would continue to build our self-esteem as Indian people. We want to see our Natives in schools. We want to see them in collegiate areas in athletics and the NBA and WNBA. NHL, NFL. Major league baseball. *Slowly*, it's happening."

Another stereotype upset him during visits to Florida. As is widely known among Native people, the Seminole Tribe of Florida owns the Hard Rock Café chain, among other enterprises. "I think it's cool that the Seminoles down there have become so successful. I think any type of success is good, as long as it's good for the people, it encourages the people to continue the culture and their way of life. But at the same time, with that power and that money comes a lot of illusions and a lot of opportunists." In Florida, he saw "a lot of non-Natives wanting to get with Natives. . . . They'd never want to talk or date or be with an Indian [otherwise]. That's really upsetting to me, to see my people believe that lie. Those non-Natives, they see money."

Years earlier, in 1997, the motivation of a military recruiter made him suspicious too. The experience still tightens his face. "I was going to join the marines, out of high school. They really wanted to be my *friend*," he said with an edge. "But they never really knew me. They wanted to 'relate' to me. The thing about it was, in high school I acted like I was from New York [because a "cool" friend was from there]. It's kind of a funny story. The recruiter they sent was from New York, because they thought I would relate to a New Yorker. He talked about New York all the time. Hip-hop, New York this, New York that. In my mind I was like, fuck, I'm not even from New York. This guy knows nothing about me."

Finally, he told the recruiter no. "Good thing, though, 'cause if they would've sent a [recruiter] from the Midwest or Native American my way, I might be a veteran."

During Quese's years after high school, he went to "a little college" in Arizona, which he did not name, and took various jobs to support himself. "I had to get up at like freakin' six A.M. every morning and go to Pizza Hut and freakin' make the dough and spread the dough in freakin' pizza pans and get it all ready for the day. I got so tired of the smell of freakin' dough. It was gross. Where else the hell did I work? I worked at a Sunglass Hut. That was pretty cool. I worked at RPS, shipping boxes and stuff. Loading boxes in the trucks."

He also attended Haskell University, in Kansas. A century ago, it was infamous as one of the first boarding schools where Native children were sent to be "civilized." Now, as a tribal college, it is a different place. "It was awesome. I met some of my bros there. They're still my brothers today. They didn't drink, so we all connected on that level." He knew its old reputation. "The spirits are still there. It's a really haunted school, traumatized school. But you can find your success there, you can find beauty there." He went on: "A lot of little kids, a lot of traumatic things happened, a lot of abuse. Sexual abuse, physical, mental. But I think it becoming a tribal university where Native youth can get their education and empower themselves is probably the greatest thing that could happen there. . . . It was all out of whack. Whenever the white folks were up in there doing all those dirty things."

"That's one of the main things that destroyed our people. Like in boarding schools, residential schools, all the rapes that were committed by these priests and nuns. You got priests raping little boys, you know? A whole freakin' line of them doing that. Nuns doing the same thing. Priests raping little girls. Evil. Darkness." (He did not mean Haskell specifically, which was not under the Roman Catholic Church and thus had no priests and nuns.)

"It's one thing that never belonged to us, that way of life. Physical, sexual, mental abuse never was a part of our culture. It infected our culture. It embedded itself within our people's minds. There was a lot of healing that needed to be done and is still being done."

Quese sees himself "as part of a spiritual movement of empowerment for our people." After all, he is a young man who does not drink or do drugs, who wants to change the world for the better, and is ambitious on all counts. Driving his purple VW past a sidewalk movie set after a sushi lunch, he exclaimed "Cool!" and revealed he had a small part in Sterlin Harjo's *Barking Water*. He would like to be in more movies, in addition to producing more CDs, doing more gigs.

He has done all kinds, including a Def Jam MTV MC battle in New York. There is a YouTube video of him in another. He explained the back-and-forth word rivalry this way. "You battle off the top of your head against somebody. Kind of like take what they say and turn it around, or just try to diss somebody in a funny way. Get people to laugh." On the YouTube battle, the audience shouts Quese the victor.

"We want to perform everywhere, you know? For white people, black people, Asians, Mexicans. Filipinos. Everyone. We want our music to go across boundaries. But it comes from where we come from, where our ancestors come from, so we don't want to put ourselves in a box, you know what I mean? This music is universal. I think the spirit within the music can speak to anybody." He had no hesitation naming people with whom he would like to share billing. "I'd like to open for Lauren Hill, Damien Marley." He paused. "Mos Def, Tribe Called Quest, people like that."

To earn a living, Quese makes money from CD sales, especially *Bluelight*. He also earns money from producing CDs and videos for others, and from working in an indigenous, mostly Mayan-themed, Echo Park gift store,

Nahui Ohlín, run in part by Votan. It features handmade earrings, including renditions of the eternal Frida Kahlo, soaps, clothes, mittens with appliquéd skeleton heads, books and magazines about indigenous peoples. Quese also works for a number of tribal youth programs, especially in Oklahoma. "Usually prevention programs such as suicide prevention and alcohol and drug prevention, as well as cultural programs," he e-mailed.

He works for free too. The gig in Oakland paid only gas money. "I like going up there. I believe in it and I support it. And I enjoy the visitation and the people putting it on. Otherwise I gotta get paid, because I gotta pay bills. But I still love it. I still operate out of that gift."

At some point, I decided to ask him about a phrase that nettled me, and I imagined must nettle him: Cherokee, Chickasaw, Choctaw, Creek, and Seminole people being grouped as the "Five Civilized Tribes," or as historian Peter Nabokov among others put it, the "so-called Five Civilized Tribes." From what I read, civilized meant taking on European habits. Yeah, including slavery, a Choctaw woman once told me, scoffing.

"I don't think any of us were ever civilized," responded Quese, evenly at first. "We're civilized because we learned how to speak the white man's language a little bit earlier than anybody else. That doesn't make us civilized. That just makes us the ones [who] maybe signed a couple of treaties that were later broken. What's the word 'civilized'? I've heard people say, 'I'm part of the five civilized tribes.' That means all the other Indians are uncivilized? We're *primitive*? I think Indians need to lose that word, civilized. A long time ago, that was the white man saying, 'You're okay now, I can talk to you, yet I don't like you because you're Indian.'" His voice sped up. "We shouldn't care about how the white man views us. We shouldn't care about how the black man views us, how the Mexican man views us, the Asian man, the Jewish man. We shouldn't care about that. Why? Because that says we're living to the expectations of somebody else's opinion or somebody else's upbringing.

"We're a people that live with *all* things, all creations. We have that understanding about the earth, the animals, Mother Earth, the moon, the sun, the stars, the Creator. That's what makes us different. If that's what makes us uncivilized, I'm uncivilized.

"They called us uncivilized, because they didn't understand us, because our beliefs were far beyond what they could ever imagine. Our beliefs surpassed their science and their creation. That's what a lot of Natives have forgotten. When people say, 'I'm from the five civilized tribes,' I think they need to understand that they're saying, 'I want to make sure that I'm validated by the white man.' Why would you want to be like that? That's what I think of 'the five civilized tribes.'"

———

The idea to affect the world with music, he said, came from a feeling. "When I first started doing it, it moved me. I could feel something, so in my mind I could see other people feeling it. That really encouraged me a lot. Somebody had to feel something, because I can't just be doing this just for no reason. When I do my music, I know there's a reason behind it. Something will happen, in a good way, in a spiritual way."

Music is part of his home routine. "Typical day is wake up in the morning [anytime from 7:30 to 11:30], "brush my teeth . . . get up, check my e-mails and get on line. Then start working on beats or start working on a song. Writing. Recording. Go eat, come back, work on music. Then usually take a break and go to the store, kick it and work for a little bit and come back, work on music. Then call some friends, maybe go out. Come home, work on some music a little more, watch a movie, and go to sleep."

The friends he goes out with are "probably some of my bros. Go hit a club or something. Go dance, hip-hop or a house club, soul, reggae. I love to dance." The subject of dancing turned to relationships. "I have a son, straight Indian. I think that's beautiful." The boy lives with his mother. What about mixed Native and non-Native marriages? "If it works, it works. But if somebody in a marriage that's not Native doesn't understand Native culture and doesn't make any effort to learn about it, that's sad. If I were to marry a Chinese person or a Palestinian or a Tibetan monk or an African female, why wouldn't I want to know about her culture? I would want to know."

It was the end of a long day, and Quese was on a roll. "People have a lack of knowledge of who we are as a people. They know more about African

Americans, or Asians or Mexicans than they do Native Americans. What part of education did they miss? Obviously they missed it at the root of education, because the people who write these books are not Native and they're speaking from a non-Native standpoint. It still puts us in a stereotype. 'This is how I think Natives are.' Yet those same people don't go to Indian country and see who we are as a people. We're just commodities."

"That's why things haven't changed, because people don't make those journeys. There are people who do, because somewhere in their mind or their spirit they have some sort of sympathy." He changed that direction fast. "I don't need anybody to sympathize for me. Help is action, and action is far more better than somebody saying, 'I really feel for you.' We don't really care what people think of us. That's just their ignorance.

"We don't really ponder on their ignorance, unless it directly affects us, like people trying to build on sacred sites. They don't understand what a holy ground is. *Then* they cross the line because they're ignorant, because they follow stereotypes. It's then we'll speak up and we'll take action." When people make supposed war whoops, though, "We don't waste our time.

"Changing mascots is a different thing, because that's where it starts. That's why a lot of mascots got changed in Oklahoma, because the Natives stood up against that." As for the University of North Dakota's Fighting Sioux, since retired, he mocked excuses to keep it. "'Now we're doing it in a sensitive way toward Indian people. We're using an actual Native on a horse.' It's like saying, 'These aren't real slaves.' But we know the root of it. We know the root of where slavery started. Why would you honor that?"

Marcus Frejo/Quese IMC wondered if America's current problems stemmed partly from "a lack of knowledge" about Native people. "We're standing over here knowing who we are, knowing where we come from, knowing our ceremonial ways and songs, understanding the earth, all creation and how it's affecting what's going on right now in the world. If people were to listen, and there are people out there who listen, they would understand. But a lot of people that listen, they want to control. They want to control land, they want to control borders, they want to control thoughts and ideas. Control words, control the media. Now they want to control the weather. They want to shoot lasers into the atmosphere that can affect the weather. As a people, we know that you can never have control, and if you try to have control, you'll be humbled in a devastating way."

His thoughts seemed to collide. "That's why we haven't as Natives been given the opportunity to speak, to be seen, to be heard, because us as indigenous people are a chosen people. Caretakers of this land, with the gift of spirituality. What we have, because we were prophesized from our ancestors, from the Star People, is the ability to bring healing to this earth. The powers that be don't want that to happen. They've put a blanket over us. But unfortunately [for them], the blanket they put over us is deteriorating. We're growing through that and we're coming through strong."

"That's how I speak, from a Native standpoint. We're not overseas in Africa. We're not in China. Tibet. We're not in Palestine. We're not in Russia. We're here on *this* land, our land where we were put, so we have every right to speak about these things. I could never say these things over in another continent where my ancestors weren't put. I would have to listen and I would have to embrace and accept and humble myself, to know that I must be a good follower.

"Here, in this country, people don't understand that. People want to take the lead that were never given the right to be [leaders]. Yet they might be the greatest followers. If they were the greatest followers in a humble way, they might be blessed to become great leaders." He wound up. "That's what my music is. That's why indigenous athletes are, that's what doctors and lawyers are, that come from indigenous blood. We are that opportunity. We are that change. Maybe that opportunity wasn't given to us, but now we're coming though so strong that we're just taking it and we're going for it. And eventually it will happen. It will happen for our people."

———

From "Greencorn," on the *Bluelight* CD: "my culture my pride / I'm taking it back to my tribe / from singing greencorn to singing hymns / I'm singing the side of why my people died / to bring it back and kill the division / between the spiritual hymns and tradition / the crusades and missions / fulfilled the visions / of dividing our people on their expeditions."

CHAPTER 8

Tales from Pine Ridge

KAREN ARTICHOKER, WITH HEATH DUCHENEAUX AND DWANNA OLDSON (LAKOTA)

KAREN ARTICHOKER

"We got along well enough," Karen Artichoker said of her white dorm-mates decades ago at St. Olaf College in Northfield, Minnesota. "I even went home with one girl. She was really young. She was sixteen, really smart." The girl's parents invited Karen and another friend to their home in La Crosse, Wisconsin, for a holiday weekend, and picked them up at the college. "All the way her mother told me about the big Indian [statue] in the Wisconsin harbor. The whole trip. These girls actually were a little bit better than their parents. 'I told my mother not to be talking stupid to you, and she's doing it anyway, I'm sorry.'" The group arrived at a home whose grandeur still gives Karen pause. "We sit down in this formal dining room. I kid you not. This mother . . . These are the nicest people in the world. I mean, there are *way* worse people in the world than this family. This mother says, 'So. You're Indian! Tell us all about it.'

"I looked at her and I didn't say anything, 'cause I didn't really know what to say. She says, 'See dear, you tell us all about it now, then we don't have to bring it up again all weekend.'"

"My friend was mortified. '*Mom*. Come on, Karen, let's go watch TV.'"

"Those girls," Karen mused, "did not live the same life I did."

———

Nor do they probably lead it now. Who else, in her early fifties, was raising the sixth such child to come into her life—a four-year-old whirlwind named

Devina—while running an organization acclaimed as the most innovative program in Native America to stop the abuse of Native women? It is Cangleska, on South Dakota's Pine Ridge Indian Reservation. Pine Ridge, known for Wounded Knee, both the bloody massacre in 1890 and the confrontation in 1973, stands out nowadays for dispiriting statistics. The unemployment rate is over 75 percent, the alcoholism rate 85 percent, Karen said. Among the population of 5,000 are some forty gangs. (A small indication of the poverty: at a gas station in the town of Pine Ridge, as I was about to fill my car, I noticed the pump displayed the previous purchase of $2.00.)

Within this scenario stands Cangleska, the sole shelter for women on a reservation the size of Connecticut. Its rooms are so often full that Cangleska is building a larger shelter. It will include a "visitation room" for women and children to have supervised encounters with the men who hurt them.

In parts of the country, locations of women's shelters are closely guarded secrets. Secrets this large do not work here. The first stranger I stopped, in the small town of Kyle, pointed to the wooden one-story shelter, right next to the seniors' home.

No sign announced its purpose, but clues revealed themselves: metal doors with intercoms and coded entrance systems, curtains over every window except those of the staff.

Inside, a hodge-podge living room (couches, bureaus, TV, piles of donated clothing, a star quilt on one wall, an old-fashioned china cupboard at another) and adjoining kitchen comprised the building's center. Off on one side were offices for advocates (women who help the abused women), a bathroom, and bedrooms for the women and children. The other side contained offices for administrators, including Karen. Out a side door was a scruffy side yard—surrounded by a tall fence—with play area, clotheslines, and a patch of cement under an eave. The more obedient smokers light up there.

Everywhere inside was the image of *cangleska*, Lakota for "medicine wheel," a circle divided into quadrants, four feathers hanging from it. Never far away was the printed exhortation, "Violence Against Native Women Is Not Tradition."

Because of Karen's strong telephone manner and her reputation as a leader in a tough arena, I expected to meet a mighty figure. Oh, that always happens, she said. She is shortish, with long brown hair, dark skin, a perky nose, glasses, and, to correct a longtime tooth alignment problem, was wearing braces. She goes all out with makeup or forgoes it entirely, seems most at home in comfortable clothes, is a fan of hamburgers and curly fries, and occasionally moans about the pounds she would like to drop.

She spends a lot of time in her office. "It can be interesting, during the day, where you're talking with someone from a shelter or an advocacy program and a tribe that's a thousand miles away about their code and their law enforcement response. You're trying to help develop a technical assistance plan for them, and the next minute you're revising a budget so you can get it off to a federal agency. The next minute you're catching up on signing paperwork, and the next minute you're trying to help some local woman get into a home. And the next minute you're plunging the toilet, or cleaning the bathroom, because we don't have those little niceties in our budgets for cleaning people. So you're doing the dishes or shoveling the sidewalk. I mean, all work is women's work."

Her work also includes meeting with tribal and federal government representatives, but she travels reluctantly. She has Devina to think about. Also, Pine Ridge is no transportation hub. It is hours by car to the Rapid City airport, no hub either. For a Minneapolis-area meeting with federal officials about the 1994 Violence Against Women Act, Karen decided it was easier to drive the eleven hours each way. An amendment of the act, Title IX, called Safety for Indian Women, mandates meetings between representatives of the federal and tribal governments. "To see tribes assert that position [as sovereign nations] and, for the record, state how they would like to see Title IX in the Violence Against Women Act work, was very gratifying."

Gratification has been hard won. Karen described, often with theatrical flair, a road that only in retrospect seemed made for her.

"I was born in Igloo, South Dakota. I-G-L-O-O," she shouted in her car over Devina's chants and nursery rhyme CD on the twenty-mile drive to Kyle one morning. "Igloo was a federal army depot. They stored mustard gas. It's a lovely little town, 100 percent employment." She always wondered about domestic violence there, she added. Karen and her two brothers lived in Igloo with their parents (married sixty years! she exclaimed) until their father, a welder, was transferred to Pueblo, Colorado. "The big city," Karen joked. "Everyone thought we were Chicano."

Her father, Benjamin David Artichoker, is Hochunk. The unusual name Artichoker is an Anglicized version of Ah Who Choe Ga. "It translates to Blue Wing. The name was my great great grandfather's. My grandmother is Lakota. My grandfather came to live in 'her country,' so we are enrolled as Oglala Lakota citizens."

Karen's father "was not very cultural in terms of participating in Lakota spiritual rituals, et cetera. He was very cultural in that he hunted, was into 'Indian food,' and lived Lakota values." He used to claim his family was well off even in the Depression, that with a team of horses and a buggy, they "lived like white people." His mother expressed the same sentiments. "I'd say, 'Grandma, what does that mean?' 'Oh, it was this, this and . . .' 'But Grandma, those are good human values. Those are Lakota values.' Of course, the church taught her that anything Lakota was bad. These human values were good and were white. So we're all confused and we're all finding our way back to who we are." Karen's esteemed grandmother Artichoker was an Episcopalian with a sweat lodge.

Karen's mother, the former Hortense Louise Horst, is of German ancestry. "My mom's one of those good traditional woman" and "very much her own person." German heritage, however, leaves Karen unimpressed. "There's no culture there, so we never had any to relate to. What's the culture? Sauerkraut?"

Later, she wrote me that perhaps her mother initially resented the children's growing involvement in Lakota culture, but whether from "maturity, wisdom, and security that comes with age, or what," became more supportive. Her father, she said, "was always able to respect my mother's discomfort" about Native life. He often politely declined invitations to Native events to spare his wife. His qualities did not impress the Horsts. His own father-in-law, said Karen, spoke of "damn Indians, lazy drunkards."

Benjamin David Artichoker was neither. He did go on one binge, which his mother told Karen about. While stationed in Japan shortly after the first atomic bomb was dropped, his grandmother died. "My dad loved his grandma. They wouldn't let him come home, wasn't an immediate relative.

My grandma said, 'Garfield Eagle Feather told me your dad AWOLed and went on a four-day drunk and got thrown in jail. He was so upset they wouldn't let him come home.'" As soon as he returned to the United States, he went to his grandmother's grave and slept on it two nights.

————

With her parents' encouragement, a scholarship, and ambition, Karen went off to college. She knew she wanted to get an education but not why. "I was seventeen years old, what did I know? I just know, we pulled up in our little Ford pickup with the camper on it. I never had a radio in my life. They'd bought me this little AM/FM transistor radio. I really thought I was uptown. Walked in, my roommate had this huge stereo. She had a car and a checking account. My clothes took up this much of the closet," she indicated the dimension of the steering wheel. "Her clothes took up two closets. But she was really pitiful. Her father was alcoholic, even though they had money. Her mother was a bitch. Her parents were going to kick her out because she was dating this Mexican or whatever. Kick her out! I was telling my dad. He said 'Let me talk to her.'" Karen listened in. "He said, 'You're Karen's friend and you're going to come home with her this summer. Maybe it will give your folks time to cool out. You can get a job around here, and you have a place to stay.' She was crying," Karen did a mock sob, "'You don't even know me.'"

"My dad would never let me go stay with them. She wanted me to spend the summer with them and work at this resort where their summer cabin was. Their cabin was nicer than our house. I was like, 'Why not, Dad?' Finally he said, 'I am not going to have you go stay with white people. That's how they'd see it, that I can't take care of my own daughter. If she wants to come here, she's your friend, that's fine.'"

At St. Olaf, Karen adjusted, sort of. "There were all these Norwegians, we ate lutefisk [dried cod steeped in lye], oh, pewww. I went there for two years. It was okay, but it was a hardship on my parents. Even though I had a scholarship, the transportation they had to pay for."

During her freshman year, the confrontation at Wounded Knee began. St. Olaf's Indian students immediately had a meeting. "That's the first time

I smoked a cigarette. It was nerve-wracking. We were making phone calls, trying to find out what was going on. Several students, including my cousin, made a decision to head for Wounded Knee. I thought about heading that way but, quite honestly, I was a goody two shoes and thought about what my parents would say. I knew they would tell me to stay in school."

"I do think the American Indian Movement and Wounded Knee made all of us more aware of who we are as Indians and what that means. We saw and heard some really good, even great, things. We also saw and heard some not so great things, like male attitudes toward women involved." Some accounts came from women who were there. "They'll say they wrote the speeches, braided the guys' hair, and cooked supper, all at the same time, of course." Karen also heard, she later wrote me, "about behavior that was confusing. Drinking, woman beating."

One effect of the activism was that "we were trying to out-*Indian* each other. Very confusing. Very confusing."

After her fill of lutefisk, Karen transferred to the University of Colorado in Boulder. "They had the EOP back then, the Educational Opportunities Program, so I went in the summer. There were Indian students. We had a blast. Then the fall came and here's 20,000 white kids. We were looking for each other desperately. By then I was twenty years old and I get this little seventeen-year-old white girl roommate. I think, oh no, I can't do this again. I went and asked if there were any Indians I could room with. They gave me the room number for this girl, an Osage. I'll never forget it. I knocked. She opened the door and her eyes got big and she grabbed me and pulled me into her room. 'You're an Indian!'" Karen started laughing. "'I'm so happy to see . . . ' Blah blah blah, 'I want to be roommates.' 'Yes! Yes! Oh God,' she said. 'Let's go eat. I'm scared to go to the cafeteria, there's too many white people. I've been eating out of the machines, I'm starving to death.'"

What could be scary about white college kids?

"They didn't live in the world. I don't know what world they lived in, but it sure as heck wasn't ours. They were self-centered, very narcissistic." Karen said "the Indian kids" shared whatever money any received, whether thirty dollars from Karen's brother Benjamin after he got paid for a roofing job, or ten dollars from her grandmother. "We had our little group and surveyed each other's needs. The white kids could never understand anyone but their parents sending money. 'Why would your brother send you money?'"

Karen was not comfortable as an "Indian kid" herself. "Being the product of a white mother and an Indian father, there was that time I didn't feel worthy or able to practice our customs, our traditions, our spiritual practices. I felt people were going to be saying, 'She didn't grow up like that, so who does she think she is, trying to be an Indian?' I feel really fortunate I found a group of friends who were able to inspire me and encourage me. Oh heck, there's none of us that know everything. Lots of us have found this way, or some of us grew up with it, but went away from it and we're coming back. We come in all shapes, sizes, and experiences."

With her revitalized sense of herself, and a sociology degree, Karen got work as a "mental health technician" at a group home for emotionally disturbed girls on the Rosebud Reservation. (Rosebud adjoins Pine Ridge and shares many of its social horrors; in 2007, a Rosebud leader declared a state of emergency over youth suicide.[1])

"That's really where I got started with domestic violence. I didn't think much about it until then. We received referrals from Indian Health Service units in the Aberdeen [South Dakota] area, so it was a lot of tribes. The women were coming to the unit for depression. They were invariably battered women and had experienced incest and rape. I started to see the impact of men's violence on women." She mocked the term "domestic" violence as "such a nice word. Even nicer is 'relationship' violence. What does that mean? This relationship isn't violent, *he* is violent."

While working at Rosebud, Karen met Tillie Black Bear, a founder of the National Coalition Against Domestic Violence and "one of the icons of the battered women's movement." She became Karen's mentor. In time, Karen became director of White Buffalo Calf Woman Society, the oldest shelter for Native women, and was elected to represent South Dakota in the National Coalition Against Domestic Violence. "People sort of didn't know what to do with me. To start talking about Native women and tribal issues, it made people very uncomfortable. I don't know if that's guilt or what. Everyone would get very quiet," she said, grinning. "I didn't have a lot of experiences with other races. My experience was pretty much Indian and white, so on a national scene to interact with African American women, Asian American women, I felt very isolated. I was happy when Tillie and I could do things together. In spite of whatever cultures the other women might be part of, they all seemed the same to us, because none of them knew anything about Indians."

A turning point for Karen occurred when a hospital psychologist recommended she take a "very, very, very battered" Native woman to a support group in Rapid City. "The first time I went, she and I were the only Indian women around the table. This was probably about 1980. I'm sitting there thinking, this is bunk. These women are a bunch of whiners. They're taking zero responsibility for their behavior or their choices. The facilitator, to her credit, gave the Indian woman ample opportunity" to speak, but she "sat with her head down and didn't say anything." On the drive back to the hospital, though, she "was chattering away," said Karen. "'When she said *that*, that sounded just like him,' and '*He's* done that before.'"

We were now, according to my notes, talking in Karen's office, where she lit up a Doral. (She is not among the obedient smokers, but she did open a window.) At the hospital, she recalled, she reported that the encounter went "okay," but thought the women all needed assertiveness training. "I didn't hear too many 'I' statements in there." Still, plans were made to return the following week. By then, "the Indian woman" had talked up the session to other Indian women in the unit. They all wanted to go. Karen complied. The same dynamic took place. Instead of one Native woman not saying a word, a group of Native women did not say a word—until they got back in the car. Karen went into chatter mode: "'He said that to me.' 'When she said that, that's *exactly* what he does.'"

"I thought, maybe there's something here I don't understand, 'cause these women are very excited about the information they're getting." Puzzled, Karen went to see the group's facilitator, who gave her a number of books that opened Karen's eyes. "I'd never thought about sexism. I always thought about oppression in terms of racism. Even when I graduated from high school eleventh in my class [among about 275] and the school counselor was encouraging me to go to cosmetology school because the home ec teacher liked how I did somebody's hair." The home ec teacher "even said something about Indians, we were really good with our hands." Karen groaned. "It never occurred to me this whole thing about cosmetology school had to do with being female. At that point in my life, to start thinking about being an Indian and being a woman, and that they were both who I am, was an awakening." She paused. "I started hearing sexism everywhere. I remember being really angry. Of course, I was always angry as an Indian, but now I was angry as a woman."

She visited the facilitator twice a week to talk about the books and the issues they raised. During one visit, Karen burst. "I'm like, 'How do you do this? I'm mad all the time.' I always remember her telling me, one day a week I could be angry. The other days I had to work. Use talking about anger as an inspiration to doing something, as opposed to paralyzing you."

Karen got on the board for the shelter in Rapid City where the support group met. "Pretty soon there's lots of Indian women sitting around that table." She was "amazed" that despite the noise in the shelter, the women paid close attention to one another. "Kids could be fighting and screaming and whatever, [women] were focused. I saw a process there that was *so* wonderful. Women who had the same batterer. One woman, her nephew had raped [the daughter of] another woman at the group. These two women having this conflict and yet they were connected by the abuse they had both experienced at the hands of men."

"If women could come together and be real with each other, maybe we could change the world," she said softly. "We could get beyond race, we could get beyond class. Because there were women with money there, they were at the shelter, but he'd frozen all the bank accounts or whatever. They were just as pitiful. It was a great equalizer. Violence was a great equalizer."

The work, Karen said, "became my passion."

At the same time, she had become a foster mother. She was twenty-one. "This [Rosebud] social worker—she was an Indian woman—and I got to be really good friends. She was telling me they didn't have foster homes. I was actually quite naïve. I thought, well, I can take care of a kid," she said. "I thought it was my responsibility as a tribal citizen. There were so many children in need and so many children that were being taken off the reservation and away from tribal families and communities, because they didn't have Native foster parents."

Karen was told the child's parents were going through treatment and would get themselves together. "I didn't think it would be a lifetime. When they brought her to me, she had pneumonia and was ready to be discharged from the hospital. Come to find out she'd been in foster care five times previously"—with the same foster parents. "They'd get her healthy and then she'd be back with them again. They weren't going to do it again."

The little girl's name was Coya, she was eighteen months old, and appeared to have been neglected and starved. "My folks had a fit. My dad was like, 'You do not understand the responsibility of having a child, you just got out of college,'" and so on. "She was like a zombie. I mean, move her around like a pawn on a chess board. She would eat and eat and eat and eat." She even grabbed at photographs of food in magazines. When the Artichoker family relaxed after supper, "she would walk around and eat everything that was on anybody's plate and anything that was in the middle."

As much as she craved food, so did she fear other things. Sirens made her "hysterical." The drinking of alcohol put her in a panic. Karen recalled an evening her parents had friends over. "Usually the men would have a beer, maybe a mixed drink," the women a tiny glass of wine. Karen's mother liked using Avon candlesticks as glasses. "The cup's about that big on them"— about an inch. While the men played cards, Edith, the wife of one of the men, visited with Karen's mother, who offered her a glass of wine, then poured the droplets into the diminutive glasses. Coya "went over to my mom and she was tugging on her and tugging on her. 'Grandma, please don't drink that. Because you're going to get drunk and then the cops are going to come and take you to jail.' My mom put her on her lap, and said, 'Edith and I are going to sit here and drink this. You're going to see that no cops are going to come and nobody's going to go to jail.' Coya's this little nervous wreck. They finished their little glass of wine. My mom said, 'See? No cops came, nobody's going to go to jail.' You see all these trauma issues that people have." For trauma, of course, read "historical trauma," a term attributed to the educator Dr. Maria Yellow Horse Brave Heart (Lakota). Karen adopted Coya at the age of five.

Now thirty-two and "a lovely young woman," as Karen described her, she writes poetry, including a moving poem for Father's Day. (Coya's birth mother died of alcoholism.) "[Her] father, who was a chronic alcoholic, sobered up and got a PhD in education and teaches at Iowa State University. She has made a relationship with him over the years. Her biological family [is] quite known for their knowledge of culture, of language." Lakota culture itself, Karen said, helped Coya in various ways, from herbal medicine for a skin ailment, to a sweat lodge (Karen has one in her back yard) during emotional distress. Karen also unofficially adopted a young woman, Lisa, who worked at a shelter where Karen met her, and who is now a nurse with three children Karen also helped raise.

Karen's household is a census taker's challenge. One October, she and Devina were the only residents, apart from Karen's brother Benjamin, who stayed there during the week while overseeing construction of the new Cangleska shelter. He spent weekends with his family in Colorado. The following February, after several dramas, her household numbered eight females, plus Benjamin. "As you can see," Karen e-mailed, "Indian households are quite fluid."

Hers never included a husband. "Never met anyone that I could imagine spending the rest of my life with." She even dated men she later realized were abusers. "One of those 'There but for the grace of God go I' deals. Plus, I wanted an Indian man, and I don't think they're by and large healthy." Or self-sufficient? One boyfriend lost favor when she learned he did not rotate his own tires.

Karen herself is the vision of a domestic multitasker. One weekend morning at her farmhouse in Allen, which is technically within the Pine Ridge Reservation, she was cooking an elaborate breakfast, playing with Devina, and shaking out throw rugs—all while counseling someone on the phone. She works fewer hours than she used to, though. "Having a young child in my life at my age and this stage of my career has severely curtailed my workaholism." But Karen was raised to "do what you got to do to get the job done." It is how Cangleska came to be.

Earlier, Pine Ridge had a small program for battered women but no shelter. "I'd say, 'Somebody will rise up to do it.'" In 1996, Running Strong for American Indian Youth, an organization led by Lakota Olympian Billie Miles, suggested Karen be "the Johanna Appleseed of shelters," going from reservation to reservation to start them. Her answer was no, it does not work like that. "You have to be part of the community." Running Strong later offered to fund a shelter on Pine Ridge. Because nobody else offered to lead it, Karen said yes. "In 1997, when we started with this, I'd be sleeping on the shelter floor for a few hours and up writing another grant. You don't build a program working forty hours a week."

"I don't think Indian leadership had a clue all of this was going on." The assault of Native women was not "on the radar screen for tribes." Then two things changed. More advocates for battered women brought the situation to the attention of their tribal councils. Also, "we knew tribal leaders weren't going to come to our trainings, so we went to them," including sessions of the National Congress of American Indians. "I do feel like we're a progressive people, because the first few meetings there was a lot of that attitude, 'It's a women's issue,' 'What about shelters for men?' We talked about a women's caucus. My God, even the women had fits. 'Our circle is Indian people.' But we kept passing out the information.

"When statistics came out in 2000 and 2002 about the rates of violence against Native women, that was very, very helpful for us. It was the first time the United States government had released any sort of figures [about the abuse of Native women]. We used those statistics to our advantage to bring it home to tribal leadership, that this was a big problem." In Karen's opinion, the problem is worse than reported. "The [U.S. Justice Department] statistic says one in three Indian women will be raped. You're sitting in a room full of Indian women and invariably at least one woman will say, 'Don't you think that [statistic] is kind of *low*?'" In some Native communities, particularly in Alaska, the abuse rate is considerably higher.[2]

Karen added that, unlike other groups of women, "we are more likely to be raped and/or battered by men not of our own race. African American women are in danger from African American men, Asian women are in danger from Asian men, et cetera. We're in danger from all men."

Once statistics convinced male-dominated tribal leaderships of the problem, "we started making the links with economic development. Women are a major work force in tribal communities, and the violence perpetrated against women is impeding the economic development efforts. That's when we produced our little brochure about sovereignty, specifically designed to attract the eye of Native leadership. They would see 'sovereignty' and of course they're going to think it's about them as a government. Then they open it up. 'Sovereign women strengthen sovereign nations.'" Another brochure Karen co-wrote describes tactics used for controling women, including physical violence, intimidation, economic abuse, cultural abuse ("Telling her she's too Indian or not Indian enough"), and ritual abuse ("Saying her period makes her 'dirty'").

Native leadership came around. "We touched key leaders who spoke in support of us. To hear a tribal leader stand up and say, 'My sister murdered her husband.' Or, 'My sister was murdered.' We started sponsoring receptions at the NCAI conventions. We did a wiping of tears. 'If you've had someone in your family killed or you have a domestic violence situation you're grieving about, come forward and get a wiping of tears.'" The traditional ceremony was effective. "When we utilize our customs and our protocols, it's pretty hard for them to be flippant or disrespectful about the issue."

"In all of our materials and presentations, we relate our belief that all of this stems from colonization. That we are a colonized people and don't believe [violence against women] was typical of our people. That's not to say that it didn't exist. Mary Louise Defender tells a beautiful story about the first battered women's shelter, and says it was a cave and the first advocates were the wolf nation.[3] How a young woman made the mistake of going to live with her husband's people—a moral right there—and he abused her. She tried to make her way back to her people and couldn't. The wolf people found her and took her to their home in this cave and nursed her through the winter. In the spring they helped her get back to her people."

Another example, she said, was on a winter count (a pictographic record of memorable incidents, usually drawn on a hide). One year the incident involved an abuser who was followed by the woman's people and killed. "Winter count is smallpox and war, and here is this incidence of domestic violence."

Amid all Karen had to say about violence and colonization, her most provocative comments involved "internalized repression" relating to Native support for U.S. armed forces. "I've never been a big fan of the military. When I went through my phase of all I read was books about Indians, getting more in touch with the history of the United States government and its actions toward indigenous people, I could not twist that around in my mind. Why in the heck as Indian people we're defending a country that tried to wipe us off the face of the earth. I still don't get it." Her father's own military service "wasn't necessarily the best experience in the world for him as a tribal man, getting called 'Chief' and all of that, [but] he'll still defend the flag and the country. Yet he'll make jokes about how if he'd have been born a year [earlier] he wouldn't be a citizen." She spoke of Native Vietnam War veterans being "messed up personally, spiritually, and psychologically. Listening to a Vietnam veteran being drunk and crying about killing somebody that looked like their uncle . . . very, very, very traumatic. Some days I'd wonder [if] maybe a purposeful, intentional lack of opportunity for Indian youth shapes our behavior and herds us toward the military." Her voice softened. "There's even days I wonder if maybe we aren't breeding farms for the military, those days when I think about slavery. Is that what they are doing to us with this military thing? There was a time I couldn't even go to powwows, because there was such a strong military presence. Then I would subject my poor friends to this tirade about all this military brouhaha."

"I do think there is an element of that concentration camp dynamic, where you bond with your oppressor," including from the boarding school era. "You see the impact of removing children from their homes, forcibly, putting them in a concentration camp type of setting, a POW type of setting, the boarding schools, and telling them anything Indian is not good, then sending them out into their community to do their work and to raise children they don't have a clue how to raise. We see our bonding with the oppressor still when we don't see each competent as Indians. We don't see each other as being honest. We don't see ourselves as having a work ethic. If we don't have that mainstream type of thinking about what's honorable and ethical, we're still sort of 'savages.'"

Native Americans proving "they are better American citizens and more patriotic than any American," she believed, is an extension of bonding with one's oppressor.

Adding to the misery was what she called a chemical weapon in a genocidal war against Native peoples. Alcohol. "It debilitated us." Karen estimates that because of alcohol, more than half the schoolchildren on Pine Ridge have heard or seen their mother abused emotionally or physically, and are likely to be abused themselves. "We know that alcoholism and other substance abuse is going to impact children's performance in school and their behavior, we know FAE and FAS [fetal alcohol effects and fetal alcohol syndrome] is a big problem, but we hadn't really talked about the impact of children witnessing domestic violence. Now, we know that experiencing trauma at a young age, even preverbal, actually affects the development of the brain."

Asked (reluctantly) whether she thinks Native people have a genetic predisposition to alcoholism or whether the problems are sociological, Karen all but shouted, "I don't *care*." The answer is "irrelevant to me."[4]

There are "circles and circles of sober people now" (a tribal election flyer on a store in Pine Ridge included how many years of sobriety the candidate has), yet "as we're getting healthier, it's also creating an environment where we can begin to address other social issues," including meth and gangs. To Karen, all such problems are "engrained, embedded, enmeshed, becoming interwoven, because there has been a lack of attention paid to tribal communities" by the United States government. Modern America itself is another dilemma. "Even though we tend to be somewhat isolated from American society, we do live in American society and what impacts all Americans impacts us. We've been affected by a 'me' generation that is selfish and self-absorbed." And yet, and yet, "we also see a resurgence of culture. We see families teaching their children Lakota ways, so these children are growing up naturally who they are, unlike many of us who either had to be who we are in a secret kind of way, or learn who we are."

———

When Cangleska began, there were no programs for batterers. They got arrested, served time, were put on probation. "We set out to help them. I think it was also a way to find a role for male leadership and to minimize criticisms we might get from [them]." Karen is definitely pragmatic. "We knew that in our community women were not going to throw away their male relatives," no matter how "messed up." Her strategy was to include them. We were now at a Kyle café, with extra ranch dressing for the deep-fried mushrooms. "I've had this conversation with other Native women. 'Look, we had this guy call and he wants information. He's in your community. Get him to some other trainings. Make a relationship with him.' These guys, you love 'em up, you feed 'em, then you can chew 'em out. They'll accept that from you. If you just reject them . . ."

The program Karen and her colleagues started for counseling abusers focused on a separate message. "You say you want to be a Lakota man. This behavior is not the true Lakota man." It worked. "If we use the mental intellect we've been given and the inspiration we have through our spiritual channels, we can create something meaningful for people. I think the reason the men who've been touched by our work and have joined our work is because," she paused, "it made sense. It provided them with some answers and helped them understand some things better about why women in their lives behaved the way they did. I think it was also a healing for men, that their mothers didn't willingly abandon them. That the pain and oppression and violence their mothers and sisters and aunties and grandmas lived with prohibited them from loving them the way [they] should."

"I believe the thing that's going to pull us through is that we are all Indian people and have a shared genetic memory of what that means. That's part of our work, to give those genes a little jump start, so we can release whatever in our brains will help us to remember who we are and how we're supposed to be in the world." Once Native people fulfill responsibilities to one another, she said almost cheerfully, "I feel like we will have something substantive to offer the world and will make our contribution to world healing."

There was a little more. "We don't really know what our population was at contact, but we know there was a lot more Indians then than now. We survived an attempt at genocide. We're a miracle."

HEATH DUCHENEAUX

"Hello, Cangleska probation. Yes, sir. Tuesday at 1:30 or 5:00, whichever you'd like. All right, thanks for calling." At his desk in the modern Lakota Express Building in Kyle, a short walk from Cangleska's shelter, probation coordinator Heath Ducheneaux was setting up counseling sessions with abusers. Heath, Lakota from the Cheyenne River Reservation, was thirty-one, with a black ponytail, lean physique, and deliberate motions. He could be described, even when seated, as tall, dark, and handsome. As he brewed an afternoon pot of Folger's, a man fiddled with a pencil at a nearby desk. Heath took no evident note of him but in retrospect may have hoped to be overheard. In contrast to Karen's quick and at times theatrical way of speaking, Heath uses a slow, uninflected cadence. It made his candor and intimacy almost unnerving.

"This is the third year I've been doing this work specific, but I've been doing work on myself for about nine to ten years now. The first four years was getting sober. The third to fourth year was figuring out I was still an alcoholic without drinking, and a drug addict. About six years ago, after I went through a divorce and began dating another woman is probably about the time I started to pay a lot of attention to how I grew up.

"I didn't grow up in a home where I saw a whole lot of physical abuse. I saw a lot of emotional abuse, verbal abuse, and even psychological abuse my mom went through with one of her boyfriends. He was with us in our home, in his home, that's probably how he'd still say it, for about fifteen years. And for about fifteen years, I didn't want to be in that home." Heath said he stayed because he did not want to leave his mother alone with the boyfriend, but then became him. "I was the re-creation of what I grew up with, with a little bit of my mom's good nature worked in, which made me seem like I was a pretty good guy, to women specific. The other side of me was him." And him, he hated.

Heath began being "disrespectful," treating his mother as the boyfriend did, and doing chores not to help out but to get money for his habits. "I drank my first half bottle of wine when I was nine. After that, it was whatever I could get my hands on as a kid. When I got into middle school and high school, I was smoking pot. LSD, mushrooms, cocaine, crystal meth."

When he met his current wife, Tawa, "she was very healthy coming into the relationship. She knew what she wanted in her life and knows who she is. I, however, coming into the relationship, had no idea who I was." Heath recalled with chagrin an incident that occurred when Tawa was six and a half months pregnant with their first child, a boy they named Cetan Cikala. They had gone to a Lakota sweat lodge outside Albuquerque. Driving home that evening, Heath asked Tawa why she had talked with one of his friends so long. She replied that both had gone to the University of New Mexico and were reminiscing. "I said, offhandedly, 'It seems to me there's maybe a little bit more going on between you than just friendly conversation about school.' Things slowly started escalating from there."

"I wasn't yelling, but I was talking to her in a voice that was very condescending." At one point, "I put my hand up. I hit the steering wheel." It broke. "I don't remember ever hearing somebody crying and sob like that before. I didn't know what to do, but at the same time, being as unhealthy as I was, I didn't know how to handle someone else being hurt, even though I was the one doing the hurting. I don't really know how to describe the sound she was making." He took Tawa to her mother's and drove off.

The next day, they talked. "She said, 'If you ever raise your hand at me again, don't come back or don't expect me to come back.' Right there, pretty much, I knew if I didn't make some kind of change, even something minor right away, she was going. I hear a lot of people we work with talk about not wanting to lose their children. I didn't want to lose my son either, but I really didn't want to lose her. If it wasn't for her, I wouldn't have a son to begin with. And I was in love with her. That seems pretty odd to say, given the story I just told you."

The young man at the desk had become still.

"Very fortunately for me," Heath continued, "my uncle and Ben Artichoker and Karen Artichoker wanted to have the first-ever men's retreat camp that Cangleska sponsored, back in 2000. My uncle said, 'You will be there. I don't care what you're doing, you're going to be there all week.'" Heath had been alcohol- and drug-free several years but "had not looked at any of my behaviors. There's a difference between being sober and changing your behavior. That's what brought me into what Cangleska does as an organization."

The now annual retreats include Lakota ceremonies, healing practices, and aspects of Lakota culture from sleeping in tipis to riding horses (in some cases, learning to ride), and attempts to instill Lakota values. According to various accounts, the retreats are wrenching and life altering. As for Heath, said Karen, he "was a kid" who needed to learn to be a good relative. She cited the Lakota phrase *mitakuye oyasin*, which implies "this yearning to connect with each other as relatives. He wanted to be a good man. He just needed a little guidance."

Did he ever. During the retreat, Heath dreamt that the counselor, Marlin Mousseau, himself a former abuser, was having a friendly conversation with Tawa in front of him. Heath woke about 3:30 in the morning, infuriated, ready "to go outside and handle business" with the dream flirter. He was dissuaded but later told Marlin about it. "That one dream was the turning point, because Marlin didn't know my wife. That dream was telling me who I really was."

Heath has seen a lot of violence committed by men as sober as he was. His clients, who range in age from fourteen to fifty-nine, attend twenty-four weeks of Cangleska classes and get counseling from him. "I've heard of people talk about batterers not being intelligent people, but I'd have to say that is very much to the contrary. In order to be able to manipulate people, you have to be a thinker. I've done that myself. You have to think fast and be able to think ahead of everybody else to stay one step ahead, to keep the manipulation going to suit your own needs." Many batterers he counsels engage in emotional, verbal, and psychological abuse, as he had. Because police cannot easily prove such abuse, such cases "are usually dismissed." Nine of ten cases, however, involve physical injuries.

Wincing, Heath recalled an older Pine Ridge woman who needed some sixty stitches to her face and jaw after a drunken Pine Ridge man attacked her. "It gets very extreme. There's a lot of things that go unprosecuted here on the reservation. There's probably a very high rate of sexual assault. I don't want to say we have a bad public safety system here, because we don't, but we do lack resources heavily all over the reservation. The incidences are very high. Very high."

In the minutes before leaving to meet his son's school bus, Heath mused about the abusers he meets. Some days they seem to want to talk, other days they do not, apart from saying they "didn't do anything wrong." Other days they are angry. There also are days "when people are happy and are getting a lot out of the information we are giving." He seemed especially gratified when men he is about to give up on surprise him. "That very same person I'm thinking about does something very special, very small, that seems like a step for them." Glancing at his desk, computer, and files, he almost smiled before his earnestness triumphed.

"Every day I'm at my job, I get the opportunity to continue growing in something I believe in. As far as seeing that light bulb go off, it's because I've seen my own light bulb go off many times in one day since I've worked here. Not to be selfish about it, but it enriches my family. It enriches the relationship I have with my wife, it enriches the relationships I'm having with my son and our daughter.

"When I first started doing this, I told a friend of mine I was going to have to get used to being lonely." Some men, he figured, would not go along with the "different way" Heath wanted to live. "That's certainly been true, but on the other hand, I've gained a whole lot of really wonderful friends. They're trying to make changes similar to the ones I'm trying to make. We're doing it because we have a belief. That makes it much more powerful, because it's not just a job. It's really about what you believe in your own life, how you want to live."

Dwanna Oldson

Among the victims of violence on Pine Ridge is Dwanna Oldson. The same day Heath was in his office, trying to change men around, and Karen was in her office, trying to change women, men, and policy around, Dwanna was on the other side of the Cangleska shelter, hiding.

It was an unusually quiet day. The Oldsons—Dwanna, her son, Nash, almost thirteen, and Alice, eleven—were the only people being protected. Tomorrow, another mother and her children would show up, and the following week more still, but today Dwanna had the run of non-staff areas. A middle-aged woman of sparkle and nerves, she was slender, tall, dark-skinned, with long, dark brown hair and the tentative smile attempted by people missing some teeth. Busying herself in the communal kitchen, she prepared meals for her children with what looked like happiness. Indeed, the tasks of opening a can of soup, heating it, and ladling it out must have been cherished moments of peace.

Absent were her two older sons. A seventeen-year-old, "the one that's still with the father," she said, vows to join her as soon as he turns eighteen. Her eldest son, twenty-two-year-old Dusty, was in Kyle's jail, "because he's too old to be here with us." Cangleska does not allow males eighteen or older to stay under the same roof with abused women. "He's over there for protective custody, but they let him out. He's the one that's set on turning informant and turning our lives around. I guess we're on a mission to stop our family from being the biggest drug dealers in South Dakota." Her husky voice emitted a partial laugh.

Dwanna and the younger children get rides from staff members to visit Dusty at the jail, a quarter mile or so away. They cluster in the jail's vestibule, Nash and Alice surrounding the quiet young man in an orange jumpsuit, JAIL printed in big letters on one leg, Dwanna looking loving and hyper-vigilant. The three could walk the distance, for Cangleska allows freedom of coming and going, an important consideration for women who have felt incarcerated in their own homes. Dwanna avoided such exposure, though. The threat of violence was so much on her mind, she did not even sleep in a shelter bedroom. (Alice told me her mother is "a protective freak.") When I stopped by one morning, Nash and Alice were each lying on a couch in the living room, Dwanna stretched out on the floor between them. She felt more secure here, she said. If someone broke in through a bedroom window at night, the three could be outside in a flash.

For a private talk during the day, she did choose a shelter bedroom. It had three bare beds, limp curtains pulled across a window. She shut the door, sat on the edge of one mattress and leaned forward. Her family is known on the Pine Ridge Reservation as "the Mansons," she said, then proceeded to describe a "slew" of aunts who were "well-equipped in loading guns, having shootouts, bootlegging, drug dealing." She spoke of at least two shooting deaths involving her family. "It was like the Hatfields and McCoys when I was growing up. They think nothing of busting a woman's skull if she's out of line." Her grandma Rita, she said, sold marijuana. Dwanna herself, as a child, sold liquor, which was and is prohibited on the reservation. "I was a very, very good bootlegger, all my life. I remember being three or four years old, going to the door with a pint of wine."

Her childhood, she said in an undramatic voice that marked most of her accounts, was "very abusive." Her first abuser was her mother. "My mom used to come home drunk and make us"—Dwanna and her two brothers—"get up out of bed and fight each other, and bet on us." Her mother also beat her with a belt buckle, which "laid me out for about four days, with my head swollen and cut up." Dwanna wanted to flee, but "I didn't know left from right. I didn't know how to read nor write or anything." At school, a therapist ordered pictures taken "of my backside, I was so beat up. My mother was turned in numerous times for child abuse. My auntie would hide me, my uncle would take me," but her mother "always had some way of paying off somebody" and Dwanna was returned.[5]

"My dad was pretty good. I didn't really know him. He kind of left my mom. He was a white man. We got the shit knocked out of us for having white blood in us. It was usually my mom doing it. 'I hate you little white bastards. I wish to God I never had you!' But she was the one who slept with him, so how it was my fault I never did understand." Dwanna twisted her mouth on that sentence.

At twelve, Dwanna stabbed a schoolteacher she thought drank with her mother, "causing a lot of my abuse." The courts stepped in. Apparently because of few options for violent girls, Dwanna was sent to Lookout Mountain School for Boys in Golden, Colorado. There, she said, counselors abused her. She started writing poetry. Later she was transferred to a Denver facility, New Horizons. "They put me in with a heroin junkie. I started shooting heroin and selling heroin out the back bedroom window."

Somehow, the wife of a Denver police sergeant stepped in. "She taught me proper etiquette. How to read. They used to call me Cousin Itt [a hair-covered character in the fictional Addams Family] because I such long hair; I held my head down so it covered my face." The woman, whom Dwanna referred to as Mama Kirsch, taught her "there was something other than violence on the reservation." She said Kirsch also tied her down and sat with her for three days to get the heroin out of her system, then took her to a methadone clinic.

Once clean, Dwanna returned to Pine Ridge. She took classes at Sinta Gleska Tribal College on the Rosebud Reservation, until she became pregnant with Dusty, the son hiding in jail. "A very good boy."

And so we arrived at her current situation. Unlike most of Cangleska's shelter residents, Dwanna was not trying to escape an abusive boyfriend or husband. Her problem was her nephew. He wanted her dead.

The convoluted story she related involved a house she inherited in the town of Pine Ridge (a forty-mile drive from Kyle), a will disappearing, a brother stealing equipment, corrupt tribal council members, an attempted land share negotiated for packets of cocaine, and Dwanna's turning the alleged negotiator, her aunt, over to the FBI. Then there was the nephew, whom she let stay in the house while she served time at the York, Nebraska, Correctional Center for Women for "kidnapping my own daughter and failure to appear in court." It seemed Alice had been in foster care, ran away when an older boy tried to molest her, and Dwanna brought her back to Pine Ridge.

While in York, Dwanna consented to her nephew having temporary custody of Alice and Nash, since he was living in the house anyway. "I didn't know he was selling cocaine; I didn't know there was fifty thousand people living there and trafficking drugs. It was more or less a crack house and I had no idea. When I came home, my daughter informed me she was made to sleep in the dirty laundry downstairs in the basement. There was bedbugs, cockroaches, the house was completely trashed. People would pass out, piss on the couches." Her nephew, she said, has "gotten very powerful for such a young boy, but his power is mostly Miss White: cocaine." Dwanna inferred he made Nash sell marijuana and smoke it, "and subjected him to pain medication" that she had to get him off with the help of a doctor. "It was a nightmare."

Amid several narrative detours, Dwanna said she got a female police officer to the house to evict everyone, at which point her nephew, in an armored vest and full of cocaine, pulled a gun. Next, a call for backup, an arrest, FBI involvement, wrestling with a gun, a search warrant, tribal police finding an arsenal of various weapons and drugs, including "some packets of cocaine, which never showed up in evidence, so one of the cops ended up with those."

Dwanna refused protective custody. "I figured if I didn't stand my ground, they would bully me all the time." While her nephew was in jail, she said, he made death threats through his lawyer's son and "orchestrated about fifteen people to gut my house. They literally took the doorknobs, the locks, stripped the house, vandalized it," leaving only a dresser, a lamp, clothes, and a kitchen table. "We had to bar the door shut and sleep in front of the living room door, because they terrorized me all night long, saying they were going to burn the house down, shoot us. They would run through the yard, hit the house with things." She said her nephew's mob called her a "turncoat" and a "traitor." (She was also excoriated as "white," she said.)

At this point in Dwanna's whirring tale, Alice, a lanky beauty who seemed to yearn for anything of interest within the confines of the shelter, entered the bedroom, ostensibly to give her mother an address. "You need to knock," said Dwanna, taking the slip of paper. "Okay, shut the door, please. Thank you." Alice left at her mother's soft urging. It was clear the family held onto courtesy like a lifeline.

Dwanna's mind returned to the terrifying night her nephew's mob threatened to burn the house down. She and Dusty "put the two little kids in the middle and I slept against the wall," Dusty on their other side. Early the next morning, she got the younger children up and off to school, "where I figured they'd be safe." The next episodes, delivered in a rush, involved Dwanna and Dusty getting restraining orders, being directed to the tribal housing council, a neighbor driving up, saying the house was on fire, an organization called Violence Assistance in Indian Country getting the Oldsons a motel room. "While we were at the motel room, the sheriff came and took custody of my two kids."

Now, Dwanna said, she has custody of them and rights to the gutted uninhabitable house. That was about it for the good news.

"My nephew wants to shoot me, the FBI wants me to turn state's evidence against all the drug dealers, and I've got nowhere to live, no money in my pocket. But, I do belong to the Mansons, which brings me to today."

Well, not quite yet. About ten years ago, Dwanna informed authorities which family members, including her mother, were dealing. As a consequence, "They beat me up really bad" on her mother's orders, she said, "and left me in a ditch in Pine Ridge. I was a couple of weeks pregnant with my daughter and having internal injuries from being kicked and pummeled.

My eye was swolled shut and my cheekbones were fractured and my nose was broke and my teeth were busted in half." At that point, an FBI agent named Mark Vukelich, "who ended up more or less pitying me, took me to Nebraska to stay with my dad, 'cause my dad's not scared of my mom and them." Although reeling from the awful account, part of me wondered if it was true.

Sipping a cup of coffee across from FBI headquarters in Washington, D.C., Special Agent Mark Vukelich said yes it was.[6]

Vukelich, a prematurely gray-haired, mustachioed man whose FBI assignment included western South Dakota, allowed that Dwanna differed from often shy, downward-glancing, self-effacing Native women he met there. Despite Dwanna's problems, she was notably forthright. And he did drive her to her father's home in Nebraska (not really a by-the-book action) because he wanted her to be with someone who cared about her. She was wrong about his motive, though. No pitying involved. Just doing my job, ma'am.

"I stayed with my dad and laid on his couch until I healed. The month I had my daughter I applied for a job in a bar, and Bruce was the owner." He was "a wonderful man," she said. "He fell in love with my kids, first of all. He loved kids. And Nash had been retrieved from being kidnapped and was . . ." she briefly stopped. "Was injured and molested."

"When I turned my mom in and she had me beat up, she took my kids and gave them to their dad who was shootin' heroin and cocaine. The grandfather, they figured, was the one who molested and abused them [her now seventeen-year-old son and Nash, then only thirteen months]. He doesn't know nothing about it. We did a lot of therapy. You couldn't touch him at one time to change his diaper, without him biting himself and screaming bloody murder."

She added, "I've had my woes, I've had my faults, I've screwed up plenty, but I've never let my failures diminish my family values all the way."

Back to Bruce. Dwanna, clean, sober, and "an awesome wife" in her assessment, and her two youngest children lived with him in his "beautiful home" in Nebraska for years. There were two problems. "My nephews and nieces and one fuckup after another would show up at our door. Disrespectful, obnoxious shit. It's just . . . I think inside he just liked the bigger women." Ah, the other problem. Dwanna came home one day and caught Bruce "with a great big huge 200-pound woman on my floor." The Oldsons departed.

Now, Dwanna semi-laughed and recited calmly (this is only part of it) her physical insults to date at the age of forty-three. "I've had most of my teeth knocked out. I've been beat up with a hammer by my Uncle Chuck; I have seizures due to severe head injuries. I've still got a couple of ribs that need to have surgery on them. My brother Les knocked my eye out of its socket and cracked my cheekbones and tore my sinuses. I have tubes in my sinuses."

There is another opening of the door. "Mommy, mommy." It is solemn Nash, reporting that "Alice is cussing." Dwanna assures him she will be there in a minute. He nods and leaves.

She watched the door. She worries about schooling being interrupted, she said. "They're A students; they're very well-mannered. I get tremendous compliments on my children. The only time I've ever spanked them is if they've been caught fighting each other or lying to the authorities." She stretched her long arms. "It's been a hell of a road and I'm tired, and there's not a day that don't go by, I wish I could put my kids to safety and kill myself." She did try by overdosing on pills, a scene she described in haunting detail, but a counselor found her.

Amid the horrors, Dwanna managed a peaceful closure with her mother in the months before she died. "I think most of all she needed to forgive herself, but she wanted me around to get that approval" and offer her own forgiveness. Dwanna seemed empathetic as she related her mother's own story of being raped and beaten by her stepfather.

There is yet another stirring at the door. Alice could not seem to stay away, then left again. Dwanna said, after a summary of what Alice has been through, "she went from a very protected little girl to wide exposures," adding softly, "it's caused a lot of crying."

"Somehow I manage to always really screw it up." Still. Dwanna is safe, for today. She also has a palpable bond with at least her two youngest children. In trying to give them a different perspective, she tells them they are all having "adventures."

CHAPTER 9

"Get over it!" and Other Suggestions

PATTY TALAHONGVA (HOPI)

"When we had our winter ceremonies," said Patty Talahongva, one January afternoon in her Albuquerque office, "our schedule was like this. My dad was a baker. That's the wonderful job"—she raised her eyebrows with "wonderful"—arranged for him after the Talahongva family relocated to Denver. "King's Bakery," she recited. "He would get off at, say, two in the afternoon. My mom would have the car packed. He would come home, load up, we'd jump in the car, and start driving. We'd come all the way down through here, cross over into Arizona, and go to Second Mesa. We would get there at night. I remember getting in that car and falling asleep. Wake up at my grandma's house. She always had a big pot of stew for us, and bread. We would come in, she would feed us. That's the last I would see of my dad for the weekend, because he would go up to the kiva [an underground ceremonial space] and stay in the kiva for the ceremonies all weekend long."

"Then early Sunday morning when he would come out, my mom would have everything packed up, we'd have our meal for the road, we'd get back in the car, and turn around and drive all the way back to Denver. We'd get there in time for him to shower. Then he would go right to work. That was how our life was during the winter for the ceremonies, like coming up pretty soon."

Pretty soon, indeed. On a frigid day later that month, in the Second Mesa village of Songoopavi, ceremonies were about to begin.

If you had no knowledge of them and were driving for the first time along Arizona's two-lane Highway 264 through the lower elevations of the Hopi

Reservation, you would find no clues. Certainly no sign announces "Authentic winter dances today!" If, in fact, you kept your eyes only on the road, you might not even see that villages exist high on all three mesas. If you did wind your way up to them, you might not find clues either. The Hopi Cultural Center on Second Mesa includes a hotel, whose stationery informs guests this is the "Center of the Universe," but it posted no notice about the dances. Nor did I see any in any of the villages, such as Kiqötsmovi, Hot'vella, or Orayvi.[1] There are no notices because none is needed. Like the better-known kachina dances, Hopi winter ceremonials have been going on about a thousand years.

Obviously, they are not meant for tourists. Neither are they meant for the Hopi people. They are meant for the Hopi spirits. It is up to them to send rain or, in this freezing month, snow. The Hopis' ancient mainstay, corn, requires it.

The setting for the dances that January was undramatic and monochromatic; Hopi was in full winter camouflage. Everything from the packed-flat frozen earth of the ancient plaza, to the stone and earthen homes surrounding it, to the unpaved alleys and kivas beyond, to the other villages of Second Mesa, and beyond them to the villages of First and Third Mesas, and farther still to the base of the distant and sacred San Francisco Peaks, was mud brown. Even the overcast sky looked muddy. The day's bitter brownness was broken only by remnants of snow and, rather startlingly, by neon-colored acrylic yarns. These were blankets nestled around some of the Songoopavi elders who hunkered into lawn chairs lining the plaza. They, everyone, was waiting.

Then, heralded by drums and voices, the retina-exploding dancers arrived. Perhaps because the day was so cold and the dun so obdurate, they looked especially resplendent: buffalo dancers, in red sashes and leggings, carrying ponderous shaggy headdresses; eagle dancers, from grown men to small boys, lifting wing arms of feathers; deer dancers, wearing racks of antlers with pine sprigs tied between them. Throughout the day, more and more dancers arrived—men, women, children—all in intricate regalia, most dancers performing barefoot. Each dance lasted close to half an hour, with the dances as a whole lasting throughout the weekend, and preparations and prayers in the kivas lasting throughout the nights.

The few shivering non-Natives in attendance were consigned to stay off the plaza. (One never knows when an ignorant interloper—"It's a party!"—might try to join in.) Forbidden the plaza, outsiders had climbed steep wooden ladders or crumbling steps to houses' flat roofs. The higher vantage point afforded so perfect a view, it had attracted others. Hopi teenagers in baggy pants and chains, restless in the timelessness, were there. (Rather than mix vibes, I decided not to ask them about reggae, which young Hopis are crazy for.) Children were everywhere, perched on mothers' and aunties' laps on the plaza, running along side alleys, sitting on roof edges, their legs dangling over the side. Most people looked economically stretched and attentive. On one roof a woman videotaped the proceedings, an apparent affront to some. She must have been Hopi, with special permission; non-Natives were forbidden to use cameras of any type, or recorders, or pens, or pencils.

If an advantage of the roof was the view, a disadvantage was the wind. It made freezing temperatures that much colder, collective exhalations of breath that much more evident. Some rooftoppers occasionally sidled up to waist-high metal smokestacks that emitted warmth, as well as chokes of coal smoke, from homes below. Conversations often were in Hopi, with some "How are you doing?" English thrown in. Nobody talked much. Attention centered on the controlled glory of the spectacle below.

Oh, the eagle dancers! As each man, youth, boy, in tall-to-short progression, entered the plaza, he squatted, tilted, and flapped winged arms in gestures entirely birdlike while slowly standing. The last was an eaglet, whose little arms were wrapped in eagle down, his gestures practiced and perfect.

The dancers moved as if barely aware of their surroundings. Toward the end of any dance, women walked up to offer gifts of food. A plate of paper-thin blue corn piki bread or robust rolls was accepted by a dancer's touch, perhaps held for seconds, before another woman took it away, the act of giving and acceptance repeated constantly. Blessings seemed to be given too. At the conclusion of the bear dance—a slow movement of older men who wore bearskins over their backs, the bears' ferocious-looking opened-jawed heads resting on their own—a woman brought a small girl to one dancer, who made gentle motions above the girl's placidly upturned face. Another bear did the same for an elderly woman who struggled to him with her walker.

What did everything mean? I had little idea. Even within the intricate Hopi clan system, not every Hopi knows the significance of every dance or what transpires in every kiva. The only certainty was the pull the ceremonies have on the Hopi people.

———

Patty Talahongva could not attend the ceremonies I watched, but "Hopi-ness" is never far from her mind, nor are attendant puns. "Hopi New Year!" she e-mails. She quotes a popular slogan, "Don't worry, Be Hopi." Patty is so hopi-ly Hopi-centric that one evening at a Chinese restaurant in Albuquerque, after I asked jokingly, "Are you card-carrying?" she answered, "Oh yes. Want to see my card?" and pulled it from her wallet. It read, "Patty Talahongva, enrolled member of the Hopi Nation. Blood quotient: four-fourths." You cannot get more Hopi than that. "That's a lie," she said of the four-fourths, "I'm part Tewa." The Tewa have lived in their own village, Hano, on the First Mesa of Hopi, for three hundred years or so and have their own language and ceremonies. Still, "part Tewa" is hardly as foreign as being, say, Navajo.

In physical description, Hopis are considered, in a word, short. Patty is no exception. She stands "five feet, one and a *half* inches tall," she said, laughingly describing herself further as "pottery red" in hue.

She never laughed when talking about Hopi culture and its birth-to-death commemorations. "We have our naming ceremony when we're twenty days old. Traditionally, the babies were born in a home. You're in a darkened room, all the windows are covered up. The family comes in. It's a transition time for the baby to meet the family—everybody he's been hearing or she's been hearing in the womb—and the family to bond. It's the father's mother who comes and takes care of the new mother—her daughter-in-law and her grandbaby. She feeds them and washes their clothes and everything else. Baby gets comfortable with the family. On the morning of the twentieth day—the night before, they're starting to pre-pare—it is the mother's family who makes the big feast. They prepare the stew and make the pikami [corn pudding]. They do everything.

"Everybody gets invited. If fifty people show up from the father's side and they all have a name for that child, that child gets fifty names. They all bring a present for the child. They wash the baby's hair, they wrap him in the new clothes and new blanket, they bless him, they get their ear of corn, and then one by one each relative comes up and offer their prayers for that baby's life, and offer their name and offer their present.

"Then the baby's mother and the father's mother take that child out as the sun is coming up and present the child to the sun. Cool, huh? They say, 'This is your new child. Thank you for this new child in our family.' They read off the whole list of names. 'This is what we are going to call the baby.' Typically, the mother, being politically savvy, will use the name her mother-in-law gave the child. Then they offer their prayers for the child's life. They come back in the house and say, 'Okay, let's eat.' The mother's family has set the table, all the father's relatives come and sit down. The grandmother takes that baby and the pikami, and puts it in the baby's mouth and tells the baby, 'We're Hopi. You're Hopi. This is our food. It's the corn. The absolute sustenance of life. You eat it, you pray with it, and you better take care of it.' They give the baby the food, everybody eats, the mother's family eats, and then they go home. You're done by 7:30. It's a great ceremony."

———

For nearly three years, Patty Talahongva was the anchor of the program *Native America Calling*, broadcast from station KUMN, 89.9 FM, located in what once was a University of New Mexico dormitory. Her office, carved out of a dorm room, included a built-in bureau on which lay a number of photographs, including one from her days as president of the Native American Journalists Association (NAJA). She was standing with then UN secretary-general Kofi Annan. "Coffee with Kofi," she smiled.

Patty hosted *Native America Calling* with verve and with humor, which, she said more than once, is essential to Native life. "How would we have stayed sane without it?" Her on-air voice was modulated and regionally unaccented. To an older woman in Patty's mother's home village of Sitsomovi, the name Patty Talahongva elicited a nod of respect. "Even though she's Hopi, she speaks English really well." Patty laughed at that.

As anchor, she was equally courteous to guest experts and often less sophisticated callers. It is not easy to bridge the demands of live talk radio (get on, make your point, get off) with Native conversational traditions (be polite, be patient, do not interrupt). "Go ahead, please," Patty told callers, after answering, thank you, she is fine. "You're on the air."

Her job included planning upcoming programs, which reflected what anyone in "Indian Country" knows; Native people are concerned not only with issues such as tribal sovereignty and treaty rights but with issues virtually all Americans share. There is much overlap. A program about cell phone usage included questions about cell phone etiquette during powwows, as well as how those darn teenagers rack up the minutes. A program about the aftermath of Hurricane Katrina dealt with which tribes had been hurt and which were helping. A program about Internet entrepreneurship dealt with tribal businesses.

Scheduled programs one week in June, for which the multitasking Patty wrote the descriptions e-mailed to subscribers each Friday, included "Protecting Our Borders" ("Last week representatives directly from the Department of Homeland Security toured the Tohono O'odham Nation in southern Arizona. Are border tribes finally getting a seat at the table to discuss homeland security?") and "Cap and Gown Quarrels" ("Some Native students are decorating their caps and gowns with beadwork and eagle feathers to reflect their heritage. Many students say it's a way to honor this rite of passage and their heritage. Critics say it takes away from the unity of the ceremony.")

"When you tune into us, you're going to think a little bit more about Native people, how our world is, and how we manage to walk—and I hate this analogy—in two worlds." One Friday, a day she was not hosting but directing, she sat in the former dorm's well-used studio 49, listening on headphones for input from call screeners, updating the substitute anchor, Camille Lacapa, about the calls, reading the computer screen for information, typing in questions to feed Lacapa, checking with the audio technician about who was on which line, and following the on-air conversation. That day, the guest—by phone—the "Native in the Spotlight," was especially prominent: Joe Garcia, just named leader of the National Congress of American Indians. He not only was president of NCAI, but had been a senior engineer at Los Alamos and was governor of New Mexico's Ohkay Owingeh, formerly San Juan Pueblo. At one point on the air, Lacapa addressed him as "Joe." Patty, as soon as she could interrupt, pressed a button to remind her he should be referred to by his title.

Later, she acknowledged her intervention. "Even though he's 'Joe' and he's very cool and he hangs out and has coffee, when we're on live and we're doing a national program, it's important to pay that respect and honor of that title and call him either 'Governor' or 'President.' That's a stickler for me."

Another world of Patty's was traveling saleswoman. Several months after the Garcia program, Patty, chic in a red tailored suit and heels, French manicure, and lip gloss, her long black hair combed off her face, her eyes merry behind her glasses, stood on a riser behind a podium in a conference room at the Wyndham Hotel in downtown Washington, D.C., and smiled mischievously. She earlier had moderated a panel titled "Addressing Lack of Indigenous People in Mainstream News," part of a two-day Quaker-sponsored symposium, "Hear Our Story: Communications and Contemporary Native Americans." Her assigned duty completed, Patty promoted. Holding a fistful of paper doorknob hangers, she asked, Who knows how long *Native America Calling* has been on the air? Answer: ten years. She cheerfully handed the winner, or guesser—it hardly mattered—the prize, a hanger that read "Do Not Disturb! I have nothing on but Native America Calling."

During her years hosting the program, it was evident she empathized with virtually all matters Native yet did not exempt Native people from her scrutiny. One program focused on a video game that involved killing an enemy tribe. A twelve-year-old tribal member called to say he liked it. Patty questioned him gently, explaining to me later, "He's not the only one out there like that. So much is said about 'our youth is our future.' Well, that's your future talking. If you agree with it, support him. If you don't agree with it, you better figure something out."

She was all too aware of how violent youth could be, remembering when news came to *Native America Calling* offices in 2005 about shootings by a teenager at Red Lake Reservation in Minnesota. Her first reaction, rather than hustle to get correspondents to the site, was to gather her staff to pray.

Another subject that concerned her was tribal identity. "I've known—I've said this on the air too—full-blooded Native people and they have no connection to their community. They don't speak the language, they don't know their culture, traditions, nothing. Just because they're full blood, that makes them Native?" She also did a show about "black Indians," as she called them. "These tribes in Oklahoma are disenrolling their black relatives. That's racism. All these blond-haired, green-eyed Cherokees are telling their black-skinned, kinky-haired relatives, 'You're not Indian.' By doing that, they're saying white blood is better than black blood. They don't see it. Whose standards are we following and how traditional is that?"

About a year after her Washington symposium appearance, Patty Talahongva was fired as NAC anchor. She was given no "good" reason, she said by phone, sounding more grim than upset. "Indian drama," she later termed it. The show's previous host, about whom she had spoken with careful praise, had been rehired to take her place.

Now Patty was busy with other projects, from working for the Hopi Education Endowment Fund, to writing articles for the glossy *Native Peoples* magazine, to making a video about World War II code talkers. They included Hopi, she said more than once.

In an impressive documentary Patty made for the Inter Tribal Council of Arizona to educate freshman lawmakers about Native issues, she included efforts to rename Phoenix's mountain for Lori Ann Piestewa, a Hopi and the first U.S. female soldier killed in the Iraq War. Patty mobilized climbers to lug to the summit a huge banner reading "Piestewa Peak" and hired a helicopter crew to film the results. It is a great scene.

On the day the U.S. Board of Geographic Names was to rename Piestewa Peak from the insulting name Squaw Peak, which Patty avoids saying, she suited up in visor, shorts, and a T-shirt honoring Hopi Olympic runner Louis Tewanima, and clambered up the steep and rocky switchbacks. At the summit, she pulled out her cell phone, got the news that the renaming was official, and spread the word. After the descent, she impishly suggested we walk behind a television reporter doing a live story on the peak's renaming, to get in the shot. My hesitation squelched her impulse. Later that day, she posted an account of our climb on an Internet site, Arizona Native Scene.

———

After *Native America Calling* hung up, Patty relied on her enormous extended family. Through the years, it had had its own setbacks. "Let me tell you my parents' story," she said abruptly one day, and began with her mother's village, Sitsomovi, on First Mesa. "The house where she was born is still there. That's where we go back to for every ceremony." The house, which a local resident had pointed out to me, is a tiny earth and stone structure. In the slightly larger village of Polacca below the First Mesa, on her mother's clan land, her father built—as expected in Hopi tradition—a slightly larger home. It lacks plumbing, mostly because "it's too much of a hassle" to have it put in, said Patty. Nobody lives there year round anyway. She and her relatives, like others, drive to a windmill-powered well a couple of miles away and fill water canisters. The Polacca house does have electricity. Her mother "had a phone line in there, so she had her Apple computer and could check e-mail, but couldn't take a shower or flush the toilet. I told her, 'Mom, you should be the poster child for Apple.'"

Patty's father was born in a village on Second Mesa, a long up-and-down eight miles from Patty's mother. The couple met not as children but as nineteen-year-olds at a mutual job site, the Grand Canyon. "My father ended up working at the Grand Canyon at the Hopi House. It's now a trading post, a tourist trap, but back then they had Hopi dancers who would sing and perform different social dances for the tourists." Her mother worked as a maid in the lodge.

The relationship almost soured before it started. "My dad had been singing with this group for a while and told her, 'I would like to take you out.' She said, 'Okay.' He said, 'But tonight, they want us to record our songs. When we're done, I'll come get you.' She said, 'I'll be here waiting.' He had no idea what it takes to record a record. He thought, 'I'll sing four songs. Thirty minutes, I'm outta there.' Of course it was all night, so he stood her up. She was mad, and hungry. It took his friends to convince my mom that no, he wasn't out running around. Ultimately they got married and had all of us"—five daughters and a son.

The couple moved back home to Hopi, had their first child—Patty's older sister—but in 1959 decided to leave. "Not very many job opportunities," as Patty put it. In the Polacca post office on First Mesa, her mother saw a poster about relocation, the push to get Native people off reservations and into cities. The Talahongvas applied. "My parents chose Denver, Colorado, because it was close enough to where they knew they could still drive home."

The move "wasn't forced, but when you have no economic opportunity on the reservation, what are your options? They've got a young family, no work. What do we do? Where do we go?" The federal government sent her parents money "for gas and for hotel lodging and for meals," a "grand total" of about twenty dollars, she said. With that, they packed up and moved.

"The host family who met my parents, we're still in touch with them. They were good people. They welcomed my mom and dad and my older sister, helped them find an apartment, helped my dad find a job, and then went out and bought my mother everything she needed to set up house. Pots and pans. Sheets, blankets, towels, silverware, whatever we needed. Total assimilation. 'Here's everything it takes to be an urban person, in a box. Okay, start living the American dream.'"

The dream was not in Hopi. "My dad only went to sixth grade, at the most. He was not literate in English reading or writing. My mother graduated from high school and had one semester of junior college at Haskell and that was it. She realized, our kids are going to need to learn how to live in this white society. They decided to speak English to us and later on teach us Hopi," while speaking Hopi to each other.

"They found out that their conversations they thought were private were actually not, when my mom's brother came to stay with us." Assuming Patty's older sister spoke Hopi, he would say such things in Hopi as "Pass the salt." She did. "They were astounded. Then they realized, 'She knows what we've been saying!' Then I come along and they were more relaxed. As a result, I speak more Hopi, but understand less. I'm more willing to say the words and make the mistake than my older sister is." The two still argue about who is saying what right.

From their father's clan, Spider, Patty was named White Spider Girl. "*Qotsa kookyangw mana*," she pronounced. "*Qotsa* is white, *kookyangw* is spider, and then *mana* is girl." She fingered a spider necklace made for her. "As you get older and you initiate into other areas, other societies, you will get other names. It's up to you to choose how you want to be called. Some names you'll only be called during different ceremonies."

Her English name comes from a less traditional source—her mother's pen pal. The two, put in touch by Catholic missionaries, not only stayed in touch, but both happened to move to Denver. "When my mother met her pen pal, she decided she wanted to name me after her. So my name is Patricia Ann. It all kind of ties together."

The tie is that Patty became a pen pal fanatic. Archie comic books, which "back in those safe days" provided fans' names, ages, and addresses, gave Patty her first connections. She wrote to fellow fans of Betty, never vain Veronica, and was thrilled when they wrote back. From addresses furnished by *Tiger Beat* fan magazine, she wrote to stars such as Donny Osmond. She also wrote to her many relatives, including an uncle stationed unhappily with the marines in Puerto Rico. She remembered he wrote her that rain is a blessing for Hopis, but ten days of rain is too much of a blessing.

In Patty's childhood, blessings were literally mixed. Her father never wavered from the Hopi religion. Her mother "always stayed with Hopi, but she went to Catholic boarding school and became a Catholic. When they got married, they were married both in the Catholic Church and had a traditional Hopi wedding. My dad took the classes, or some instruction, and promised the priest he would help raise all the kids Catholic. He said, 'But they're going to learn Hopi, too, because that's my way.'" The priest, she said, agreed.

"My dad, in some ways, was a better Catholic than my mom. He would get all of us little girls up on Sunday, brush our hair, braid our hair, and tell us, 'Get ready. You've got to go to your church.' He took his religion seriously, and he figured if that's what we're going to do, we should take it seriously. We should be there every time, on time. He'd have all of us out the door. 'You better go. It's starting. Your God is coming at 10:00.'"

Patty's father attended Catholic mass on Christmas Eve, Easter, and Father's Day, and "helped when the church needed to be expanded. He was the first one to show up with his box of tools and his ice chest of beer. I loved my father," she smiled. "He was really good. He was good about instructing me and my older sister [about the Hopi religion]. He told us a lot about the importance of different roles in different ceremonies."

While spending a summer with relatives on the reservation, Patty, about thirteen, decided to learn the butterfly dance. Her parents "got all flurry. 'We've got to get everything ready.' They had to run out to the reservation and take care of me. Then I had to pick my partner. You have to go to your uncle's house and talk to them. 'I would like to dance with your boy in the butterfly dance.' Then that family has to measure your head, because they make the headdress. It's a big process." The butterfly headdress, made of wood, is enormous.

By tradition, "the boy can't say no. Because of the way the Hopi society is built, they are considered our sweethearts, our dear ones. They do things for us, including dancing with us. We take care of them, they take care of us. You'll hear the term 'her boyfriend,' but it's not sexual. It is like my uncle and my uncle's boys. They're my *mooyis*. There's no good translation for that. I'm his *kya'a*, his auntie, for lack of a better term. What it boils down to is a relationship. If I need wood chopped or coal or water hauled, he's going to come and help me do the physical hardcore labor. I'm going to make the bread. I'm going to take care of his moccasins. In turn, he's praying for me, I'm praying for him. It's that interdependency and really nice structure of family, that Hopi is just wonderful at."

"From the time I was that big," she said, flattening her hand about two feet off the floor, next to her desk, "your uncle walks in the house, he better have a cup of coffee before he sits down. You better be offering him some bread, some food. You treat them with the utmost respect. That's your mother's brothers and your mother's blood and clan relatives."

Relationships and ties to Hopi were so important to Patty's parents, they moved back to Arizona. "None of these relocation programs work," she said. "My mom sold everything. I remember my dad going, 'My fishing poles!' My mom says, 'Where are you going to fish in Arizona?' Poor dad." Because the reservation still did not have many jobs, her parents moved to Snowflake, Arizona, which did. Her father got work at a paper mill. "Snowflake was close enough where we could zip out there for the weekend and come back."

In Snowflake, Patty became a prodigious reader, thanks especially to her mother. "We had more books than we had any toys. That was partly because we were so poor." Patty happily recalled trips to the library and "reading about different people around the world."

In high school, she took journalism classes and kept writing. "But when it came to think about a career, I thought I wanted to get into law school. I was trying to figure out, what can I do? I like writing. Someone said, 'Lawyers have to write a lot, too, and they argue a lot.' Someone said, 'Well, you like to argue, so that sounds perfect for you.'"

The reason Patty considered law was a family tragedy. "My father died when I was fifteen, and my mother had a really hard time trying to get all the legal paperwork organized and everything else. She got the runaround from the bank and from other establishments. And he didn't have a will so we had to go through probate. She hired a Hopi man, who was a lawyer. When that man walked into the bank, they couldn't argue with him. He knew the law and he knew what the rights were. I was very impressed with him, and very, very grateful."

The cause of Patty's father's death was suicide. "Who can ever explain a suicide? I gave up a long time ago trying to figure this one out," she wrote by e-mail. "People are complex beings. I know he was very strong in his Hopi beliefs. So that doesn't explain why he did what he did, because the Hopi way frowns on suicide. It also frowns on any substance abuse, but he was still a functioning alcoholic. It's just a terrible thing and it really hurts the people left behind: questions, anger, and even guilt for not realizing or recognizing or whatever to try and prevent the suicide. As a Hopi—we have four days to mourn the person's death and then we let their spirit go. We are not to continue mourning for them, and we don't go back and visit the grave ever. As women, we don't even go to the grave when the person is buried. If you continue to cry and mourn for them, you are hindering their journey into the next world."

At his death, "everything in the family went phhhsst. Flipped upside down." Patty's mother moved with her youngest children into a small apartment on the campus of Northern Arizona University in Flagstaff. "She returned to college twenty years after graduating from high school. She knew she needed a career so she could take care of all the younger kids." Patty shook her head in admiration. "This is from a woman who did not speak English until she was eight years old." Patty grew up speaking with her mother's heavy Hopi accent. "I used to say 'cloding' instead of 'clothing.' She couldn't say wolves. She would talk about, 'I want to see that movie, *Dances with Wooves*.' 'What's a woove, Mom?'"

Her mother graduated from NAU with a dual degree in English and art history, Patty said, earned a master's, studied at Oxford University for two summers, and became an English teacher. At the time of our talks, she was teaching at San Carlos Apache Reservation high school during the day and at a community college in the evening.

When her mother returned to college, the apartment being too small for all of the children, Patty and one sister were sent away to Phoenix Indian High School. "I truly believe everything happens for a reason. If my dad had been alive, we would have stayed in Snowflake. Maybe ten people went to college. The rest of them just got married. Get married, have babies, have a little house, and run around town. I think back, who left town? For the guys, it was join the military. What did the girls do? My best friend, bless her heart, had five kids. She has a daycare in her house. She was talented and funny and who knows what she could have done if she'd decided to go off to college and try something else?"

At Phoenix Indian High, Patty got what she smilingly called "my first paying job as a journalist. I wrote for the *Teen Gazette*," a weekly insert in the *Phoenix Gazette*. "They had never had a correspondent from the Indian school." Her counselor thought of the idea, even contacting the paper on Patty's behalf. "They said, 'We'd love to have her.' I wrote every assignment, I enterprised on my own. I was constantly saying, 'What about this story?'" She started getting paid per column inch.

Her mother, meanwhile, managed to get a larger apartment on campus and told Patty to come "home" to Flagstaff. "Being the ungrateful teenager that I was, [I] did not like coming home for my senior year. I'd finally gotten to make friends, then I'm going into a whole new school, I don't know anybody? Oh big hurrah."

Nonetheless, she enrolled at Flagstaff High. There she met a "good ol' white boy," Cameron Ferguson, she still extols. He urged her to join the school newspaper, she did, and apply for a job at the television station where he worked. Patty was hired. "It boiled down to this. FCC regulations. Since they broadcast on the Hopi and Navajo Reservation, they needed to have that representation on staff. The one Native person they had was leaving." Patty learned the technical side of broadcasting, such as running studio cameras, then, thanks to Cameron, learned how to direct. "I was seventeen years old and I was directing the five o'clock and ten o'clock newscasts in Flagstaff. After school, I'd come in, 'Okay, where's my script? Camera one. Camera two. VTR A, B, and C,'" she chirped. "I can't believe the owners trusted me. We were high school kids."

"We covered the Iran hostage crisis." An Arizona man was among the hostages. Days were marked using "a felt thing with stick-in letters," like for hotel meetings. "That was my first introduction to big breaking news, watching that Iran crisis unfold and everything Carter went through. The minute Reagan was sworn in as president, they let [the hostages] go, the ayatollah. I remember thinking, 'My God, Carter worked so hard.' Anyway, that's how I got into broadcasting."

Her ambitions circuitously led also to marriage. When Patty first dated, she kept the number one Hopi stricture in mind. "'What's your clan?' Right away you identify family. Or, 'Okay, I can have an interest in you.' We know you do not marry into your own clan. That knowledge came from who? The Creator. How did we settle on this?" she half-asked herself. "I never even consider dating anybody who's Water clan, [her own] Corn clan, Spider clan, or a related clan like Snow. Because those are your relatives. Today, it's not so hard core, but I wouldn't and my family wouldn't stand for it."

She took Hopi tradition only so far; she never wore the eligible-for-marriage maiden hairdo of two tight coils by the ears, similar to Princess Leia's coif in *Star Wars*. Patty laughed about Hopi kids doing double takes at the movie. Is Princess Leia secretly Hopi?

Clan restrictions were sometimes superfluous. "In high school in Snowflake, there weren't a whole lot of Native people around. I did go out on a couple of dates before my dad died. They were all white guys. He was pretty cool about it. He never told me you can't date a non-Native person or a non-Hopi. He was more open and understanding, like it's a different world we live in. I didn't have the pressure from my mom, either."

At college, Northern Arizona University and Arizona State, where she transferred to focus on broadcast journalism, dating was more varied. She went out with a "Chinese guy" she liked a lot. "I had some Natives, too, but even the guys who were in college drank a lot. I knew from the time I was little, being around alcoholism and everything else, I would never, ever be in a situation like that. People in those kinds of environments tend to become victims or they become the abuser. I said no way."

Patty's quest for career-enhancing summer work led to the Phoenix Zoo. "I wanted to drive the trains and give the tour, because I thought that would help me develop my broadcast voice. I wanted to be a reporter *so* bad." But "this white guy" named Paul got the job. Patty was hired to work concessions. He asked her out. "I had no interest. Plus, I had a Comanche boyfriend I really, really liked." After she and the Comanche broke up, Paul and Patty got together. "Everything happens for a reason. We were brought together to have this baby."

One morning, when Patty was in terrible pain, Paul carried her to his car, "drove me to the Indian hospital—that was his first time, white guy at the Indian hospital." After an all-day wait, she learned she had a kidney infection and was pregnant. "That to me was a clear sign and an indication our Creator has blessed me and this is what's meant to be." When she told Paul the news, he immediately responded, "We're getting married!"

The ceremony was not traditional Hopi, including, as it did, a Chinese banquet, but the sentiment was. "Paul wrote in his wedding vows that he would support [their son] Nick and his Hopi upbringing however he needed to do that."

Paul even tried to learn Hopi. "It was hilarious. My other sister married a white guy too, and we were having dinner one night and wanted to know who could speak the most Hopi, [of] our husbands. Nick's dad won, because he rattled off all these commands right away. 'That's because Patty is the bossiest.'"

"I don't claim to be fluent by any stretch of the imagination, but I try hard and communicate with [Nick]." When he was little, Patty's English commands had little effect, so to tell him "Don't pick up that disgusting cigarette butt," she used Hopi. "I'd say, '*Iste-eh-heh*,' and he would drop it. To this day, if I say '*Iste-eh-heh*,' he'll stop and go, 'What?' and start looking around." Hopi was also handy for correcting him in public without embarrassing him.

Her marriage lasted, Patty calculated, fourteen years. In traditional Hopi marriage and divorce, as in most familial matters, the woman rules. "If the man was unfaithful or he was lazy or whatever, the woman bundles his clothes up, puts it outside the door. He comes home, 'Oh. I'm divorced.' Picks up his clothes and goes home to mom. I didn't do the Hopi thing. I moved out. I still regret that. He should have moved out." As for their divorce, "Let's just say 'irreconcilable differences,'" she later wrote. "I will say that in the end Paul was a bit fatigued with the Hopi way. It's hard for anyone who is not Hopi to accept all that is required. Many Hopis don't do all they are supposed to do with regards to the traditions and ceremonies. He made a gallant effort." The effort extended past the marriage. "In our divorce decree [he stated] he would continue to support Nick however he wanted, when it comes to Hopi."

Nick thus grew up in the Hopi manner, such as considering his cousins his siblings. "There's no word for 'cousin' in Hopi, because your mother's sister and all of her kids are your brothers and sisters. I have four sisters, all of them have kids. All of their kids are considered his brothers and sisters." She smiled. "When he was in kindergarten, one of the first things they tell you is, 'Draw your family.' He's coloring and coloring and coloring. He's coloring Lawrence and he's coloring Rachel and he's coloring himself and he's coloring Suzanne. The teacher's looking at all the kids. . . . I had to clarify it when I got there. 'No, physically they are not my children, but, in our way, these are his brothers and sisters.'"

———

"There's this huge disconnect from Native life and mainstream society," Patty said, pursing her lips. "We don't even cover Native American history in our schools. That is compounded through the years, even at the college level. I've said this on the air, too, that's why we graduate so many ignorant politicians, also journalists." She was particularly upset when a CNN reporter called the Red Lake shootings a Trail of Tears—as if the deadly forced exodus in the nineteenth century could be invoked so casually. "Inappropriate!"

"As a Native person, I have to know the Constitution," she continued. "I have to know how the Supreme Court works. I have to know and embrace the larger society we are a part of." Why then does "mainstream America totally ignore" Native society? She does not expect mainstream America to understand Hopi governing systems, which include the tribal council system imposed by the federal government as well as other approaches. "At my village, we still recognize the traditional leader, the *kikmongwi*. Other villages have chosen to elect a governor. And the representatives to council are made in various ways. They all come together and try to hash things out—we are very complicated!"

But basic matters, she feels, should be basic knowledge to all Americans, including fellow journalists. Take freedom of the press. "It doesn't exist in Indian land, so get over it!" she said, in mock frustration. "I used to tell this to reporters in my newsroom and producers, everybody. Act like you're going to Mexico. Act like you're going to Canada. Act like you're going to some other country, because that's what you're doing when you step onto federal Indian land. *Sovereign* land. They have their own laws. Yeah, they can take your camera away. Hey, guess what? They can destroy your notes. You don't have the protection of the U.S. Constitution."

Native journalists, including Patty, have pushed for freedom of the press on reservations anyway. "We're telling tribal leaders, 'Our traditional ways, we had freedom of the press, so what's wrong now? How come you don't learn?'" Even though she understood the situation, it continued to frustrate her. She e-mailed, "Many times tribal leaders won't even bother returning our phone calls requesting interviews or information. . . . It seems some tribal leaders are fearful of exposing too much negative information, but they don't realize that if journalists can't expose the problems, they will continue to grow and hurt Indian people. Here's an example: Jack Abramoff. It was a journalist who noticed some irregularities and started asking questions . . . it led to uncovering his terrible deeds."

The e-mail continued: tribal matters such as these should be taught in schools. "That's my main point! Not just for non-Native people, but for Indian people, too! Many Indian people don't even think why the appointment of the Supreme Court Justices is so important! Or why we should fight to get more Natives appointed to the federal judgeships. We need to care!"

Maybe, just maybe, such knowledge would help bridge the "huge disconnect from Native life and mainstream society," a disconnect Patty memorably experienced in San Diego.

"When I was at Phoenix Indian High School, we had some foreign exchange students from different parts of the world. It was really great, because they lived in the dorms with us. We took them around. Part of their experience was to come to boarding school and meet the Indians. They came with very open minds." She recalled students from Turkey, Iran, and Sweden. "They loved learning about all the tribes and the language and everything else. They did not prejudge us; they did not have stereotypes about us." As part of the exchange, Patty's school selected a few Native students, including her, to visit schools the foreign students were attending in San Diego.

"These are our *American* brothers and sisters who lived one state away from us. We're going from Phoenix, Arizona, to San Diego, California. The year is 1978. We get in vans and drive over to San Diego to go spend a week there. We were paired up with a family to host us. I remember being all excited. San Diego, the beach, cool!

"When I got off the van and got paired up with my host family, my first thought was, this is going to be a long week. They just stared at me. They didn't talk much. They put my stuff in their car and pretty much drove me home in silence. I kept thinking, 'What's wrong? They don't like me?' They showed me where I was going to stay with my host sister. She still wasn't talking to me and wasn't being very friendly. I stayed in the room. I unpacked.

"Their youngest son had some sort of learning disability. He was in a special school. That was a Sunday. They were having dinner with him and were going to take him back to the special school. His name was Christopher. Little Christopher is sitting next to me and blurts out, 'Well, she can speak English fine,' or something to that effect. I said, 'What?'

"He said, 'They told me that you couldn't speak English. That you couldn't do this and you couldn't do that.' He started spilling the beans. 'You look like we do. You have blue jeans on.' The whole family was horrified. The mother was trying to get him to be quiet. But he's got this learning disability. He's being very honest."

Christopher's outburst "broke the ice. Then I found out the head lady organizing this exchange had brought all the families together and said,

'You're going to be hosting these Indian kids who have never been off the reservation, who have never probably seen a mall or have gone bowling, so these are some of the things you might want to take them to. You might want to introduce them very carefully, because they probably don't speak English very well.'

"I'm sitting there like, 'I bowl a good game, okay? And I've been to the *mall*.' I couldn't believe it. It was *San Diego*. This is not ancient history," Patty all but sputtered. "It's recent. Since then, I've had questions like, 'If you're a member of your tribe, does that mean you're not a U.S. citizen?' 'No, I have dual citizenship.'"

She took a long breath.

CHAPTER 10

The Former President

CLAUDIA VIGIL-MUNIZ (JICARILLA APACHE)

Claudia Vigil-Muniz suddenly jumped to her feet.

She was among a hundred or so Native women attending a conference at the Gila River Indian community's Wild Horse Pass Resort and Casino outside Phoenix. For days, the women had gone to workshops such as "Understanding Tribal Budgets" and "Rising Impacts of Meth" in Indian Country.[1] The stated theme changed each year, but the unstated one remained constant: Native women are wonderful.

Accordingly, at today's conference luncheon, a designated woman from each table extolled her tablemates in particular and Native women in general. At the table of Claudia Vigil-Muniz, though, something else happened. Radiating fervor, Claudia—a compact middle-aged woman in blouse and skirt, practical haircut, practical shoes—introduced herself as the former president of the Jicarilla Apache Nation. Then she challenged the unstated theme.

"We women can be each other's worst enemies." If it were not for certain women, she told her startled audience, she might still be president.

———

The Jicarilla Apache Indian Reservation in northwestern New Mexico is mostly forested and mountainous. In early March, swaths of snow covered the land, but the roads were clear, the skies crisp, and—apart from smells of oil—the air clean. In a valley within the landscape lies the reservation's sole town, Dulce, which contains tribal headquarters and most of the reservation's 4,000 residents. It also contains a modern supermarket, a success of former president Vigil-Muniz's administration, new spiffy-looking schools, a small tidy library, and a public gym in which, one afternoon, plump older women chatted on stationary bikes while young men lifted weights. A few blocks away, empty used FEMA trailers were positioned near abandoned houses whose roofs were caving in. Throughout Dulce, the inhabited homes ranged from run down to kept up. Many barking dogs were chained or not. Toward one end of town stood the tribally owned Best Western motel, which includes a small casino. Steps from the motel was what? The Apache House of Liquor?

Most reservations ban the sale of alcohol, for reasons underscored in Dulce. One young man in leather biker clothes, his handsome face pock-marked, his body swaying, held out a hand to me and said he'd found Jesus. What would Jesus do? I shook the hand. Apache House of Liquor, indeed.

Dulce seemed a place of uneven and uneasy circumstances.

Sitting alert in the Best Western lobby, nearly three years after her memorable flair of dissent, Claudia Vigil-Muniz looked as I remembered her, although slacks and sweatshirt replaced skirt and blouse. Her lovely brown eyes were as intense as before, her honey-colored skin as unlined and un-made-up, and at fifty-three her dark hair showed no gray. Over the next few days, we met when her work schedule permitted, including in her Dulce living room, which featured, next to a large flat screen television, a larger—indeed enormous—buffalo head, its eyes the size of bowling balls. Unable to stifle romanticized images of yore, I asked if pursuit of the buffalo had been difficult. "No," said Claudia, "we just drove up and shot it." The Jicarilla Nation owns a game park.

Claudia also talked to, from, and during dinner in Pagosa Springs, Colorado, fifty miles to the north, her husband Bill at the wheel of his Toyota. The distance was nothing, they shrugged. Perspective counts; Claudia's great grandmother carried her grandson on her back four hundred miles in 1888 when fleeing Mescalero Apache territory in southern New Mexico. "That's *our* longest walk," Claudia said.[2]

Mostly, over my visit of several days to Jicarilla, Claudia talked in her small van, which afforded privacy and an exit from town. Her discomfort in Dulce was palpable; it was where her political enemies still lived. One, a large man with a long ponytail, had rushed past us in the motel lobby. "I could sense it was bothersome to him." Another adversary and Dulce resident was a woman who was "very adamant about getting me out. I don't know what I've ever done to this woman." Claudia boldly did try to find out. "She was standing there and she was shaking. In our language, she says, 'I hate her *sooo* much.' I walked up to her. 'What did I do? Did I take your husband?' In our culture, that's the first thing you ask. 'What do I have of yours?' She walked off. Even to this day whenever she sees me, she completely avoids me." Why? "I still don't know."

Before Claudia seemed ready to talk about what I specifically had come to hear, she suggested a tour of the reservation. It began in Dulce with a point of personal civic pride. "That's our trash disposal facility," Claudia said, pointing out the window. "Under my administration, this has been the number-one thing we had to get in, our waste water and drinking water delivery system." The next stops were on higher land. She parked before a handsome two-story building cresting a hill. "That's our new clinic. That was built under my administration." She spoke in detail about it being built under a joint powers of leasing agreement with the Indian Health Service, that the building measures 52,000 square feet, how patients' medical records are kept and usage rates determined, that it contains departments for "behavioral health," a pharmacy, an emergency room, x-ray rooms, an eye clinic, and space to expand, if necessary, into a dialysis facility. She pointed to the second story. "This is all dental. So when you sit in the dental chair, you could look out and see these beautiful mountains."

We finally got out of the van and entered the clinic. The lobby resembled an enormous masonry and glass tipi, artfully embellished with tribal references. Steps away was a small prayer/meditation room.

"We opened up in November of 2005. I was out by then," said Claudia evenly. "But I was asked to participate in the opening. My name is on that plaque by the door." "Claudia Vigil-Muniz, President," reads the plaque at the entranceway.

"Claudia Vigil-Muniz, Executive Director, Department of Education," reads her business card now. "I'm in charge of Early Head Start and Head Start. The library, Department of Youth, the language program, scholarships for higher education, the audio-video, the Community Education Learning Center." She also heads the federal education programs, she said, including education specialists and researchers. "The way I see it, my role is to help the directors keep their people in line because of that chain of command. As things come up the ladder, when it gets to my level, I have to figure out where does it go and how do we get this resolved. That's what I'm doing right now, but my stupid computer—it had a glitch last night. We had a power surge."

The glitch, which she remembered on a road out of Dulce, led to her unfavorable opinion of the local power company. "We get all of our power source from an independent company called NORA [Northern Rio Arriba] Coop. They've been playing mind games with us." The tribe was considering setting up its own power company, she said.

Driving on, she pointed out ill-planned projects by HUD and BIA. "For some reason, the people from Albuquerque area always thought and still think, we're equivalent to Zuni climate." Zuni Pueblo, south of Jicarilla, lies mostly in a desert. "They give the specs for the roads and the houses. Both of them are worthless. The roads have fallen apart," she said, shaking her head. As for the houses, they initially had flat roofs. In the mountains, yet.

She was upset, too, that the Jicarilla tribal council had just fired a particular planner. "We got things accomplished with that man. He knew his stuff." She fumed, as she had to tribal council members who opposed him. "You guys are so stupid. You guys are *dumb*. People don't care if you don't like [him]. It doesn't matter."

It was clear that Claudia Vigil-Muniz, out of elective office, was not out of the fray.

———

The Jicarilla were one of nine Apache bands that migrated from Canada between A.D. 1300 and 1500, according to the tribal Web site. The best-known Apaches, at least to non-Apaches, were Cochise and Geronimo, of the Chiricahua band.³ "We're all different," Claudia said. For centuries, the bands more or less coexisted because there was so much land. Arguments or strained hospitality could be solved by moving on within the vast territory the Spanish called Apachería. (The word Jicarilla is Spanish too, for "little basket.")

The Jicarillas commanded roughly the lower third of present-day Colorado and the upper third of present-day New Mexico, as well as western parts of Kansas, Oklahoma, and the Texas panhandle. Because people lived far apart, they saw each other maybe once every three months, Claudia said. "The relationships were good. They cooperated with one another. My father told us this story about when their barn burned, people came from all parts of the reservation." They brought their wagons, their tools, their horses, set up camp, cut trees, dragged them back by horse, and rebuilt. "He says, 'We got our barn back.'"

"There's our elementary school." She pointed to a modern building ahead. "The view is so gorgeous. I just love it." Gorgeous it was. Snow- and tree-covered mountains sloped to valleys, pastures, and a river, vistas all untouched by the less than felicitous human hands that fashioned Dulce. Claudia's mood improved the farther away she drove. Look, a golden eagle!

Twenty miles from Dulce, we reached flatter land. "This is our feast grounds," she said happily, indicating a grassy area. "It comes to life." Every September, it is the site of a major event, the Jicarillas' footraces by the tribe's young men. Young women do not race "because we bleed."

The race begins with four older runners, including Bill Muniz. "When they get near the kiva and cross an imaginary line, the head runners are released. They run full speed." Runners come from the Jicarillas' two clans, white and red. White represents mountains and meat. Red, to which Claudia belongs, represents lowlands and vegetables. The track represents the world, the runners various animals, the laps the seasons. When the race is over, people know if it will be a good year for hunting meat or for growing vegetables and what kind of weather to expect. "RED CLAN WON! Which means another wet winter with lots of snow!" Claudia e-mailed.

The races are a remnant of Jicarillas' history, the reservation a remnant of their domain. In the nineteenth century, the combined force of the United

States government and its favored citizens, ranchers, were squeezing the Jicarillas out. On the ranchers' behalf, the government displaced the Jicarillas five times in fifteen years, asserted Robert Nordhaus, a New Mexico lawyer. One trek, he wrote in *Tipi Rings: A Chronicle of the Jicarilla Apache Land Claim*,[4] was marked by hardship, smallpox, and six deaths. It led to Fort Stanton, the Mescalero Reservation in southern New Mexico, where the Jicarillas were unwilling to go, and where they were unwelcome. "Our people don't get along. We fight too much," said Claudia.

The government provided for the Jicarillas at Fort Stanton so miserably, New Mexico's acting governor in 1854 reported, that they had to steal or starve to survive. A military observer wrote, "If they have to starve and freeze they prefer to do so elsewhere." (The Mescaleros, meanwhile, were pretty miserable themselves.)[5]

As soon as the Jicarillas trudged back north to putative reservation land, "powerful interests (settlers and stockmen) once again forced their removal to the Mescalero Reservation," wrote Nordhaus. It was not a good time to be on the move; in 1864 the Arizona Territorial Legislature adopted a resolution to kill all Apaches.[6]

The Jicarillas' struggle to secure some of their land included the help of Claudia's great grandfather Augustine Vigil. "The story goes that he translated from Jicarilla to Spanish to the German man who was the trader here. The German man translated it into English, to Congress. That's how they negotiated this property."

The Jicarilla Reservation, made official in 1887, is part of the original homeland, but only a fraction of it. The question of compensation arose. The Jicarillas essentially told the government, we never sold our other land to you, there is no ratified treaty, and we have always been here. The government said to point three, prove it. Then we can talk money. Enter the research of anthropologist Frank C. Hibben.

Decades earlier, Hibben had explored the territory with two "Jicarilla gentlemen," as Claudia referred to them. Along the way, he noted tipi rings, a circle of stones that held down buffalo hide–covered tipis. When the Jicarilla moved their tipis to another campsite, the rings remained. Hibben cited more than eighty tipi-ringed campsites and villages, thus proving the

Jicarillas had lived and hunted where they said they had, and for centuries.[7] "In addition to that," said Claudia, "the bones of the animal that is butchered? Jicarillas are the only ones known to kind of repackage it and give it back to nature. Some of these bone remnants, the skulls, everything, were found in bundles, which determined that was Jicarilla territory."

Once the Jicarillas' original acreage was established, the question centered on how much they should be paid for leaving it. The Indian Claims Commission actually ruled at one point that the U.S. government had no liability, because "prior sovereigns," Spain and Mexico, had been in power. Nordhaus, hired by the tribe to get as fair a deal as possible, kept working. In 1970, the commission calculated the value of lost land, more than nine million acres, at $9,950,000. That was a little more than a dollar an acre in 1883 dollars. "My father always reminded us we were *only*, as he put this"— Claudia gestured with outstretched hands—"*only* given ten million dollars for what we thought was our land."

Even more outrageous, the federal government then asked for $2,189,850 back "for expenditures made by the government for the benefit of the Tribe." The lawyers reached a compromise, tribal members approved it, and in 1972 Congress signed off—almost a century after the reservation was established.

No wonder the Jicarilla people, including Claudia, are reluctant to leave.

The land has its drawbacks. The soil contains too much clay for good farming, although Claudia's grandfather had success with some crops, including corn and potatoes, and her grandmother put in a vegetable garden. It does have an abundance of water. And it proved to have an abundance of oil and natural gas. The Jicarillas became the first tribe in the United States, asserted Nordhaus, to own and operate oil and gas wells on their own reservation—hence the fumes inhaled while stopping at a scenic overlook.

Money did not settle old scores.

Some people, said Claudia flatly, "don't like the Vigils. They just don't like us." Was it jealousy dating back to Augustine Vigil, or jealousy about Vigils getting good educations and good jobs? "For some reason we've always been treated like outcasts." For having too much, though, or too little? Claudia's mother, Ella Mae Vigil, had an upbringing so miserable,

Claudia did not want details made public. "My mother had a rough life and because of that she was pretty sensible. Because she didn't drink, that's what really saved us." Claudia's father, Nossman Vigil, an artist who designed the Jicarilla Nation shield and painted almost daily, "was an alcoholic during all the years we were growing up."

Raised mostly by an older brother after their parents died, Nossman Vigil did not come from an enviable situation either. He used to tell the children to learn all they could, including English, "so that nothing is taken away from us again. My father always told us, 'You have to remember where you came from. When the train tracks came down and when the rations were given out to the people, your grandmother had to sit there and sift through the dirt to get the flour out of it.'" The U.S. soldiers, he said, had slit the sacks open and thrown them on the ground. Her father also warned that the reservation might one day be rescinded, so be ready to survive without it.

Ella Mae Vigil's survival, or refuge, as Claudia put it, was the Dutch Reform Church.

The Vigil children, six girls and a boy, attended its social events from Christmas celebrations to skating parties, mostly with non-Natives. Through church missionaries, their mother helped sort shipments of donated clothes and was allowed to take first choice. "We were always dressed really nice, despite the fact that my father was never home half the time. It amazes me how we survived, because there was never any food." Claudia carefully noted exceptions: her father sometimes provided game, and her maternal grandparents butchered animals on trading days, to trade meat for produce that Pueblo Indians carried in on their backs. The Vigil children also picked piñon nuts and herbs, among other things, which their grandmother dried. "In the wintertime she would add water and we'd have instant berries, or instant pumpkin." Claudia's more prevalent memory, however, was that food was as scarce as comforts.

"We lived in a one room shack, literally. It was a nine-by-twelve building my father had bought. Before that they had lived in a tent." After land claims were settled, the family was able to get a house.

Of six Vigil daughters, only three are alive. Claudia is the second oldest. "We had a sister in between, but she died from an enlarged heart." The youngest died of a brain tumor. Decades later, the second youngest sister, Dawn Charmaine Vigil, who had succumbed to drug addiction, was found dead—murdered, said Claudia, a footprint found on her back. Claudia talked about the horror, and mystery surrounding it, mostly in the darkened car on the ride back from Pagosa Springs.

For a child of her circumstances, Claudia did have a remarkable adventure. When she was sixteen, she traveled to Europe with the music-oriented youth group Up with People. The invitation followed a local Up with People production and an interview, and came at a time of particular estrangement on the reservation. "I was always reminded of who I was and where I came from. A lot of times it was not done in a kind manner. It was done in a mean way. So when I was young, trying to fit in, it was hard at times." Her parents were mixed about the European adventure. Claudia's mother thought her too young. "My father was like, 'Let her go see the world.'"

Claudia went, along with a cousin, and toted less cultural appreciation than she later wished she had had. "It was like oh, Venus de Milo, okay." Europe did provide a memorable experience about the reputation of her own people. A host family in Antwerp invited her and her cousin to dinner because a family member had married a Vigil in the United States. "They showed us a picture of this man standing there and they kept saying, 'Vigil. Vigil.' We really couldn't communicate very well. The man was pointing [to the photo] and saying, 'Apache.' My cousin says, 'Yeah, Apache.'" Pointing to herself and Claudia, she repeated, "Apache."

"The man literally freaked out. He grabbed all the knives on the table. And the forks. We were kind of stunned. He didn't want us to have anything sharp because in his mind, what he knew of Apaches as Indian people, what he read about, was that they were vicious people."

Where did she think the reputation came from? Claudia laughed. "It's true! It's true!"

———

As an adult, Claudia compounded her unfavorable social status when, "to make matters worse, I married into another family, the Muniz family. They too aren't very well liked." The sin seems to include pride of accomplishment. "Well, I'm sorry if our children are educated." Claudia and Bill's two children, whom she did not want named, attended college. Their daughter, a firefighter with the BIA, lives with them. Their son, a radio sports announcer and would-be coach, lives outside Dulce with his Navajo wife and their two little boys.

Vigil and Muniz, ironically, were not even family names to begin with. Neither Claudia nor Bill has any known Spanish heritage. At some point, a government agent wrote down names of tribal members as he heard them, she said. Two years later, another agent took over but could not read the former agent's handwriting. "They were all in Apache. When he pronounced it, the people couldn't understand what he was saying. It's like they threw the whole thing out and decided, 'Okay, you're going to be a Velarde. You're going to be a Vigil. You're going to be a Largo. You're going to be a Vicenti. You name it. They're all Spanish surnames." Claudia has no idea what her ancestors' real names were. "So we got stuck with these names."

––––––

Claudia Vigil-Muniz's decision to run for president of the Jicarilla Apaches resulted from disappointment, rejection, moxie, resolve, frustration, and surprise, in roughly that order.

Decades earlier, when the tribal secretary repeatedly hired her high school dropout relatives rather than high school graduate Claudia, "I ended up working for Indian Health," whose director encouraged her to get a college degree. "I also worked for the Bureau of Indian Affairs. That's where I got most of my experience." In 1977, she found work in the BIA's forestry department, becoming one of its first two female firefighters, along with a sister-in-law. "We had to prove ourselves. We worked our butts off, but it was a good experience." Bill is now a firefighter with the BIA himself.

Troubles in the early years of their marriage, which she did not want spelled out, led to another career step. When their children reached school age, Claudia arranged to "acquire a skill" by getting a degree at the College of Santa Fe. "It became obvious that I could not support myself and my children. My husband was off doing whatever. I didn't tell him anything. My parents knew. I applied for a scholarship. I paid off all of our bills. I worked till the last day. That last day I asked him to come to a going away dinner. He didn't know what it was all about. He showed up. All the people I worked with gave me little going away gifts. He says, 'You quit your job?' I said, 'Yeah.' He said, 'What are you going to do?' I said, 'Well, starting Sunday you're going to have to be responsible enough to take the kids to your mother's house in the mornings so they can eat breakfast and catch the bus and then you pick them up at five o'clock.' He looked at me. 'Where are you going?' I said, 'I'm going back to school.' " It took her two years, she said, to convince him she was not seeing another man.

Her surprise decision had a positive effect. "The tables turned. I could see things happening. It put him in a different position. I found that my own strength helped me get to that point." He "changed his ways," she smiled.

Four years after entering the College of Santa Fe, Claudia was graduated at the age of thirty-one with a BA in business administration and a major in public administration. Among the proudest of her accomplishment was Bill. "He was just beside himself."

Despite "that joy, all that hard work," the family celebration was private, to tamp possible resentment by other tribal members. "No one knew that I had a college degree until I was inaugurated into office." She did cite her degree in asking for a raise from the tribe's finance department, where she worked after graduation. After being turned down and told a degree did not matter, she quit.

She started working in the education department, which she liked, but was "frustrated and so disgusted with everything that was going on" within the tribal government.

"Political Woes Hit Jicarillas" read a headline in the *Albuquerque Journal* of March 1998. New tribal council president Arnold Cassador, "who campaigned on a platform promising more openness, efficiency and accountability of tribal government," was at odds with the tribal council, whose actions he questioned. The council wanted to impeach him. (Cassador's predecessor resigned after charges that included being a "chronic abuser of controlled substances.") Cassador, continued the *Journal,* was "fighting an ill-matched legal battle against the tribe's virtually limitless financial resources."

Claudia was upset also about a personal matter. Her father had died, and she was mourning too long. "You have to get your crying done once and for all." Days are sanctioned. She was taking years. Complicating her emotions was the fact that in his older years he stopped drinking. A priest, who had often sobered him up and reminded him "about his family and his responsibilities and the gift that he received from Creator," frequently hired him to work at the church. While painting a statue of Mary, Nossman Vigil "had a spiritual experience," thought Mary spoke to him, and never drank again.

After his slow death from prostrate cancer, Claudia turned her grief into outrage that his pension, after many years working for the tribe, totaled only $9,000. The outrage led to reforms in tribal health insurance packages. Yet tribal problems were enormous.

"By 1999, we had a council that was pretty bad. Things seemed so depressing, and it didn't help I was still grieving. It created some health problems for me as well. By the time 2000 came around, I decided I need to do something else." One day in May, as Claudia stood at the copy machine at work, preparing for a trip to Portland, pondering law school, and wondering whether the tribe would help pay tuition—she remembered the moment—"one of the girls that worked in another department approached me."

" 'Claudia. What do you think about running for office?' I looked at her and I went, 'Yeah *right.*' "

"Office" meant president of the tribal council. That meant president of the Jicarilla tribe.

The job is both prestigious and not. A product of the federal government's Indian Reorganization Act of 1934, however well meant by its authors, who included Indian Affairs commissioner John Collier, the tribal council system remains controversial. Washington bureaucrats liked it. With an IRA tribal council headed by a president, "Take me to your leader" became a simplified command. Many tribes, however, preferred various systems they had worked out over the centuries for their own needs. In short, being elected president of the Jicarilla Apache tribe was an honor but was not like being Geronimo.

"I froze. She says, 'I've got the money in my pocket and I'll put the money up for you.' I'm like, 'You're kidding me!' That day was the deadline. She says, 'There's nobody running against this individual [Rodger T. Vicenti, who replaced Cassador.] We got to do something.'"

Claudia asked for time. She went home and talked to Bill. His answer was an adamant no. The job destroys families. "I looked at him and thought, 'Okay, you feel that way.' I went across the street and asked my mother." Her response was, you know what to do. "At the same time she says, 'But let's check and make sure.' I went around to different elders. They were all happy about it. 'You have our blessing.' One person even said a prayer for me right there. I went back. This is quarter to twelve. I told her, 'My answer is yes.'"

When Claudia returned from Portland, she was primed. She started planning strategy and goals with five other like-minded tribal council candidates. The Jicarilla tribal council has ten members, whose four-year terms overlap. "We had a lot of meetings. We couldn't really do it here at home because we were being watched, so we would meet a lot of times off the reservation. Tribes are sovereign. Because there's sovereignty, they think they can do whatever they want, which is technically true. But a lot of times they do things in a fashion that is not really acceptable to the rest of the United States. There's no real freedom of speech, no real freedom of congregation."

The strategies worked.

"Associated Press—July 19, 2000—DULCE—The Jicarilla Apache tribe has elected Claudia Vigil-Muniz as its new president, ending several years of political turmoil on the northern New Mexico reservation."

Claudia's inaugural address was largely in Jicarilla. (She and Bill speak it at home and to their children, who understand it but do not speak it fluently. She said they need to be surrounded by it and are not.)

Early press coverage was favorable. "First Woman to Head the Jicarillas Carries Sense of Patriotism," said the Associated Press in May 2001. "More than six months into Vigil-Muniz's term, the Jicarilla Apache Tribe has changed its name to the Jicarilla Apache Nation, placing a new emphasis on its sovereign independence. The nation has also celebrated the addition of more than 5,000 new acres to its reservation trust land. . . ."

In August 2003 the AP reported, "The Jicarilla Apache Nation has become the first tribe in New Mexico to take advantage of a new state Board of Education rule that lets tribes decide for themselves who is competent to teach their native language. Jicarilla Apache President Claudia Vigil-Muniz recently signed an agreement. . . ."

It seemed that all of Claudia's education and work for the Jicarillas, paid and unpaid, from being on the radio board, the housing board, the school board, the powwow committee, not to mention employment in Indian Health Service, finance, and education, was being put to use. She even did some historical housecleaning after a staff member discovered a closet crammed with documents—plans, drawings, blueprints, maps—some in Spanish, some dating from the time of the Louisiana Purchase. Recognizing their value, Claudia put them in a safe. Also in the closet were "some really nice paintings that my father had done. One of that rock right there," she pointed out the car window to Dulce Rock. "I washed it and I cleaned it off." She hung the painting in her office, along with a couple others. They were part of her downfall.

When Claudia became president, two council members "from the old regime" opposed her. "You could feel the tension." With the 2002 election of several new tribal council members, the situation worsened. "That group was so arrogant. They did not greet any of my staff. It wasn't even a 'Good morning.'" One new member, said Claudia, "got herself elected to get me removed as president."

The clash was on. Before long, some members were encouraging Claudia to do things she objected to. "Council was trying to get me to be flown around the country by this private jet, by somebody that was catering to the tribe. 'No. I won't.'" The pressure continued. Around September 2002, "I got chased" to a meeting in Chicago after the tribal council "demanded" that she go. At the meeting, "I was wondering what am I doing here?" The answer was not immediately clear. "They introduced some oil people and they introduced a geologist." The tribal attorney and the BIA regional director arrived too, she recalled, as puzzled as she. Finally, a tribal councilman announced that he and others had met with an oil company that earlier had outbid the Jicarillas to buy back Jicarilla property containing oil wells. Turns out, she said, the company did not have enough money. So, the councilman announced, the Jicarilla Nation itself would raise a bond for $95 million, to help the oil company buy back the wells. "In cahoots" was her phrase for what seemed to be happening. "They took us for a ride. Even at that time I was leery. But everything was already lined up and ready to go. Paperwork was to be signed."

More than a year passed. Claudia's work as Jicarilla president continued, as did her uneasy relations with certain tribal council members. Then, on a trip to Washington, D.C., in January 2004, while crossing a street with Bill, "I froze. He looked at me and he goes, 'What's going on?' I said, 'Something bad's going to happen.'"

In her family, Claudia is known for her premonitions.

————

Claudia Vigil-Muniz's political troubles as president may have originated in old or new jealousies and may have increased over her impatience with special interests or substandard performances, but they topped out over one issue. It was her response to allegations she was hearing about the tribal police force. One allegation was that some officers raped female detainees. Claudia hired a director of public safety, Eric Frame, to discover the truth and act.

"What we were trying to do," she said, "was to get our law enforcement back in order in preparation for our new facility," the Ishkoteen Judicial Center. It was named for an outstanding tribal police officer of the past and was one of Claudia's proudest accomplishments. She did not want it tainted.

Frame "had years of experience. He was a nonmember, but he was willing to help us and train people." His investigations into the allegations led to his firing two officers. The tribal council, no longer comprised of a pro-Claudia majority, responded in a fury. "The council fired him. They took it upon themselves. They were micromanaging. And they wanted him to leave the reservation." Frame's dismissal is "what kicked off everything."

The *Albuquerque Journal* returned. "Apaches at Odds over Police," read a February 2004 headline. "There's a power struggle between the legislative and executive branches over the tribal police department on the Jicarilla Apache Nation, its director of public safety said. Describing 'corruption' within a department he oversees, director Eric Frame said police officers have been fired, re-hired and fired again for offenses like drunken driving, using excessive force and mishandling drugs seized as evidence. . . . Frame said he was hired by President Claudia Vigil-Muniz to clean up a police department." The article quoted Frame as saying he had "to remove all investigative materials off the reservation to a safe place" and has been fired and rehired three times.

Claudia went outside again. She appealed to then vice president Dick Cheney. " 'Mr. Vice President, please understand that our situation is not stable and an immediate federal presence is essential,' " said the *Journal*. Cheney reportedly passed her letter to the Justice Department and the Bureau of Indian Affairs. The *Journal* named the two officers, both non-Natives, fired by Frame and added that a BIA report included nearly four hundred signatures by people who say one officer's "abusive treatment of tribal members has been long-standing ever since he was first employed with the tribe."

Charges of corruption in tribal police forces were not unique to the Jicarillas. In a 2007 *Denver Post* series about high crime rates on reservations and the maze of understaffed and overlapping law enforcement entities, one article cited problems with tribal police forces thought or known to be corrupt. The article included the Jicarillas.

Part of Claudia's dilemma was that none of the alleged rape victims would speak. "I don't know what these guys did to them, but they're all afraid to testify. We had hope of one fourteen year old. She's eighteen now. If she had stepped forward, everything would have fallen apart on everybody, and there would have been some people that would have gone to prison."

Absent testimony, the tribal council majority refocused its ire. "What they chose to do was to get rid of *me*, because I didn't enforce what the council had wanted to do—to fire this man and get him off the reservation. What I suspect is that Mr. Frame also found out some things about those council people they didn't want to get out."

"Jicarilla Council Locks Out Leader," headlined the *Albuquerque Journal* toward the end of February.

It was literally true, she said, perching on a stool in her living room. "I didn't have much time. There's a police officer standing there looking over me to make sure I didn't take anything, that I only took my stuff. We cleaned up as quickly as we could. My sisters came and my husband was there. My children were there. The mistake was not documenting it or signing off on it. Anyway, I left. I took those paintings and I took those baskets," which some women had contributed to her office décor. Everything else Claudia and her family threw into the across-the-hallway office of the tribal secretary, a friend.

One tribal member later struck an exceptionally low blow. "She went as far as accusing me, and convincing many people in the community, I stole my father's paintings." Claudia pointed to her living room's mostly bare walls, where she wants to hang some of her father's paintings. But "I refuse to do it because of what this woman accused me of. I'm afraid somebody will come into my house and either steal them or confiscate them and say they belong to the tribe."

The *Journal* article continued: President Vigil-Muniz has "been charged with negligence for asking for federal help from outside agencies and for failing to follow the council's orders." It quoted "Vigil-Muniz supporter Troy Vicenti" as saying, "We had a review of the police department several years back, and to find out that there was some corruption in the police department. And also some abuse and some police brutality, so to speak, on some tribal members." Claudia's spokeswoman Stacey Sanchez was also quoted. "I got the heck off the reservation because it was getting spooky up there."

The tribal council's next step was to do to President Claudia Vigil-Muniz what an earlier council had done to President Arnold Cassador. Even the template was the same, said Claudia. The maddeningly imprecise charge was "malfeasance."

"Jicarillas Plan Impeachment Vote," announced the *Albuquerque Journal.* "The president of the Jicarilla Apache Nation was scheduled to face impeachment charges by the Tribal Council today, a situation she says was generated by her drive to rid the tribe's police department of corruption."

On March 4, 2004, the tribal council voted five to three for impeachment.

———

"Our culture has developed into this society where it's like people are out to get you. They want to see you fail. When I got removed from office, my mother told me, 'You keep your head up high and you walk among your people. You didn't do anything wrong.' But people have a tendency to make you feel like you were the crook and you were the criminal and therefore you have to hang your head." Holding her head high proved all but impossible. "I knew I was really depressed because I, my pattern . . ." She finally got out the words. Her bedroom became her cave. "I'd get up and I'd move around, but it was just motion. I didn't even cry. I lost all my emotion. I detached from everything. My younger sister took me to Pagosa Springs. She wanted to go try to cleanse herself, so we went to the falls up in Wolf Creek Pass. She cried. I just sat there and I watched her. Yet I'm the one that's very emotional. I'll cry at a movie or whatever. I don't have that anymore."

After months "moping" in her cave, months including eating a lot and not exercising, Claudia went to a doctor, gave a blood sample, and learned she was borderline diabetic. The diagnosis shocked her into life. She went to a naturopath, who gave her massage and acupuncture treatments, put her on a regimen of colon cleansing, and a new diet. "We're still in the process, changing to a lot of whole grains, a lot of fruits and vegetables, cutting back on the meat." Despite homage to the new diet, temptation is not far. After the reservation driving tour, Claudia stopped at the stand of an enterprising Pueblo Indian couple who drive to Dulce almost daily to sell items like home-baked bread and burritos. Claudia settled on a well-named Frito pie.

What helped her as much as the mostly better new diet was going with a sister to visit a medicine man. "We would sit in the tipi with him. We'd listen to him sing and watch the kids dance. That whole summer, I went to I don't know how many ceremonies. He told us a lot of stories, and he would invite me to his house. I got to know him and his wife very well. I love to hear him talk. I always ask him to talk to me in Jicarilla so I can practice. He has the real old language and the true language. Some of our pronunciations are

lost. They tell us we sound like a white man trying to speak our language."
She recalled her grandfather—the boy carried to the Jicarilla Reservation by
his grandmother—speaking no English to the day he died, at 106. His
Jicarilla was so old, even Claudia's father had difficulty translating. The
grandfather chided them all. "'We have a word for every color that exists,
but you guys don't know that. You guys only know the language today
where things are clumped together.'"

Jicarilla is difficult, Claudia acknowledged. There is a glottal sound hard
to master. A number of basic English words, like "sorry," do not exist. "To
apologize to someone, we would run on and talk about everything else and
how we feel. It's supposed to define 'sorry.' But there's no one specific word
for it." She looked sad. "We're taught that if our language goes away from us,
we die as a people. Our children only hear the words. They don't understand
the depth of what it truly means. They live literally in the white man's world.
Everything they know is material."

Meanwhile, what about the two officers?

Claudia said the council later "recanted, and they rethought it and they
got rid of them anyway. But the individuals still exist here." They do not
work as police officers, yet are employed on the reservation. "From what I
was told, last July [one of the two] raped one of the co-workers in the department. I've been waiting for that family to come forward. Nobody has. But
guess what? Yesterday the young lady they're talking about was sitting in the
lobby at the tribal building with a brand-new baby." Claudia looked closely
at the baby. "She doesn't know that I know. This is real strange. One of the
relatives was drinking and called me. In her drunken state, she told me
everything. 'What are you going to do about it?' I said, 'I can't do anything
about it, because I'm not in *any* position. What are *you* going to do about it?'
When I see her, she's hesitant to talk to me. She knows she told me a little bit
too much."

———

Some five years after the headlines, Claudia Vigil-Muniz seemed as involved
in, or concerned about, the Jicarilla Nation as ever. She mentioned numerous topics troubling her, from the Nation's being "locked in to a situation

where we don't get much for our oil," to per caps, the blessing and curse of wealthy tribes. How much is too much for an individual to receive per capita from a tribe rich in natural resources or, less relevant to Jicarillas, casino income? The Jicarillas also have tribal trust funds for young people. How and when should the money be distributed? The Jicarillas are considering an idea adopted by their neighbors in Colorado, the Southern Ute: not granting the trust until high school graduation or a certain age. "You have to think like a parent."

Another concern was identity. Outsiders address her in Spanish, as they did her father. He answered in Spanish and did not bother correcting them. "Now it's more important for us to keep our identity, so we try to wear our beadwork and things like that [to] distinguish us as being different," even though non-Natives in nearby Farmington still mistreat Native people, she said. "To other nationalities, all Indians look alike."

Intertribal relations worry her too. "As tribes we don't stick together. I've seen it even at NCAI." Some tribes will talk openly about an issue, but "others will talk about it in their own languages. There's no real togetherness like there should be." Then there is the matter of infighting among the Jicarillas. "That's the hardest part. We take a step forward, but we take ten back. That's so frustrating because the potential for the progress we could make is enormous."

Alcoholism is obviously a problem that troubles her too. So, what is with the Apache House of Liquor? Her answer stunned me. A railroad used to run through the reservation to various off-reservation towns, including Lumberton, where many people, including her father, went to drink. "Understand, they had to walk to get there. They walked on the railroad tracks" for several miles. After many, many people walking to and from Lumberton liquor stores got killed by trains, a tribal chairman pushed for a liquor store on the reservation. It was such a success reducing train-related deaths that a bigger store was built. "That's the Apache House of Liquor."

———

Amid everything happening on the Jicarilla Reservation, it was clear that Claudia cared intensely about its governance. Being on the sidelines was not easy. Regarding certain new council members, "what really gets me is that

overnight, when they get elected and put into office, they're these individuals that know everything. They're making decisions on our behalf on
finances, that they have absolutely no idea about." Same thing with legal
issues. "It's so frustrating because in my opinion, they don't have what it
takes to fill that capacity."

"The reason why it was so traumatic for me when I was removed is
because it made me feel I didn't complete my mission. It left me hanging.
I started a task, but I didn't finish it. I'm still trying to cope with it and deal
with it the best way I know how." She believes her enemies suffer too. "The
people that removed me walk around with a lot of guilt and regret. Because
what they did to me, in turn, they did to themselves. I've been told, in my
traditional belief, I was removed from the picture to be protected from
something that wasn't meant for me. That I can accept. I can deal with it.
That's what has kept me moving forward."

She was again considering law school.

CHAPTER 11

Practicing Medicine

HARRISON BAHESHONE (NAVAJO)

"I'll formally introduce myself, as is tradition in Navajo. My name is Harrison Baheshone. I am of the Rock Gap clan. Tsédeeshgizhnii is my mother's maternal clan. My father's clan is Kin Yaa'áanii, Towering House clan. My grandfather on my mother's side, they're Chishi Dine'e, which is the Chiricahua Apache clan. Then on my paternal side it's the Tl'aashchi'I, Bottoms Red People clan, which are closely related to the Many Goats and the Many Mules clan. I am originally from a place called Coalmine Mesa, which is about thirty minutes east of Tuba City, Arizona."

––––––

The ceremony would take place on the Navajo Nation in the hogan of the Goldtooth family, relatives by clan to the medicine man, by blood to the patient. Directions, which the fastidious medicine man Harrison Baheshone sent by e-mail, included such instructions as "Enter cattle guard and turn diagonal east."

The Goldtooth Ceremonial Residence, as he labeled the eight-sided cement block and stuccoed hogan, was at an elevation of about 6,000 feet. The setting was desolate and gorgeous. A mile away, vistas opened into buttes and canyons, but the prevalent view here was flatness softened with scrubby grasses. About a hundred yards from the hogan was a combination cooking and sleeping building—upright split logs at one end, a trailer at the other, tires holding down a plastic and chicken-wire roof area in the middle. Walks away in two directions led to a wooden outhouse and a reclaimed Port-a-potty, its walls scratched with graffiti in Spanish. Apart from the four disparate structures, earth met sky in a straight line. The air was clean and thin, the peace embracing.

During a four-hour drive north from Phoenix to the hogan, I carried directions, fruit, a digital recorder, and a pack crammed with a sleeping bag. Nestled within was a triple-wrapped contribution.

"I think it would be a nice gesture to our family," Harrison had e-mailed, "if you could bring a small bottle of water. I usually prepare water from a natural spring. It would be great to use water that feeds into the great Pacific Ocean. You will need to offer a sacrifice to the deities and offer a prayer on behalf of our family. We make offerings such as corn pollen, corn meal, small jewels (white shell, turquoise, obsidian, jet), powdered mirage stone, etc. Pray that the water will provide cleansing, blessings, harmony, prosperity, and a good harvest for those that use it during the ceremony."

Days earlier, I had clambered under the Golden Gate Bridge onto slabs of broken concrete by water's edge, placed corn meal on one slab, prayed as specifically as I could, gathered Pacific water in a bottle, and avoided a uniformed guard training binoculars on me.

At the hogan, I stopped my car and bolted out. Seconds later a dark, trim man in jeans, baseball cap, and boots emerged from the cooking/sleeping shelter. Silence.

Years of Navajo protocol gleaned from the mystery novels of Tony Hillerman, I realized with chagrin, had eluded me. According to Hillerman heroes Lt. Joe Leaphorn and Sgt. Jim Chee of the Navajo Tribal Police, when a visitor drives up to a home, the visitor waits in the car for a few minutes. This gives those inside time to see who it is, collect themselves, and come outside leisurely.

At this man's silence, I regained a fraction of protocol and introduced myself, if without the majesty of maternal and paternal clans. More silence. There seemed reason to add that Harrison Baheshone invited me. Then, I'm looking for the Goldtooth residence.

"I'm Goldtooth."

Freddie Goldtooth led me from silent sunshine to the lively smoky shelter, where cooking for the ceremony was in full swing under the direction of his wife, Stella. An ample woman with a bad knee (she planned to get a new

one), she had a commanding presence even sitting. She is the youngest of
several sisters, someone later whispered, but assumes the role of the eldest.
More Navajo etiquette à la Hillerman was returning: shake hands softly, not
firmly, don't stare into another's eyes, and, a point of pan-Indian politesse,
shut up and listen.

The central cooking, eating, and relaxing area, into which gusts of red
dust flew each time the door was opened, featured a homemade metal oven
on the earthen floor. A fire blazed within. On the flat top, pots of coffee
boiled, skillets of potatoes steamed, and meats sizzled. Cinders occasionally
were shoveled out a foot or so into the room, a grate placed on them to
receive Stella's slapped circles of dough that became chewy tortillas.
Someone else was making fry bread. A large sack of Blue Bird flour dimin-
ished with each hour. Huge coolers fastened with duct tape held other pro-
visions. Bottles of water towered nearby. (There was no plumbing or well.)
In the coming hours and days, various family members placed food on the
room's long picnic table. Meals within the smoke-filled space seeming never
to begin or end, as generations were welcomed from morning into the night:
Stella's and Freddie's infant grandson laced into a cradleboard, energetic
toddlers and older children, a quiet boy with Down syndrome, a fuchsia-
haired teen, young adults overweight or lanky. In earlier days, young people
would be home tending livestock, I was told. The older people as a group
were slender, the eldest showing ramrod posture. The young people mostly
spoke English, the older mostly Navajo. (To a non-Navajo, one sentence
sounded like this: Navajo word Navajo word Navajo word Hannah Montana
Navajo word Navajo word.) Many visitors came to honor and acknowledge
the ceremony but did not enter the hogan. Therefore they never would see
the medicine man, who, except for outhouse forays, stayed within the hogan
from Friday evening to dawn Sunday.

The three-day Blessingway was to begin that evening, Good Friday, end at
sunrise on Easter, and had nothing to do with Jesus. Amid the foodstuffs
piling up in the Goldtooth kitchen area were a carton of Easter eggs and a box
of Easter-themed cupcakes, but those were for the children, later. Confirmed
a friendly young masseuse nicknamed Cee, here Easter is considered a
holiday for children, "but the real meaning, no." I thought of a photo

Harrison sent me of his baby wearing a Halloween pumpkin outfit, remembered a Native radio program dedicated to Valentine's Day, and wondered if any consumer group supports Americanized holidays more than Native Americans.

Close to sundown Friday, there was a cry, "Harrison's here!" A small crowd rushed outside to the hogan.

An SUV had pulled up. Harrison Baheshone got out and said good-bye to his wife and three young children, wiggling his fingers at the baby. They drove off to her parents' place, a good hour away, as he turned from the role of husband and father to that of medicine man.

Harrison, forty-two, is slim and stands straight, yet almost everything about him seems soft—his manner, his eyes behind glasses, his cheeks, his handshake, his voice, his unselfconsciousness. A year earlier in a Phoenix steakhouse, with fork and knife in hand, he closed his eyes and said a lengthy blessing (softly) in Navajo, finishing just before our waitress asked (not softly), "How you guys doin'?" After that lunch, it was back to work at the Indian Health Center in Phoenix. Harrison, who received a BS in graphic design at Arizona State with a focus on architectural design, is a facility planner there. One project he was overseeing was widening doorways so that obese patients in bigger wheelchairs can get through.

When he arrived at the hogan, Harrison was wearing casual clothes, including a baseball cap that read "Ireland." (Harrison seems quite fond of baseball caps.) The only cultural marker was his black hair, which he sometimes wears in a braid, but more often, when I have been with him, in a traditional bun called a *tsiiyeel*, the hair looped and bound at the nape of his neck with a strip of white cotton.

We were connected through a mutual friend, Randella Bluehouse, whom I met via INDN's List, a group that helps Native people run for elected office. Randella described Harrison as "a modern medicine man." This was true technologically. At his Phoenix office, he had handed me a computer printout that looked like a family tree. "That's lineage in the Blessingway." To guide me around the people depicted, he held a laser pointer, his tapered hand seemingly carved from a light brown stone. The laser's red dot first landed on his father, whose parents died of illness at a young age, leaving him in the care of grandparents, themselves medicine people. "He started as a young boy doing these ceremonies. One of the ceremonies that he did was the Blessingway. When he passed away, I started wanting to know more about it, so I started following different people around. Finally I met this lady here, Pearl," the red dot went to her name, "who was a clan sister to my father, that took me in and told me the ins and outs of the ceremony." Pearl Yazzie's pursuit of becoming a medicine woman was remarkable. "Even today there are certain ceremonies that females aren't allowed to attend or witness. It was more like a gentlemen's society. But she had a will to learn." As a young girl, Pearl sat outside a hogan, listening to those inside. "Eventually the men folk, they took her serious, so they started bringing her in. [My father] started taking her to different ceremonies."

Pearl Yazzie, whose name had been Aszda Lchee Horseherder until Catholic missionaries changed it, taught Harrison the Blessingway in "bits and pieces," then completely, using her own medicine bundle meant specifically for Blessingway. "She did the ceremony for me initially. Then she did it again when I started learning. When I had my bundles come together, I did one for her, as a final graduation-type thing, I guess. After that she said, 'Okay. You're on your own.'"

Harrison's laser dot moved up the page. "These people are back in the late 1800s. These are the real traditional people. Beyond that, we're carrying on what little we have. There's so much involved. Everything's got to be detailed out and the stories that goes within the prayers. They say that the Blessingway, xójǫ'-djí, is the backbone of all these other ceremonies," some of which are used "for pregnancy, some for the puberty ceremonies, some are for marriages and some for home blessings."

Under Blessingway also are subceremonies such as Monster Way. "The Monster Way ceremony is probably the one that's used for people coming or returning from war." Along with other tribes, the Navajo attempt to help traumatized veterans, including those from Iraq and Afghanistan, by holding ceremonies to vanquish their minds' troubles. "It parallels with the stories of the twins that went off to destroy the monsters. Two of our deities in the Navajo myth [are] hero twins that were created by the White Shell Lady, who gives birth to the twins to destroy these monsters."

White Shell Lady, more commonly known as Changing Woman, is the major force in the Navajo creation story, *Diné bahane,'* from whom the first clans are believed to have emerged. *Diné bahane,'* even in its English translation, is at times wildly sexual—appropriate for the subject of creation.[1] The creation story, or myth, as Harrison called it, encompasses all the ceremonies, including Blessingway.

His laser dot then went to his brother Frank, also a medicine man. Frank had died unexpectedly only weeks before at the age of fifty-seven, following an eye operation. Harrison clearly was affected by the death yet was trying to proceed according to tradition. "We buried the body on Saturday," he said in a low voice, "and we had four days after that. There are certain things you do. Four days, you can clean yourself, put certain things on, and get out amongst the community. That's when I returned to work. Navajos, our way's that you don't really deal with death. You don't talk about it. There were certain things said in that period you don't talk about at other times. Navajo elders, they talked about these things, what was done in the past. Things that are done a certain way for medicine people. How you act and what you say. How you dispose of his things and how you carry on." His voice became stronger, as if by effort. "All these other passings before, they never discussed it with me. This time around it's all this information coming in. 'This is it. You're the person to handle this for us now.'" The funeral was the first ceremony of its kind Harrison had done on his own.

———

Almost a year to the day after our laser-led conversations in Phoenix, he was about to perform the Blessingway—often known as a sing—for Michael Riggs, thirty-eight, a jovial, worldly, heavyset man. Michael was a nephew of Stella's and one of Pearl's fifty-seven grandchildren. Like Harrison, Michael grew up on the reservation. He worked for the World Health Organization in Washington, D.C., and had flown back for the ceremony.

That the medicine man worked for the Indian Health Service and the patient worked for the World Health Organization, both purveyors of medicine that had nothing to do with the kind about to be practiced, was one of many ironies I noted only to self.

Harrison thought Stella probably instigated Michael's sing, he told me later. "Most of the ceremonies in that family go through Stella, to keep things going good for [family members] and to give something back to the spirit, to say, 'Thank you for bringing me this far. I'm your grandchild, Grandmother Earth and Father Sky, and these different holy beings. I'm here to say thank you and help me to continue.'"

In the Goldtooths' hogan, whose door properly faces east and whose packed dirt floor properly symbolizes Grandmother Earth, a square iron woodstove crouched in the middle of the floor, a smokestack leading out the conical roof. Cedar logs were stacked nearby. A washstand stood to one side of the door. Lining the perimeter were a few chairs, a couch, a television that was never turned on, and mattresses of various thicknesses, some covered with quilts or blankets. By one wall was a china cabinet, whose plates Stella and I earlier scrubbed. Instead of using them, though, we ate on plastic dishes. On one wall, Stella had hung a photo of smiling and newly sworn-in President Obama. Michael did a double take, then said with a laugh, "Barack will witness my whole sing!"

The Blessingway ceremony, in a sense, began without ceremony.

As light from the hogan's two windows faded, someone turned on a kerosene lamp. Chatter turned to quiet. Harrison and Michael sat side by side on blanket-covered mattresses, their home bases for the next two days. Harrison had carried in with him a brown leather briefcase and red vanity kit, each repurposed to contain a medicine bundle. "One of them's more for the Protection Way," he later explained. "In these ceremonies, my approach is to get the evilness, the bad energy, the negative things that people are going through in their inner soul, their spirits, try to get that away from them. That's what one of the bundles is for. The other one is to promote blessings. Everything dealing with Blessingway." He had arrayed the contents of the first night's bundle on the floor in front of him, as orderly as operating tools. They included leather pouches with drawstrings, a bound bunch of sage. Confronting such formality, I was flummoxed about how to present my water properly. In a private moment, I finally said, "Here's the water," and handed him the bottle. He said, "Thank you." That was that.

In the early evening, people carried in a cavalcade of food, placing it on the floor in front of Harrison. The offerings included corn on the cob, mashed potatoes, chicken, ribs, many warm plump tortillas and rolls, pasta salad, and a dessert of strawberry and bananas in a sugary sauce. There was also a large container of fruit punch. What would have been served fifty years ago? Mutton and bread, someone answered. There seemed no proto-col about serving, although Harrison and Michael served themselves first. Younger people then filled up plates and passed them to the others. Conversation was entirely in Navajo.

Up to a point. Dinner eaten, dishes removed, Stella turned to Michael and asked in English, why don't you tell Harrison your situation and what you need?

Michael, who understands much Navajo but speaks little, talked for about ten minutes of his work, that he is moving higher in the organization as people retire, and has more exacting responsibilities, that he travels 40 percent of the time and encounters mostly people with AIDS, TB, malaria— a lot of dying. There are also challenges with foreign governments and fund-ing. Furthermore, his roommate lost his job, so Michael is paying rent for both. Poor Michael, I thought. This was, though, not the whole Michael; a social network page presents a Michael who likes "movies, good food, hang-ing with friends, bike rides, travel, music, politics, drinking beer, softball, shopping, reading, art"—and "dating men." That preference presumably was known to the group and irrelevant. Homosexuality is not the issue for Native people it is for others.

In the hogan, throughout Michael's frank and somber recital, Harrison listened attentively, nodding. He was now wearing a bandana headscarf, jeans with suspenders, a white shirt, ankle-high moccasins with silver but-tons, and impressive turquoise jewelry, including a ring and necklaces.

After Michael finished talking, Harrison began singing. And singing. The songs reverberated so deeply, I longed to keep them. In a pause between them, Harrison picked up a short stone pipe. A younger man lit a dried corn cob from the now crackling stove fire, passed it to Harrison, who lit the pipe and passed it around, clockwise. After an inhalation, then exhalation, people smudged themselves, passing the smoke over their heads with one hand, then inside their shirts, and down the front of their body, waving it along. Michael was not a smoker and coughed a bit when he inhaled, to the merriment of the group. Stella's impressive exhalation enveloped her like a cloud. Not until Cee, on my right, passed me the pipe did I realize with a start, I was not an observer of the Blessingway. I was a participant. She whispered, move the smoke to the parts of your body that might be sore, like your legs and back from your long drive today. (How did she know?) The smoke—which gave me, a nonsmoker, a lovely light and temporary buzz—smelled nothing remotely like that from commercial cigarettes.

"I use different types of tobacco," Harrison later explained. "The one on the first night was more for Protection Way. The primary ingredient, they call it Deer Ear. Then White Tip tobacco." It was a good sign, he said, that all seemed to enjoy the smoke with no ill effects. "In a different setting, different ceremony, people might get sick from it, and they start throwing up. People get headaches. It's the spirit that's working."

That first evening, when the pipe completed the circle back to Harrison, he emptied it into a bowl filled with water. The ashy liquid was passed clockwise around the room and sipped.

Between songs, he next passed a small pouch around the room. Each of the fifteen or so of us took out a stone arrowhead. "Do not drop it," whispered Cee, who had become my unofficial cultural translator. Each person passed the pouch to the person to the left, clockwise. After we all had an arrowhead, another bag was passed, containing gritty white powder. We put a little on each cheek, then on the arrowhead, and rubbed it toward the center of the hogan, then moved it in a clockwise circle. This was to help vanquish bad spirits weighing down Michael.

"That's all part of the Protection Way ceremony," said Harrison. The powder was a ground stone, resembling marble. "Symbolically we're going back in time to that setting where some of these things occurred. The powder is more to make ourselves transparent from those energies so they don't sense us, don't see us. So we're a ghost to them, essentially."

As Michael sat upright, cross-legged, a bandana around his forehead, Harrison continued singing and passed another pouch around the circle. Ground corn pollen, Cee whispered. The pouch was to be held in the left

hand, while the right dipped in, and placed a bit on the tongue, the top of
one's head, the rest scattered on the earth, to return it to the place from
which it came.

Not every moment was serious. Throughout the ceremonial rigor, which
ended about 10:30 P.M., a casual counterbalance hummed—one auntie
asking another to pass her a Diet Coke from a cooler, a toddler granddaughter in a Gap sweatshirt cuddled.

As people left for the night, I prepared to spread my sleeping bag in my
rental car, a type chosen for this exigency, but learned that one auntie and
I were to sleep in the hogan to keep the fire going. (Harrison and Michael
were not allowed to cook during the ceremony, nor tend the fire.) Logs near
the door were indicated. Not to worry, just wake up every two hours, I was
told. Right.

Then everyone was gone but us four, the kerosene light blown out. In the
stove's glow, I barely could see Harrison leaning back, one knee raised.
Michael, by flashlight, was reading. (It was Anita Diamant's *The Red Tent*,
about the biblical character Dinah.) The auntie, Marilyn, hefted a couple
logs onto the blaze and stretched out under a blanket. After wriggling into
my sleeping bag fully dressed, as were the others, I tried to set a mental alarm
clock. The only sounds were pages turning, logs popping, and, yes, snoring.
Sleep eluded me until sometime after I put more logs on the fire, about
two A.M. The next unofficial round of the ceremony was supposed to start
about five, with the making of breakfast.

Suddenly it was 6:30. The Stella-led aunties and others crashed in, wield-
ing a huge enamel coffee pot, bowls of scrambled eggs, tortillas, blue corn
mush, a plate of fruit. One then assertively poked the fire's embers. Uh oh.
Not only had I let it go out but had overslept and not helped. Stella was not
pleased.

The ceremony resumed after breakfast. Harrison again donned his silver-
buttoned moccasins and prayed in song. He then poured about a gallon of
red powdery sand from a plastic pail onto the floor. With a carved wooden
spatula, he smoothed it into what resembled an elongated key without the
notches—the key's circle about a foot in diameter, the key part about a yard
long. He worked deliberately, like spreading frosting, as all watched. On the

final form, about two inches deep, he sprinkled white corn meal in a triangle shape, attaching it in a line to another triangle shape in the opposite direction, then made two more. A sprinkled circle was divided into four quadrants with four X's. The triangle represented footprints, the lines connections between journeys.

The sand painting finished, Harrison touched different places of the hogan, by the door, the windows, the walls. Prompted by Stella, Michael stood, removed his shirt, socks, and pants, leaving on his briefs. Harrison took him by the hand and led him onto the sand, pointing out he was to step on each triangle, then turn in the circle.

Next, pulling out a disposable shower cap, Harrison placed it over a shallow woven basket, emptied San Francisco Bay water into a pail containing other water, and poured some of the liquid into the basket. He took a piece of yucca and beat it in the water until suds formed. With the sudsy water, he washed Michael's hair. Next, he gently put drops of it on the soles of Michael's feet, his legs, chest, back, his palm, jawline, and forehead. Stella took the remaining water to the side and washed her own hair in it, then the toddler's, who did not make a sound.

After the cleansing, Michael dressed. Another lengthy prayer recital followed, then Michael headed toward the door. He knew to leave in the clockwise direction, but Stella had to remind him to drape his blanket around his shoulders. When he returned, the morning prayers were complete.

The ceremony was slated to resume at midnight, with an all-night blessing sung until dawn.

People stood and stretched. Most left, although visiting in the hogan was allowed, even encouraged. Harrison seemed contemplative. He acknowledged he was thinking about the night to come, what prayers, what songs, what medicines would most benefit Michael. He was gearing this Blessingway specifically to "somebody that journeys a lot. There are certain prayers, certain songs that accompany a person in his status. It's a special thing for people that travel on the water, under water, and in the skies. It's to promote that blessing for what he does. I know he's been going through a lot." This ceremony's purpose was for Michael "to have a good journey, that he won't be inflicted by these negative energies and negative feedback he gets from people, like his co-workers or colleagues."

In the kitchen shelter, people ate leftovers, cooked, and visited. One auntie in the adjoining sleeping/supply room listened on a battery-powered radio to a gospel program in Navajo. Cee the masseuse rubbed people's backs or feet, Freddie stoked the fire, and Stella eventually set out a lunch feast including two hams and a stuffed turkey. Then, her knee paining her, she sat back and wondered out loud what to cook for dinner. She also parted with a few opinions, including that Tony Hillerman got a lot wrong in his mysteries. At some juncture, she asked what exact steps I followed to gather the water. Upon hearing the answer, she pursed her lips.

As the hours increased, the Goldtooths' slender son, a horse racer and father of the adored baby in the cradleboard, brought his horse in a trailer and rode around. Children played catch in the windy outdoors. Freddie Goldtooth, while surveying the scene, told me he is a mechanic for a power plant, and has an hour and a half commute. He parted with a few smiles like small rewards, but never was as garrulous as his relatives.

At one point, Michael joined the kitchen visitors, almost as if playing hooky. He said he wanted to go on a long walk, but Harrison told him no, stay near the hogan. Michael seemed the same—earnest and open. I barely dared ask, had he felt a moment of change? Yes, a sudden connection with the earth. Would he like me to record a song or anything? He looked aghast.

That afternoon, I drove Stella to her home in Tuba City, about fifteen miles away, to pick up supplies. The modest house was neatly crammed with paintings and photos. In the bathroom, decorated with framed jigsaw puzzles of fish, I availed myself of the bliss of warm water. The Goldtooths live in Tuba (from Hopi leader Tuve or Toova) but drive to the hogan as often as every evening for the beauty and peace. Tuba, like other reservation towns, can be a cacophony of "rez dogs," hot-rodding, and other noises.

At a Tuba City supermarket, having volunteered a side dish for dinner, I bought various vegetables, olive oil, and herbs. As my concoction simmered that afternoon atop the steel oven, the Navajos regarded it with polite curiosity and little interest. Next to it roasted slabs of steak Stella had vigor-ously cut from a massive part of a cow. Sitting at the long table, slapping more dough into rounds, she brought up her annoyance with English-only initiatives and bilingual ballots. Everything with *Spanish* she said, looking peeved. Navajo has been spoken for a thousand years here and someone wants to make English the official language, or accommodate Spanish speakers? Her pique moved to non-Natives who think all Natives are the same. They ask if we live in tipis, she snorted. "We never lived in tipis."

Another afternoon arrival, a Navajo language teacher, was piqued, too. Her parents do not speak a word of English she said, as if challenging me. She added, if you plan to be around Navajos, learn some words. (Neither she nor anyone else used the increasingly popular original word Dinéh, for Navajo.) She wrote down the common greeting, *Yá'át'ééh*, one of few expressions I knew. *Ya* means universe, she said, so the greeting is in essence "How is the universe and you within it?" I also know *bilagáana*, I said. It means foreigner. (Admittedly, I was alert for it.) The teacher was piqued anew, wanting me to use another word. What country are you from? she demanded. This one, I said. No, what country? Having recently done a Google genealogical search, I had found family on my father's and mother's sides back to 1660, before the trail led to England. Three hundred years American, I said. She dismissed that. What *country*? I gave up. Both my father's name, Owings, and my mother's maiden name, Roberts, are Welsh. Wales, I said. Where's that? she said, still annoyed. Europe, I said. Most of Europe is Germany, she replied, right? Michael, overhearing the exchange, strained to suppress a smile. Wales is not in Germany, I managed to announce to a now attentive table. Anyway, you're a *bééshbich'ahii*, she wrote out. Much nicer than *bilagáana*.

The grammar and geography interlude ended with the revelation that *hózhó*, the final word I knew, meant not only beauty but a state of grace and harmony.

Throughout the afternoon in the kitchen area came hints of *hózhó* divides—one auntie's daughter having problems, someone in Michael's family being absent, Harrison's 105-year-old grandmother (who still wove rugs and lived in Tuba) not attending because she is "a Christian lady." In a later conversation, Harrison spoke of her affectionately. "My grandma still digs roots, and she'll put her stuff together for certain ailments, if you have a tummy ache or if you have a headache or if your back's hurting. She has her own little recipes for certain things. She'll prefer that to sitting in the waiting room for hours. I hear she's not doing too well. She's facing skin cancer now, and I think her body's kind of shutting down on her. But what can we do? She's lived a full life and seen things most Navajos haven't seen. She's been around the world a couple times, been to Egypt, Jerusalem." That trip involved "becoming Christian and seeing where Jesus walked the land."

"The medicine bundle I have for Blessingway, that was made for her when she was young. Maybe early '70s or maybe the '60s, I think she turned to Christianity, so she gave that bundle to my mom."

Harrison's mother, born in 1924 as the first of several girls, is, unlike them, not Christian, mainly because she was not taken away to boarding school. "They hid my mom when the crew came by, because they wanted her to herd sheep. Some of her sisters they sent to school. She's had mixed feelings about that through the years. Sometimes she'd be mad at my grandma for not sending her to school. Sometimes she's okay with it, that she could carry on the traditional side."

Harrison's mother never learned English, although he and other siblings tried to teach her. "She didn't have any education at all. It's all traditional lifestyle." Her husband, Harrison's father, was a medicine man. "This was my father's full line of work" after retiring as a laborer. "Sometimes he'd be gone for weeks and weeks. She was home with her kids and had stuff to do." Harrison is the second youngest of eleven children, including two sisters from his father's first marriage.

In his family, beliefs are wide-ranging. Apart from his late brother Frank, also a medicine man, "I have a brother George that is familiar with it. Sometimes he'll come follow me, but he's more into the Native American Church, the peyote ceremonies." Another brother, "if he needs to have a ceremony done, he'll agree to it, but beyond that I don't think he would choose to go out to ceremonies." Of the sisters, some go to church, a result of boarding school experiences in which they lost much of their traditions. "It's not like they were away for a year. They were gone five years at a time." They managed, though, to keep both their language and their family ties.

"That's probably one of my blessings. We get along. I've heard horror stories about other families, that they're divided because of their spirituality."

Harrison himself went through a number of influences. In his early teens, he was baptized as a Southern Baptist and later as a Mormon, after his father sent him to Utah to get an education. "It was a Mormon family, a Mormon high school, a Mormon town, a Mormon state. Everything was Mormon." Then his father developed Parkinson's disease. "I went to go care for him. I stayed home with him for almost a year, caring for him and just had a yearning to know who he was." The time together was "a life-turning event for me."

Harrison started to learn how to be a medicine man. There were no formal lessons. "He was going through his own thing. It's not like he was sitting down with me and saying, 'I think this is good.' We didn't really have that type of a conversation. It's just caring for each other."

"My father used to always say there's different levels of ceremonies and spiritual wellness. There's those that think good things, they have positive outlook on things, and that's who they are. There's others that are brought down by some of these negative entities, evil entities. That's where some of these ceremonies play a role in ridding the spirits from them and bringing them back up. There's other ceremonies that are more [for] the mental, physical type people," and some for physical ailments. "We kind of grew out of that because of the modern-day hospitals. If somebody breaks a leg or cuts themselves, we send them off to the hospital. But back when my father was younger, he talked about somebody falling over in a sweat lodge, burning a hole in their side, so they relied on herbal medicine. He's brought people back. There were ceremonies for that."

"It's just like the medicine field. There's all these different professions and specialties." He listed some within the main branches. "There's God Impersonators branch. There's the Male Shooting Way branch. Then there's a Life Way branch, which includes like Bead Way or Flint Way. That deals more with people inflicted by certain things, lightning," but are used today for people who undergo surgery. "The last one is probably Game Way," used long ago in preparation for a hunt. "A lot of these ceremonies are extinct."

Harrison learned ceremonies not only from his father and Pearl but from his brother Frank. "I started tagging along with him. He was learning the

Night Way chant. It's a nine-night winter ceremony" commonly called (with varied spellings) the *Ye'iibicheii*. The third major ceremony Harrison learned from his Uncle Michaelby, "who does the Red Ant Way ceremony, which is from the Evil Way branch." The uncle and his wife were talking about Michaelby's "health conditions and his getting older. They were saying he's the only one on the reservation that does that five-night ceremony for Red Ant Way, that he traveled the entire reservation trying to find somebody. They agreed they wanted the ceremony to continue." They decided to teach Harrison, or more properly put, "to bless him with the ceremony."

Of the major ceremonies Harrison practices, what he uses from them varies. "Sometimes it's a simple prayer. Sometimes it's a matter of smoking tobacco. Sometimes it's just talking with people. It could take anywhere from fifteen minutes to the full-length ceremony, nine nights, which involves the entire community almost." The ceremonies require a daunting amount of memorization, which Harrison indicated is not his strong suit. Instead, he thinks of the stories, which then tie the songs and prayers together.

Each ceremony requires its own medicine bundle, which in turn requires strict protocol about how its contents are gathered, who can use it and when, and how it is passed on. When it was time for Harrison to have his own Night Way bundle, "it took me about a year and a half to gather everything. It's a big undertaking." Some items were given him, some lent, some made. Contents vary according to the practitioner. Frank's contains "certain sub-bundles . . . that are strictly for certain animals that I don't have with mine. I have certain protection-type medicine he doesn't have with his."

Harrison uses herbal medicine "to some degree. I'm not a medicine digger. I have specialists that go out and dig medicine for me. They know the names, they know the prayers that go for a certain purpose, and they know where to locate them and how to prepare them. At my end, I know how to administer them. Depending on which [ceremonial] branch you're under, there's different uses of different herbs. You don't have herbs on hand for certain ailments until you're asked to go get it. Then you find out who the patient is and what's wrong."

When a medicine person dies, the bundle is given to another medicine person. "It continues to live." While the disposition of Frank's bundles was being decided, a sister cared for them. "Because she's had the ceremonies done for her and they shouldn't be in other people's hands that haven't had the ceremonies for them. They're a living thing and they can harm you."

Whoever later received a bundle, Harrison said, probably will refresh it. There are ceremonies to do so. "We'll untie the main bundle and wash everything down. Renew it. Put new medicine in there. Then whoever's taking on the medicine, they're actually blessed and initiated with it," blessings eventually extending to the patient.

Harrison seemed uncharacteristically aggrieved when I asked whether prayers and songs or medicine helped Michael more. "I wouldn't be able to do what I do without my medicine bundle. Just with the history that goes with the bundles and how it's been carried down from the moment it's been created. There's certain Navajo spiritual elders, medicine men, that came together to create it. Knowing that and who's been involved with it, that carries certain weight." Some people who want a certain ceremony, he said, probably choose less the practitioner than the bundle.

Modern medicine was something else entirely. What does he use? "I use it all! There's a pharmacy across the street from where I live. If my children are coughing, I'll go get some cough syrup for them. If I lived out by the Grand Canyon and the pharmacy's a day's horseback ride and another couple hours by vehicle to the pharmacy, I'll go dig roots and boil something. But I'm not going to drive up to Grand Canyon to dig roots if there's a pharmacy across the road."

At the Goldtooth hogan, as Saturday afternoon turned to Saturday evening, Harrison spread out the contents of his second bundle. Few people were in the hogan, for a basic reason of hospitality; aunties were serving food to visitors, one after another, in the kitchen area. "You have to feed people immediately," I was told.

Torn between the quiet of the hogan and bustle of the kitchen, I went back and forth, once arriving in the hogan when the fire was almost out. Michael called out tips, to peel the bark off a log for kindling, smush it into loose pieces. It worked wonderfully.

Dinner in the hogan was served in haste, the aunties rushing back to the kitchen to see to more guests. Once we had eaten, Harrison, Michael, co-fire-tender Marilyn, and I lay down to sleep. Around eleven P.M., the other aunties, led by Stella, charged back in, upped the kerosene light, and placed a box of assorted doughnuts and a pot of coffee in front of Harrison and Michael. Both men ate and sipped in silence as others arrived.

The pre-ceremony atmosphere became jovial and entirely in Navajo, with Harrison repeatedly making people laugh. "I tell stories about certain things and certain people, and people find humor in that. In English, you're making fun of people. In Navajo, it's different. Sometimes a lot of stories are about my uncle Ram Herder, who I highly respect. But he's a character and people know him that way, so I was telling stories about my visit with him. He was sitting on his bed early in the morning and was asking about my mom. He said, 'Next time you go out there, tell her you saw your uncle. And tell her he is infested with lice and that's all he's busy with.'"

As if by an unspoken signal, conversation in the hogan stopped. Protocol tonight was stricter than before. Under no circumstance could one leave the hogan until after the first round, which might end around one A.M. A burly man seated to my left, a Vietnam veteran, signaled to me and with a wink uttered his first words of English that night. "There's certain do's and don'ts."

Around 11:30, Harrison leaned back, clasped one knee as he often did, and began to sing, and sing, and sing, to Michael sitting next to him. The melodies were again mesmerizing. Off and on, he sang for some five hours. At times, he paused to spit into a glass or sip some water from a metal cup hooked on a pail of water. Sometimes Stella and others joined in what seemed the songs' choruses. The lovely word *hózhó*, repeated often, became a caress. Michael was being blessed.

Throughout, Harrison paid close attention to him. "I'll gauge certain ceremonies depending how he responds and how he behaves and how he acts. Sometimes [patients] don't respect what I do. They'll be over there talking on the phone or arguing with people. Sometimes they don't comprehend things. So I kind of lower myself down and let things go. It ranges." At times, during a large gathering, "I'm there in the back of the hogan, kind of overseeing the entire ceremony and seeing what the family goes through and how they interact with each other. . . . If something's going on back there and it's tense and people fighting with each other, it eventually affects the ceremony." Despite such struggles, he has never stopped a ceremony.

On occasion, the family of the person seeking help is so uninvolved, only Harrison and the patient show up. He also encounters scoffing. "I hear rumors about some [people] saying stuff about me and my family and people I learn from, that we're all fakes. I'm sure people are like that."

Ceremonies that go well made him smile in recollection. "Some, they're so positive. The spirit's different. Sometimes, even though it's a tiring ceremony and being there for several days and having to put up with being there, and even with the last night having to sing all night, I actually feel better at the conclusion."

He is alert to moods from the beginning. "You start picking up on these things when you enter that person's home. How they greet you, how they treat you, how they treat each other. Then sometimes you start seeing images. All these things, they play a factor [in] how you administer your medicine and how you talk to a patient." Some factors are beyond his powers. "I've witnessed various levels of being in danger. Some of them, when I'm actually doing the ceremonies, all of a sudden I'll lose my voice. One of the most powerful things is probably when the female, when they're mensing, and they come into the ceremonies. That spiritual thing, that energy, that's what causes you to do that." He said that at one large ceremony, an entire group of male singers with him was struck mute.

"I've done ceremonies for people, prayers for people, I'm taking that spiritual from them, what they're going through. I carry that with me. Sometimes I have nightmares when I get home. I find myself fighting with certain animals or certain deities. There's that piece of danger I go through."

It is one reason he receives money for his work. "I don't think a lot of these people subject themselves to this without being paid, and traveling all these miles, and wear and tear on their body." As for what he receives, his first teacher helped here, too. "What Pearl said was, 'You will never ask for a certain fee for a certain ceremony. It's up to the people you're doing the ceremonies for. But you will gauge your ceremonies based on what they give you.'" Usually the person who initiates the ceremony will hand over cash or a check before it begins and clarify what he or she expects. "I've done ceremonies for as low as maybe twenty dollars, and I've been flown into Albuquerque and set up with a hotel stay and brought in to do an opening prayer, just to give a few minutes' speech on Blessingway, for a couple hundred dollars."

Harrison dutifully reports all fees to the IRS. "I've been ranging about seventy ceremonies per year. Most of them are weekends up in Navajo. Sometimes I'll do stuff on weekdays in Phoenix." He does not double-dip. "That's *my* time. My personal annual leave." His IHS co-workers not only know about his ceremonies, many ask for them. "I get a lot of calls, either for advice or for ceremonies." He suggests they call him at home or meet at lunchtime. He also performs ceremonies in a patient's room, but only if requested.

If strangers ask about his work, he answers he is a facility planner in a hospital. "I don't advertise that I'm a medicine man. Again, this goes back to my teaching. Even Navajo people, they'll ask, 'I hear you're a medicine man. What do you do?' I don't outright tell them, 'Okay, I do Blessingway. I do Red Ant Way. I do the Night Way, I do the Enemy Way ceremonies.' It's through conversations and communication they'll find out," such as a parent inquiring how he might help a child. Harrison focuses "on Navajos and within the four sacred mountains" but does not rule out helping others. That summer he did a ceremony for a non-Native child adopted by a Navajo couple. Quoting his uncle Ram Herder, he said, non-Navajos "walk the land and have five fingers like us."

———

Harrison's day begins unceremoniously. "I get up, go into the kitchen, make my coffee, come back, take a shower, go back out, have my cereal and have my coffee. Sometimes I'll stand outside just to stand outside and wonder why I am and why things are the way they are. To think. Whatever's out there. That the earth will continue to sustain us and that we can continue to walk upon her and that we walk below the sky that's above us and that the two continue to nourish us and everything in between, whether it's physical or mental or spiritual. Whatever role they play in my life, whether it's negative or positive and whether it's a blessing or if it's a hex on me. There's a reason for all this. I stand out there and watch the darkness turn to light and breathe it all in."

———

Tonight in the Goldtooths' hogan, the feeling was uplifting. Harrison's singing was magnificent; the fire sparked like a friend. Then came a sudden onslaught of rain and hail. People looked up joyfully. "Sometimes they'll say if you get rain like that, the spirits are happy," explained Harrison. Michael was happy too. "Rain is a blessing, we believe," he later e-mailed. "It indicates the gods are with us."

About one A.M. Sunday morning came the first major pause, signaled by Harrison's simply getting up and walking outside. Others in the room helped themselves to now cold coffee. Some said goodnight and left. Before the ceremony resumed, Harrison's wife, Davina, arrived with their three young children. The little boy, Dylan, immediately ran to his father's side and slept. Davina carefully unfolded stacks of cloths on the floor, making a pile close to a foot high. Everyone put valuables on it. It was unclear to me they would be returned, and I hesitated offering my entire purse (driver's license! credit card!). At one look from the Viet vet, though, I obeyed. Also on the cloths went a cluster of dried reeds that had been hanging on the wall and Harrison's two medicine bundle cases. Freddie Goldtooth brought in two saddles, placed them there, and left. He supports ceremonies, Harrison commented at one point, but does not take an active role in them. The pile complete, Davina, with daughter Leilani and the baby, snuggled in next to me.

The ceremony resumed with the passing of another pipe. This time, Michael had an easier time inhaling. This mixture, said Harrison was "a blend of different types of tobaccos. One form of tobacco I also use, they call it White Shell Woman's tobacco, which grows on the San Bernardino Mountains." When Davina received the pipe, she passed smoke over the head of her sleeping baby and did the same with Leilani, then herself. Davina, a nursing student, is luminously pretty, and contrastingly plump to Harrison's slimness. She is not fluent in Navajo, but understands it and can do what he asks during a ceremony.

She and Harrison had an arranged marriage. "It still occurs," said Harrison matter-of-factly. He had dated some, but "my focus was learning ceremonies." Because his and Davina's families both were Navajo and knew each other through ceremonies, there was no need for introduction, but there was for instigation. One of Davina's brothers approached Harrison's mother. "She liked the idea and she respected the family. I was in my thirties and they said," he laughed, " 'we need to do something for this boy. He's not going to do it himself.' It kind of happened. My sisters and my mom and myself, we went out there and they made arrangements." Davina was "about seventeen, eighteen. She was young." He figured her family recognized his positive feeling about the marriage and liked that "she's marrying a medicine person, somebody that will stand there with her and her family, and for them."

The Baheshones married in 2003, twice. "We had a regular walk-down-the-aisle type ceremony where we had a judge officiate." After changing out of that ceremony's clothes (white dress, tuxedo), they put on color-coordinated velveteen and had a Navajo wedding. Two hours later, by eleven P.M., they were a Navajo couple.

Davina passed the pipe to me, on her left.

Throughout the night Harrison continued singing, with every song, every prayer, every word in Navajo. He sprinkled pollen on the objects on the cloths, blessing them. Around three in the morning, during another pause, more people left, and more casual conversations took place. A young man who sang Blessingway songs almost as well as Harrison asked me where San Francisco is.

As the hours went on, I struggled to stay awake. And struggled. About five A.M. there was another startling turn up of the kerosene lamp. The ceremony was over? The Viet vet leaned over and growled that among the do's and don'ts, you are not supposed to sleep. I was mortified. But hadn't others nodded out? Davina smiled and said it didn't matter.

Then the items on the cloths, thankfully, were returned. Davina collected the cloths and gave one or more to each person in the hogan. Harrison and Michael walked outside. The rest of us followed, facing lavender sky streaks presaging the rising sun. Someone handed me corn meal. Imitating the aunties, right arm outstretched, I offering blessings to the four directions.

It was over.

Within an hour, Harrison and his family had driven off toward Phoenix. Stella, remarkably, had a second wind and was planning out loud the day's further activities. Amid good-byes and thanks, I apologized to Michael for falling asleep. Draped in a blanket and blinking at the lightening sky, he was kindness itself, naming others who slept too, and said he had been close, but figured that would be bad form. A smile for a farewell.

Minutes after getting in my rental car and heading west to Tuba City, amid enchanting dawn colors, an unexpected wave of loneliness came over me. For company, I turned on the Navajo radio station, 95.1, that one auntie liked so much. Amazingly, a person beloved by Native Americans as well as me was starting a gospel song that evoked both Easter morning and *hózhó*. I drove on, listening happily to Elvis singing "Peace in the Valley."

POSTSCRIPT

Many important topics Harrison and I touched on only briefly or not at all. There was the Indian Health Service and its precarious budget situation, as well as its infamous reputation of sterilizing young Native women in the 1970s without their consent. There was the uranium mining on the Navajo Reservation that has led to much cancer and deaths among tribal members. There was Navajo tribal politics, including the imprisonment of former tribal council president Peter McDonald for conspiracy and fraud. There was the Navajo–Hopi land dispute that forced Harrison's family to move from its home, but spared the patch of Goldtooth land several miles to the west. (The dispute, begun by and exacerbated by federal government actions, led to misery for people in both tribal nations, spawning resentment that has not ceased.)[2]

All the topics were important, but my focus was the ancient work of a modern medicine man. My remaining question was, why did he consent to an interview?

He answered late one night while leaning back in the worn armchair I have in my study. A window behind him glimmered with lights of San Francisco through the fog. He was at my home as a guest; at the end of the

Blessingway weekend, I had invited him and Davina to visit. They did, bringing little Leilani. Why I expected their interests to reflect Blessingway seriousness, I do not know, for they returned each evening from a day's outing with evidence from every top tourist spot in the Bay Area: Davina in a Haight-Ashbury T-shirt, Harrison in a Chinatown baseball cap, Leilani in endless cute outfits. Fisherman's Wharf, Muir Woods, Alcatraz, Ghirardelli Square—the Baheshones reached them all. Their vacation coincided with an especially cold summer fog, but, clad in borrowed scarves and so on, they were uncomplaining.

After dinner, Davina and Leilani crashed, while Harrison talked on. Late nights, after all, were nothing to him. So, why did he say yes? "I consented to sharing about my general views. What I didn't share with you were some of these medicine men type of stories and why certain prayers are done, certain songs, what they mean. You have to be initiated at kind of different levels of training. I knew coming into these interviews, I wouldn't share those. These books you have here," he gestured at *Navajo* by Susanne and Jake Page, and the *Diné bahane'* creation story, "has all that information."

The answer was disappointing but about to improve.

"Throughout the years, all I pushed for was learning the ceremonies. I don't want to say my priorities changed, but with my family, my wife and my kids, they made a strong impact. I'm glad they're created. I don't know if it's changing the views of my world or my ceremonial life, but it's making things more special, I guess. I think, why didn't I do this sooner? Then I hear my uncles or my aunts or my sisters say certain things happen for a reason and a certain time. Each person has their own destiny and their own journey. Even meeting you, I'm sure there's a reason for it." He gestured to the fogged-in city across the bay. "Somebody out there in a dark alley of San Francisco . . . maybe this will be printed on paper and it will blow into the alley and they'll pick it up and change their life. I don't know. Things happen for a reason." He paused and laughed. "Or maybe it was just to get my family out here in the coldness of San Francisco."

CHAPTER 12

The Kin of Sacajawea

EMMA GEORGE AND SUMMER MORNING
BALDWIN (LEMHI SHOSHONE)

EMMA GEORGE

"I remember my dad telling us pretty much all our lives, from when I was like six years old, 'Don't you forget who you are. You come from chiefs. Chief Tendoy is your great great grandfather. Your ancestor is Sacajawea.' But when you're young, you go, 'Okay Dad, yeah, all right.'"

Emma George, curled on her springy couch, smiled at the memory. Light through seen-better-days Venetian blinds warmed the living room of her house on the Fort Hall Reservation in southeastern Idaho. Photographs of relatives hung everywhere. Behind her, on a yellow wall, was one of her father, Wilford George, often called Willie, wearing the regalia of the Lemhi Shoshones. His mother died when he was a toddler, and his father, who was also known as Willie George, went off to earn money, including working as a showcase Indian for the Buffalo Bill Cody Wild West extravaganza. His grandparents raised him.

Willie's grandfather, Emma continued, fought in the Bannock War of 1878, one of several between Natives and Idaho settlers. "His Indian name was Topa-dah. That means 'breechcloth.'" Topa-dah's wife was Weetoi'-si. "That means 'drumming' in Shoshone. My dad's great grandfather was Naki-zaka, which mean 'breaks belt.'" Clearly, each name was precious to her.

The name that brought Emma George to my attention was Sacajawea. The Lewis and Clark expedition member who joined the group in late 1804, Sacajawea proved vital to its success. When the expedition got under way, she was some six months pregnant and married (not necessarily of her own volition) to French Canadian fur trapper Toussaint Charbonneau, who had been hired as an interpreter. In the course of the exhausting trek, Sacajawea famously was reunited with her brother, the Shoshone leader Cameahwait. In Shoshone lore, the two were separated after the Mandan Hidatsas kidnapped her as a young girl. Without her and Cameahwait's help, Lewis and Clark and their doughty but sometimes starving group might never have reached the Pacific.

Only four generations separate Sacajawea from Emma Lou George.

The connection is Cameahwait, which in Shoshone, said Emma, means "Won't Go." One of his children was the esteemed Lemhi Shoshone chief Tendoy, who, according to the family, called Sacajawea "auntie." Born around 1834, Tendoy managed not only to keep his people from joining Indian wars, distracting them by initiating bison hunts into Montana, but built relationships with white settlers in and around Salmon, the area's only town. Tendoy also attempted to retain his people's beloved homeland in the mountains of Idaho's Salmon River country.

That meant thwarting enormous pressures to vacate it for their assigned place of exile, the flat and unwelcoming Shoshone-Bannock Fort Hall Reservation two hundred miles to the south. In 1868, Tendoy and eleven subchiefs reluctantly signed a treaty granting the Lemhi Shoshones some land along the Salmon River in exchange for increasingly needed annuities. The U.S. Senate, however, never ratified the treaty. In 1875, President Ulysses S. Grant approved a reservation, described as "tiny," along the Lemhi River. The land could not support the seven hundred people who occupied it.[1]

Finally, in 1905, even Tendoy gave in. The exodus of his destitute people to Fort Hall began in 1907, their weeping reportedly so loud it was heard for miles. The Lemhi Shoshones may have been crying not only for their homeland but their leader. Chief Tendoy was dead.[2]

He was Emma's great great grandfather. His son, Hoorah (pronounced HOOR-ah) Tendoy, was born in 1858 and died in 1912 without leaving a sizeable historical legacy. His daughter, Emma's grandmother and namesake, Emma Tendoy George, was the woman whose early death, in 1929, left Emma's father, Wilford "Willie" George, in the care of his grandparents.

His daughters, Emma and her two older sisters, Rose Ann and Rozina, thus are the great great great grandnieces of Sacajawea and, following the death of their younger brother years ago, are her closest known blood relatives. (Sacajawea's two children are not believed to have reached adulthood.) Other individuals claim connection, assertions Emma generally shrugs off as irrelevant or sad.[3] Because of public appearances about the disputed Sacajawea coin,[4] Lewis and Clark bicentennial events, and various setting-the-record-straight writings, Rose Ann and Rozina are better-known kin than Emma. She was always shy.

As a schoolgirl in the 1960s and 1970s in Salmon, where her family returned to live, Emma remained silent whenever a teacher gave a lesson including Sacajawea. "I thought, 'Oh. She's my relative.' But you didn't really go, 'Well, *I.*' To me that was too vain or whatever." Almost all her classmates were white and unaware who Emma was. "'She's Indian.' They didn't really know." Emma did not discuss the connection much with her ex-husband, who came from a chief's lineage too. Nor does Emma generally volunteer the information today. "I'm one of those people that don't want to talk about it. I think our issue is when history becomes misinterpreted or whatever, that's when you want to stand up." There was also envy. "Different people get upset and say, 'Who do they think they are? Do they think they're better than we are?' I don't like conflict. I'm just peace, looovvve. Come from the '70s."

While attending Utah State University, Emma read the Lewis and Clark journals "to some degree" to find references "unique to our culture" through Sacajawea. "Not only the language, but medicinal practices. There were some words I know Lewis used in his journals that were Shoshone. Also, when she got really sick, Lewis had to take care of her. She told him what to get." The sole description of Sacajawea in the journals, said Emma, was "comely."

Sacajawea, furthermore, is only one factor in the full life of Emma George. She works in Fort Hall's planning department and is trying to finish classes at Idaho State University in Pocatello, including dreaded math, to get a degree in mass communications. Also she helps care for an enormous network of family and friends, takes part in cultural ceremonies, including powwows, must feed her fish and small manic attack dog, and tries to have a semblance of a private social life; she also tries to keep her coffee and cigarette "vices" in check, strives to make ends meet financially, and thanks the Creator constantly.

In a way, Sacajawea is no more important to Emma than is the land both came from, the land to which Lemhi Shoshones have been returning to visit, or live, ever since being forced to leave. She planned to show me the land, too, despite non-optimal timing; it was the day before Halloween, and Fort Hall was in a decorating, eating, and costume-assembling frenzy. Rozina, who wanted to join us, had to be back the next evening to trick or treat with a little girl she is raising, a little girl all but exploding with excitement about her Michael Jackson costume.

On the eve before Halloween Eve, a much-cheered costume contest for grown-ups took place in Fort Hall's Buffalo Horn casino. One Shoshone woman dressed, um, well, as an Indian. We missed seeing Emma's daughter Summer outfitted as Sarah Palin, toting a rifle and hauling a fake bear.

During much of the contest, Emma and I sat in the adjoining Buffalo Horn Grill with her cousin Cookie, discussing the then recent deaths in a Sedona, Arizona, New Age sweat lodge run by a non-Indian. Cookie said her mother feared "people will blame the Indians." Emma said she was appalled by "the plastic medicine man." She forwarded me a public online message from Lakota spiritual leader Arvol Looking Horse condemning such behavior. He also wrote a message, called "A Great Urgency," that she later forwarded about the oil spill in the Gulf of Mexico. "The dangers we are faced with at this time are not of spirit," he wrote. "The catastrophe that has happened with the oil spill which looks like the bleeding of Grandmother Earth, is made by human mistakes, mistakes that we cannot afford to continue to make." Emma certainly agreed.

———

The next day, on the cusp of nasty weather, I offered to cancel the trip to Salmon, but Emma and Rozina insisted we go. So, with Emma at the wheel of her rattly Ford, we headed north for the three- to four-hour drive from Fort Hall. They wanted to be home, even for one night, they said. Home, clearly, was not where they lived.

"I was born in Salmon, Idaho, in 1959, on a cold wintry day," said Emma. "When I was to be born, normally Indian men would go out and jump in water for the strength and endurance of a child. My dad took the easy way out. He went and took the hot bath. I was somewhat insulted by that." She smiled. "As a small child, I remember living at different places. There was a little log cabin, on Water Street." We drove by as soon as we reached Salmon. The dwelling was abandoned but memories remained. "When my sisters and I were growing up, I thought everybody spoke Shoshone. We used to have neighbors, and they were white women. We spoke to them in Shoshone. Eventually we learned not everybody spoke Shoshone. We were living at the Indian Camp for a while too, I remember."

Indian Camp, a place of crude homes and tenacious hold, now looks like a sandy spit at an inlet, but resonated to both sisters. Emma recalled her family's home there, "a little one room shack with a wood stove, no running water and I guess I could say no electricity. I was going to be starting school and my dad, there was a kerosene lamp burning, and he was teaching my A-B-C's and my 1-2-3. I went to school, I think it was in the first grade. I remember standing up and was able to say all my A-B-C's in front of the class. Some of the other students weren't able to." Life was basic. "We'd have to haul water, and we'd use outhouses. When you're a child, you don't know the disparity or the economic situation. You're just grateful. It was wonderful, the wood stove burning. It was comforting. During the wintertime there was a little creek, and I would skate on the ice amidst cattails." The Georges maintained Shoshone traditions. "To me there was things that were normal, like burning cedar and stuff like that for prayer, and if somebody was sick."

Today, Emma and Rozina turned in every direction, mountains in the background, a few warehouses and a picnic shelter in the foreground, a lone muskrat in the water. There was no trace anyone had lived here. They posed for some photos, both dark-complexioned, lovely, slender, dressed for the chill in sweaters and slacks, Emma more carefully made up, her black hair shoulder length (she had cut it after a nephew died), Rozina, taller, striking, making a goofy face, her hair waist length.

Indian Camp, a final attempt by Lemhi Shoshones to stay in Salmon, was—city officials reported—unsanitary and dilapidated. While Emma's relatives were visiting family in Fort Hall, Indian Camp was bulldozed. Not for the first time was the observation made that honoring Sacajawea did not necessarily include honoring her people. "I say I'm the last of the Lemhis, meaning those people that came [to Fort Hall between the] 1970s to the '90s, that migrated here after getting government homes," said Emma.

Before the Georges removed to Fort Hall, they spent blissful summers within the Bitterroot and Beaverhead mountain ranges, a landscape that encompasses river valleys thick with fish and other food. Willow grows too, its supple branches used to form frames of babies' cradleboards, which Rozina makes. (One aspect of the U.S. Mint's 1999 commemorative Sacajawea dollar that the Georges object to, aside from a Shoshone-Bannock rather than a Lemhi Shoshone being used as the model, is that in the image Sacajawea carries her baby not in a cradleboard but a blanket.)

The summer mountain idylls were prompted by jobs. "Some farmers would come pick us up. We'd be in the back of this stock truck, and they would take us up to the mountains in Salmon where they were doing farm-ing. I remember the gunny sacks with the hooks and the little wire baskets," part of equipment her parents used to harvest potatoes. "We weren't literally forced to help, but we did help. I loved the smell of the dirt. At that time, agriculturally, they didn't put a lot of chemicals in it, so they were natural potatoes. They were really good. We always had fresh fried potatoes, Bannock bread [a quick bread sometimes cooked in an open fire], and deer meat." Many potato fields today, like those across the road from Emma's house, are leased to non-Natives who use so many pesticides that children no longer are allowed to cool off in the irrigation ditches between fields.

Emma's parents also worked in forests around Salmon to cut lodgepole pines for fencing, again taking their children with them. "That was one of my fondest, fondest memories," Emma said, almost rapturously. "We were children of nature. We would camp up there for a month or more and we would have one of the ranch hands come and bring us supplies. In the mornings, my mom would get up and she'd start coffee. Today in our life we're always busy and we don't enjoy the simple things and the beauty of nature. At that time when I was a little girl, I remember coming out of the tent and I could smell the coffee. It's just cowboy coffee and it smelled soooo good. You could smell the essence of the pine trees, and your view would be sweeping greenery. There'd be wildflowers growing as far as you could see.

"My sisters and I and my little brother, we'd go play in the creek. We'd pretend we were fishing. Then we would play. I didn't have a doll, so I went and got myself a piece of wood that was laying around and I got some charcoal and I drew a face on it and wrapped a towel around it. That was my doll." Her father played too. He would gather bread crumbs, then call "his pets." Woodpeckers and bluebirds flew from the trees to eat from his hand.

"Also in the mountains, there was wild strawberries. Before we would find them, you could smell them. They had aroma that was unbelievable." The family slept on mattresses in an army tent. During the day, big sister Rose Ann was in charge. "She took care of us, and she made sure we had something to eat if we were hungry and kept us together like a little flock of chickens. One time there was a bear come snooping around. She threw us all under the mattress. We were quiet until it left." They missed a cougar, or vice versa. After a man shot it, Emma saw it "draped out," as long as the width of the road.

The children traveled to Fort Hall too. "When we were young kids, my father goes, 'You need to introduce yourself.' He'd bring us on the reservation and introduce us to the different elders. I'd go, 'Ne naniha Emma George. Ne agai-dika.' That means, 'My name is Emma George. I am a Salmon Eater. Ne again-bah nai' keem-up. I come from the Salmon River country.' Sometimes we'd go, 'My parents are, Ne uppa, Wilford George, Ne bia, Camille Navo George.' We'd even go further into who our grandparents were, so those elders would know who we were related to. 'Ne genu, Willie George. Ne hutsii, Emma Tendoy George,'" her paternal grandparents. "Ne dogo, Charlie Navo. Ne cagoo, Zuni White Bear Navo," her maternal grandparents.

Through Emma's childhood wafted the dark cloud found in many accounts: her father's alcoholism. Could the key in his case have been disjuncture? "He was raised by people at the end of the era when they were free to roam, and the reservation period began. They were the last of the way Indian people lived." In 1943, at the age of sixteen, he enlisted in the navy and was sent to the Pacific. One of his many medals was the Bronze Star for a feat that became family legend. "Some kamikaze pilots were going to crash into their ship. There were over a thousand men on [it], navy men. It was the USS *Tulagi*. People were running and scammering, and he got up on the aerial gunner and he shot them down. He saved all the men."

In 1946, after the navy said Wilford George was too disabled, from saving two men in a boiler room accident, to be sent to Korea, he joined the army. "That was very interesting because his grandfather *fought* the U.S. Army." He maintained the motivation was the same—to protect the homeland. He left the military in 1949, having received the World War II Victory, Bronze Star, Philippine Campaign, and other medals, she said.

He returned to a mixed welcome. In Blackfoot, a small town outside Fort Hall, signs read "No Indians or dogs allowed."

"In their midst was a war hero that was never accepted." Emma said her father talked about the signs, but not "what he had actually seen" during the war.[5] He also drank, especially with other veterans.

During our visit to Salmon, Emma and Rozina took me to a Main Street bar, the Lantern, where their father often went, to show me an oil painting of him. The excursion had a furtive feel. They mulled going in a back door to avoid notice, but in the front we walked, quickly, early on a sparkling Saturday afternoon. The place was dark, full of cigarette smoke and acquaintances. The principal's daughter, drinking at that hour! exclaimed Emma later. As soon as we entered, Emma and Rozina were surrounded. As the smiling bartender, the only person who seemed sober, pointed out the painting, a man with rheumy eyes managed to leave his stool and wobble over to Rozina. He slurred, "How are you, you good-looking squaw?" We gasped. At this worst of epithets, I expected dauntingly direct Rozina to deck him. She said only, "Stop that, don't be mean," and turned away. We soon fled.

On our one evening in Salmon, we went to a cheerful-looking restaurant, where, with the sisters' encouragement, I ordered a Sacajawea Ale. I thought the waitress had regarded them warily and said so. They said they had not noticed, but Rozina recalled a time in the 1980s when she and Rose Ann "had a bad experience" at a Pocatello restaurant, Myrtle's. "We had sat down and waited for a waitress. We looked at them and they looked at us. Then they ignored us. They wouldn't serve us. We didn't understand at first. We realize now it was a case of who we were." They left.

"I do experience prejudice from time to time, but I figure it's their own ignorance," said Emma. "Maybe one day they'll learn." Sometimes she gets stares after going into a store. "I don't like that. 'Oh my gosh, there's an Indian in here! What are they doing?'" The possibility that her beauty attracts attention seemed not to occur to her. In Salmon, "you don't know whether they're glad to see you or they're *not* glad to see you."

Some people confront her. "'You get per capita and I'm paying for your taxes and you don't pay any taxes and the government's sending you money every month' type of people. 'Why do you have to keep living on the reservation? Why don't you move off and become mainstream? Why don't you get over it? History's done with.'"

———

On the drive to algebra class at Idaho State University in Pocatello, Emma's first recorded words were disconcertingly candid. "My oldest daughter, she took her life when she was fifteen. This is when I was going to school as well. At first I felt like I was thrown off the edge of a cliff. I was falling, falling, falling. Nobody was there to save me and nobody could save me. I realized I have to do it myself. 'You're going to have to get yourself together. You've got four other kids.' They're the ones that helped me be strong. I probably wouldn't have survived if it wasn't for them."

Emma then recollected a more recent time, when she was thinking about deaths of other people close to her, including elders. "I was walking along, I heard my boots clicking on the ground, then I felt my heels vibrate with the ground. I felt a spirit near. It was Mother Earth. She seemed to have said, 'It's okay. Don't be sad. That's life.'" Emma paused. The message she took from the experience was that we spend our lives "to make a difference, no matter how small or how big." She added, "You might meet someone on that road of life to walk with you, but nobody's path is the same."

Emma's path included a teenage romance with her future husband, whom she has since divorced. They had six children. Their first was stillborn. Their second was Loreal, who took her life. Surviving are three daughters in their twenties who live nearby, and a nineteen-year-old son who lives with Rose Ann's family in Sacramento.

Emma's path has always included work. After transferring from Utah State to Idaho State, "I got an associate degree in marketing and management. I had been working for our tribal housing." Her assignments ranged from billing to "move in and move out inspections" to prorating rents. She later became northwest advertising sales manager for *Indian Country Today* and helped edit the tribal newspaper *Sho-Ban News*. She also taught "basic elementary Shoshone" at a grammar school. She speaks the language "like a child," she said. This did not seem the case during a visit, several country blocks away, to her mother, a diminutive and lovely woman who lives with Rozina and Rozina's girl. Emma's Shoshone and her mother's English both seemed better than she claimed. "Very traditional woman," said Emma of her mother. "She had to quit school when she was nine years old" because her own mother went blind. "There was no type of government things to help people, so she had to stay home and take care of her. That's why she's tried to push us to go to school."

Emma's employer, Fort Hall's Shoshone-Bannock planning department, pushes too, making a BA degree a requirement for Emma to move up from her current position. Emma also has considered careers in graphic design, in which she has notable talent, and in writing Native American "stories that weren't told before, that I felt would be lost forever."

Her planning work "has been a real learning experience as far as our land base. Our goal is preserving the reservation. If you look across America, it's all about development." (All Emma's opinions are "my own personal perspectives," she asked me to state. "I do not represent the tribe's.") As on other reservations affected by the calamitous 1887 Dawes Act, which sold "surplus" land to non-Natives, Fort Hall today clashes with its numerous non-Native residents, whether property owners or renters. A common feeling among them, said Emma, raising her voice in imitation, is "'It's *my* land, doggone it, and I will do whatever I damn well please. I'm not going to have no Indian tell me what to do.'"

They all need education about tribal law, she said, and at the same time must be treated fairly. "I thought our land use did a good job as far as being fair with those polygamists."

The polygamists! Dozens of members of the Church of the Firstborn and the General Assembly of Heaven, a sect led by self-proclaimed Mormon prophet Terrill Dalton, now excommunicated, rented a house on Fort Hall (from a non-Native owner of the property). They then added mobile homes and planned a dormitory. The motive was, supposedly, to bring religious guidance to the Shoshones. "It is an irony," said Emma dryly. The now undistinguished suburban-looking site, which she drove me past, had reminded her of Indian Camp in Salmon. "That's what I also told the land use commission. It was an encampment they had over there, not a single family unit." That is not all she told the commission. "'Keep in mind what happened a long time ago, when the Pilgrims came and said they were going to Christianize the Indian people for their own good, that they were savages.' I says, 'What happened?'"

The EchoHawk Law Firm, counsel for the Shoshone-Bannocks, where Emma's daughter Summer is the firm's receptionist, took up the case. After much wrangling, the Sho-Bans won and the polygamists left, with Dalton telling Mark EchoHawk, one of three brothers at the firm, "God is watching you."

Emma herself owns no land. "I'm a landless Indian." She makes payments on her prefab house, "but I won't own the land." If she could own any, it would be in Salmon River country. "A place just to be *there*," she said, before tearing up.

The trip to Salmon was emotional. "I felt really good. I felt like crying. I did cry. I felt like the spirit of the old people and the land when I was there. I felt the mountains were joyful and the rivers were joyful. It was like glad to see an old friend. I felt there was some things I didn't want to face and had this block in my heart. But when I got there, it kind of let go." Back in Fort Hall, she seemed there again. "It's one of the most beautiful places, the mountains, the rivers, the skies. Everything."

Despite a century of living on Fort Hall, the five hundred or so Lemhis there now, including the Georges, remain a mostly distinct entity. By being counted as Fort Hall citizens, however, they lost the claim to having been a separate intact unit since time immemorial, as the government requires, and therefore seem even more unlikely to be granted their own reservation.

In lieu of having her own piece of land, Emma dreams about traveling to other lands—South America, Italy, and Japan pull her for their old buildings. She did once take a dream travel vacation of sorts, part comic and part glamorous. It happened after heeding a niece who said she needed a vacation. "I'm one of those people that live on the edge. I didn't have that much income." (Emma gives money to anyone who asks, from strangers to relatives, I noticed.) Finally, she bought a plane ticket to Florida, to participate in some Native events there, including a powwow. Her eyes alight, she talked of seeing "varieties of people" in Florida cities speaking different languages. "It was kind of flavorful."

In Florida one evening, while driving back to a hotel after a dance performance, Emma and the group she was with passed a dead otter on the road. "For Native people, we use those otter wraps. They're worth about maybe two to three hundred dollars for a hide. We thought, 'We're not going to let the otter waste on the road.'" They retrieved it, skinned it at a nearby fish-cleaning site, and slid the body down a chute into a pond, hoping alligators liked otter. While carrying the rolled-up hide back to the hotel, Emma and her friends met a group of local people sitting around, chatting about their nice life. Their pond, they said, even has an otter.

"I was like, oh *great*."

The group said a fast good-bye.

Instead of heading home to Idaho, Emma accepted a cousin's invitation to join her and her husband, a leader of the Seminole Tribe of Florida, in New York. The fairy tale that followed included a stay at the Four Seasons, dinner at a fancy restaurant, and a tour of the restaurant's wine cellar, where famous people stored their vintages. Emma is no drinker but, trying to be a good guest, managed a glass of Merlot. The next day included a carriage ride in Central Park, breakfast at Tavern on the Green, captured in a souvenir photo, and a performance of *Phantom of the Opera*.

"Then I came back to Fort Hall. I felt like Cinderella!" she laughed. "My clothes were turning into rags, my carriage turned into a pumpkin. Pretty soon I dropped down into the dirt in the potato field."

Emma reciprocated the hospitality in spirit, putting her cousin up at her decidedly unglamorous house. One of two toilets is inoperable, the vanity door in the working bathroom is off its hinges, the kitchen has no table—Emma gave hers to a woman with young children—and the front door is so hard to open from the outside that Emma keeps a stool handy, which she puts under a particular window and climbs in. As for dining at the Buffalo Horn Grill, Emma's cousin fortunately loves Tater tots.

As the autumn afternoon in her home wore on, Emma became philosophical. "There's things you go through in life and they're hard, but other people have had harder lives. It makes you humble and grateful to be blessed with life, no matter what the situation is. To live another day." She spoke of Shoshone creation stories, in which everything and everyone had duties and made sacrifices, and "was given its good and its bad services to do," such as water providing drink, "but also maybe a flood." She shifted about on the couch, spoke of the Creator, of gratitude, and of proportion. "Even though we're not perfect beings, we try to be good people, to be better people, and to live our lives, and not to be too gluttonous, not to take too much, only what we need.

"I think the most important thing is to have understanding. You can't make somebody do something they don't want to, but it's been a life effort trying to bring about understanding. My great great grandfather Chief Tendoy, that's what he did in his life, strived to bring people together. In today's world, we're fighting other people. We're fighting other cultures we don't understand." She was talking primarily, but not exclusively, about wars in Iraq and Afghanistan. "I think we need to reassess the situation and really look at the people, not the people in power making the decisions. Go to the people and find out what they want in those other countries. I mean, if we are truly desirous of helping, fighting war is not the answer. That's because it's happened here. We have gone through genocide and annihilation." She went on, in a paean to humanity, "We all have heart. We have laughter, joy, pain. What makes another person's more important?"

As she spoke, my mind returned to Salmon, Emma driving slowly down Main Street and past the local high school whose sign promoted its football team: the Salmon Savages.

We had spent the night in a half star motel overlooking the Salmon River, mostly so Emma could be close to it. Early the next morning, while Rozina slept in, Emma—having wept at river's edge—drove me up and around the town's outskirts, to places various relatives had lived, but which mansions and ranches now make inaccessible. Finally, she pulled over on a mountain road. In silence, we walked up a hill and picked a few sprigs of wild sage, Emma putting down tobacco to thank the Creator for taking them. She stood, inhaled, and looked at the magnificent views. Snow-capped mountains glistened light blue and grey as sunrise reached the peaks. In the foreground, through morning fog, appeared pinkish yellow aspens. All was still. Emma held the sage to her heart, closed her eyes, and sang in Shoshone a "simple song," she called it, of thanks.

SUMMER MORNING BALDWIN

She is curvaceous, bright-eyed, and, in contrast to her mother Emma, often speaks dramatically, merging words quickly and softly like a whispered aside. And that laugh! It seems squeezed out of her, as if in response to a sneak Heimlich maneuver. The effect is charming and very young. Summer was born July 26, 1983.

She and her partner, William Temoke, also Shoshone, have a seventeen-month-old boy. "His name is William Jr. but I call him Tun, Tunners, or Tunz." (Full disclosure: I babysat Tunz during a hectic Halloween night when Summer and William, having duct-taped themselves into unrecognizability, headed to the second Fort Hall costume contest of the weekend.)

"Most of my [childhood] memories are of us playing outside in the potato fields, but we weren't supposed to," she said, introducing the laugh. "Because they sprayed chemicals. We swam in a ditch and we got in trouble." Sometimes dead livestock were in the ditches too. "Now that I think back, I would freak out if my son did the things we did," like climbing on a roof. "That was when I was younger, when my parents were still married. As I got older, we moved closer to Blackfoot, on the other side of the reservation. It was pretty good." She hesitated. "Well, I became the older sister later, when I was about ten, because my older sister passed away. After that I had to be more responsible and look out for my younger brother and sisters."

Summer remembered the awful time of her sister's suicide as a child might. "She would have been sixteen in December, but she passed away in July. Right before my birthday." Her sister Loreal "was beautiful inside and out. I can't remember her ever once getting mad at me. Or being mean to me. My mom, she had a difficult time with it too."

Foremost in Summer's childhood picture of her mother is that she was always there, cooking, cleaning, and taking the children to powwows.

The trips launched Summer's powwow passion. She started as a jingle dancer, but, she said almost confessionally, was pigeon-toed. "My Aunt Rose Ann suggested I try traditional because I'd be going slower and be able to try to focus on keeping my feet straighter." It worked.

Women's traditional dancing involves wearing a fringed shawl folded over the left arm, and making the fringes swing rhythmically, as one. "When I was little, that was my main concern, make sure my fringes were moving. Now that I'm older," she is less concerned. "They'll move with the movement of your body when you're dancing."

The first regalia Summer wore to dance in was a red dress with cowrie shells her mother gave her. "Later I got an elk tooth dress from my Aunt Cookie. My mom let me wear her outfit off and on when I started getting to be a teenager. When I was sixteen, my grandma made me an outfit, with beads and buckskin."

Having grown up in a home where primarily English was spoken (Summer's father does not speak Shoshone), Summer's Shoshone is not enough to converse with her grandmother, whom she calls "my *cagoo* Camille. I could listen to people and pick up on words, and I have an idea of what they're talking about, but I couldn't have a conversation. Sometimes when I say a Shoshone word, she laughs at me." Summer has never seen her grandmother, either, get mad at her.

"About two years ago William and I went to go over to her house so she could show us how to do deer hides. It takes a lot of strength in your forearms because you have to pull in a downwards motion," she said, imitating holding a skinning device in two hands. "I did something incorrectly and created a hole in the hide." The hole was in the middle, ruining it. "I was like . . ." she drew her breath in sharply, "because I knew that I had messed it up. I felt so bad. She just laughed and said, 'It's okay.'"

Summer began dancing competitively at powwows while very young. "Each powwow, it's a celebration." Making a "let-me-see" face, she ran through recent appearances. "I've won all different places, first, second, third. Some powwows will have a ton of places. I recently went to San Manuel powwow—that's in southern California—and I got first. I think that was a thousand. The weekend before that . . ." the list went on, ending with almost winning a Chevy Malibu at a Labor Day powwow in New Town, North Dakota.

She got first place at Morongo's powwow, too, whose casino must be among the flashiest in the world. She liked it and its shopping outlet. Morongo, as is typical of powwow sponsors, offers only the space and prize money. "You provide your own travel, hotel, everything." Summer reports her winnings and expenses to the IRS. "Yep! W-9." For a celebration and competition in Coeur d'Alene, she camped out. "I kept my tent receipt. I hope they'll take it when I go do my taxes this year."

There is debate throughout Indian country about whether powwows should offer prize money. Many do, although more ceremonial ones do not. Summer relishes both and was looking forward to a non-prize powwow the following Saturday for veterans.

Powwow dancing being more pleasure than occupation, Summer also has a day job. She gave me an enthusiastic tour of her place of employment, the EchoHawk Law Firm in Pocatello, including an introduction to each person and a survey of each area, including the supply room. She was considering, though, pursuing an earlier goal in childhood education. The goal started in high school, when she and others tutored children at the Fort Hall Elementary School in reading. "I want to help other Native American children to find a path they want to go on and know that things aren't always so bad."

She has held a number of school-related jobs, including that of substitute teacher at Sho-Ban High School and "interim attendance clerk." Squirming in a chair in my Super 8 Blackfoot Motel room, where the interview took place, Summer looked uncharacteristically troubled. She did not enjoy making calls to say a child had not shown up for school and learning the parents did not know where the child was. "I would get a little insight into their home life."

Summer's first attempt at college, the University of Idaho in Moscow, Idaho, was unsuccessful. She blurted, "I was irresponsible. I'm not embarrassed to admit I used to have really bad problems with waking up early." Finally, she moved back to the reservation, later attending Idaho State University, but "kind of lost focus of what I really wanted to do. I started powwowing. I feel like I powwowed nonstop."

Then there was William Temoke, whom Summer first noticed at a sun dance in the Bannock Creek district of Fort Hall and has known since they were teenagers. "One day we were skipping school, a group of us kids—it was kind of at the end of the school year—and we went swimming 'down bottom.' It's a preserved area on the reservation, where there's creeks and rivers." While playing catch football with friends, William accidentally landed on Summer. "He realized he knocked me out, and he got me up and pulled me out of the water and saved me. We always joke around that he saved me."

When the relationship evolved years later, so did Summer's plans. Her slogan "I need to get back in school" ended when she found out she was pregnant. It became "I need to get a job." A friend told her the EchoHawk law firm was looking for a receptionist. Summer recounted every step of the subsequent interview process, including her lunch choice at Buddy's Italian restaurant in Pocatello. The job was offered her. "I was *so* excited." She also told the EchoHawks she was pregnant. They responded by offering maternity leave.

"I am learning a lot more about tribal history and zoning and different types of law that apply to my tribe. It's really exciting. Even my boss will give me a paper with an old treaty and say, 'You should read this.'" The case involving the polygamists was difficult for her, but in a way different than for her mother. "I guess I'm the wimpy sister," she said, squirming. "I told William, 'I feel really bad for the children. Everybody needs a place they could call home.'"

Her own child was born at 4:50 in the morning on the last day of May 2008. She and William knew what he was supposed to do. "He left probably at 5:30 or 6:00 in the morning from the hospital to go jump in the river." The local

Chubbuck police pulled him over, for no reason she or William knows. After he explained Shoshone tradition, "they let him go. He jumped in the river."

William LaSalle Temoke Jr. may grow up strong not only from his father's early morning, and very cold, dip. He carries the lineage of six chiefs, plus Sacajawea, within him. From Tunz's maternal side, Summer listed by later e-mail, are Chief Cameahwait and Chief Tendoy, as well as Chief Eagle Eye (Weiser band of Shoshone) from her father. From Tunz's father, William Temoke, are Chief Pocatello (Shoshone), Chief Tetoby (Bannock), a signer of the Fort Bridger Treaty of 1868, and Chief Te-moak (Western Shoshone). Te-moak obviously became Temoke.

By another tradition, insisted upon by William's grandmother, he and Summer were not to see each other for a week after the baby's birth. "It was sooooo hard for me." Summer tried to make a tragic face through her smile. "That night after he was born, William and I were talking on the phone. I was like, 'I don't think I can do it.' He was like, 'Me, neither.' I was like," she rushed-spoke, 'Why don't you come see me tomorrow?' 'Okay.' We didn't last. But at least we lasted that whole day."

The challenges had not ended. "Both of our families are traditional. They believe you're not supposed to go out in public for a month after you have your baby." That was also hard on the new mother. "I'm more of a person who likes to go to the store, I like to go do things. But it's kind of for the baby, you know? For the mother and the baby to bond, so they have that time together. Also because there's lots of sicknesses and diseases you don't want your child to be exposed to right away. The only time I left my house was to go to a doctor appointment." Actually, not the only time. "I went to a grocery store where I didn't think I'd see anybody I knew and I seen someone I knew and I was *so* embarrassed," she all but squeaked.

When Summer went back to work at EchoHawk, the plan was that William would care for the baby at home. "Right now he's unemployed. He does a lot of beading, though. That's how he's been helping provide as well. He's beading on a men's traditional outfit. It's a heck of a lot of work. It takes a lot of patience, a lot of time." William's work is exquisite, judging from a change purse Emma gave me. The minuscule beads form pattern progressions both bold and subtle.

William cared for Tunz at home for about ten months, until he acknowledged that beading and baby is a difficult combination. Tunz now goes to day care. William also works as a carpenter. "He does cabinets and shelves, woodwork. He's more of an artist. He's restoring a dresser that was my sister Loreal's my mom gave us."

One concern the couple has is teaching their six-chiefs boy Shoshone. William speaks "a little bit more" than Summer. "But some of his words are different from mine because his is more Nevada Shoshone. There's different dialects. He likes to tease me and say I'm saying it wrong. I'll say, 'No, you're saying it wrong.' But we try to say Shoshone words around our son so he'll know."

The couple did unite on tribal affiliation. "William recently became enrolled in our tribe. His dad lives in Elko and his maternal grandparents live here in Fort Hall and his mother lives here in Fort Hall." The reason he changed his enrollment from the Western Shoshone to the Shoshone-Bannock tribe was partly pragmatic. "As a tribal member, you could get your wood, you could hunt, you have those rights. He wasn't a tribal member here, so he wasn't able to do that to provide for his mother and his grandmother, and for us."

As Summer well knows, each tribe can decide its own membership criteria. She e-mailed me a copy of the Shoshone-Bannock Tribes Tribal Enrollment Application Checklist, which included many contingencies, including "Enrollment's Paternity Affidavit Notarized (if NO marriage certificate of biological parents)" and "DNA REQUIRED for unwed NON-Member Mother."

Years ago, the tribe held an election to decide how future membership would be determined. "You know what was really funny? This all goes back to being Native American and everything. We voted . . . either it be based on blood quantum or ancestry [meaning a person had to have at least one Shoshone-Bannock ancestor]. If blood quantum, how much. A quarter, half, eighth." She spoke earnestly. "I always vote. I think it's important." At the moment of voting, though, she changed her mind from blood quantum. "I said, 'I don't think I'm going to end up with a Shoshone guy and I don't think I'm going to have children with a Shoshone guy, because all the guys my age, they're my relatives or they're not the best husband material. I'm going to vote for ancestry.' Now I'm kind of kicking myself."

"I learned at school about pan-Indianism, and I don't want to be an enabler for pan-Indianism." She sighed. "Blood quantums have always been the subject for Native Americans. I have a theory. You know when the white man first came, they wanted to basically get rid of the Indians completely and they weren't able to? Now this is kind of a way later on. 'Let's let them all kind of blend in.' I'm teasing." Maybe.

In the vote, ancestry won. Summer would prefer blood quantum now, she admitted, laughing, "but that's a little selfish." The reason has to do with per capita payments generated by the two Sho-Ban casinos. Summer, William, and little Tunz have a high Sho-Ban blood quantum, putting them in a smaller group than people who simply have one Sho-Ban ancestor. If blood quantum were the criterion, they would be entitled to more per cap money. She declined to name the amount but said "we usually receive it around Christmas time, so that's nice."

Because of the Fort Hall housing shortage, she, William, and Tunz live in Chubbuck, a small suburb outside Pocatello. There are so many Sho-Ban restrictions on housing, she later e-mailed, that "the only way I would be able to live on the reservation is if I lived with my parents! Lol, I don't think so. I'm a grown woman!"

She and William discuss "a lot" where they might move, without being too far from their families. "We both want to venture out and try a different piece of life, so we discuss all these places." They were considering Salt Lake City, which would allow Summer to keep dancing at local powwows and other cultural events. "I'll always want to have that part of my life. I also want my son to know that part of his life, that's who he is." She added, "Then my mom and my family. My mom's such a nice lady and she's so sweet. I want the best for her, and I don't want her to . . ." Summer started to cry. "I don't want her to be sad. I know that's so nerdy, but I want the best for my mom and I want the best for my family."

Summer also wants to finish her education. After reapplying a month ago to Idaho State, she was denied because she owes too much money. "They said I have to pay it off completely before they'll let me enroll." Her bosses indicated they might help, until finding out the amount. Summer knows it is her responsibility. The EchoHawks also offered to let her work part-time if she returned to school. "A little bit of stress was raised off my shoulders."

To her bosses, primarily Mark EchoHawk, she explained she wants to teach not only because she likes helping children but because she would get Christmas break, spring break, and summers off. "It so happens the pow-wow seasons falls on summer vacation!" She is torn about how to do the most good. "Working here at this office, I could help a lot of people," including tribal members. "If I was to be an educator, I could go back and be more of an influence on one person at a time." She knows Native children could use that influence. Summer made a full body sigh. "I do want to go back to school. I feel like, oh man, I'm getting older and time is ticking away."

—————

Like her mother, Summer has gone through various sentiments about her most famous relative. "At first I was really swelled with pride of where I'd come from, but sometimes there's people that put you down. There's a thing people say. Indians are like crabs in a bucket." Summer, too, now generally keeps the connection private, "because I don't want to deal with people's negativity." One group, however, is unanimously thrilled about the Sacajawea connection: white people. The recollection got her going. "It is a really neat thing to come from such a valiant person that is a part of our American history. William likes to tease me. When I was in labor, I said, 'I'm too wimpy. I can't do this.' He said, 'What would your ancestor Sacajawea think of you?'" She laughed. "I can't even imagine traveling from Pocatello to *here* on a horse with a baby! She traveled all the way from . . . oh my gosh."

When Summer was a child, family history repeated itself on road trips to Salmon. This time Emma sat in the front as parent instructor. "We'd pass Chief Tendoy's grave, and she would tell us about that and she would be pointing things out and talking about the history of the area. But it was more like Charlie Brown, 'Waa, waa waa waa . . . ' I was little and you sit there, kind of listening."

CHAPTER 13

Indian Humor

CAROL CRAIG (YAKAMA)

Is there a joke within the infinity labeled "Indian humor" that Carol Craig does not know? All attempts to stump her have failed. Okay, how about this one under the heading "Don't Mess with Indian Women," which I forwarded from a Native Web site?

A Native man with six beautiful children is so proud of his achievement, he starts calling his wife "Mother of Six," despite her objections. One night at a party when it's time to leave, he shouts across the room, "Shall we go home, my little mother of six?" His irritated wife shouts back, "Any time you're ready, father of four."

Carol e-mailed in response, "That was always a good one!!!" and said she first heard it in the early 1990s.

To receive Carol's humor is a private pleasure, but to see it affect a wider audience is a measure of the woman. Picture hundreds of people gathered in a Seattle airport hotel banquet room for the Native Women's Leadership Development Forum. They had bowed their heads for the opening prayer and listened to panels about the challenges of nurturing women in the arts and education. They had heard the keynote speech about Native youth, including the wrenching problem of teen suicide. Later in the day, the program read, they would hear from Native women who established a cancer survivors network. They also would hear about upcoming "canoe journeys."

Could that be the day's one high? What began as Paddle to Seattle to mark Washington's centennial is now an annual celebration. Members of Washington and Canadian nations paddle some eighty dugout canoes for weeks, stopping at reservations and ending triumphantly at or near the host tribe's reservation. (The year I saw the journey's thrilling end, the host was Carol's maternal tribe, the Muckleshoot outside Seattle.) Canoe participants today would talk of commitment and preparation, and display copious planning notes, such as "best time to arrive w/current," and safety equipment lists. Then, one participant would break down, describing how "canoe journeys" helped cure her addiction. "I'm still facing the battle of my temptations." Another would describe the pink canoe paddles publicizing breast cancer awareness.

In sum, the day's prevalent tone was solemn. The Enduring Spirits Honoring Luncheon portended nothing less. Oh dear, I thought. Enduring.

Yakama tribal member Carol Craig, Endurer No. 1, was called to the podium. In her late fifties, a bit short, a bit stout, her gray hair in a smooth page boy, Carol was introduced as public information manager for the Yakama Fisheries Program, as an educator, journalist, and public speaker, particularly on the subject of treaty rights, and as someone who helped fellow Washingtonians, the Makah, manage the uproar over tribal plans to kill a whale.[1]

After accepting the award and applause, she acknowledged her widowed eighty-four-year-old mother, beaming at her from a nearby table. Then, within sentences, Carol proceeded to change the day's mood. How about those clueless non-Natives she encounters in her work?

"College students, *college* students, ask me, 'Are you full-blooded?'"

The audience held its collective breath at this, one of the rudest questions non-Natives ask.

"I say, 'No, I'm a pint short. Just came back from the Red Cross.'"

The room exploded.

————

The following summer, in and around Toppenish, the "heart" of the Yakama Reservation as Carol calls it, more such jokes erupted from her. "What do you call a white guy surrounded by sixty Indians?" Answer: "The bingo caller." "What is worse than tennis elbow?" Answer: "Tennis balls!" "You know how much a tribal baby costs? A little under a buck." Whenever she is asked if she has lived on a reservation her whole life, she answers, "Not yet."

Like all good comedians, Carol is also spontaneous. After the Yakama Nation police chief discovered marijuana growing on the reservation, he made what Carol considered a pompous announcement that he intended to burn it, asking her to photograph his civic-minded action for the Yakama Nation magazine she edits. She told him, yes, she will photograph the burning. Furthermore, she will stand downwind and bring snacks.

The occasion for many of the jokes was a long drive to and from an event she helped organize at a remote forest site within the Cascade Mountains. The event, entirely serious, concerned Yakama Nation rights.

The rectangular-shaped Yakama Reservation sits in southern Washington, much reduced. Yakama who signed the 1855 treaty establishing the reservation relinquished 12 million acres of original homeland, said Carol, quoting the document. "'We reserve that original portion'—that's where the word 'reservation' comes in," she added. The treaty included access to "ceded areas," places where the Yakama assiduously maintain a number of rights, particularly to gather food, including their sacred fruit, huckleberries.

The only food as important to the Yakama is salmon. Before there was a reservation and ceded lands augmenting it, the "heart" of Yakama used to be a prodigiously salmon-rich site on the Columbia River. According to William Dietrich in *Northwest Passage*, "North Americans lived on the Columbia for at least eleven thousand years before European discovery. When it was drowned by the Dalles Dam in 1957, the Indian fishing community at the river's Celilo Falls . . . was the oldest continuously inhabited community on the continent. Whites came to the Columbia very, very late."[2] The Dalles Dam was constructed despite much protest by Washington tribes, including the Yakama. "We had the largest delegation go to D.C. to talk to the president, Congress, and Senate, but it fell on deaf ears," said Carol.

The Yakama have not moved on emotionally. On a hillside overlooking former Celilo Falls, above the reach of the now wide and placid Columbia, is an elegant new wooden longhouse used for community ceremonies, including anniversaries of Celilo Falls' destruction.

Its destruction meant the Yakama had to rely more on inland territory for sustenance. For Carol's family, that meant land her father inherited outside Toppenish as part of the catastrophic Dawes Act. When he inherited his parcel, it was down to eighty acres. Carol's share is divided between seven siblings. (In breaking up reservation land, Dawes either did not take inheritance into account or did so cynically.) Descendants of the non-Native homesteaders who bought the "surplus" land within the Yakama Reservation now proclaim, "'We're fourth-generation farmers.' I tell them, 'We've always lived here.'"

The Yakama town of Toppenish looks like any small western city. Downtown murals depict "pioneer days." A slaughterhouse advertises itself by stench. There are smatterings of shops and restaurants, schools and offices. One might need directions to find Yakama tribal headquarters or its Legends casino, not to mention the nondescript fisheries offices. Yet Toppenish is part of the reservation, despite what some white residents want to believe. "They say, 'The city isn't the reservation.' 'Where do you think you *are?*'" A non-Native city councilwoman refuses to pay local taxes because she cannot vote in tribal elections. Carol sighed and cited a Native mantra that "the most prejudiced people live in and near Indian reservations." A non-Native city councilman "was a grade below me in high school. When I would go by, he'd say, 'Injun. Squaw.'"

Not even all of the Yakama tribal members understand the situation. At a meeting to discuss having a protest march through Toppenish to ban alcohol, some fretted they needed a city permit. "I stood up and I said, 'This is heart of the Yakama Reservation! Why would we have get a city permit?'" The march was held without one.

Where did Carol Craig learn such moxie? At home, for starters.

She was born in Tacoma to doting parents, her mother from the Muckleshoot Reservation, her father from Yakama. When young, both had lost their mothers. "That's why they were sent to the boarding school. 'Oh, you Indian men can't raise these kids. Here, let us take them.'" Carol's mother, ordered to St. George's Catholic boarding school outside Tacoma, remembered hanging onto the back of a buckboard wagon, while crying, "I don't want to go!" She later told Carol, "I guess it was good."

Carol's father was "shipped off to Chemawa Indian school in Salem [Oregon]." As was the norm, children were punished for speaking their own language. "They were told to forget all of that. But some tribal people, I hear elders talk about it today . . ." They dreamed in Yakama and "would keep it in their mind so they wouldn't forget it." Her father salvaged words and phrases. Her mother lost them all.

They met as teenagers at a dance on the Muckleshoot Reservation. "She was telling me last week, 'When Dad went over to ask my dad to get married, my dad told him, Don't bring her back!' She still does have a sense of humor. To me, she was the tribal Lucy." If her parents quarreled and her father stalked away, her mother—Carol imitated—made a face, thumb on nose, fingers wiggling, to the delight of Carol and her siblings. The instant he swerved around at the giggles, tribal Lucy was straight-faced.

"They'd have their differences, but she always packed his lunch. He went to work, and he'd come home and have dinner. Back then, we'd have dinner for ten of us altogether. Eight kids! We would have Kool-Aid or milk to drink. We would have dessert and later on in the evening fresh fruit. It was always provided. It was all there, growing around us. Dad, he was a hard worker." The eighty acres outside Toppenish were not sufficient to support his family, and he became a bricklayer. Often traveling to construction jobs, he returned on weekends. "He'd bring home stuff he knew we liked. My dad was a great inspiration to me, too."

When the tribal agency posted a notice about rifle hunting classes for children, Carol was intrigued. "I've always been a tomboy." She told her father she wanted to learn, and he took her to the sign-up. "I think I was ten. We had to walk down to the basement of the building. There were all these tribal men and their sons. They asked what am I doing here? Dad said, 'She wants to learn how to hunt.' 'No, this is just for boys.' He argued with him for a half hour. Finally we left. He held my hand. We were walking upstairs and he says, 'They're wrong. You know what? You'll remember this all your life. When you know you're right, you hang in there.'"

When Carol once chattered childish questions about directions while riding in his pickup, he gave her another lesson. "'You always have to pay attention. Watch where you're going,' he says. 'You don't want to be lost all of your life.'" After his death, Carol learned her father was also sentimental. He had made scrapbooks of everything family-related, including an article Carol wrote in high school about her "Indian girls basketball team."

In those school years, Carol once approached her mother about a delicate matter. "'I understand we have a pinch of French blood in us. Where did that come from?' She said, 'You know the French and Indian War?' I said, 'Yeah.' She said, 'Well, it wasn't all war.'"

Carol laughed as she steered the fisheries van onward. The landscape, once freed from the uninspiring confines of Toppenish, had burst into vistas of scrub desert, pine forests, and snow-capped mountains. "Sometimes I think about things my mother taught us when we were younger, how much sense it made. I remember when we first went into outer space, my mom says, 'They're poking holes and it's going to ruin the earth.'" Later, Carol connected the warning with holes in the ozone.

The subjects of her mostly sunny childhood, followed by an often fractious adulthood, had come up over dinner the evening before in a lively Toppenish Mexican restaurant, where Carol listed her ex-husbands as "the kids' dad, my first white husband, and my second white husband." Three times and she struck out, she put it. Now when people ask, "Are you married?" she tells them, "No. I'm happy." Her children, a daughter and son, both work in Oregon and are raising her three grandchildren.

"The kids' dad" was part Yakama and part Mexican. After the young family moved to Tacoma, said Carol, he was so controlling and physically abusive, particularly after drinking, that she feared the children would be next. A Catholic priest in whom she confided advised her, despite Church policy on divorce, to leave him. His counsel gave her strength. With no money of her own, she hocked the precious flute she had bought in monthly installments, bought bus tickets, and fled with the children back to the reservation to live with one of her sisters.

First white husband impressed her as ultra polite. "Mannerly, would open the door." She and the children and he moved to Salem, where he installed heating and air conditioning systems. She began attending a community college. Then he began acting like husband number one. "Carol," she mockingly asked herself, "do you see a pattern here?" The pattern started with something she was learning about in her college psychology classes: isolation.

"Second white husband" happened along much later. Carol was working for the Columbia Intertribal Fish Commission in Portland. He was a Vietnam veteran who became ill, both were convinced, from Agent Orange. He told her it was sprayed on the trees, then dripped onto the soldiers, who were told not to worry. After he collapsed and became immobile from Guillain-Barre syndrome, and after the veterans' hospital where Carol took him refused to acknowledge Agent Orange symptoms or help him, she offered to marry him so he could get physical therapy through her health insurance. He agreed. Gradually, he went from being motionless to walking on his own, to complaining about Carol's daughter living with them. The parting was mutual.

While Carol was still a young mother, she witnessed something whose recollection brought her to tears. The reminder came en route to the forest event, as a stretch of the Puyallup River curved below us. What she remembered was a 1970 "fish-in" by Native people to protest Washington State's announcement that it controlled fishing within its borders. The announcement denied fishing rights that the Yakama, among others, had assumed for millennia, rights written into the Treaty of 1855 emblazoned on the Yakama Nation shield.[3] Carol's father, among many other Native people, long had fished the Puyallup. When Carol and a sister heard about the protest, they decided to investigate. "We put our babies in the baby seats and went out to the Puyallup River. We were in shock. There were all these camouflaged soldiers carrying what looked like huge machine guns, going up and down and pulling the boats out and pulling the tribal people out of the boats." Carol stared ahead as she drove, but her voice broke. "Pulling the women out of the boat with their long hair, dragging them up the banks. It still makes me cry," she said, choking. "What they endured and what they stood up for."

After several court cases in which sport and commercial fishermen protested the claims made by the Yakama, the Yakama recovered their rights.[4] Native tribes of the Northwest were declared, in Carol's phrase, "co-managers of the resources." Along the way, Carol Craig found her calling: to help her tribe.

There were hurdles. After fleeing her first husband for the Yakama Reservation, she went on welfare "for probably less than a year. I hated it." Then the *Yakama Nation Review* needed a reporter/photographer trainee. Carol got the job. "I thought, Wow! I really like what I'm doing! I'd run around, start doing the news stories." After the editor left, another man took over who became Carol's mentor. When she told him she wanted to "better myself," he encouraged her to complete her education. It was a defining moment, Carol said. "I wrote to several colleges, including the local one in Yakima." (The city is spelled with an *i*, but the tribal nation, to reflect its closer-sounding origin, spells itself Yakama.)

The only college that responded, and enthusiastically, was Portland State University. Carol started classes there in 1978 at the age of thirty-two. Everything was looking up. Her daughter Karen was starting sixth grade, her son Andy third grade. Then Andy came home, shoulders slumped. He finally admitted he was being put into remedial reading and math.

Carol, knowing he was the only Native boy in his class, got into "militant tribal mom" mode, went to the school, and demanded, "Has he been tested?" He had not. It turned out that Andy, too scared to answer questions, had been labeled "slow." Once he was tested, however, he was put into regular classes. There, other boys hassled him, made "war calls" in the hallways, she said, and got in fights with him. Following such fights, only Andy was held after school. "Militant tribal mom" kept returning.

Apart from such forays, she went to PSU full time. "All that time I would get Pell Grants [and] tribal money. I would save money, so during the summertime I would have enough to pay the rent for three months. I always made sure I had early morning classes so I'd be home when the kids got home from school. We'd all sit at the table and do our homework together." After three years, the pattern abruptly ended. "Reagan got elected. All the funding was cut. I had to quit in my fourth year." (It took Carol ten years to get her bachelor's degree.)

She interrupted her tale as we searched for directions or signs from now unpaved roads that may, or may not, be pitching us closer to our goal. Mammoth cedar trees made visibility no closer than the next turn. We were lost, and on what Carol termed a "*very* big day."

The event was to commemorate the seventy-fifth year of a handshake. In 1932, the Yakama Nation chief and the supervisor of then Columbia National Forest, now Gifford Pinchot National Forest, shook hands to confirm that Native people have the exclusive right to pick huckleberries in certain ceded areas of the forest. The significance of the anniversary was not only about access to the huckleberries, but that a treaty involving a white man, sealed with merely a handshake, has held.

Today the heads of the Yakama Nation and the forest, both women, to Carol's delight, were going to shake hands. There would be prayers, gift exchanges, speakers from the tribe and forest service, and informational handouts. Carol's van contained boxes of brochures she had written, including "Protecting the Huckleberry Fields Forever." A photographed huckleberry was captioned "*wíwnu*—our sister."

For refreshments, Carol had suggested juice, water, and cookies, but the women elders insisted—only a week earlier—that the occasion warranted a feast. Such an event involved considerable more planning, including killing a deer, digging traditional roots, collecting bowls of huckleberries, and assembling a phalanx of people to cook and serve the food, and clean up.

The big event was to start at noon. Where was the pile of logs marking a turnoff? I tried to follow Carol's cheerful lead and told myself that being late to a Native event, even if you are the emcee and main organizer, is no cause for alarm. Native people joke about "Indian time," but it was one avenue of humor Carol did not take.

"Did we come down here?" she asked, peering over her dashboard. In lieu of certainty, she told another joke. "At the entrance to the reservation," she said, managing a dirt-spewing U-turn, "there's a tribal guy, and he's got his ear to the ground. This white guy's driving up and stops. He's right in the middle of the road. He says, 'What happened?'" She rasped in a stage voice, "'White man driving a red Cadillac convertible. Woman have blond hair. Two dogs in back.' He says, 'Dude! You can tell all that just by putting your ear to the ground?' He says, 'No. Ran over me half hour ago.'"

Carol roared as she steered us wherever and, while morning became afternoon, resumed her own story. After the PSU funding cuts, she stayed in Portland, working various jobs, including waitressing at a Mexican restaurant.

"Because of my color," she said, customers assumed she was Spanish and asked if she spoke it. "Sure! Nachos. Tacos. Enchiladas. Tamales. You want to hear anything else? Salsa." She loved waiting tables, of course; she got people to laugh.

The income did not go far, though. Carol Craig became a pool hustler. After a boyfriend taught her the basic shots, she joined an "all-tribal-women pool team." (Carol almost always says tribal rather than Native or Indian.)

"We kicked butt." She also had a solo act utilizing her secret weapon of being left-handed. "I would challenge men, 'I'll play you left handed.' 'You don't have to,'" she mimicked their solicitous reply. She usually won. When men tried the pickup line "What is your astrological sign?" she replied, "Dollar."

One time when she did not have many dollars, she saw a sign saying Pool Tournament Saturday. "Steaks for the first prize." She told her children, get ready. Off she went for a long evening. After beating the owner, he said she also had to beat a man named Turkey, best out of five. She did. Asked how gracious Turkey was in defeat, Carol answered tartly, "Men are not gracious." She took the hard-won steaks home to a happy reception.

In a more sophisticated ruse, she and a Yakama friend named Gwen— both single mothers needing food money—worked as a team. First, they scoped out a pool hall's clientele. If they saw a lot of men, Gwen would go in alone and challenge them to a game. "Then I would walk in and challenge her. The men would start betting." After Carol, or Gwen, collected the money from whichever men bet on her, she left. The "loser" later followed her to a designated spot, where they split the winnings.

For pleasure, Carol played softball. She accepted an invitation to join a team of "gay girls," and in the process gained more friends and joke material. "They had a great sense of humor, so we'd sit around and laugh and talk. I'd tell them a tribal gay joke," one that a gay "tribal guy" loved. Carol made me promise I would not be offended. "Do you know what you call a tribal gay guy?" No. "One brave sucker."

She then remembered "one young tribal man, we would kind of giggle. He was a boy back then. He'd walk," she semi-demonstrated, with kind of a swing. "He wanted to be a woman. He finally did get a change. His sister is one of my good friends too." The sister calls him Auntie. "I don't think it's ever bothered anyone on the reservation. There's several gay girls, too, tribal girls." She shrugged.

Throughout her adult life, Carol was less interested in sexual orientation than financial captivation. She still scrambles for extra income by holding yard sales. "When I go to Portland, there's this used bookshop. I buy the old *National Geographics* that have tribal people in them. I put the names in there and I sell those for a dollar. They always buy them up." Her entrepreneurial efforts make her impatient toward a group of Yakama she referred to as "the disgruntled chronically unemployed."

When Carol landed a steady job at the Intertribal Fish Commission, she was financially secure but socially awkward. Much of the job required public speaking, like teaching schoolchildren how to raise salmon from eggs. In her first class, she froze. "They were second graders staring at me. 'What's wrong with this lady?'" She chastised herself, "Goldarn it. I'd never spoken in front of anyone before." Then she realized she could loosen up the children with jokes. "How do you keep a salmon from smelling?" Answer: "You cut off its nose."

To this day, Carol never misses a "teaching moment." She recently noticed a group of Portland children with feathers in their hair. "They had two feathers each. I told them, 'Oh! So you're supposed to be tribal people!' 'Yes!'" In her imitation, she is the happiest person imaginable. "I said, 'Do you know what it means when you have two feathers in there on your headband?' 'No.' 'It means you're married. So all of you are married?' 'Noooo!!' 'Then maybe you better take one feather out.' 'Okay!'" She paused as the moment of levity passed. "It's an ongoing education process."

In her job with the fish commission, Carol ran information booths at convention centers, state fairs, sports shows, and salmon festivals. After taking a seminar called How to Present Yourself, she learned that sitting at a booth makes people think you are bored. Carol Craig always stands. Before long, she was a one-woman show. She got wall calendars from the tribe and "real cheapie things," such as fortune teller fish. She gave the presents away, but only if the booth visitor, adult or child, first took a short quiz about the Yakama Nation and salmon.

After living in Portland for seventeen years, she found that the reservation again tugged at her. "I had been seriously thinking about moving back home. I was the only one out of the eight kids that ever moved off the reservation." The impediment was finding a job. Then Yakama's fisheries program director paid her a visit and told her to write her own job description. Soon Carol was back home, and doing work she loved, including writing, editing, and taking many photos for the thrice-yearly sixteen-page magazine *Sin-Wit-Ki* (All life on earth), published by the Yakama Nation Fisheries Management Program. It included articles about fisheries programs, digging bitterroot, returning sage grouse to the reservation, and memorials and birthdays.

Meanwhile, she educated anyone she could about the fisheries program and how it has undone destruction from state and federal programs. Along the drive to the forest huckleberry site, she pointed out one of the tribe's hatcheries. "It used to be run by the state. They finally handed it over to us because we're doing the right thing." The state, she said, raised the fish in the concrete hatcheries, and the fish returned there. "That's why there was no salmon in the Yakama, no salmon in the Umatilla River." If the saying is true, "When the salmon are gone, we will be gone," it is clear why the Yakama reintroduce salmon as naturally as they can. They cannot replicate the way a female salmon whisks her tail, broomlike, in riverbed gravel to form a nest for her eggs, but they can raise and release baby salmon as early as possible, so adult fish think the river, not the hatchery, is the place of return. "They'll lay their eggs in the river, and their progeny will come back to that spot in the river and will become natural spawners. That's what we had to fight for, for almost two decades, before the state and feds would let us do it."

The divide between the sophistication of salmon and the unsophistication of bureaucrats is remarkable. *Individual* salmon bodies evolve genetically, putting on a specific amount of fat to match their individual situation, including water temperature and distance to be traveled. Compare such subtleties with a government idea to help salmon upstream. I thought "fish story" when Carol told me, but a federal wildlife biologist confirmed it. Because a dam blocked the salmons' route, the federal government proposed collecting them in a truck, driving them past the dam, and dumping them back in the water.

The Yakama prefer more natural routes.

Former tribal opponents, including sports fishermen, are now supporters. "A lot of people would come up to me and shake my hand. 'Would you
go back and tell the tribe thank you? We know if it wasn't for the Yakama
Nation we *still* wouldn't have any fish in the river.' It's taken that long,
twelve years, for people to understand."

"We were taught to think and plan seven generations ahead of ourselves.
We're not here on Mother Earth just to live and go away. We're preparing
Mother Earth for future generations. We're borrowing the water. We're
borrowing the salmon." The well-known Native concept of thinking seven
generations ahead is especially true for Carol Craig. She belongs to the
seventh generation born after the 1855 treaty.

Long into what seemed like the eighth generation, a good four hours after
we left Toppenish, we arrived all at once—a turn in the piney mountain forest shooting us to the huckleberry event site. Carol hopped from her van and
started saying hello. Everyone—running children, ambling adults, including
forest employees in pressed dun-colored uniforms—seemed to be in familiar
surroundings. I, however, gaped. The trees, no longer fleeting images, were
breathtakingly magnificent. Almost as intoxicating was their bracing smell:
sun-warmed high country pine. It managed even to supplant the considerable scents of parking area dust, wood smoke, searing deer meat.

In a clearing amid the trees stood a large tipi, temporary home of a man
who had helped prepare for the ceremony. Near it stood a party tent, the
type with plastic Palladian-style windows. Overheard conversations indicated that getting it up here had been a monster. A few yards away at an outdoor kitchen, men flipped meat, while women, wearing lovely cotton dresses
from which ribbons flowed, cooked other dishes. The dresses, often called
ribbon dresses, are wing dresses to Yakama, said Carol, and signify cooking.
Throughout the area, including within the tent, grew the tiny guests of
honor, knee-high glossy-leaved shrubs full of small dark huckleberries.

Eventually, friendly commotion outside became a respectful and earnest
ceremony inside. Once the eighty or so folding chairs were full, people stood
along the walls. Many were in regalia, but not Carol, who wore her usual
outfit of shirt, shorts, and sandals.

She introduced each speaker. Some prayed in Yakama. Others complained in English, mostly about encroachment. Forest service personnel dutifully listened. Encroachment turned out to be a repeat problem. As people in the Depression had taken huckleberries, leading to the set-aside area for Natives and the famous handshake, now immigrants, particularly from Southeast Asia, did so. Speakers said the newcomers either had no regard for, or knowledge of, rights of aboriginal people, literally spelled out on road signs: "This side of road reserved for Indians." Furthermore, today's intruders were not handpicking, as per tradition, but using metal rakes, aggressively. Some of the pickers cut limbs off the fragile bushes and then found a shady spot to strip the berries. "They're killing the huckleberry plants," said one speaker.

From a wheelchair, Elsie Billy Dick, eighty-nine, spoke in Yakama as a younger woman translated, about gathering huckleberries here before the 1932 treaty, about children playing a stick game, about gathering and roasting pine nuts, about making berry baskets from cedar bark, and of thinning the trees to help the berries grow. Carol later explained that certain trees and underbrush were burned to bring light and nutrients to the huckleberries. People picked in another area until the burned acreage grew back.

The "invasion of the different races," in Elsie Billy Dick's phrase, led to the treaty. She returned repeatedly to problems posed by non-Native pickers. "They're called the Cambodians, taking over the mountains. They're picking and they're selling the berries. Who gave them the right to do that? Being a native of the United States, I would never go to their country and do things like that."

After her long disquisition, it was time for the shaking of hands. Tribal chairwoman Lavina Washines and Gifford Pinchot National Forest supervisor Claire Lavendel rose to do so, and to exchange presents and words of cooperation. Lavendel said as far as she knows, there is no other treaty in the United States like this one. Afterward, Carol—ever alert for a photo op— hustled both women outside to shake hands again in front of the tipi.

Meanwhile, Yakama people set up long tables in the tent and moved chairs into place. Once all were again seated, all took a drink of water. "You're thanking the Creator for bringing all the resources back," Carol explained. "Without water, nothing on Mother Earth would be able to exist." Along with mounds of food passed on platters, glistening bowls of garnet-colored cooked huckleberries adorned the tables. Because they were being honored, they were eaten last. Only at feast's end did spoons dive into them. They tasted soupy and delicious.

Suddenly a post-huckleberry surprise of two birthday cakes appeared. A male chorus sang "Happy Birthday" in Yakama. One cake, from an elderly man to his wife, was preceded by a short speech about "some difficulties" a while back and his wish to be "lovey dovey" again. Such a public apology, explained Carol, means "he's truly sorry. That's part of the tribal ways, so he can get out of the doghouse." The wife, seated to my left, indicated satisfaction.

On the trek back to Toppenish, Carol said she felt everything was worth the time and effort, including letting the Forest Service know the sentiments of the huckleberry guardians.

Yet for her, everything that helps tribal people is worth the time and effort. No, she never tires or gives in, she said. Whether driving from one salmon festival to the next, or from kindergartens to college classrooms to various organizations, she tells one and all about salmon restoration, treaty rights, and "whatever else they want to talk about." She smiled broadly. "I love it. I just love the traveling, the driving. Because there's just me, so I can do what I want."

She has become fond of young audiences that once intimidated her. "The younger they are, the more inquisitive. Ask you all kinds of questions. They don't care. Once they get into middle school and high school, they're quiet. I don't know if it's peer pressure." In ways, she said, college students and adults are as uninformed as children. "That's what I tell the public schools. 'There is no curriculum or requirement to learn anything about tribal people. That's why you don't know anything about us.' They glom us together."

The phrase "ongoing education process" passed her lips once more. Recently, a friend of her son's mentioned "you Indians, when you worship totem poles." (Totem poles, of course, are vertical histories of a sort. They are not worshipped.) Carol's response included the sentence, "John Wayne and Bugs Bunny didn't kill us all."

On Sundays, when she is not traveling, Carol attends services at the longhouse. "I say my prayers every morning." It took her a while to leave the Catholicism her mother brought home from boarding school. By high school, "I was thinking I really haven't learned very much from them. All you have to do is memorize things." Later, in Portland, she attended various Protestant churches. They would have Bible studies she found "real interesting." One reason she moved "back home," though, was to join the longhouse. A man who leads services is "very kind. Some of them aren't. He explains everything. 'This is why we do this.' He'll say it in Yakama and then he'll say it in English." One of Carol's sisters mocks her for embracing the tribal religion. Carol said she does not care.

She also takes secular breaks. In August, there is Portland's Mount Hood Jazz Festival. Her "smooth jazz" favorites include David Sanborn, Dave Brubeck, George Benson, and Diane Schuur. She plays jazz CDs at work. Evenings alone are another source of pleasure. After working from roughly seven in the morning into the late afternoon, Carol gets in her '94 Pontiac Grand Am. Five miles later, she is in her apartment. She locks her door and opens her curtains. "I like lots of light. Then I'll usually take something out of the freezer" and put it in one of her yard-sale collection of cast iron pans. "I love cooking, and I've always had cast iron and remember mom saying, 'Cooks the iron right into your food.'"

Meanwhile, if it is summer, "I get right in my shorts. I throw off my shoes. I get as comfortable as I can. If I want to relax, I'll bring my computer home and play the computer games or word games. In the wintertime, I do the puzzles. I always want to keep my mind going." She loves jigsaw puzzles and prefers the Springbok brand. Sturdier.

In the hour or so her dinner cooks, Carol may watch national news or the Discovery channel. She added, grinning, "I can't miss *Jeopardy*. I've been watching that since I was a kid," and is a longtime fan of the host, Alex Trebek. Once she wrote to show.

"I said, 'Dear *Jeopardy* Writers. I noticed that when you have a Native American category, it's always about tribal people that [were] a long time ago, like we're not here. We're a live people. We're different nations.' Just kind of educated them. I said, 'It would be nice if you had questions like

"This author received the Pulitzer Prize back in 1962 for his book *House Made of Dawn.*"[5] I said, 'We do have smart intelligent tribal people *today.*' I signed it, 'Respectfully Submitted, Carol Craig, Yakama Tribal Member, Yakama Nation.'

"Two months later they had a Native American [category]. They said, 'This is the largest reservation in Washington State.'" An exuberant look crossed her face. "All right! Yeah! It was Yakama. And they spelled it right, with an *a.* Of course the people didn't know it, the contestants."

Carol Craig, endless educator, did not care. "Hey, they read my letter! I loved it."

CHAPTER 14

Powwow Power

TOM PHILLIPS (KIOWA)

On a sticky August evening in Sacramento's O'Neil Park, hard by a highway underpass, master of ceremonies Tom Phillips opened the city's thirteenth annual powwow by invoking timelessness. "Over the year we've lost a lot of our loved ones. A lot of our people have left the circle," he intoned into a microphone. "But we still want to continue on, because that's the way they would want it. They would want us to dance and to carry forward these traditions that Creator has given us and blessed us with."

Tom, a man of medium height, rounded features, glasses (he was considering Lasik surgery), and a long thin black ponytail, possesses an unrushed, graceful manner and an extraordinary resonant baritone that seems to massage his cadences. "Be with us and bear with us and stand with us for these few moments." He called upon Wilma Mouman, an elder from California's Ione band of Miwok Indians,[1] to give a prayer. As she walked to the microphone, Tom raised his voice a fraction to enunciate the expression of acknowledgment and thanks common among California tribes. "A-ho!"

"A-ho!" answered some seventy people.

Sacramento's powwow is on the small side of a spectrum that tops out at the gargantuan Gathering of Nations in Albuquerque. Yet all powwows are simultaneously intimate and formal, as well as welcoming of well-behaved outsiders who, for example, do not hop into the powwow's sacred inner circle, here in Sacramento a worn lawn, to join a ceremonial dance. "Miss

Dances with Daisies" is not welcome. Virtually everyone else is, and no more so than when Tom Phillips holds the mike.

He emcees an average of thirty powwows a year, mostly in California. His experience shows. To open one session of Sacramento's powwow weekend, he strolled from his car to the announcer's table, briefcase in hand, with the other hand swooped up the microphone, switched it on, and greeted the gathering as if he had waited for that moment. He receives an honorarium ranging from $500 for a long weekend's work to an atypical $3,000 at a big casino-sponsored powwow. He also holds two other jobs. Twice weekly he drives from his home in the central valley town of Manteca to San Francisco's Mission District, where he trains counselors at Friendship House, a substance abuse treatment center focusing on Native youth. He also teaches at Cal State Stanislaus's graduate Social Work Department in Turlock, thirty miles from home.

As Sacramento's Friday opening ceremonies unfolded almost lethargically, Tom was enthusiasm itself. "Find a good place to sit on the ground. If you didn't bring your chair, throw your blanket out there and enjoy yourself! Relax. Hope you each and every one have a good time tonight. We welcome you," he said, making a point to include dancers, sponsors, vendors, and visitors. Among them were a few Phillips family members, including infant granddaughter Michaela, nestled in a modern beaded cradleboard.

It was good to be with Tom's family, but how disappointing the powwow was so small, the attendance so modest, the dances so few. Only two of five scheduled groups showed up that evening. Tom announced that one no-show had a car accident, another had a death in the family. As he said prayers for them and relayed the updated schedule, I dreamily recalled the first powwow I attended.

It was on the Kumeyaays' Sycuan Reservation in the desert hills of southern California, a few hundred yards from the tribe's hugely profitable casino, and was one upscale powwow. The sacred inner circle was fresh sod, brilliantly green. The audience sat under roofs of freshly cut willow branches on sturdy wooden supports, not white plastic canopies on metal sticks like here in Sacramento. The Kumeyaay emcee and other dignitaries presided from a well-built grandstand. In Sacramento, Tom sat at a folding table.

That Friday evening at Kumeyaay, skies over sage-scented hills were dark, blazes of artificial light bright, the contrast a dramatic setting for the unfolding explosion of sound and movement called Grand Entry. First, drumbeats pulsed the air. Then the tribal chairman, moving his feet slowly to the rhythm and carrying the eagle staff—a symbol of Indian history and culture—entered the inner circle. In chronological second place came the American flag, carried by a solemn color guard of Native veterans. Then! There arrived in single file at least a hundred dancers and singers of all ages and numerous tribes, also moving to the drumbeat. They entered clockwise, slowly filling the circle with blazes of color and movement. The dancers' regalia ranged from lavishly beaded buckskin and elaborate feather head-dresses to less fortunate raiment of polyester. The dancers' bodies swirled, swooped, spun, swayed. As spectacle alone, the Sycuan Grand Entry was thrilling. Okay, not everyone was thrilled. There were then, as there often are, sleeping babies and bored teenagers. "This is like my thousandth powwow this summer."

Sacramento's Friday evening proceedings revealed no evidence of casino riches. Admission cost four dollars. And, sigh, there was no Grand Entry. That would happen the next afternoon, under bright skies, and be minimal in size. Yet in a way, everything about the Sacramento powwow was thrilling too; it exists.

Thanks to people such as Tom Phillips, hundreds of powwows take place annually. Despite differences in cash flow, geography, and population, among other circumstances, the basic layout is the same. The sacred inner-most area, whether sod, dirt, or linoleum, is meant only for the invited. Tom's daughter Josephine all but pushed me onto Sacramento's to join in the Blanket Dance, used to raise money for dancers and singers or someone in need. Although participation merely requires dropping a donation on an open blanket and shaking the hand of each veteran—including Navajo code talker Joe Morris!—standing beside it, I feared a "Miss Dances with Daisies" expulsion.

Surrounding the sacred area is the audience, primarily extended tribal families. Old-timers tend to nestle into aluminum lawn chairs their grand-children set up, while younger attendees unroll the newer canvas variety.

Families tote in coolers, too, containing copious amounts of food and soft drinks, powwows being adamantly alcohol free. Most people wear comfortable modern clothes, sometimes with a signifier such as a silver bracelet or a ribbon shirt. Tom's signifier, other than his ponytail, was a polo shirt with the embroidered words Kiowa Nation on the breast pocket. One day he sported a T-shirt on which was printed Michaela's photo and "Grandchild #7!" Tom looks resplendent in ceremonial Kiowa regalia but otherwise does not stand out as a fashion plate.

More or less surrounding the audience is a promenade space, used for strolling, visiting, introducing the baby. In Kumeyaay, the space was desert dirt, but sprayed down and raked daily, like a Japanese garden.

Surrounding the promenade area are the ubiquitous vendors, with wares of jewelry, dream catchers, blankets, wall hangings, clothing, paintings on leather, and food. The clothing vendors have the edgiest items, like T-shirts with Calvin Klein's CK logo, which on closer inspection spells out "Custer Killer." An especially popular T-shirt features a photograph of four armed Native men, including Geronimo. Above are the words "Homeland Security." Below, "Fighting Terrorism Since 1492."

Because many vendors make the same rounds every year, they are part of the ongoing reunions among participants and visitors. During a break, Tom walked to virtually every stall, getting caught up, and spreading greetings and cheer, before heading back to his table.

The busiest vendors sell food, in big helpings. Some powwows offer roasted corn on the cob and other healthy fare, but most veer toward dishes based on the beloved/discouraged staple of fry bread, dishes that lead to sales of XXXL T-shirts and an intertribal scourge of diabetes. (A Lakota friend who works on the Pima Maricopa Reservation told me it has three dialysis centers for a population of 1,000.) Among the vendors' circle are also representatives from organizations offering help with housing, job training, AIDS prevention, and treatment for meth, alcoholism, and diabetes.

"One more time, we say thank you to all the vendors *all* the way around the circle," Tom continued on opening night. They "traveled many miles to be here this weekend with us." After an invitation to "take a look and take something home with you," he effortlessly switched gears to introduce the bear dancers, "whose songs are for healing, for medicine, for longevity. A-ho!"

"A-ho!"—the accent on "ho," the "a" so soft as to disappear, is close to the expression Tom spoke in the Kiowa language of his native Oklahoma. "I grew up using 'A-hoh, dey onh day!' as an expression of gratitude throughout my life," he told me.

Thomas Carlisle Phillips has reason for gratitude. For starters, unlike two of his great grandparents, he was not captured as a child by a raiding party. Tom's maternal great grandfather, a Mexican named Calisay (the spelling is a family guess), was captured by Kiowas in a raid in the mid-1860s. Calisay's future wife, Tom's great grandmother, Mary Hamilton, was taken as a child in the mid-1870s. As he explained in an e-mail, she was "a White captive and she was captured by the Kiowas, including Set'tien day (White Bear) and Tien Goodle (Red Heart) whose sister could not bear children and she wanted a child to raise." In the raid, Kiowas captured Mary and her older sister and killed the rest of their family. The older girl cried so much, "the Kiowa feared they would be found with her and her sister. They took the older girl to the [Indian] Agency and told the agent they found her walking alone on the prairie." They kept Mary. Tom's e-mail continued, she "became They-gome gah day which translates to 'Stands Behind the Tipi.' She was a brave young lady and was the inspiration for Michael Blake in his book *Dances with Wolves* for the character named 'Stands with a Fist.'"[2]

Because neither relative is known to have written about the capture, Tom's rendition is as close as both came to the literary genre of "captivity narratives." Mary Hamilton/They-gome gah day/Stands Behind the Tipi is also known in the family for the following story. During a flash flood, the chief's pony was swept into a river. Young boys of the tribe stayed on the banks and watched, afraid to intervene. She, still a young girl, dove in, grabbed the halter and saved the pony, much to the boys' humiliation.

After marrying fellow captive Calisay, she had six children, among them Tom's grandfather, Carlisle Calisay, born in 1894. He became a skilled wrangler and ranch worker: an Indian cowboy. He "was always on the road, always working. He was a bronc rider. He would be hired by different farmers and ranchers to break their horses." Carlisle Calisay worked for Kiowa ranchers and white homesteaders, the former eventually losing out to the latter. According to accounts I read, in the early twentieth century white thieves stole Indian stock with no fear of reprisal, and Texas ranchers purposely grazed their herds on Kiowa lands. "I heard that, too," said Tom. His wrangling grandfather, he added, "was also a ceremonial leader." Tom's middle name, Carlisle, honors him. The name Thomas honors his other grandfather.

The first genetic Kiowa to enter the Kiowa family was Carlisle Calisay's wife, Bessie Ko-kom, Tom's grandmother. "She is full-blood Kiowa and also a daughter of one of our principle chiefs, Ko-kom." She died shortly after giving birth to Tom's mother, from tuberculosis. "It was pretty rampant among our Kiowa people."

"So, my mother is half Kiowa by blood and one-quarter Mexican and one-quarter white, but on the Kiowa tribal rolls she is full-blood Kiowa. My grandfather [Carlisle Calisay, whose last name government officials some-how changed to Kodaseet] was also enrolled as full-blood Kiowa, although he was a [child of captives]. He and his brother and sisters were all culturally, tribally, and linguistically Kiowa. All spoke the Kiowa language and are held in very high regards as prominent members of the tribe." Tom revealed this lineage only after I asked his mother's name. Short answer: Roxie Kodaseet.

Tom, a member of Kiowa's Zodlh-Tone band, which translates as Stinking Creek, remains fluent in Kiowa, which he described as "clicky" and "guttural." He inserts it into prayers, even if nobody understands. No matter. Prayers at Native events often are given in a Native language—an increasingly valued medium—which the speaker might translate all, some, or none of. People bow their heads for all options. The rhetorical question goes, "Who cares if anyone can understand, as long as the Creator can?"

Tom's father's family is Muscogee Creek from Eufaula, Oklahoma. (Muscogee is the restored tribal word, Creek the anglicized one—and Muskogee the town.) The name Phillips does not point to a British ancestor but derives from the missionary practice of trying to save souls, Tom explained in another e-mail. "I am told that the Creek people with English surnames were baptized and given English names to 'transform' them from Pagans into Christians. The Muscogee Creeks who retained their Indian names were not baptized, i.e., Talassee, Minitubby, Solasee, etc. . . . nor were Indians with 'translated' names, i.e., Tall Chief, Ten Bears." Tom, who was born in 1944, in Lawton, Oklahoma, has no idea what his surname would be without Christian intervention.

His comments came between emcee duties on an increasingly hot Sacramento Saturday. Under the canopy today were more Phillips family members, including Tom's son-in-law (father of baby Michaela), Michael Singh, who danced at the powwow too. Singh? I asked Tom later. *Singh?* Yes. One of Michael's great grandfathers is Punjabi, thus making Michael, well, Indian and Indian. "We tease him," Tom chuckled.

Also here today, besides baby Michaela and mother Josephine, were Tom's youngest child, Samuel, a slim good-looking teenager, who is deaf, and a deaf friend. They cracked each other up in sign language. Tom signs too, but some of Samuel's laughs involved his father's mis-signs. Josephine, a classroom assistant in the San Joaquin County school district, attained ASL certification to communicate with her brother.

As an amplified voice urged vendors please to move their vehicles to avoid getting a ticket from Park and Rec, Tom continued talking about his mother. After various family members raised her to school age, she was sent to government-sponsored boarding schools, including one in Oklahoma's Fort Sill, essentially part of Lawton, and to Riverside Indian School farther away in Anadarko, a flat town whose all but deserted downtown streets today include the Redskin movie theater. Boarding school experiences have been recalled with fury and sorrow by earlier generations of Native children, but Tom implied his mother did fine. "The boarding schools for the Kiowa were right on the reservation. They weren't thousands of miles [away], like many other tribes," at most "maybe a day's travel by horseback from their families. But certainly [there] was the requirement of the school matrons, the teachers, to prohibit the speaking of the language. I'm sure the intent was to try to acculturate the Kiowas to speaking English and becoming knowledgeable of [the] English language, so they could become more self-sufficient in the new world."

That was a most generous interpretation. He agreed, adding that "intent" did not leave many Kiowas happy. "They were lonesome, they missed their children. Their children ran away from schools. They were whipped, they were beaten, they were abused. Certainly that was the experience of many of the Kiowas that went to boarding school."

Roxie Kodaseet, however, managed to progress to the University of Kansas. She studied business, but not for long. She had met Tom's father at her last boarding school, married him, gave birth to Tom's sister, and dropped out of college to care for her. "When my mom got pregnant with me, it was World War II, so my father enlisted in the United States Army and went overseas." Somewhere on the European front is all Tom knows. "When he came back, I was born. I guess like many other Indians, [he] got caught up in alcohol and drinking, which was a part of military life at that time. He became abusive and kind of violent with her, and she wouldn't tolerate. . . ." he trailed off before adding, "She wasn't raised with that." Tom shook his head as powwow announcements continued. "I have very early recall of one incident where I hid under an ironing board. In those days they were boards, they weren't metal. I heard him yelling at her and kind of pushing her around." From under the ironing board, "I remember yelling, 'Stop! Stop! Stop! Leave her alone!'" His parents divorced "when I was just an infant child." Tom never had the "desire" to see his father again.

At the age of four, Tom contracted the same disease that killed his grandmother. His tuberculosis ate away the socket of his left hip. "Transplant surgery was new, so they did experimental surgery and grafted some of my shin on my right leg to my hip socket. I spent a year going through that process" at the University of Oklahoma Children's Hospital. "After that, the doctors didn't think I'd be able to walk, but I was able to get full recovery." The problems were reason enough for his mother to make sure Tom was not sent to boarding school. Furthermore, there were hospital visits every month. "We went before the sun came up and came home after the sun came down."

The silver lining in the struggle was that by not attending boarding schools, Tom maintained fluency in the Kiowa language and learned Kiowa culture, often from elders. They spoke about pre-Columbian days and "Kiowa traditional protocol." Tom added, in his typically diplomatic under-statement, "The reservation era kind of changed a lot of that."

"That was the time when the tribes were at war with the United States to resist removal from their homelands, when America expanded westward. There was a move toward eminent domain, so the railways came through. Then after the railways, the cattle drives came through, and after the cattle drives, the land rush came through. Indian people were kind of a barrier to that development, and so they were forcibly removed from their homelands into reservations." Understatements continued. "We adapted to a changing and evolving lifestyle. Reservation lifestyle took away the dependence on the land, so we became dependent on the government for sustenance. . . . Then we began to see the industrial revolution take over, and became a more mechanized world."

The announcer was telling people to keep children off the center powwow grounds. "Let your kids know it is something sacred still in America, that it's a circle. It means a lot."

Tom's mind was on the past. "Pre-Columbian times, we didn't have a need for weapons. Bows and arrows were used for hunting. We didn't have weapons for defense. When we had that contact with Europeans, particularly with the Spanish, they were a very fierce people and would attack our Indian villages, thinking we had gold and all kinds of things. We had to adapt to that." Adaptation meant weapons.

It used to be, Tom continued, "Indian people lived and died within a short distance of their birthplace. Fifty miles, if that." But once the Spaniards brought horses, Kiowas mounted, and the world opened. "Kiowas were curious. They were adventurers, they were explorers." In addition to hearing "the old ones" tell of Kiowa journeys "up into the ice land where they saw the white bear," he heard about tribal explorers going into Mesoamerica and returning "with tales of seeing the little men in the trees with tails." All tales were told in Tom's native language. "Maintaining the language has always been a part of the Kiowa culture. Storytelling was in Kiowa. Ceremonies were in Kiowa. Family gatherings were in Kiowa." Intensive use of the language ended when "our young Kiowa men" went off to World War I, a time, incidentally, before Native people had the right to vote.

Tom was about seventeen when elders nudged him into a ceremonial role, asking him to come forward and greet families at a gathering. It would

have been called a dance in English, he said, today a powwow. His primary
teacher was Carlisle Calisay/Kodaseet. "My grandfather was one of our tribal
orators." So was Tom's father.

The duties of today's powwow master of ceremonies have expanded far
into modern life. He (it's usually a he) must know not only social and ceremonial protocols. He is also the watchdog, picking up the mike to warn
people when cameras are not allowed. He is the introducer of dancers,
singers, drum circles, religious leaders, elders. He is the cheerleader, encouraging applause before or after dances ("How 'bout that!") and encouraging
onlookers to visit the vendors. He acts as emergency go-between, making
announcements about lost children. He is often a comedian, expected to
make groan-inducing jokes and puns. Judging from times I have heard Tom
emcee, he is no jokester. He also may act as historian, giving background
about a particular dance. That is Tom's specialty.

At the Sacramento powwow, he introduced the gourd dancers, older men
who sang while moving slowly to the beat of a gourd rattle they shook in one
hand, a feather fan in the other. The gourd dance is said to originate with
the Kiowa, thus perhaps Tom's full-throated fervor in explaining, over the
singing, the dance honoring those who guarded Kiowa encampments
against enemies and wild animals. "These warriors put themselves in harm's
way each and every day, twenty-four seven, [to] patrol the perimeter of
our encampments." He went on, his cadence steady, Kiowa chiefs Satanta,
White Bear, Lonewolf, Guey-chaga, Great Heart, all part of the encampment
society, wrote some of the songs that "recognize the role the chief plays as
the leader of the people. The chief will never put his family in jeopardy or in
danger; he never puts the young men in danger. He always goes out in front
and first. This dance honors that warrior spirit." The men continued singing
as Tom's voice rang out, a coda to the music and movement, explaining that
the gourd rattle "is symbolic of their position as camp police. They dance in
a whipping motion, replicating and emulating driving out the enemy. The
dance is very solemn, very respectful. Dance around Mother Earth, dance
around the encampment.

"The fan they're carrying, as Indian people we use these feathers because
the birds fly up to the heavens. They take our prayers with them. When we

have our ceremonies, we use the fans to smudge and smoke and cleanse ourselves. These gentlemen that carry these fans, that is their purpose as they dance. They may be offering prayers, they may be sending thoughts for good people."

He went on to describe the symbolism of the colors in blankets draped over the men's shoulders. Just before he seemed to be ending, he added an entirely new element.

Notice that the dance is repetitive, he said, but that the tempo picks up. "That also reminds us of the process of life. When we're born into this world, things are slow. In that first year the child develops, learns how to sit up and to crawl and later on to walk. Life begins to pick up speed after that. These songs, they replicate life. As life progresses, it gets a little bit more speed, a little more tempo." Seniors like him may find, "My, that year went by fast. The tempo of life and the beat of life begins to pick up faster, and that's the song you sing."

———

For a long while Tom lost the culture he so cherishes. As a teenager, he became part of the flawed federal experiment of relocation. "A brain drain," Tom called it, with unusual bite. "Many of our Indian people now believe it was a conspiracy by the government to remove the brightest and best thinkers from the reservation, so they could not promote the intent and recovery of the tribe. [The government] introduced programs that appeared to be helpful, but the intent was to have us removed from our homeland."

The young Oklahoman went west on a relocation program in the 1960s, to become a merchant seaman. "I didn't even know what a merchant seaman was. Had never been to sea, had never seen the ocean."

Through the Bureau of Indian Affairs and the Pacific Maritime Association, Tom was sent for training two hours north of San Francisco at a retirement home for merchant seamen. The home, he said, almost smiling, was a "really beautiful facility. There was *ducks*."

He lived with some 120 students, including several Natives, thanks to a Native union representative who tried to give them opportunities. "We were trained in the stewards union, which were cooks, bakers, room stewards, waiters." The goal was to work on cruise ships. "We learned how to be waiters. We learned how to be dishwashers. We learned how to work in the larder, and we learned how to work in the cooking station." They not only fed the retirees three times a day, but "after the meals were served, we would go up and make up their rooms. It was full training on how to be a proper room steward, how to be a proper waiter."

After graduating, Tom's virgin voyage was on a cargo ship with twelve passengers.

"I never will forget the first time I saw a foreign country, Yokohama, Japan. I was really amazed how small a scale things were. The bathrooms were small, the cars were small, the mechanisms that operated the loading and unloading of cargo were small. The highways were small, the people were small."

Tom, if intrigued, had not said sayonara to Oklahoma. "I missed the ceremonies, I missed the songs. I would find myself on deck singing the ceremonial songs. Pretty soon I'd look around and I had a whole congregation of people standing around me, listening. I didn't get far from the practice. I still had my own meditations, my prayers, my thoughts and missing family and being lonely. Maybe I wasn't as lonely as I just missed birthdays and missed the family gatherings, because it was an adventure for me as well. Being out on the sea. Being able to see different lands."

Through a fellow seaman from the Sac and Fox Nation of Oklahoma, Tom met and married "an Italian lady" in California. They annulled the marriage after six months. "She went her way and I went mine." He later married a "very fine Indian woman," a Navajo named Helen Devore, now Waukazoo.

Helen is the major force behind construction of Friendship House's handsome modern facility, which has rooms for some seventy residents, and an outdoor space with meditation garden and sweat lodge. In the dining hall on a day Tom was to conduct a graduation ceremony, he pointed out an old black-and-white photograph of the staff, including attractive young Helen. Attractive young Tom was in the photograph too. They have a daughter, Crystal, who is a legal secretary in Oakland. Tom calls her "inspirational." His marriage to Helen lasted about three years. "There were philosophical differences and emotional differences and all those kinds of things." The two now have what seems like a cordial relationship. "My current marriage," he called it, to the former Wanda Gene (formerly Gene-hah, pronounced jen-nay-hah), is in its thirty-fourth year. "She's Walapai from Big Springs, Arizona, and half Navajo. She's a good woman, and we have four children together." He named each by location, marriage status, and grandchildren. Josephine and her family live with Tom and Wanda. "That's common in Indian families. My youngest lives with us as well."

None of Tom's children is fluent in Kiowa, although he speaks it with them. Mostly he uses it by phone with family members in Oklahoma or powwows there. "To be fluent in it, I have to be home. Very few fluent Kiowa speakers out here in California."

As a young man, Tom kept his language but "got away from the culture, got away from the family, got away from relationships, came from Oklahoma to San Francisco into a new world where the tallest buildings are on New Montgomery. Buildings of finance." Tom earlier cited an observation that a culture is judged by its highest buildings.

In a passage that sounded often repeated, he said the new culture drew him in as if into a spider web, that he got confused about what was real, needed to escape, and "many times we find that escape and that relief through alcohol, or through drugs, or through other kinds of, quote, 'deviant behaviors'—pornography." Tom's spider web did not engulf him long. He has been sober for decades.

Meanwhile, he was sent to Vietnam. He was 4F because of his tuberculosis but deemed fit enough to be a merchant seaman. "I was on commercial freighters up the Saigon River, transporting supplies for the troops. We didn't supply munitions, but we brought all their dry stores, soda pop, beer, cigarettes, candy. We were shot at."

Asked his feelings about the war, he looked thoughtful. "I did not see the need for it. In my mind it was commercial exploitation to advance the status of war. Goodyear, Goodrich, rubber plantations needed protection, and the only way to get that protection is to declare it a war zone or to have a conflict so the military presence would protect the plantations. I didn't see it as a war of necessity. Similarly, I don't feel Iraq is a war of necessity. I don't believe we should ever have *war*. We've had enough on our people. We have lost generations of children and family because of war. I don't think any Indian person believes in war, but we do have a sense of dedication and commitment to defend our homeland." The motivation is "not necessarily a sense of patriotism, but certainly a sense of commitment as a warrior."

Part of Tom's time back San Francisco coincided with the takeover in 1969 by Native people of an abandoned prison island in San Francisco Bay named Alcatraz. "That gave opportunity for a lot of Natives, a lot of American Indians, to reconsider what they wanted to do about this"—he paused—"realization that our government had not been treating us fairly. Kind of gave us a wake-up call. 'What are you going to do? How are you going to help your community?' I began to really think. What are my priorities? What do I want to do with my life? Began to listen, began to watch. And I helped on the shore side, volunteered some time to receive donations for Alcatraz for the ones on Alcatraz Island." Did he not want to get on board and join the occupiers? Not at all. "I'd lived on ships for eight, nine years."

After the Alcatraz occupation ended, Tom felt at loose ends. Having heard about Friendship House, then located elsewhere, he decided to stop by, if only to see Native faces. "I missed family. I went and met a lot of people. And lo and behold!" Two men Tom knew as merchant seamen were on the staff. "They said, 'You ought to come and work here.' I said, 'I'm shipping out now, but I'll certainly think about it.'" When he returned, he filled out an application for a social activities coordinator. He got the job, eventually became a counselor, then gained his current position as instructor of counselors. His career as a merchant seaman was over. Heavier lifting had begun.

———

When Tom counseled incoming residents, he tried to determine "their level of assimilation" into Western culture. "If they're operating from a totally Western dynamic, certainly my interview technique is going to be a little different." He first introduced himself, then asked what brought them here. "Indian people, when they meet someone for the first time, they'll say,

'Where are you from?'" The answer helps counselors frame the person. "'I'm from Redding.' They begin to put that together. 'Okay, Redding. That's around the Wintun area, the Wailaki area.' We're trying to set up, what is their belief? What is their practice? We're beginning to develop point of contact." The next questions involve relatives. "We might know their family. They may say, Jackson. Okay, Jackson family, they're loggers." The inquiry continues. "Who are your people? It's very important to Indian people. . . . We say that we're all related, so there might be a common denominator between me and the client sitting across the table."

Everything is relevant. "Age differential, gender differential, region, area, kinship, those all have a connecting part. You have to be familiar with the Indian culture to understand that and how to apply that. A noncultural counselor may not understand. 'Which theoretic framework shall I approach? Shall I go into Jungian? Shall I go into Gestalt?'"

Some clients knew little of their culture. "'All I know is I'm Indian.'" In such cases, counselors go to questions related to what got them there, what treatment if any they have had. Then came assessment. "What kind of behaviors are they displaying?" In addition, counselors determine how intense someone's "addictive history" is and what "psychosocial factors" are involved. They also determine when the person last used whatever substance. If the answer is "every day for the past six months," end of probing interview for now. After detox, treatment starts.

All along, Tom used himself as a point of reference. "I bring my life experience to the table for the clients and say, 'I've gone through what you're going through right now. I know the loneliness. I know the despair, the frustration, the anger, the resentment. Part of that is the further I get away from my culture, the more I'm going to experience what you're going through. But when I get back, the closer I get to the culture, the stronger I become in the practice. I'm coming back to that *cangleska*, back to that medicine wheel for those four sacred components we all have, the mental, the physical, the spiritual, and the emotional,'" he said, as if again counseling. "'That's what I want you to know. I've sat in that chair you're in. I was fortunate to find my recovery by going back to the practice of custom and tradition and knowing who I was as an Indian man. Once I got back into it, it became my sanctuary. It became my healing circle, my wellness, my balance. That's what I want you to do. I want you to realize you can come back into the circle. You may not ever have been to the circle before, but if you come in with an understanding that you get away from the drugs and the alcohol, you're going to find balance. No matter what tribe you're from, even if you're *not* Native, you're going to find that balance by coming into that same circle.'"

The more traditional the clients, the more tradition was prescribed. "If they come from a sweat lodge family, we're going to make sure they're out there in a sweat lodge on a frequent basis. If they're powwow dancers, we're going to try and make sure they're connected with powwow. But alcohol and drug free. That's one thing we try to stress. 'Maybe in your past powwow experience you've been outside of the circle, around out in the back in the car behind the tipis, drinking and using and smoking." No more. "When you come to the circle there's light, there's community, there's children. Your behavior is going to have to reflect that. You're going to start consider- ing you need to be a role model."

At some point in discussing his counseling career, Tom said centers such as Friendship House should not exist. "It's an irony we would even have to have substance abuse treatment programs," or facilities for domestic violence. He ran through a now familiar saga, that Native traditions prohibit "aggressive behavior, assertive behaviors," that they were all brought on by fur trappers who "introduced fermented beverage, rum, in exchange for the furs," and that alcohol, along with governmental "policy toward our Indian people," including "attempts to assimilate our Indian people into the main- stream," led to sacrificing their own culture. Adding to that the impact of boarding schools, the result was "displaced behaviors, manifested hostilities and anger and resentment," resulting in "venting and violence toward relations, relatives, family. That was not a practice and that was not a part of our cultural way," he said more forcefully than usual. Now—in great summary—the job is to get back to tradition.

Tom himself has accommodated another belief. Besides "my traditional way," he is a practicing Methodist. Both suit him. "I believe there is a spiri- tualism that has to supersede the religious ritual. That's got to be your own connection with everything around you. Other Natives can't find that balance because they are constantly bombarded with the conflicts of religious practice versus traditional practice. I haven't had that difficulty." He focuses instead on "the balance" within Christianity and traditional practice, and finds both have a common "process of renewal." There is one major difference, in his opinion. "With Christianity, there is sin. With Native practice, there's not."

―――――

It was time for the Friendship House graduation. Today's was one of several held every year for residents who pass milestones of sobriety. "Because of our cultural losses, we've lost a lot of the ceremonies that were an integral part of our Indian way," Tom had said, softly. "Those included rites of passage, recognitions and honorings. We don't have that practice intact. We're trying to reestablish that by this completion ceremony."

The dining hall was crowded with about one hundred residents, staff, graduates, family members, and friends, including a group of bikers who had roared up to support their sober buddy. One, unclear on the concept, wore a T-shirt reading "Outlaw Saloon." After a taco lunch that residents cooked and served, came testimony. The most moving remarks were from role models, graduates who returned after years of sobriety and now wept in gratitude. A very wrenching story came from a recovering addict, a very young woman, whose parents stood stiffly beside her.

Then Tom, who had opened the proceedings, again took the microphone. He acknowledged the drum circle that was beating a kind of counterpoint to his remarks, he thanked various people, and he let loose. "Keep it real and not just be a wannabe," he almost shouted. "The only way you can be real is to have a real spirit in your heart. In your mind. In your body. In your spirit. In your soul."

After more such words of motivation, he asked everyone to stand for the closing prayer.

"We give thanks today that you have been here to share this experience of graduation. Once again, Creator, we call upon you. We ask you to look upon us as we bring this ceremony to a close. Thank you for the goodness and the wellness in your spirit. For the voices of those that have received these gifts of recovery. To the voices of thank yous for the families that have been here, the counselors. For the appreciation, gratitude, of our executive officer. You know the needs of each one honored today. Their families are giving you thanks, Creator. Pray that you will be with us until the next time we gather for the ceremony." He spoke for a minute in Kiowa, then closed. "All these things we ask. A-ho."

"A-ho," came whispers in return.

CHAPTER 15

Relearning for Life

HENRY FRANK (YUROK)

It seems remarkable, given the circumstances, that Henry Frank is thriving as an artist. Is it the power of art or is it the power of Henry?

As he held up his woodcuts, Henry, generally a modest man, all but beamed. A self-portrait titled *Big Bear Medicine* features the top half of Henry's Buddha-like torso, his hands clasped lightly, his expression serene behind glasses. Emanating from his wide head and long hair are myriad strands, possibly of hair, possibly of light. Henry's face and arms ("the color of copper," he wrote in an essay for a college class) are white like the paper, the rest mostly dark.

A sheet of other woodcuts—really linoleum cuts, he explained—is titled *Klamath Inhabitants* and includes a cabin, a Japanese-style riverscape, a bear grasping a birch tree. Henry signed both pieces "Hawk," the translation of the Yurok name his grandmother gave him in childhood.

A year later, he was working on smaller woodcuts, of a hawk, wolf, otter, deer, each containing geometrical imagery he hoped was Yurok. He was planning to arrange them as one larger piece, with a spider in the center. "It's going to be called *Web of Life*." Another woodcut portrayed his mother's aunt, whose existence he learned about shortly after she died.

Henry was painting, too, mostly animals with iridescent touches. "I'm a huge Liquitex fan." He had framed the paintings with branches. He was also learning to make hand drums. Several hung on a wall. One was for his father. "'I want it square and I want it eighteen by eighteen.' I had to compromise because the skin isn't that big of a deer, so I made it fifteen by fifteen. I was

like, 'Tell me how to make it traditionally.' He's like, 'You're Yurok, so whatever you make is going to be all right. Just make it square.'" His father also
wanted it painted, which was fine with Henry—paint makes the skin tauter.
"Then he wanted abalone inlay. Well, if I have the abalone and learn how to
inlay, which probably is just a Dremel [power tool] or a router, I could probably do all that, but I didn't think there was going to be that much space in
here [the studio where he works]." Henry ultimately nixed the abalone. The
rest of the drum was coming along, with some elements arriving from a mail
order trading post. "I'll probably have a bear claw hanging off this." He
gestured to the strap. "I'll have four eagle feathers on this side and four red
tail hawks on this side. I'll have a grizzly bear pattern and maybe a little frog,
because in our culture it's good luck." Henry seemed elated to oblige his
father's request. "He said he's going to play it all the time. He'll take it all
around the rez [the Yurok Reservation] and play songs."

Ever since he was "a little guy," as Henry put it, his father encouraged
Henry's artistic talents. "I'm going to share a story." (Reader beware: it is disgusting.) "I'd seen my dad draw all the time, and he would make leatherwork,
he would make regalia, arrows, and quivers. One day he was out at school,
and I was there with his girlfriend, my brother and I. I used the restroom.
And I reached in after I was done, grabbing out the stool, and I rubbed it all
over the wall. But not just any way. I shaped and everything. She was hot.
'Wait till your father comes! You can't be doing that.' As soon as Dad walks
in the door, 'You got to go see what your son did.' She's screaming, and she
walks him back there. 'Here! This is what he did!' And he's like, 'Oh, my God.
We have an *artist*!' So I get that, and he pulls me aside, says, 'We got to wash
this off. There are more appropriate ways to express yourself artistically.'

"That's when I got the coloring book and crayons, and then it goes into
pencil and pen and paper and then carvings and then on the beach with the
mud. When I was about thirteen, I started drawing my Transformers and
my GI Joes and getting my depth perception down. Later on I get into making regalia earrings and necklaces. When I got in here, I started branching
out to colored pens and mixing colored pens with colored pencils. Then it
went to watercolor. From watercolor I went to acrylics. Then they offered
this block printing class. It's a whole new world. I enjoy it. Like any artwork,

it puts me at ease and kind of focuses where I'm into the spirit of the piece, so I can get it exactly the way I envision it. If people appreciate that, cool. If they don't, well, I like it."

Such equanimity is hard won. The place where Henry Frank creates art is California's San Quentin State Penitentiary.

––––––

His case, in great summary, is this. He was "affiliated with the Eighteenth Street Gang" in Eureka, the port city about five hours north of San Francisco. (He later wrote me, "I did not ever see myself as a gang member, but a person playing a role, because when all the water evaporated, the only thing left was a Yurok Native American.") Late in the afternoon of New Year's Eve, 1993, at the age of nineteen, Henry drove the gang car, a yellow Cadillac, with two (apparent) gang members to the Bayshore Mall. "One of the guys outside said, 'Hey, take me to the store.' I'm like, 'I'm just here to say hi and bye and give my respects to Jason [a friend whose brother had died].' He's like, 'Come on, man, you got to take me to the store.'" He got in, as did the second passenger, who claimed, "I like to feel the wind on my face."

"I drive down to Bayshore Mall. And then all kinds of crazy stuff happened. Guy gets shot. And I'm just like, 'Wow.' My choice was either get out of the car or take off. I took off. That's how I'm involved. I didn't tell on anybody. I figured when I was in court, the truth will come out, and the truth was I didn't have nothing to do with the planning. There was no plan to my knowledge."

The prosecution argued the trip was planned with the goal of shooting any Asian in retaliation for an Asian gang's earlier attack. Henry contends he did not know that either passenger carried a gun, much less planned to use it. He asked rhetorically, if they had said, "'Hey, Hen, let's go shoot someone,' you think I'd have gotten in the car?"

The victim, whom Henry does not want named, had been eating dinner with family members. Did he die? I asked Henry. "He lived. I mean, he suffered, because he lost a spleen, and he has to live with that for the rest of his life. But he's still alive." The reason, Henry wrote me, that he "respect-fully requests" the man be identified only as "of Asian descent" is that "I really don't want him to suffer more than he already has. I pray that he does not view himself as a victim still and has moved on with his life and is enjoying it for all that it has to offer."

Henry refused to testify against fellow gang members. "If you're raised in a regular household, to be a good citizen," you tell authorities what you know. "If you're in that lifestyle" as a gang member, you tell nothing. "I was a loyal subject. And my father had no respect for an informant."

Henry's first lawyer, Christopher Wilson, now a judge in Eureka, said in a telephone interview he wanted Henry to testify.[1] "I think he would have made a decent witness." Henry's version: "I told my lawyer I would, but I'm not going to mention names." After some back and forth, Henry did not take the stand. Judge Wilson described him as "a pretty naïve kid" who "hooked up with the wrong people." Who knows, he mused, whether Henry put the pieces together that evening, adding with an audible sigh, "I have true affection for this kid."

He also wanted Henry to accept a plea bargain he had worked out, but the "overconfident" lawyer for the man accused of the shooting persuaded all three defendants to reject it. Instead, Henry was at the mercy of the jury, citizens of a community to whom gang violence was "very frightening," said Wilson, especially in a well-known gathering place. Jurors threw the proverbial book at all three defendants.

Henry Edward Frank, by then twenty, was convicted of multiple counts of conspiracy to murder and attempted murder, with four extra years for a hate crime. He had vented in jail about being a victim of an Asian gang. "I referred to the Asian gangbangers as rice balls. They recorded it, and it came back. 'We see this man obviously has problems with this race.'" Henry claims he is not anti-Asian. "I was practically raised in San Francisco. All my friends were Asian."

His sentence was twenty-nine years to life. "I've been incarcerated since February 15, 1994." Had he accepted the plea bargain, he likely would have been released in 2001; the sentence was for seven years.

————

Wilson filed a motion for a new trial. Henry was "clearly not the shooter," did not share the shooter's intent, and lacked "malice," among other arguments. Motion denied. Many anguished letters, mostly handwritten, then went to the sentencing judge from Henry's family and others. One woman, calling Henry "eminently trustworthy," wrote that he continually urged her runaway daughter to return home and tried to keep her "as safe as he knew how given his living situation." The letters had no notable effect.

"I did about two years at county [Humboldt County Jail]," recited Henry, "eight years in Corcoran [State Prison]. I've been here for about four years. My first parole hearing should be in 2013. At the current rate, you're not getting out on your first time," he paused, "so I probably still have about another ten years after that." His chain of appeals and state-appointed lawyers ended with a rejection from the United States Supreme Court. "It's like the space shuttle. Once you get to a certain altitude, it breaks off and that's the last time you see it."

He does not have the money for a private attorney. "I believe I have a good case. I didn't know how to argue it. I'm ignorant to the law. It's not just that. I'm lazy. I don't want to go to a law library and read a million books. I want to enjoy life."

That life was now in its second decade of confinement. "I know I'm in prison, but I don't focus on the negative stuff." He paused again, something he rarely did when speaking. "I find people that in my judgment are good people, people I can trust and rely on and I believe care about me."

His main contact and most frequent visitor is his father, Rickey Frank, who lives in Eureka and indulges Henry with whatever presents he can. After the shooting, Henry told his father not to buy him anything. "Dad raised me to be independent, then broke me of it." His father argued, " 'It honors me to know I can help you.' " Henry relented but was shocked at the cost of shampoos his father sent. Henry liked washing his long black hair with concoctions named grapefruit guava, passion fruit smoothie, mist of strawberry. "I'm very spoiled. I love that stuff." The next year we met, Henry's hair was as short as a badger's. He makes whatever changes in his life he can.

Rickey Frank also attended Henry's most triumphant moment at San Quentin: his graduation with an Associate of Arts degree from Patten University, a Christian-oriented college in Oakland. (Patten, through San

Quentin's Prison University Project, offers the only on-site degree program within California's enormous prison system.) Henry's courses included Geometry, Critical Thinking, History of India, Evangelism, Introduction to Philosophy, General Psychology, and Creative Writing. He got A+ in Sociology.

A year later, when he mailed his father the finished drum, Rickey Frank was so moved, he traveled all the way from Eureka to thank him. "He said it has made a tremendous difference in his life, it has made it better. He walks by it and he feels the energy draw him to it. I could see the appreciation in his eyes."

Appreciation shows in Henry's eyes too—about San Quentin. "I get a lot of support from my Native brothers here. A lot of enlightenment and a lot of hope comes from the sweat lodge. Also I am the chairman of the American Indian Culture Group, so I get a lot of contentment from producing the paperwork" and organizing in-prison powwows. "Seeing it all come together at the end . . . seeing the smiles, the dances, that brings great joy to me. Even working in a good environment. I'm going to classify *this*," he gestured around him, "as a good environment." In fact, he referred to "the Q" in a letter to me as "a sanctuary for 'lifers' who wanted authentic introspective to change."

———

Sharing enthusiasms for "Q" can take a while. The fortress-looking buildings, the first of which opened in 1852, contain the state's only gas chamber and a death row to feed it. Every visitor enters the same way, at a chain-link fence and check-in post. As instructed by Steve Emrick, whose official title is Artist Facilitator of Arts-in-Correction, and who had put me in touch with Henry,[2] I did not wear prison outfit colors of blue, orange, yellow-brown, or lime green, in case there were "a problem" (so that guards in the towers would not shoot me). I carried minimal belongings but—with special permission—a voice recorder. No food other than what I might need was allowed. The fruit I bought Henry to honor the Native tradition of always taking someone something? Back to my car. A terse guard telephoned Emrick. An affable and fit gray-haired man in his fifties, Emrick (always in beige) soon appeared and led me along a breezy sidewalk past the staff parking lot. There were spots for Locksmith and Employee of the Month.

The medieval entrance to the main prison complex involved another checkpoint, sign in, and inspection. Emrick and I, amid chatting employees returning from lunch, stepped into an enormous metal box, a sally port. Two sides—entrance and exit—are formed by thick bars. With a thunderous clang that nearly made me drop everything, the outside door closed. Two guards on a raised platform looked us over. The metal door on the other side then clanged open. We stumbled out (in my case) as if into a dream—a pleasantly landscaped outdoor area, with flowers. The dream did not last long. Although many prisoners strolled freely (they are "main liners," as is Henry), occasionally a man walked by in manacles, accompanied by a guard.

We continued, past a mural painted by prisoners, to North Block, where Henry lives. I peeked through the open door. Five stories of floor-to-ceiling iron bars formed what looked more like cages than cells. San Quentin is so old, guards lock and unlock each cell/cage individually. In North Block, lock up is usually at nine P.M., unlock at six A.M.

Past North Block, pavement led to an old white building with a narrow door surmounted by an arch of hand-painted lettering. Art Center. The words are misleading. They are too grand for the space and too modest for the accomplishments, including the revival of Henry Frank.

Most of the center is a 600-or-so-square-foot room featuring a large table where men worked on various projects, from collages to paintings. Stairs in one corner led to a small loft area. At its edge, overlooking the activity below, is Emrick's desk. The center burst with artwork, supplies, furnishings that might charitably be described as shabby, and a variety of instruments, including a wall of guitars awaiting repair by other inmates. The overall impression I had during two visits was of a focused (and unusual for a prison, racially integrated) and calm scenario.

The mood may be credited to Emrick. "Steve, although he's an employee and he's a ward over me, he's a decent guy," said Henry, in the loft area where we talked. Henry was not alone in his praise. At a 2009 ceremony in San Francisco, the Dalai Lama honored Steve Emrick as one of forty-nine

"Unsung Heroes of Compassion" worldwide, specifically for his prison work.

A couple of years earlier, Steve hired Henry as an Art Center clerk. Henry is there virtually all day every day, and some evenings. "Steve wanted me here because, one, for my love for the arts, and two, not to be egomaniac, but I'm an excellent clerk." Because Steve is "fair, it doesn't add more stress. I tend to let go of the stressful things I don't want to focus on." For Henry Edward Frank, that would seem to be a tall order, not only because of his sentence but what led to it.

Life started well. His parents "were ecstatic when I came out," March 25, 1974. The name Henry honored the most intelligent man his father knew. The name Edward honored the bravest, someone who had fought bullies at school on his father's behalf.

Henry's "sole identity" growing up was as a Native. "I pretty much knew I was Indian before anything else." A major influence was his paternal grandmother. "It was a very close family, so I was always around them, and I'd hear Grandma speak Yurok"—Henry then spoke it too—"and Dad always going to brush dances and all that good stuff, and jump dances, and then Pomo dances. All up and down northern California. My mom also was Yurok. She wasn't that involved."

"I'm enrolled in the Yurok tribe. I have enough blood lineage, whatever, to be on the Pomo roll as well, but as soon as I was born I was pretty much enrolled in Yurok. I'm not into switching back and forth." Henry is also Tolawa, and Karuk, and has some Dutch and Spanish from his mother. He feels Yurok down to the name he received in childhood. "When I was about three, my father dropped a needle. I was a room away." His father and grandmother got on their knees, searching. Henry spotted it immediately, by a table leg. "They're like, 'Whoa!!' Ever since then I was called Spa-gat," Yurok for "hawk."

In early childhood summers, Henry and his father stayed on family land in Weitchpec on the Yurok Reservation, some seventy-five miles northeast of Eureka. They would "live off the land, pretty much." Then his parents separated. "Dad gave us a choice either go with Mom or stay there with him. Both my brother and I chose to go with Mom. We went to Hoopa

[Reservation],” living across from a grocery store, behind a laundromat, for about a year.

In Hoopa, Henry started kindergarten. “Everybody else was Indian so it wasn't a huge thing like, 'Oooh! There's Indians!' We were all just who we were. When I went to town, it was kind of different, because I was with pretty much 90 percent white people. I was, not just me but other Indians, like their commodities. 'I know an Indian,' and 'My friend's an Indian.'”

It was the least of his concerns. “In that time, my mom developed a heroin addiction. There was a point where she went out with a shotgun and was going to shoot our neighbor. Police got involved.” Child Protective Services placed Henry and his younger brother Tom with foster parents, “another Indian family there in Hoopa, until my dad found out. My mom didn't tell my dad, because she wanted us back when she got out of rehab. Dad was mad about that. He should have been called first thing so he'd come and get us. We don't belong in foster homes because we have family.”

Throughout most of his school years, said Henry, correcting himself often about dates, he and Tom moved between Eureka and San Francisco, where their father, in Henry's words, “was a professional student” at San Francisco State University.

One return to Eureka was prompted by hope. “My mom was being clean for four or five years. I got tired of losing my friends all the time.” His father told Henry, then about sixteen, that he could stay in Eureka if he had someone to stay with. Henry's mother agreed to be the someone. “I stayed there until I got arrested.”

Meanwhile, Henry himself used virtually every drug possible. “I did marijuana. I really enjoyed that one.” After it came “pretty much everything.” He stopped at needles. “I'm going to give credit to my mom, in a weird way. When I was about eight or nine years old, I visited her. My dad let us go over there to spend the night. At that time she was on heroin. She was kickin' and she was so tore up she couldn't fix herself. She had me do it. As a kid. She doesn't say, 'Hey, hit me with my dope.' She's like, 'Mom's hurting and this is her medicine, so can you help me?' She told me how to do it.” Much later, Henry realized what he had been made to do and confronted her. “She apologized. This was when she was sober.”

"Now I'm about eighteen and at that point where I did so much dope my body is rejecting it." He said, gesturing to his face, "In my nose it would stop in the canal and then come back out. The only way to continue the high would be through a needle. That was my point. When I was about fourteen, when I confronted my mom, I vowed I wouldn't ever put anybody I love through such an ordeal. That this drug has so much power over me I would lie to my son to get my high. I don't want anybody ever to feel that way. My homeboys are on me. 'The only way you can do this is through the needle.' I'm like, I can't, because my dad taught me, your word is your word. That's the only thing somebody can't take away from you almost. They're on me and on me. I'm like, 'Check this out. You offer it to me one more time, I'm going to smash both of you.' They got the message I'm serious, I'm not tripping anymore. So I went to sleep. I'm proud to say I haven't ever shot up." He has long been clean.

Henry's current weakness is food. He is a wide man from head to foot. The first time we met,[3] he was wearing, along with extra large prison blues, gargantuan Nike sneakers his father gave him, EEE width. "I have a Fred Flintstone foot," he grinned.

Feet and all fit into a space measuring, he stretched his arms to figure, four by nine feet. For two. (San Quentin was meant for some 3,300 prisoners but holds nearly twice that many.) The cell is furnished with bunk beds. Henry's "celly," a Filipino who participates in all available sports on the yard, takes the top. "He's a skinny guy." The two "get along pretty good" and make sure "little moments" get resolved quickly.

Within the limited space, prisoners may each have twelve books. Henry's mostly are from college assignments. "I've done a *ton* of reading. I've got *Reminiscences of a Yurok Woman*,[4] and I have *Yurok Spirituality 1850 to Present*. I have *Dream Interpretations*. I have the *Seventeen Success Principles*. What else do I have in there? I have *Fingerprints of the Gods*, which is a book that connects all the mysteries of the world into one hypothesis." He has not finished it. "I also have Plato. The *Writings of Socrates*. I have David Hume and René Descartes."

Essays Henry wrote for Patten courses were, to my mind, impressive. In "Only Death Can Change Me," he wrote, "I maintain my identity by breathing" and "I knew I was Yurok before I knew I was a boy." Especially compelling was an essay for an Evangelism course in which Henry addressed "you brothers" as if they were about to enter a sweat lodge. He wrote of different stages of prayer, beginning with the "selfish round" of sweats by praying for oneself to be cleansed, "so that when we pray for our loved ones and each other['s] loved ones, no negative baggage transfers to them."

The object of the essay, San Quentin's sweat lodge, the first in a California prison, has existed since 1972—a result of Indian activism, including the takeover and occupation of nearby Alcatraz Island. Henry heard about "Q's" sweat lodge in county jail. Shortly after arriving at San Quentin, he went to see it. "It was a fenced off area and like a little park. It *is* sacred land. The medicine man comes in and blesses it. I was like wow, to see such beauty within these walls."

We decided to visit it together, he and Emrick leading the way out of the Art Center and past the yard. The ground around the elongated chest-high carapace of willow branches was raked pristinely clean, the blankets that would cover the frame were carefully folded, the stones that would be heated and put inside were piled neatly. Fuel for the fire to heat them, said Henry, was scrap lumber from the prison's furniture-making shop. The men have to look out for nails.

Hanging by the lodge was a dream catcher he had made. Arrayed nearby were six bundles of tobacco in colored cloth, holding prayers—one for each of the four directions, one for the Creator, one for earth.

Henry sweats almost every Sunday morning, then sits around with others. "Usually we sing songs or we just BS and then come in. I'll sleep, because it drains you."

The first sweat of his life was right here. "I stayed the whole four rounds." A fellow inmate later reported the accomplishment to Henry's father. "Then Dad comes and tells *me*." Henry seemed embarrassed and proud. "Prior to, I didn't participate on the outside. Reason being 'cause my grandmother, although she was a medicine woman, she was a Christian as well. That's a hard walk to walk, really." Henry quoted her in his Evangelism course essay as "always" saying, "I want to be known for two things. The first is, I was the best Christian I could be. The second, I was the best Indian I could be."

Not all of Henry's relatives were so ecumenical. "Uncle Squeaky was anti anything that wasn't Indian. Then I have an aunt that was all Christian and let go of the heritage." As for his father, said Henry with the usual mien of respect, he "didn't want me to be exposed or brainwashed by any religion and let me find my own connection with the Creator."

We headed back to the Art Center, where Henry brought up the subject of differences that in prison lead not to a richer belief system, but racial tensions and power plays. "Do you got ABs? [Aryan Brotherhood.] Do you got Skinheads for the whites? The same with blacks. Do you got the Crips running it? Do you got non-cliqued up blacks running it? With the Native Americans, we don't really have shot callers," but rather "a council of Natives" in which everyone has a say. "But within that group, you get city Indians and reservation Indians. 'Why are you going to be like the BIA?' 'Are you the BIA?' 'You should just be an Indian like everybody else.' Then you got Indians that had problems with blacks in their past. 'We don't mess with blacks and we don't . . . ' I'm like, 'Ohhhh dear.' I didn't have an easy road, because I'm not letting another man tell me what to do if it's not logical to me or if it's prejudice based. Just because one black man did something to you doesn't mean they're all going to, and it doesn't mean they're going to do it to me. I'm going to take people as individuals." He added, "Because you're Indian doesn't mean nothing to me. You could be a jerk like anybody else can be a jerk. I'm not going to rush up to you, 'Oh, oh! Indian!' I'm going to stand back and see how you walk. I don't want [to take the consequences of] something you're doing, say drugs or you're messing with homosexuals or you're gambling, you can't pay your debt, and then you get jumped on. If I'm there, I'm kind of obligated to back your play.' "

"The point is, I don't do it, so why should I get in trouble for you doing it? Usually when I get to a yard and we get into the circle, I let everybody know that. If it's racially motivated, I got your back," meaning, he clarified, "If the dispute is solely based on my brother being Native American, then I will defend him." However, "if it's your debt, you're on your own." He shrugged. "I kind of keep people at a distance at first. When I see they're just trying to go home or they're trying to learn about the sweat lodge," he tries to be "courteous and friendly to them." Otherwise, "I mainly don't mess with shady people."

To help prepare Henry for San Quentin, other county jail inmates (including at least twenty older cousins he met for the first time there) offered advice, as well as instruction in games he was told were essential to know: cribbage and pinochle. The advice included the common nicety of how to meet people like yourself. "One of the things was, when you get to a prison, on a yard, it's not their job to find you. They don't know what you came in as. Because there's northern Indian, there's southern Indian, that run with gangs, and some might come in and maybe were raised by white parents, so they consider themselves white."

"As soon as you hit a yard, anybody you see will know an Indian, pretty much. 'Hey! I'm an Indian. Can you let somebody know I'm here?' It gets back to them, and they come down and they chat with you. 'Who are you and what tribe are you from? Is it your first time?'" In some yards, said Henry, unless you can show proof of tribal enrollment, you cannot join certain groups. "You can hang out with them, but you're not going to sweat lodge, you're not going to powwows." Henry said he and other Native inmates tried to replace such attitudes with "an Indian's an Indian if they have 1 percent or 100 percent of Native American blood, and if they claim it when they come in."

Despite all the advice, Henry's initiation into San Quentin was uneven. "I went up to North Block. As soon as I was walking up the hill, I seen the Indian secretary. To me he looked like a Mexican, so I wasn't even tripping. He's like, 'Hey, you skin?' I'm like, 'Yeah?' He's like, 'I'm So and So and I'm Apache Mescalero.'" He then gave Henry some basic information, like where the showers were. So far, so good. Then Henry met his cellmate. "I talk to my celly, and I'm programmed for a different way of pulling out my prison paperwork, showing I'm not a rapist or a child molester, and then my other paperwork saying I am enrolled in a tribe. The Filipino's like, 'Whoa, what are you doing, man?' 'I'm just letting everybody know I'm clean, so there's no madness about anything.' He's like, 'You pull that out here, man, by the time you hit the yard, ten people will drop a kite on you and you'll be gone.'"

Why the drama? "Dropping a kite" is prison-ese for snitching, but something else was going on. Henry and Steve clarified. In prisons with a reputation for violence, such as Corcoran, from where Henry came, it is customary for inmates to know each other's crimes. A new prisoner showed his paperwork, then chose friends and enemies accordingly. Henry was used to showing his paperwork, proving he was neither a rapist nor a molester, and thus protecting himself from inmates who beat up rapists and molesters—the most hated inmates in prisons.

San Quentin, despite its infamous prisoners and its death row, is considered relatively calm in comparison to Corcoran. The majority of inmates think about parole. They do not want to see an inmate's paperwork for the simple reason that if they know he molested or raped, they are obligated to beat him up, and perhaps his cellmate and anyone else he is friendly with. This lessens chances for parole. Also, if someone like Henry shows paperwork proving he is not a molester or rapist, other inmates might feel obliged to show their paperwork, and molesters or rapists would have to be dealt with. Much better if nobody knows anything. As Henry put it, "My celly was letting me know this yard does not do paperwork."

At the time, the outburst so stunned him, "I go down to the yard and I talked to the Indians. 'Yeah, that's pretty much true.' I said, 'Well, check this out. I'm showing somebody,'" he laughed in the telling. "'And somebody's going to show me their paperwork.'" Henry got his way. "I said, 'All right, we're all good now.'" Introducing yourself into prison life must be learned as you go, said Henry. "It's not like senior orientation."

———

During his initial time at San Quentin, Henry was put in a restricted category called Level IV. He "couldn't separate the days," started playing practical jokes on co-workers and having arguments with guards, and was in a "mentality" to follow up any slight "with a physical engagement." A phrase in the Yurok language turned him around.

"It came to me after I got my final denial from the United States Supreme Court appealing my case. I made a commitment to myself to do crazy stuff at that point, because there was a sign of no hope." Yet by then he had taken "many different classes that gave me new tools and new ways of thinking outside the box." He no longer wanted to do "crazy stuff."

To resolve his conflict, he did "a lot of praying and a lot of crying" privately. "I sat there and talked to the Creator for two or three days. Finally I heard my grandma say, 'Trust the Spirits. It's going to be all right.' I went and looked at my [Yurok] dictionary, translated it, and wrote it over and over and over. It was the sign I needed for me to change my path and create a new one. From there, it turned into a song, which now I use in the first round in the sweat lodge to call the spirits." His grandmother's phrase, Trust the Spirits, is now tattooed in Yurok across Henry's smooth broad chest: ROK-CHIM KU TE-NU-MO-NOK.

Thanks to trusting the spirits, to the sweat lodge, to a job he likes, to making art, to anger management classes, and to wanting parole, Henry wants nothing to do with fights. He has not been in any, he said. "I try to alleviate the problem through words, because I don't have anything to prove to anybody. All I have to do is go home. That's my main goal."

He does all he can to stay positive, sometimes in stunning ways. Regarding the North Block, he said the top floors are hot and the bottom ones are noisy, but in his third-floor cell, "I'm perfect."

Staying positive also means being a productive, peaceful Yurok man. One element of that goal includes relearning his language, or trying to, through his Yurok-English dictionary. (He estimates there are about fifty Yuroks in San Quentin and not one speaks the language.) "I spoke it pretty good when I was with my grandma and my dad, but that was a long time ago and I forgot it since. Now I'm reintroducing myself and learning more. Most of it is from songs. Songs have been coming to me, my own songs, so I've been translating them. That helped me out a lot. I know I can learn more about it if I had the right instructors or right teachers, the right elders that would like to share some knowledge with me."

He yearns for help from the tribe but until 2010 had received little. "I can understand why they wouldn't want to write it through the mail because, you know, officers read this and that. But in my opinion, I'm not really a concern to the tribe because I'm incarcerated. I've written them time and time again, asking certain questions and asking [for] certain materials they can give me. They did give me my enrollment number papers and the bylaws and the constitutions of the Yurok, and they did send me some basket patterns, but they didn't send me the meanings. I don't want to use them, because I don't want to clash them." Putting the energy of one spirit with the wrong design concerns him. The painting of his mother's newly discovered relative includes a "basketweave kind of thing" in the design, she having been a master basket weaver herself, he said. "I figured it was appropriate."

The only time he seemed stumped for a positive answer was when I asked, gesturing around the Art Center, What would you do if this didn't exist? "Wow," he said, his eyes wide, then paused. "I don't know."

———

For Henry Frank, staying positive also means avoiding the negative, including the news, although he does get into "huge arguments" with inmates about fighting in Iraq and Afghanistan, "because you've got patriotic people" among the inmates. And, yes, he does think about why Natives total about 7 percent of San Quentin's inmates, triple the percentage they make up in the U.S. population. "In my opinion it would be intolerance. A lot of reservations are poor, and they don't have job skills." He wonders if jails are a way to take Native people "out of society, so they don't have to look at them."

Another negative he tries to avoid is yard talk about execution. "I don't want to sound cold, but he's the one dying, not me. After I know he was killed, I might say a prayer for him, like 'Find your way home in a good way.'" (The best-known inmate executed since Henry has been in San Quentin was Tookie Williams, a founder of the Crips gang in Los Angeles.)

On a pragmatic level, and Henry is pragmatic, executions mean lockdowns, and lockdowns mean Henry cannot go to the Art Center. Once he prepared in advance. "I knew a lockdown was coming. Somehow I found out. I took a bunch of supplies with me and stored it in the cell. We were locked down seven days or something. I painted and beaded and wrote. I did that from six in the morning till about one in the morning."

For Henry, virtually everything, including the adornment of the sweat lodge, comes back to Native art. He regrets not having more imagery to work with. "I would have been taking pictures of all the lands. I would have had pictures of my favorite oak tree and my creek. I'm saying 'my' because we own it, so technically it is mine, but it's the Creator's, of course. It's my favorite tree, and I could have took pictures of all that and the woods and the river."

Henry gets artistic encouragement from his family. He thinks often of his father, Rickey Frank, and his mother, Valerie Beck Tuey, and of his aunts Jewell, Carolyn, and Itsy. He has countless cousins and thinks about being free among them. "I think I'd be a positive role model in their lives because they're kind of running amok. They don't want to hear it from people who haven't been there." He spoke longingly of a baby niece, his brother's child, he saw once. "She was just adorable. She couldn't talk yet except for 'Uncle Henry.' I have no contact with her now because my brother got arrested because he was in gang involvement. He got eleven years." The baby's mother was a heroin addict, Henry added. Maternal grandparents were caring for the child. (He since has had "communication" with the girl.)

He was also concerned about his mother. "My mom is in Hoopa right now. She's recently fourteen months clean again, so she had a backslide. She was living in Arizona for about nine years, and then she came back. It's rough for her. There's something to be celebrated that she is staying clean there. Everybody knows her from way wayyyy way back in the day. It's kind of hard to cut off those friendships," he said as if to himself. He appreciates, as he does any shred of Yurok or family information, that she sent him a photo of her newly found aunt. His mother "just got reconnected with that side because she was adopted out."

His earlier words about her not being "that involved" with Yurok now resonated. How many Native American children were adopted by a white family, however kind, and then eventually felt estranged both from that culture and their own?

Henry once asked his mother to write to him, but truthfully. That Christmas she sent him a card. It read, "Hi Hen, I tried to commit suicide, but a friend found me. I hope you have a Merry Christmas."

He looked amused. He had asked for honesty and got it, for she did try to kill herself and a friend did find her. And she did want him to have a Merry Christmas.

Henry's family includes a wife. He is in infrequent contact with her, and did not name her. Can they have conjugal visits? "Nope. No lifers do." He offered to divorce her and filed the appropriate papers, but she did not follow through. "When she wants to marry somebody else, she'll contact me and we can get this over with." He was upset when she did not visit as promised, but more upset when she inconvenienced one of his friends. A San Quentin program calmed him down. "I got into nonviolent communications, which helped me a lot."

Prison itself has "freed me, it helped me emotionally and spiritually," he said. In offering him art and a sweat lodge, as well as enforced opportunities to rethink his life, it also helped take him back to his roots as a Yurok.

Some questions I did not ask. For driving a car from which a gun was fired and a man wounded, how long did he think California's Department of Corrections should keep him locked up past the years a current judge felt were appropriate? How much more can you, Henry Edward Frank, be corrected?

CHAPTER 16

Eskimo Ice Cream

CHRISTINE GUY (YUP'IK)

Christine Guy, a thirty-six-year-old Yup'ik, sat on the linoleum floor of her kitchen in Kwethluk, in western Alaska. A beaded barrette, one of many in her collection, held the end of her black braid, which almost reached the floor. Her back was straight, her legs in a V-shape, pinioning a huge metal bowl. On the floor around her she had arrayed various ingredients. Beside her, or on chairs, or standing, were about eight other people. They included her oldest daughter, Christina, nicknamed Pooh (a lovely teenager, who crochets while watching James Bond videos), her youngest son, Big Boy (so named by a hospital nurse because he weighed three pounds seven ounces at birth), her husband, Bobby, and a number of visitors.

That evening there would be a dinner to honor the birthday of Christine's late grandfather. About fifty family members would attend. In a village of some eight hundred people, of whom nobody is unknown and many are kin (Christine is directly related to about a tenth of the village), fifty is an average-sized family gathering.

In her opinion, Christine was in the optimum position for making what she promised would be a special dessert for the dinner. The table would be too confining. First, she said, reaching into a large can, you take two hand-fuls of Crisco. Plop. Plop. Then, reaching for a large bag, you take equal amounts of instant mashed potato mix. She stirred them together with both hands as family members looked on. Some stole glances at me, the baffled visitor. Then, she said, you add two handfuls of white sugar. She now mixed with one hand, her other holding the bowl. The final ingredient came from

Alaska itself, but much farther away than Kwethluk's almost produce-free grocery store.

In the summer, once ice has melted and rivers run, the Guy family members, like most people of Kwethluk and other Yup'ik villages, abandon their close-together prefab government-issued houses, and ride their motor boats up the Kuskokwim River into the tundra to set up fish camp. For weeks or months, depending on other demands, Yup'ik families live in tents amid the glory of Alaska's outdoors. They catch and dry fish, hang them on stretched lines, occasionally shoot a bear (Bobby devoted almost an entire photograph album to one such event), and pick many, many wild berries. The Guys covet salmonberries, named for their color. They also harvest other varieties—Alaska has about fifty—including blueberries and a kind of sweet cranberry Christine called a bogberry. The summer berries, a traditional mainstay, once were dried. Nowadays any berries not eaten immediately are brought home, put into Ziploc bags, and stashed in the freezer.

The Guys' kitchen, essentially part of the living room, features a large refrigerator from whose freezer compartment had come a bag of beautiful, glistening berries gathered last summer: the coveted salmonberries. Christine picked up the bag, its contents thawed, and emptied the berries into the Crisco, instant mashed potatoes, and sugar. Then she resumed stirring.

Ever clueless, but thinking fruit cobbler, I asked, How long do you bake it?

Christine smiled, eyes behind her glasses especially lively. "You don't. It's ready."

The others looked on, grinning.

It's amazing, she continued, as she got to her feet, how the same recipe comes out differently depending on who makes it and how their hands blend the ingredients. The dish, she said cheerfully, is called Eskimo Ice Cream.

It is the modern version of *akutaq*, someone explained. Before Crisco, we used seal oil. It was unclear what had preceded the instant mashed potatoes.

———

That week and weekend, Christine Guy was especially busy. As usual, she worked all day, Monday through Friday, as assistant to the principal of the

Ket'acik and Aapalluk Memorial School, also known as Kwethluk School. She also coached the volleyball team. A big game, the regional championship, was that Friday evening. There was the family gathering to prepare for, although her contribution of Eskimo ice cream was ready. There were also her roles as wife and mother. Finally, there was the big event Saturday afternoon.

"It's a throwing-away ceremony," Christine had said weeks earlier on the phone, extending an invitation.

The ceremony was to honor her older son, Sarge, she said through a fuzzy connection. A throwing-away ceremony? Like recycling? It sounded as if she said Sarge had caught his first bird. An image presented itself of a canary in a cage. "It's for women only," she said. A women's recycling ceremony for a son who caught a bird? It would take place in late November. Ah. Late November.

"We don't have plumbing," she added. "We use honey buckets."

Honey buckets? The term sounded disconcertingly cozy. Anyway, who could resist the opportunity to recycle in cold rural Alaska on behalf of a boy's caged canary? Was there anything she would like, or needed? She professed repeatedly, no, nothing, but finally relented. Tangerines would be nice. What about something for the throwing-away ceremony? No, she had flown to Anchorage, stocking up. All the way to Anchorage to buy things to throw away? The misunderstandings mounted.

When, days later, I told her my plane would arrive in Bethel (the closest airport to Kwethluk where Air Alaska flew) at four P.M. Friday, her response was, "I'll order a plane for you." This sounded rather jet-setty, but no. There are no jets in Bethel. There are no roads either, between Bethel and Kwethluk. If it were summer, she told me, she could take the boat up the river to the airport. If it were later in the winter and the river were completely frozen, she could reach Kwethluk by dune buggy. November was an in-between time. So, recycling for a bird now entailed four flights: San Francisco to Seattle, Seattle to Anchorage, Anchorage to Bethel, Bethel to Kwethluk.

When Christine (her Yup'ik name is Ciuk'aq, after her mother's cousin) invited me to the throwing-away ceremony, I was, if mystified about specifics, honored. Thanks to her help with a freelance assignment I was working on,[1] I knew something about Yup'ik culture and Kwethluk. I knew that men still were subsistence hunters and shot moose, caribou, and any variety of birds for food, that the village, as it was called, was officially dry. (Christine's aunt, a friendly information conduit during the freelance work, asked me to bring a bottle of red wine, but don't tell Christine.) I knew most villagers lived in subsidized government houses, that government stipends kept people from poverty, that graduating from Head Start was a big deal but graduating from high school was not, that people ate moose all summer and salmon all winter. And, I later learned, honey buckets may at one time have held honey but are a sweet name for five-gallon receptacles placed under toilet seats. They are, in fact, ubiquitous in rural Alaska, where permafrost inhibits installation of septic systems or outhouses.

After weeks of telephonic delicacy, I also learned that Christine's parents had an arranged marriage, as had been customary. But her mother, she said, did not initially love her father and had not allowed him to touch her for the first year of their marriage. Eventually he must have, I said, then immediately felt like a cheap comedian. Yes, she said without levity. Now, "when they are apart for as much as a day, she longs for his return."

Christine e-mailed from her office, "I'm counting the hours for your arrival."

Hagaland Aviation Services, up the road from the Bethel airport, was packed with people waiting for flights to Yup'ik towns reachable this time of year only by plane. An off-duty Air Alaska pilot, my seatmate en route to Anchorage, said one reason he likes his job is the Native Alaskans; they are so patient. In Alaska, flights get canceled all the time because of weather. Rather than act like people in "the lower 48," who rush the counters, demanding to know when they can get on which flight, Native Alaskans nod at whatever announcement is made and wait. Sometimes for days. Indeed, the only anxious people in Hagaland's waiting area seemed to be the white guy running things and me. He took and weighed my bag, which contained not only tangerines but apples, cheese, crackers, and Glo Balls. (Who knows what might come in handy?) Then he asked how much I weighed.

I deducted ten pounds before answering. Four of us boarded: the pilot, I, and a young woman and her baby.

The best way to describe the plane's size is to repeat the pilot's suggestion as I settled in next to him. "Better hold on to those purse straps, ma'm, so they won't get caught in the pedals."

After he wiped off condensation on the inside of the windshield with his sleeve, we were off, jouncing over the kinds of spectacular mountain scenery I sometimes think humans were not meant to see. Noticing my craning-neck interest, the young woman behind us, holding her baby, shouted over the engine to ask why I was going to Kwethluk. To visit Christine Guy, I answered. "You're from California, right?" she asked.

Turned out, I knew about her too. My freelance assignment, writing captions for an Alaska photography book, included photos of her chiseled-cheekboned husband Ilarion Nicolai, whom I had interviewed on the phone. Apart from learning about his hunting, I learned he took Sundays off in baseball season to watch televised games and, for reasons unclear, was a Chicago Cubs fan. As he parted with his few words, I thought of Christine. Her way of talking, like that of other rural Native people, was a rebuke to interruption. She listened, waited, and stopped if I did not have the courtesy to wait. When she spoke, her words were measured and sparse. Ilarion's responses made Christine sound like a motor mouth.

The flight was mostly smooth, but some wind gusts knocked us around so much, I thought with frantic guilt of my subtracted ten pounds. Before landing, the young woman pointed to Kwethluk's school, to Christine's house, and a few other attractions. From a few hundred feet up, the town was bleak—a sepia photograph. No trees grow in this part of the world. Some bushes struggle, but that seemed the extent of plant life. Beige houses connected by mud roadways, remnants of a snowfall here and there. Kwethluk looked rutted and cold. My companion grinned. She was home.

Christine Guy, semi-stout and about five foot two, smiled broadly in greeting, her eyes merry. We soon tromped up an exterior set of stairs to her house. The newer government ones like hers are raised, with open cellars used more or less for storage. Through a mud room, which contained a large barrel of rainwater, we entered warmth—the main living room/dining room/kitchen. A row of photos lined one wall, on another a wall of videotapes, which Christine planned to rent to neighbors. She introduced me to her husband Bobby, whose sticking-straight-up black hair looks like a hairbrush and whose smile was as warm as his wife's. Over the next two days, their four children, Pooh, Mary, Sarge, and Big Boy, came and went, as did various other children and relatives. I realized that my appointed bedroom, adorned with a poster of Kobe Bryant, a Garfield cat, and Russian Orthodox icons, was at least two of the children's, who were sleeping elsewhere to give me privacy.

The Guys' bathroom, including such amenities as a hair curler, looked like a regular bathroom, except for dry faucets. The bathtub was for storage. Water, toted in from the mudroom barrel, drained through the bathroom sink or toilet seat mounted on a platform, into the honey buckets. It was the men's job, I gratefully learned, to empty them.

We had hardly been through the front door when Christine said she had to go to school for a volleyball game. Only then did she reveal she is coach of the Kwethluk Kings, who were playing that evening against the visiting team from Akiachak.

The school is about a quarter of a mile away from the Guy house. We started walking as the sun set and cold settled, but soon hitched a ride on a dune buggy, the post-dogsled vehicle of choice in Kwethluk. Freezing wind blew straight into everyone's faces.

The K-12 Kwethluk School, built in the same prefab unadorned style as the houses, rang with the voices of teenagers getting ready to play or cheer those who were playing. Along the entrance hallway hung children's drawings featuring awake faces and tired faces. This turned out to be part of a campaign to emphasize that children should sleep. Yup'ik parents, more than one Anglo teacher told me, are beyond indulgent. Children stay up all hours of the night, watching television or videos or playing. They arrive at school both exhausted and late. I already knew, from my phone interview with Kwethluk's prom queen (one of four girls to graduate), that the prom was a bust. So many kids had so many detentions for being tardy that only a few were allowed to attend. The prom king was the only boy to graduate.

Throughout the volleyball game that evening, indulgences toward Kwethluk's children seemed pronounced. Children regularly ran across the court to adults to ask for a dollar or two, and then ran back across to a concession stand where they bought candy, melted orange cheese product on taco chips, sodas. I thought of Big Boy, a darling child of ten who looked six, flashing gold fillings when he smiled or looked up from the Coke he drank out of an action figure cup. As I silently rued what the fast food industry had wrought in Kwethluk, my heart softened by what was happening in the gym.

All ages of people sat on the packed bleachers, chatting in English or Yup'ik, the predominant language in Christine's home. Many elders, including her grandmother, speak only Yup'ik, but fluency was diminishing generation by generation. Like other communities, Kwethluk is trying to restore what was. The school has a mandatory Yup'ik-language immersion program for grades 1 to 3.

On the court, both teams, made up of boys and girls, played the game with enthusiasm but often absentmindedness. Several times the ball simply landed at a player's feet. After every play, however, all team members gave the person who had done well, or not, a touch of their fingers—a low five. The quick clustering included an often hapless boy who never managed to serve the ball over the net, and then, head down, extended his hands for all to touch.

That response, referee and teacher Jim Howard said later, is the problem. People here are so nice and so passive. Howard, a tall, slim middle-aged Caucasian with sandy red hair, paused and added, there is a lot of alcoholism in Kwethluk. A lot of abuse. Of spouses and of children. And incest. (An Internet site, "Registered sex offenders in Kwethluk, Alaska," as of May 2009 listed twelve men. Of them, seven were accused of assaulting minors.)[2]

Nobody, he all but sputtered, makes a fuss, because everybody knows everybody. "You can't report him. He's your brother-in-law's second cousin." He went on: in his opinion outsiders take advantage of Native people terribly. On the other hand, one can get ahead financially so easily in Alaska, but Natives do not bother. Who would, he added, with government assistance? It is much easier watching videos than tracking caribou. In Bethel now, there's a job offering $25 an hour, good money, to clear snow from the runway. Nobody is applying.

Jim refereed the game with humor and firmness. "If you don't stop your children from running across the court," he announced to the Kwethluk fans, "you will forfeit the game." He obviously loved his work and neighbors, but what he described as their passivity upset him. Here is a story he told, while making a pancake breakfast at school the next morning for the visiting and home teams.

About twenty years ago, he was on a boat going up the Kuskokwim River. On it, too, was "a yahoo guy" from Susanville, California, who had grown up in the South. When the boat rounded a bend, a moose appeared. The yahoo picked up his gun and shot it, for the heck of it. The other passengers, mostly Native Alaskans, were so outraged, they made him get off the boat, essentially in the middle of nowhere. Once off the boat, the yahoo started walking. Eventually, Jim later learned, he arrived at a Yup'ik village. It was an unusually beautiful village with well-crafted wooden homes. In this lovely village, where people had lived for centuries, the yahoo made himself at home. Got a job. Soon, he was the person delivering propane to people's homes. Soon, too, he was thinking of running for mayor. Before long, if you didn't support the yahoo for mayor, you didn't get your propane on time. Fast forward. The yahoo got elected and brought his whole yahoo family to the village. They took over. Anything you wanted, you had to get through the family. The village became a virtual dictatorship.

What did the people do?

They left, said Jim, grimly. They did not want the hassle. They packed up what they could, left their beautiful homes, and moved en masse to another village, one not nearly as beautiful. He fairly thundered, "It's unjust!" And, he concluded, it's typical. Alaska's Athabascans would have fought. So would other Alaskan tribes. Not the Yup'ik.

When the Kwethluk Kings beat the Akiachak Huskies, they all touched each other's hands. The game had more than average significance. The Kings now qualified for high school semifinals in Anchorage. Today's victory involved a trophy, a lineup for photos, and a stealth attack by some players who poured a pail of water over coach Christine's head.

Following the game, after Christine nominally dried off, it was time for the dinner honoring her grandfather. The celebration took place in a relative's house and was decidedly informal, with relatives coming and going, and sitting where they could. As far as I could tell, there was no moment where he was specifically honored, as in a prayer. That his family was there, and in quantity, was the significance. The Eskimo ice cream disappeared fast.

———

The next day's throwing-away ceremony, it was now obvious, was no Arctic cousin of a garage sale. Instead, the hostess was obligated to procure, in quantity, new items "that women want, like kitchen sponges," Christine told me. The loot she bought in Anchorage was stored in her and Bobby's bedroom and along the hallway. It was a staggering amount. Boxes and boxes of mostly Made in China things, it seemed, and a carton of boxed dishwashing detergent. Wrapped up as the special prize was a comforter. She graciously accepted my small offerings, which paled in volume to hers. One all but shouted sin. Not having equated "women's things" with kitchen sponges, I contributed a red satin teddy I had never worn. Christine immediately put it in an opaque plastic bag and tied it tightly. I felt like the fallen woman come to town.

The throwaway, she explained, would take place at her grandmother's house, because it had a shed out back from whose roof she could toss the presents. The throwaway ceremony, as most Native people know (who also call it a giveaway), is not unique to Kwethluk. *Uqiqur*, meaning to distribute, is the linguistic basis, according to the Yup'ik-English dictionary in the Guy home. A book lent me by another teacher said *uqiqur* derives from an ancient custom of sharing meat and blubber from the first seal of the season. Gratitude for the bounty implied an obligation to share. Later, handcrafted items were made to celebrate. Later still, the bounty was no longer limited to celebrating the death of a seal, but, as I suddenly learned on the occasion for celebrating Sarge's feat, a bear. *Bear*, Christine had said on the telephone! Not bird. And caught, it turned out, meant not caught as put in a cage, but shot. The clueless visitor finally approached cultural speed.

On Saturday afternoon, under a cloudy sky augmented by a bitter wind, Christine climbed a homemade wooden ladder to the top of her grandmother's slanted roofed shed. Big Boy helped hoist bulky cartons to the roof. Hundreds of the village's women, mostly Yup'ik, but also a few light-skinned teachers from the lower forty-eight, and all bundled to the teeth, stood below, holding plastic bags Christine had distributed.

In a formal manner, she announced in English, as snow started to fall and the wind picked up, what the occasion was for. Standing far back, I caught the word "proud." Then the tossing began. Mittened arms flew up as items flew out. Dozens of green plastic colanders. Dozens of blue plastic dustpans. Women's things! Dishtowels, beaded trivets, wooden spoons, clothespins, pot holders, the comforter, and, at some point without fanfare, a bag containing a certain piece of lingerie. Throughout the throwing, in a village where a third of the residents live below the poverty level, the women jostled good-naturedly to get what had fallen. No pushing, no shoving. Finally, according to tradition, Christine tossed sprays of hard candy. Once all pieces were collected, everyone went home.

That evening, she beamed. Her son had been properly honored.

That night, it was time for a sauna. Most families in Kwethluk, said Christine, have built one behind their homes and therefore use it whenever they wish. For whatever reason, the Guys and several other families share her mother's sauna a few minutes' walk away. Why she did not consider it her father's, she did not explain, nor did she offer an opinion on why men get to use it first. They do, though. The men were late that night. Then the fire had to be restoked. Well after eleven P.M., Christine announced it was time. Wrapped in my woefully thin coat and carrying a towel, I followed her into the bounteous black starlit sky, through frozen mud ruts, to a crude wooden building that looked like a storage hut. A few other women were arriving too. We stooped to enter.

The sauna consisted of an anteroom and the sauna itself. The anteroom, about six by six feet in length and breadth and five feet in height, did not allow most adults to stand. A single dim light bulb gave a glow. On a shelf were various shampoos. We squatted, undressed, and, taking turns, squeezed through an opening about two feet wide and three feet high into the sauna proper. Two women could crouch in front of hot embers, sweat, wash, shampoo, and change places with whoever had cooled off in the anteroom. The scene, I thought with a cliché I have never shaken, was like a photograph from the *National Geographic*: the dimness, the steam, the women's beautiful glistening brown backs in low amber light, their sturdy feet going back and forth, to and from the heat, carrying a metal basin of water to wash with, to rinse with, and to sprinkle on the embers for more steam. Voices were low.

Christine kindly guided me through the routine, proffering glasses of water through the opening when I was on the sauna side, and offering soaps and shampoos. Striking throughout was the ease and naturalness of the women with each other (although I later learned that unspecified family matters caused strain among a few of them), the quiet talk in English and Yup'ik, the modesty amid the nudity.

After well over an hour, every pore steam cleaned, we dried off, the shampooed women wrapping towels over their heads. We crouched back into our clothes, undid the latch, and ran into the still and freezing Alaskan night.

———

Christine—proficient in e-mail, faxing, video taping, computer games, air travel (she made a trip to Washington, D.C., in high school after winning a scholarship award)—sat in Kwethluk School's teachers' lounge and listed ways to ensure smooth pregnancies.

"They tell us if you want fast labors and fast deliveries, if you happen to be cutting up a porcupine and it has a fetus, you should drop it in the neck of your shirt and let it drop out the bottom." Christine did this for a friend and for Pooh, for whenever Pooh decides to have children. It worked for the friend, Christine said. Also, when a woman is pregnant, she should not eat porcupine or she'll have slow children—not mentally slow, but physically slow. There was more advice. Do not eat leftovers when you're pregnant or your baby will have missing parts, like ears, hands, or toes.

When pregnant, finish whatever you start and do not put it off, or your labors will start and quit. "That's what happened with Sargent," she added. It is also a good idea to pass a goose egg around your waist. Finally, "Don't cut anything while you're wearing it," like repairing the hem of a skirt you have on, or your delivery will tear you up badly, because the cervix will not open properly.

Christine herself had a hellish time both with birth control and two of her pregnancies, the former including devices and pills that made her gain weight and turned her once smooth complexion pimply, the latter including heavy hemorrhaging. She was sickly as a little girl, she said, then added in a rare self-description, but she was bossy anyway.

Despite belonging to a people who only recently subsisted on reindeer meat and traveled in winter by dogsled, Christine had had hopes far outside the community. For one thing, she wanted to go away to college. But by age eighteen, she and Bobby had coupled up. She abandoned such hopes, placing them instead on Pooh, who surfs the Internet, has a Walkman (this was several years ago; almost certainly she now has an i-Pod), and knows how to dress game.

In the Guy home one morning, Pooh sprawled on her sleeping bag in front of a video, while Big Boy sat on the couch, playing Crazy Eights and other card games with me and Christine. He raised his eyebrows expressively and often, a mannerism I had seen in Christine's aunt. Finally, thanks to Christine, I learned it means encouragement. Yes! Pick that card! Yes! Have more Eskimo ice cream!

As the weekend ran down, the weather turned rainy and sleeting. The prospect of being in that plane again, with purse straps again clutched to bosom, alarmed me. True to reputation, however, the people of Kwethluk take weather in stride. They are used to calling various sources, on short-wave radio, for information about flights. And they did. It seemed Hagaland was going to keep flying for much of the day, but later flights out of Bethel might be canceled. The possibility of overnighting in Bethel airport's cement waiting area and returning to work even later than arranged made me decide to try to get on an earlier plane. None was scheduled, though, and it was too late to order one. Christine decided we should go to her grandmother's house, near the landing strip, and I should run to get on whatever landed.

The walk there, over rough wooden planks that bridged puddles, past stringy tethered and barking dogs and dilapidated houses, was so depressing,

I felt eager to leave. Her grandmother's house, though, crammed and warm, and strung with laundry near an old stove, offered a convivial pre-farewell site. One aunt kept checking the short wave for updates. A male relative disappeared and reappeared with a present: a beautiful black slate scraper, an ulu, he earlier retrieved from the Kuskokwim River. I stared at how perfectly it fit into my hand. Go ahead, take it, said the aunt, raising her eyebrows repeatedly. He has more.

Every family member—there were about ten at various times—snacked from a bowl containing thin lengths of dried salmon arrayed like breadsticks. The weather seemed to clear. We, or at least I, breathed easier.

After at least an hour of conversation, mostly taken up by transportation issues, Christine's grandmother, ancient-looking and beautiful, wearing thick felt slippers, finally decided to address this stranger in her home. She told me, as translated from Yup'ik, that when you are hungry, it is best not to drink water, for that will make you more hungry.

As I had not fully grasped before, I realized this is a woman from the days of subsistence hunting and berry gathering, and no government aid. Every bite of food had been critical to survival. The recognition occupied my mind later, as I replayed again and again her sole question to me, translated by a relative.

"In the place where you live," she asked, "what berries do you gather?"

POSTSCRIPT

In later catch-up phone interviews, Christine said she is "older and heavier," and wiser. She thinks twice before buying something she doesn't need or accepting an invitation to a party. Pooh graduated from high school and was considering the Job Corps. The family still used honey buckets. The sauna has been insulated, which helps a lot in the winter. This winter it was sixty below, with the wind chill factor. There was hardly any snow, though, and everyone was worried about the berries. The volleyball team had a win/loss record of seventeen and one. Christine was considering giving up coaching to spend more time with her family. Bobby was working for the tribal corporation.

By then, years into researching this book, I knew that according to Native women involved in fighting abuse, the worst statistics come from Alaska. I knew that in some villages, the percentage of abused women was thought to be 100 percent. The question had to be put to Christine. She was forthright.

It was a problem in the early years of her marriage she said, and was connected to alcoholism, as it is with most people, she thinks. Much later, she e-mailed me that she put Bobby in jail once. "That straightened him out. I think it was jealousy, too. I think with our native men in most cases alcohol is a factor in a lot of these assault/domestic violence cases amongst my people. I sometimes wish a lot of these women can stand up and say that's enough or I'll press charges against you for treating me like this." Christine concluded, "I was not brought up to be abused by anybody."

In further e-mail updates, she wrote that her "middle children" (Sarge and Mary) had been chosen to take a trip to Washington, D.C. "I hope they enjoy their trip as much as I enjoyed mine when I was their age." Bobby's gill nets were starting to tear from snagging submerged trees on the river, so she faced the expense of buying material to repair them. Fuel for the fishing boat was as much as five dollars a gallon. "It's hard to keep the motor gassed up all the time."

In our last conversation, she was still working at Kwethluk School, Bobby had quit his job and was taking care of a relative's sled dogs, Pooh and Mary were studying nursing, Sarge, who had joined the National Guard, was getting married, she hoped, and Big Boy was taller than she was.

CHAPTER 17

Aloha from Hawai'i

CHARLES KA'UPU JR.

A Hawai'ian in a book about Native Americans? But isn't the federal government's phrase for Native peoples "American Indians and Alaska Natives" (AI/ANs), omitting Hawai'ians entirely?

Let me pose other questions. Did Hawai'i not have an indigenous population whose lives were radically changed by European arrival? Did European Americans not take over much of the land and the government? Did they not change the lives of the indigenous population by such efforts as adding their own religion and subtracting the other's language, while proclaiming their appreciation of the indigenous people's cultural output? Do descendants of the indigenous population not feel, to put it gently, irked? Are they not asked (today!) whether they live in, rather than tipis or igloos, grass shacks? Finally, is Hawai'i not one of the fifty states? I rest my case.

Landing in Honolulu on a quest for interviewees, I was greeted by a lei of surrealism. Streets leading to Waikiki were deserted, as were the beaches. Granted, previous trips to the islands made reality iffy: beach waters the temperature of the air, breakfast papayas all but offering themselves, sunsets climaxing from another world. The surrealism this time was connected to the 2010 tsunami warning. By the next day, realism resumed. Having exhaled when the waves did not endanger, people legendary for openness and generosity of spirit sat down to talk story, as the Hawai'ian expression has it. My challenge segued from surreal to real—choosing an interview from one of four compelling people for these pages.

David He'akoelekauaikalani Kalama Jr. (possessed perhaps of the world's most thrilling middle name) is an experienced filmmaker steeped in Hawai'ian cultural knowledge.

Daphne Kealalaina Ho'okana, self-described as chop suey ("I'm Hawai'ian, Chinese, Portuguese, English, Irish, and some Spanish") is an optimist recovering from drug addiction.

Bridget Manulele Dudoit Clarke is a multitalented singer (once with the Don Ho show!), musician, and "master of all trades," who conducts ceremonies from weddings to memorials.

Then, decidedly, there is Charles Kauhi Ka'upu Jr.

———

When Charles talks, the air rumbles. When he laughs, the sound seems to come from several octaves. And when he chants, when he renders Hawai'ian blessings, praises, and genealogies into music, in tones less otherworldly than extraworldly, descriptions are inadequate. Charles Ka'upu's chanting is a skin-altering event I know less from hearing snippets at a chanting class he led, or from CDs, than from an amateur YouTube video. He was outdoors, sitting on the edge of a stage, and seemingly addressed the gods.

We met at a Kaua'i deli through an admirer of his, Manulele Clarke. Both had just finished a weekend hula workshop, she as student, he as teacher. Over lunch, they discussed and discovered various extended family connections (involving at least three Hawai'ian islands). It was precisely the kind of conversation I had heard Native Americans engage in. After Charles expounded upon Hawai'i's universal health insurance program, for which he pays about $185 a month for full coverage, he suggested we talk story near his late afternoon assignments. These were to coach a women's chanting class and a men's hula class at the Grand Hyatt Kaua'i in Koloa, near Poipu beach. We made our way to an open-sided thatched-roof hut by the hotel's employee parking lot, a hut popular with employee smokers, including Charles. He has smoked ever since high school. No, he does not think it affects his voice. Maybe not.

He is an imposing person even when silent, a man of expressive eyes, tall and large body, and larger presence. (Other coming and going smokers in the hut paid him heed.) His trimmed mustache-less gray beard surrounds his generous face, giving him rather the appearance of an Amish Polynesian. "The title I hold at the moment," he clarified, "is Kumu Hula or Master of Hula. The rest of the knowledge I hold is from my *kupuna*." *Kupuna* is a respectful term for a culturally knowledgeable elder. Charles is fifty-two.

Asked how he compares himself to Native Americans, he did not hesitate.

"I think we're both in the same canoe, so to speak. The Hawai'ians probably had a little better deal in the process of our relationship with the United States. But if you really want to get down to the nitty-gritty, genocide is genocide no matter what shape or form it takes. It could be a subtle cultural genocide or it could be like the Native Americans, who were given blankets that were infested with disease to decimate the populations when they were moving them from place to place. For the Hawai'ian, that kind of genocide took place with the introduction of new people coming into the islands and exposing various diseases like measles, smallpox, influenza. Those took a major toll on the population, but I don't think that that was purposely done. It just happened. That was during the whaling days in the mid-1800s."

His own family he described in terms of later concerns. "My mother was actually Hawai'ian/Japanese. My grandfather came here for the sugar plantation as a laborer, illegal as far as age was concerned. He came from Okinawa. His name was SeiSei Higa. When he came to Hawai'i, because he was underage, they did what they had to do in order to get work, which was to change his name and identity, and came to work here in Kaua'i on the plantation. His father brought him here, then went to Oahu and worked."

"My parents were of firm belief that we needed to be educated in what was now 'the system.' To play the game, to make sure education was the top priority, but constantly feeding us our Hawai'ianess through home, like any other ethnicity that was here during those days. I'm talking about the early '60s into the '70s."

"We were true to our cultures, whether it be Hawai'ian, Japanese, Filipino, whatever the ethnicity might be. Then when it came time to party, we had the best of everything, right? The best food, the best people, the best *all* of it. It's not like it is on the mainland, where you have different ethnic groups and they're constantly at odds because of one thing or another. Here it's a little bit different. We can celebrate each other and live side by side. You're a good neighbor or a bad neighbor. It has nothing to do with one's race. Either you are or you aren't, you is or you isn't."

Hawai'ians of any background make fun of one another. "I mean, you gotta laugh at each other. That's just part and parcel of life." He made an exaggerated sigh. "Sometimes we go overboard. We grow up teasing each other to the point of making one another cry. Whoever cries first gets a licking on top of that. Gets a slap. It's true!" he boomed. "Well, it's true in my case."

His inclinations toward chanting and hula "started at the time of birth, really, with my parents." The specific gravitation toward chanting happened when he was about twelve. "I was exposed to it earlier at my grandfather's funeral, but that's a whole different kind of chant. It's wailing. It's a little more on the spooky side when you're a young kid. But when I was reintroduced to it, it was like a lightbulb moment in your life. This is what you were meant to do. I *want* to do this. I will grow up doing this. I don't know how it's going to unfold later on, but I know that this is something I need to do."

The moment took place in Honolulu's Iolani Palace. "There was what they used to call tableaus, or presentation of historical events. The celebration was for King David Kalakaua's jubilee, so the best of Hawai'i's chanters and hula masters were there to perform. It was Ka'upena Wong—the bee's knees for me in chanting. That's the one on the pedestal. To aspire to be as great as that man."

Charles described Ka'upena Wong physically as "partially bald, hair on the sides. What you would picture as a Chinese merchant, but Hawai'ian, you know? Hawai'ian Chinese. It's not the physical appearance, it is the spiritual voice coming out. It's like Hawai'ian DNA at its best. It's the sound. It's that spirit."

In Charles's youth, he briefly considered another career path. "I was going to go into the FBI. I wanted to become an agent, actually. I wanted to be a spy," he laughed. "It's every kid's dream, right?" An uncle, in either the FBI or CIA, he is now not certain, was his spy role model. Charles also considered the military, and attended a military academy, as well the Kapalama Campus of the Kamehameha Schools in Honolulu. In his schooling, he met scions of missionary families. Asked what they were like, he lit a cigarette and uttered one word. "Haole."

The word means foreigner, but as an Anglo-Hawaiʻian resident told me, it is used solely and derogatorily for light-skinned haoles like her, never dark-skinned haoles. Charles knew the word is loaded. "That's not really a nice thing to say," he added. The haole schoolmates he meant were, "Entitled. That's a really good way of describing them. Entitlement." Manulele, sitting beside him in the hut, nodded.

Charles's course for chanting had one major handicap, the Hawaiʻian language. "My dad and mom did not teach [me]. My mom spoke a little, my dad spoke fluently. My grandparents spoke fluently, including my Japanese grandfather. But for them, English education was the forte. So [Hawaiʻian] was never taught at home. I had to go to school to learn how to speak Hawaiʻian." He joked about his level of fluency. "I can get by, I can survive. At least I know when they're talking about me. That's the most important thing." He narrowed his eyes in mock warning. "You better not be talking about me!"

His life's chosen work has always supported him, although not opulently. "You learn to do without. If you have the money and you can afford it, then you get it. If you don't have the money and you can't afford it, then you just don't eat. And I have a lot of fat reserves," he laughed, "so I can get through at least one winter. If you have the gumption to get up and go, our icebox is right past the beach. Go fishing! And you can always rub two sticks together to get a fire. These are all basic survival techniques. You just *do*."

Charles travels for work about six months a year, mostly by himself, "doing what I do. Teaching or judging competitions. Or I'll go out with musical groups and things like that." One is the Hawaiʻian group Hapa. Even without the tourism industry, he believes he could support himself, although hotels such as the Grand Hyatt Kauaʻi would not exist.

Today's classes, which he taught in what he called the bowels of the hotel, in cinderblock meeting rooms off vast locker areas, past racks holding hundreds of laundered aloha shirts/uniforms, were tangentially tourist-related. The chant class was made up of half a dozen Grand Hyatt women employees, whom he taught with a combination of tough love, careful explanation about word meaning and pauses, repetition, a dose of mincing mimicry that had the women giggling, and, finally, praise.

The purpose was a "protocol for the Ritz Carlton Celebration of the Arts" in Maui, where the novice chanters would compete with chanters from other hotels. The later men's hula class (which I did not observe) was for another event.

One of Charles's steady gigs is chanting at the Old Lahaina Lu'au in Maui. There, or almost wherever he performs, tourists are in his audiences. Fine by him. "How better to educate people than to hook 'em? Gotta have a hook to get the interest. It's not that every one of them will be interested, but let's say out of ten, you get one. That's one more than you had yesterday." When a non-Native wants to learn whatever he can teach, his answer is, "Teach them."

"If you get rid of the places that we all come from and the practices that dictate how we act according to the place, we're the same. We have different appearances because of the conditions. That's simply that. The color of the skin is only our uniform. The inside is the same. We all bleed red, we all flow blue, so how can there be a difference? It's only our cultural practices that have dictated whether or not we view one race higher or lower than ourselves. I think that sucks. Because somewhere along the line, sooner or later, you're going to be in the boat that's in the bottom of the canoe and not on top of it. Why even go there? Why not view everybody on the top deck of the canoe, moving along *togetttther* and navigating our world?"

The navigation analogy came up again when Charles mentioned he married three years ago, for his first time. "I'm a newbie, so to speak. Still navigating the waterways. Sometimes they're treacherous. Sometimes they're rapids. Other times it can be smooth and easy." His wife is partly Maori from New Zealand. His voice deepened. "Like any other Polynesian woman, fiery. Well, maybe any woman in general. Don't get them *maaaaad*," he lilted. He and she (she did not want to be named) had a small wedding ceremony on a beach in Maui.

"For the common person," he said, warming to the topic, "the Hawai'ian wedding ceremony was live together. Hence the term 'shack up.' That's the Polynesian way of marriage. There's no contract. You just, oof, have babies," he laughed. "That's your wedding. Only the chiefly lines had ceremony. For us peons, nah."

One bridge joining peons to others is hula. "It's really a reflection of our world. It reflects the natural parts of our world. It chronicles our history, it's there for entertainment. It's become the basis, because all else is lost." It is also serious, he said, including the moments before commercial perform-ances. "The spirit . . . even though it's entertainment, it still carries through. We have this saying here. '*I ka olelo ke ola*,' in Hawai'ian. Then, '*I ka olelo ka make*.' 'In the word there is life' and 'In the word there is death.' It's really important we get it right, because what you put out into the world, whether it's in Hawai'ian or in English, there is a certain amount of life or death cho-sen by the words you use. You release into the world that spirit of the word.

"I know it's kind of hard on the English side of the world to understand this, but this is how I explain it better. If nothing but 'f—you' and 'shit' and 'damn it' and all of those words are used on a constant basis, what you're attracting is negativity to your life. Whereas if you stay away from those words and use only kind and loving and 'words of light,' for lack of a better term, then the paradigm shifts and there is much more goodness coming to you, rather than negativity.

"Words carry power behind them, whether we realize it or not. That is the case for us in Hawai'ian, so we're very careful with the kind of word that we use. One word can mean many different things, and another word can mean the same thing, but on the darker side of the world. So even in our composition and our poetry and our chants, we are careful to choose the words that bring life and nothing but that. No harm. Even if we might be pissed off at the person, that cannot enter into the picture, because it's a two-way street. If you call to send, it can always be sent back to you."

A major epoch of negativity for Charles and other Hawai'ians was the overthrow of Hawai'i's monarchy and annexation to the United States. He cited an 1897 petition against annexation that was ratified by a vast majority of Hawai'ians, sent to Congress, then "buried in the Library of Congress" until coming to light relatively recently.[1] "That sentiment never changed. The next fifty-nine years [up to statehood], it was still the same. They did not *want* that."

His feeling about Hawai'i being part of the United States? "Well, it's a bad deal. It's illegal. I want the recognition. I really want my civil rights back as a native Hawai'ian. That's what I wish for to happen. Now, will it? Probably not. Not in my lifetime, anyway, so I deal and move on. There's no sense going down that path of resistance where I cannot function in the manner I choose to function." As to what civil rights he wants back, he was completely clear. "I want my birthright back! I want to be recognized again as a Hawai'ian citizen."

"I think a lot of people misunderstand the fact that because we had a royal family and we were ruled by them, we just lay down and died. That's not it. We killed our chiefs who were ugly and usurped their rule. We stoned them to death. That's who we *are.* So there's a two-way street with our royal personages versus the masses. They had to take care of us. If they didn't take care of their people, their people did not take care of them. Without the people, there is no ruler. Same thing in a democracy.

"America thinks anything that's not democratic has to be wrong. It cannot be right, because we're right. Well, no we're not. Not all the time. We can pull modern-day blunders. Take a real good look without the prejudice of being an American and see the blunder for what it is. We're involved in two wars that should never have been. It's an old story, but why did we go to Iraq when we didn't finish Afghanistan? Why was it that important to do at that moment, when you haven't even cleaned your house, you're going off and changing the bull's eye from where it should have been? That was to safeguard your people. You didn't do it on September 11th. You had all of the warning signs, but you chose not to act. That's really a big blunder. Nearly five thousand people die in that and your only response is, 'I got to go after the guys who started this'? But you're a part of the start."

After running down more "blunders," such as backing the shah in Iran, Charles concluded, "I say no one way is the right way. Democratic, socialist, royalist, whatever you want to call it. A government is a government. It can be a great government if the government takes care of their people. But we don't have a very good track record as a democracy, because we still have homeless people in our country." He amended the term in regard to

Hawai'i. "We have a lot of *house*less people. This is their home, they just don't have a house. That's our fault as a society."

He lit a cigarette and inhaled. "We're like any other people on the face of this earth. Ours are specific because of where we are. We are a reflection of our world. Since our world is beautiful more than not, that's who we are. But that doesn't mean we're a welcome mat, that you can step all over us when you come here and expect us to be nice, and then ask us, 'Where's the aloha?' Aloha went out the door when you decided to step on my face.' A lot of people hear so much about this thing called aloha and they expect it. That's their free pass. But it's not that way. It's a two-way street." He spoke slowly, as if instructing a child. "'I aloha you, now you need to aloha back.' It's not something you can buy. It doesn't come with money. It comes with giving from the heart. If you can't give from the heart, then" his voice went light and bright, "there really is no aloha. It doesn't exist."

The aloha-needy are represented by two types of outsiders. One is New Agers trying to take on Hawai'ian traditions. "I call them Crystal Lighters," he said, looking amused. "All the more power to them, but what they need to realize is, this is not your culture, and you have no business telling us what it's supposed to be. A lot of them end up doing that. What do they call that? Precociousness." He added, with less humor than his words conveyed, "I laugh. I think it's hilarious."

The "Idiot Tribe," he called them. "They're idiots and every village has an idiot, okay? Contrary to popular belief, we've got our idiots too. We're even. It's not race-based. An idiot is an idiot. Since there's a rainbow of people, each part of the rainbow got idiots."

The other type of outsider made him take a substantial breath. Recently, Charles said, he went to an ATM machine. As he approached, so did a woman. Then he noticed someone already using the machine. "Surfer kid. I'm standing back, giving him room. She runs and stands right behind of him. He's still doing his transaction. He looks to me and he rolls his eyes, because he already knows what's going on. He steps away from the machine and she goes right up. He goes around to his car, he looks at me and he does this." Charles made an elaborate, sorry, but what can do you? gesture. "We're communicating that way, and laughing. She's meantime at the machine punching in the numbers and keeps on looking over to me. She did that three times. On the third time I said, '*What?* Why are you looking at me?' She goes, 'Well, you know . . . ' And I said," his voice rose in volume, "'You *knew* I was waiting for the machine.' She goes," he put on a falsetto girly voice, "'I didn't know you were coming here.' I said, 'What does this sidewalk mean and why am I standing here? Am I standing here for my health?' She goes, 'I don't know . . . ' *Screaming* at the top of her lungs. I'm looking at her and I say," he now put on exaggerated softness, "'Cousin, you knew.'" Her response, again in falsetto: "'You don't know me, you know nothing about me. You have absolutely no idea who I am.' I said, 'You're *right.* You're so right, but I know people like you, and you're exactly like them. It's all about *me*—the rest of the world be damned. It's only me I'm concerned about.'" She replied, "'You don't know nothing.' I said, 'Uh huh, I know people like you. I know your entire family. Where did you come from? Orange County?' She goes," falsetto again, extra loud, "'How did you know that?' I said, 'Because you *act* like that.'

"I said, 'You came here because of the beauty of the place and the Hawai'ian people.' 'Oh, they're so nice.' 'Yeah, we're nice until you step on our face.' I said, 'This is an experience you need to learn from. You should get back in your car, pack up your bags, and go *home,*'" he fairly thundered. "I said, 'You come here and for the very thing you love about these islands, now you change them, because you want it according to your rules. We don't work like that over here.' I said, 'You wait in line like everybody else does. And don't look at me like I'm the one that's doing something wrong, because you're wrong.'" By now Charles was all but spitting. The other smoking hut visitors were staring at him, engrossed and nodding. "I said, 'You know what? Just finish your business and get the hell out of my sight, please.' That's how wound up I was by the time I got to the end of that conversation."

"That night after work"—he had barely paused—"I'm at the stoplight, there's this tourist in back of me and this guy with his bike and trailer crossing. I'm waiting to make the left, because he's in the crosswalk. [The tourist is] sitting on his horn. I think to myself, okay, what is the lesson I'm supposed to be learning here? I pull off to the right lane, two-lane highway now. He gets into the left lane and speeds up. Well, I know the light up [ahead] is going to turn red any minute and I'm going to catch him at the light. Sure enough, take my time, he's stopped. Pull up, the window is down. I turned and I said, 'And where are you going? You rushed me. You wanted me to run the guy over?'

"Now the lady is putting up the window. I said, 'Before you put that window up, let me tell you, this is an *island*. You're only going to go down the street. You have a mile and a half to go.' I said, 'Was it that important you got to this stoplight before I did? Really?' Oh, kupuna. I know I scared the shit out of them. After they left I said, 'God, I'm sorry. I failed the test again. I yelled at them. I got it, I got it. Please, no more lessons. Patience. Patience is a virtue. Okay, I failed twice. I said, I'm not going to fail the third time, so don't test me again, please.'"

Much of these paired stories he told in semi-humorous tones, but his voice flattened with the next words. "We have to deal with that 365, 24–7." The sentiment was similar to those I had heard Native Americans express.

As the conversation continued, it turned out that Native Americans had contributed to a moment in Charles Ka'upu Jr.'s life that might be called transcendent.

"In the groundbreaking of the Smithsonian on the National Mall [for the National Museum of the American Indian in 1999], we were invited to participate with the Indian tribes. When we walked into the ballroom, it was really hilarious. All of the Native Americans are looking at us like, 'What are they doing here?' I felt like, 'Uh oh, we're intruding.' Each tribe went up and did a short presentation."

"When I went up to represent Hawai'i, I did our genealogy." The phrase "I did our genealogy" meant that Charles chanted about "the birthing of these islands and the population of it and the connection from the gods to our chiefs to us. It went on about seven minutes, which is kind of lengthy," he said, with a slight shrug.

"But by doing that, it brought us into their world. Then they knew that we were Native and understood why we were there. So the celebration began. It was really nice. Every single member of every tribe came up to me and said, 'When you guys walked in here, we were wondering, What the hell are you doing here?' And I laughed, because I *knew* that's how they felt, you know? I didn't blame them. 'This is your gig. This isn't my gig. I'm not a Native American, I'm a Hawai'ian. I'm outside of the circle, so to speak."

Missing a point, I asked about language. His genealogy chant was in Hawai'ian, right? Yes. But . . . no, he did not translate it. "Didn't have to. Because now it goes to the spiritual realm. It's our kupuna talking to theirs. Then it's their kupuna telling them what is going on, on this end. They knew exactly what it was. There was no need to explain to anybody why we were there. They knew immediately."

Conclusion

When the trips were finished, interviews transcribed, research and writing done, what stays with me most are three impressions.

The first is the rationality and reasonableness of Native people in the wake of one imposed insult or assault or disaster after another. I was stunned less by their resilience, stunning enough on its own, than by what might be called accommodation. There was much resentment expressed, of course, but virtually no hatred, and none at the level that my fellow European Americans express toward any number of other people, including Native Americans.

The second impression is (most) Native Americans' very American-ness. It included an embrace of something akin to patriotism, or patriotism itself. It also included popular culture. As someone rarely drawn to it, I could not tell if the lure was commonality with a larger society, a result of techie youthie inundation ("lol!" and "my bad," younger Natives e-mail me), or personal preference, but it was evident across the country, and it certainly felt American.

The third impression threw me. Having grown up feeling, as I mentioned earlier, American to my core, I began rethinking my place. That is, instead of wondering about "them," I thought about "us."

The rethinking started with land. What about the bits or expanses of soil we modern-day Americans rent, own, lease, trespass, farm, covet, cover, despoil, sell? Because the word "land" came up so often in the interviews, I was ever more aware that every one of us who lives in one of the fifty United States lives on what was Native land. Whether we are that precious fraction, descendants of original inhabitants who still occupy their ancestral acres, or were part of a tribal nation sent to unfamiliar territory by treaty, policy, or coercion, or moved from that territory to another for whatever reason; or whether we are descendants of the other half of the twin shame of the United States of America, slavery, and are near or far from sites where our ancestors underwent unspeakable suffering; or whether our ancestors arrived hundreds of years ago of their own free will or in indentured servitude (as did my great grandmother from the Netherlands); or whether we arrived yesterday—each of us lives on what was Native land.

Should we not at least recognize this? Should we not learn, if we do not know already, who precisely lived first on the spot where each of us lives now? I'll go first: California Coast Miwok. Such inquiry may well extend beyond a home place. Should we not know who was in the places we see or visit? Should we not know how long they were here and why they are not here now? Should we not also ask ourselves, what would they think about how I am treating their land, their—I hesitate to say this, but it usually is true—usurped property? After all, nearly every inch of the United States was in one way or another wrested from Native stewardship.

Rethinking my place in terms of land, however, turned out to be much easier than rethinking another until then basic status: that of human being. Those breathy "brotherhood of man" sentiments, everyone holding hands around the globe, always touched me, but did not cause me to think much beyond my fellow *Homo sapiens*. (Fellow *Homo sapiens* were concern enough.) After years of hearing Native people give prayers, however, that typically included not only human beings, but winged beings, four-legged beings, amid many other beings, as well as trees, rocks, wind, sun, and on and on, it dawned on me that being human was not more important than being anything else. Perhaps this is why humility is so much a part of Native culture.

Talk about a double letdown. From being a person with a book idea, I had become a descendant of interlopers, and of the mere two-legged variety. Having rethought my place, I cannot say I cherished it.

Fortunately, Native Americans, the people who changed my self-image, offered much ameliorating comfort.

Through them, both in person and in readings, I revalued compromise. Either/or has rarely been a prevailing Native mindset, in my opinion. Instead, through treaty negotiations then and through legislation now, the impulse seemed and seems to be to work things out, to have a peaceful solution. Some efforts by tribal leaders over the years to avoid confrontation took my breath away. A photograph I return to repeatedly depicts the formal signing of legislation in 1950 leading to construction of the Garrison Dam. It will submerge North Dakota lands, lands that tribes occupied for more than a thousand years. Most faces are grim or expressionless. But Hidatsa leader George Gillette, wearing a suit, covers his eyes with one hand, and weeps.

Sorrow, yes, but where was hate? Why so much compromise and so little revenge? Was loathing turned inward, sluiced so often by alcohol? Or was there not much to begin with?

I also revalued moderation. One example is demonstrated in the following story, whose source I cannot conjure. A Native man went to buy a saddle. The saddle maker showed him his wares, including a saddle that was exceptionally well made and beautiful. The customer admired it, tempted. The saddle maker added, the clincher sales pitch, this saddle will make you stand out from all your people. You'll be the envy of them all! The customer, with a shudder, declined.

The concept extended to many other areas. Be satisfied with what you have, if you have enough shelter and food for survival. Be satisfied with where you are. Do not mourn too long. Be mindful that none of us chooses the circumstances of our birth. Or, why should you not be my mother/father/cousin, just because that is not the genetic connection?

None of these concepts or values is exclusive to Native Americans, of course, and not all Native Americans, of course, are beyond wanting much more than they physically need. (After all, we two-legged creatures all are flawed.) In general though, Native Americans seem to have at the very least a working residue of common and communal values that might benefit all Americans—if we listen.

Notes

PREFACE

1. Margaret L. Archuleta, Brenda J. Child, and K. Tsianina Lomawaima, eds., *Away from Home: American Indian Boarding School Experiences* (Phoenix, AZ: Heard Museum, 2000), dedication page (the figure "tens of thousands"), 16.

2. It is also quoted as "Kill the Indian and save the man."

INTRODUCTION

1. National Museum of American History, Smithsonian Institution, *Do All Indians Live in Tipis? Questions and Answers from the National Museum of the American Indian* (New York: Harper Collins, 2007).

2. Archuleta, Child, and Lomawaima, *Away from Home*, 31.

3. Bureau of Justice Statistics report, "American Indians and Crime," http://bjs.ojp .usdoj.gov/content/pub/pdf/aic02.pdf.

CHAPTER 1 —— A MAN OF THE DAWN

1. Donna M. Loring, *In the Shadow of the Eagle: A Tribal Representative in Maine* (Gardiner, ME: Tilbury House, 2008), 4–9, 20, 25–32, 47–48, 50–53, 57, 154, 161.

2. National Museum of the American Indian, *Do All Indians Live in Tipis?* 12.

3. See also quoted references to the word's origins by Abenaki scholar Marge Bruchac, in Paula Gunn Allen, "Does Euro-Think Become Us?" in *Make a Beautiful Way: The Wisdom of Native American Women,* ed. Barbara Alice Mann (Lincoln: University of Nebraska Press, 2008), 18–19.

CHAPTER 2 —— "INDIANS 101"

1. The term, originally "Indian 101," was coined around 1970 by Americans for Indian Opportunity, an organization founded by LaDonna Harris. See more at http:// www.aio.org.

2. Maria Tallchief with Larry Kaplan, *Maria Tallchief: America's Prima Ballerina* (New York: Henry Holt, 1997), chap. 1.

3. The Bureau of Investigation's 3,274-page report may be read at http://foia.fbi.gov/foiaindex/osageind.htm.

4. See Dennis McAuliffe Jr., *Bloodland: A Family Story of Oil, Greed and Murder on the Osage Reservation* (San Francisco: Council Oak Books, 1999), 250, 251. Originally published in 1994 as *The Deaths of Sybil Bolton*, by Times Books.

5. For background and details, see http://www.CobellSettlement.com.

6. At the time of the settlement, Interior deputy secretary David Hayes, blaming "the legacy of the Dawes Act, which allotted individual Indians with interest in the trust land" and did not take inheritance into account, cited a case in which one forty-acre plot had 439 owners. The majority receive less than a dollar annually from it.

7. Full disclosure: I led one called "Collecting Tribal Oral Histories," aware of the irony of a non-Native invited to instruct Native people about oral histories. The invitation reflected WEWIN's openness and that of cofounder Susan Masten.

CHAPTER 3 — A TRIO OF LUMBEES

1. Barbara Alice Mann, "Slow Runners," in Mann, *Make a Beautiful Way*, 71.

2. North Carolina's Revised State Constitution of 1835 mandated that people of color did not have the rights of people with, in effect, no color. Walt Wolfram, Clare Dannenberg, Stanley Knick, and Linda Oxendine, *Fine in the World: Lumbee Language in Time and Place* (Raleigh: North Carolina State University, 2002), 42.

3. Adolph L. Dial and David K. Eliades, *The Only Land I Know: A History of the Lumbee Indians* (San Francisco: Indian Historian Press, 1975), 2–4, 10–11.

4. Mann, "Slow Runners," 102.

5. For a concise and compelling volume about the disaster, see Theda Perdue and Michael D. Green, *The Cherokee Nation and the Trail of Tears* (New York: Viking, 2007).

6. Ibid., 139 (figure), 117 (quotation).

7. Ibid., 133. There are six other state-recognized tribes in North Carolina. The list excludes the Tuscarora, with whom the Lumbees are often associated.

8. Christopher Arris Oakley, *Keeping the Circle: American Indian Identity in Eastern North Carolina, 1885–2004* (Lincoln: University of Nebraska Press, 2005), 49–50.

9. Fergus M. Bordewich, *Killing the White Man's Indian* (New York: Doubleday, 1996), 63.

10. A 1956 federal "Lumbee Act" recognized the Lumbees as a Native community but at the same time said they were ineligible to continue with the Federal Acknowledgment Process (FAP), leaving them in bureaucratic limbo. Oakley, *Keeping the Circle*, 126–133.

11. See http://ncmuseumofhistory.org/workshops/civilrights1/cr_oral_histories/clip2.swf. Special thanks to transcriber Sheri Prager for discovering this interview.

12. Oakley, *Keeping the Circle*, 57.

13. Gerald M. Sider, *Lumbee Indian Histories/Race: Ethnicity, and Indian Identity in the Southern United States* (Cambridge: Cambridge University Press, 1993), 10.

14. Oakley, *Keeping the Circle*, 77–78.

15. The Lumbee Guaranty Bank is "the first Indian-owned financial institution in the United States." Ibid., 114.

CHAPTER 4 — ELDERS OF THE HAUDENOSAUNEE

1. Wampum, "the traditional device used by the Iroquois to punctuate diplomatic speeches," according to Timothy J. Shannon, *Iroquois Diplomacy on the Early American Frontier* (New York: Viking Penguin, 2008), 6, was integral to the fabled diplomatic feats and treaties hundreds of years ago that the Iroquois negotiated for peace (and presents) with competing British, French, and American settlers, traders, and armies. Wampum has long confused some people (including the definition writer of my *Webster's New World Dictionary*), who equated it with money. The confusion began when European colonists noticed wampum's importance to Native people and mass-produced wampum beads as a trading currency.

2. My thanks to Laura Harris of Americans for Indian Opportunity.

3. Charles Mann says that "traditional lore and astronomical calculations" suggest the confederacy began between A.D. 1090 and 1150. Charles C. Mann, *1491* (New York: Vintage Books, 2006), 373.

4. The six nations are the Onondaga, the Oneida, the Seneca, the Tuscarora, the Mohawk, and the Cayuga.

5. Except by name, Tonawanda Seneca Nation is unrelated to Tonawanda city northwest of Buffalo.

6. A link to the document can be found at http://www.iwgia.org/sw248.asp.

7. Shannon, *Iroquois Diplomacy on the Early American Frontier*, 9, 19.

8. Mann, *1491*, 371, 372.

9. According to various references and translations, the ceremonies are the Great Feather Dance, the Thanksgiving or Drum Dance, the Personal Chant, also called the Men's Chant, and the Peach Stone Game.

10. A *Buffalo News* story, "Films Give Voice to Unsung Heroes" (December 13, 2009), reported that "at the Thomas Indian School in Irving, 30 miles south of Buffalo, children from Native American families were systematically stripped of their native culture and heritage, and sometimes abused, for nearly a century. The school closed in 1957. Such schools are the focus of Ron Douglas's documentary *Unseen Tears: The Impact of Native American Residential Boarding Schools in Western New York*."

11. Mann, *1491*, 372, 373.

12. In 1999, Hillary Clinton's printed remarks about the meeting included being "privileged to experience the accumulated wisdom of generations of Native American women."

13. Geri's words came back to me when I read this passage in Wade Davis, *The Wayfinders: Why Ancient Wisdom Matters in the Modern World* (Toronto: House of Anansi Press, 2009): "Writing, while clearly an extraordinary innovation in human history, is by definition brilliant shorthand that permits and even encourages the numbing of memory" (175).

CHAPTER 5 — CITY KID

1. It is often believed the U.S. military purposefully infected blankets with smallpox, but the truth may be more complex. See "Did Europeans Purposely Use Smallpox to Kill Indians?" in the National Museum of the American Indian, *Do All Indians Live in Tipis?* 43–44.

CHAPTER 6 — THE DRUM KEEPER

1. "NAGPRA provides a process for museums and Federal agencies to return certain Native American cultural items—human remains, funerary objects, sacred objects, and objects of cultural patrimony—to lineal descendants, culturally affiliated Indian tribes, and Native Hawaiian organizations"; NAGPRA Web site, http://www.nps.gov/history/nagpra.

2. Catlinite is named for the painter George Catlin, whose Native portrait subjects used pipes carved from what is called pipestone, or catlinite.

3. For an article about the center, see http://www.timberjay.com/detail/4637.html.

CHAPTER 7 — "HOW'S EVERYBODY DOING TONIGHT?"

1. Jake Page, *In the Hands of the Great Spirit: The 20,000-Year History of American Indians* (New York: Free Press, 2003), 260.

2. The link is http://www.census.gov/prod/2002pubs/c2kbr01–15.pdf.

CHAPTER 8 — TALES FROM PINE RIDGE

1. According to the FCLN's summer 2007 "Indian Report," there were more than 240 suicide attempts, in a population of 13,000, during 2006 and 2007, of which 6 were successful. See also "Indian Reservation Reeling in Wave of Youth Suicides and Attempts," *New York Times*, June 9, 2007.

2. Of the numerous studies about the problem, I recommend as sources the Justice Department's Office of Violence Against Women, including its report "Violence Against Native Women: A Guide for Practitioner Action," put out with the National Center on Full Faith and Credit; http://bwjp.org/files/bwjp/articles/Violence_Against_Native_Women.pdf. See also www.ovw.usdoj.gov/TribalCol.htm and the Amnesty International report on violence against Native American and Alaska Native Women, http://www.amnestyusa.org/violence-against-women/maze-of-injustice/page.do?id=1021163.

3. Mary Louise Defender Wilson (Dakotah/Hidatsa), a traditional storyteller, recorded a number of spoken-word CDs and has been honored for her work.

4. Philip A. May, "The Epidemiology of Alcohol Abuse among American Indians," *American Indian Culture and Research Journal* 18, no. 2 (1994), finds that the "myth" that Indians "have particular biophysiological reasons" for alcohol abuse "has virtually no basis in fact." His essay was reprinted in *Native American Voices: A Reader*, ed. Susan Lobo and Steve Talbot (New York: Addison Wesley Longman, 1998), 388–400. The evidence is more ambiguous in Bordewich, "A Scene Most Resembling Hell," in *Killing the White Man's Indian*, 240–269. Nichea S. Spillane and Gregory T. Smith, in "A Theory of Reservation-Dwelling American Indian Alcohol Use Risk," *Psychological Bulletin* 133, no. 3 (2007): 395–418, debunk the charge that Native Americans are genetically more responsive to alcohol than are whites. They do contend, however, that Native Americans report a different "reactivity" to alcohol, meaning that their perceptions of their level of drinking did not necessarily match reality. Thanks to Dr. Lynn Ponton.

5. A life story all too similar to Dwanna's is found in Luanna Ross, "Punishing Institutions: The Story of Catherine (Cedar Woman)," in Lobo and Talbot, *Native American Voices*, 407–416.

6. When we talked in early 2007, Vukelich was chief of the Civil Rights Unit. He was working on a case that broke days later: the arrest in Mississippi of alleged Ku Klux Klansman James Seale in connection with the 1964 murders of African American teenagers Henry Dee and Charles Moore.

CHAPTER 9 — "GET OVER IT!" AND OTHER SUGGESTIONS

1. Also known as Old Oraibi, Orayvi is considered by many the oldest continuously inhabited town in the United States.

CHAPTER 10 — THE FORMER PRESIDENT

1. The group that organized the conference was WEWIN, Women Empowering Women of Indian Nations, for which Elizabeth Lohah Homer (chap. 2) had taught a seminar another year.

2. Claudia was referring to the infamous deportation called the Long Walk, forced on the Navajos in 1864, when U.S. Army troops led by Kit Carson pushed some 8,500 Navajos from their homeland on a 250-mile trek to Fort Sumner. The year before, his troops had managed to do the same to some 500 Mescaleros. Page, *In the Hands of the Great Spirit*, 270–271.

3. Geronimo was born into the Apaches' Bedonkohe band but led the Chiricahua band, which some people say were the same. Thanks to Prof. Donald Fixico of Arizona State University.

4. Robert J. Nordhaus, *Tipi Rings: A Chronicle of the Jicarilla Apache Land Claim* (Albuquerque: Bowarrow Publishing, 1995).

5. See Sherry Robinson, *Apache Voices: Their Stories of Survival as Told to Eve Ball* (Albuquerque: University of New Mexico Press, 2000), pt. 2.

6. Richard J. Perry, *Apache Reservation: Indigenous Peoples and the American State* (Austin: University of Texas Press, 1993), 5.

7. Nordhaus, *Tipi Rings*, xi.

CHAPTER 11 — PRACTICING MEDICINE

1. A lively and scholarly version is Paul G. Zolbrod, *Diné Bahane': The Navajo Creation Story* (Albuquerque: University of New Mexico Press, 1984).

2. For much more, see Emily Benedek, *The Wind Won't Know Me: A History of the Navajo-Hopi Land Dispute* (New York: Knopf, 1992).

CHAPTER 12 — THE KIN OF SACAJAWEA

1. John W. W. Mann, *Sacajawea's People: The Lemhi Shoshones and the Salmon River Country* (Lincoln: Nebraska University Press, 2004), 28–29, 34.

2. He had died a month earlier. Whether as a result of alcohol and exposure, or alcohol and a fight with one of his sons, is not known. Ibid., 35–36.

3. See Gerard A. Baker, "Mandan and Hidatsa of the Upper Missouri," in *Lewis and Clark through Indian Eyes*, ed. Alvin M. Josephy Jr. (New York: Knopf, 2006), 124–136.

4. The George sisters are, among other things, upset that the chosen spelling was Sacagawea—that of the Hidatsa, her captors. The National Park Service fold-out brochure "Lewis and Clark Trail" also uses the Sacagawea spelling, while writing that she is "believed to be a Lemhi Shoshone."

5. Kimberly Hatch, "Man between Two Worlds," *Patchwork* (Lemhi County Historical Museum of Salmon, Idaho), May 1989, 42–49, is a loving and frank biography of Wilford "Willie" George.

CHAPTER 13 — INDIAN HUMOR

1. See http://www.makah.com/whaling.htm for the Makahs' legal response to the controversy.

2. William Dietrich, *Northwest Passage: The Great Columbia River* (New York: Simon and Schuster, 1995), 52. Hopi contend Old Oraibi is the oldest continuously inhabited village in the United States.

3. The shield reads "Confederated Tribes and Bands, Yakama Nation, Treaty of 1855." Of fourteen tribes and bands, the Yakama is the most prominent. Others include the Palouse, Wenatchapam, Klinquit, and Ohce Chotes.

4. An excellent summary of the decades-long conflict may be found at http://www.tolerance.org/activity/against-current.

5. Who is M. Scott Momaday?

CHAPTER 14 — POWWOW POWER

1. According to the band's Web site, the now-named Ione—one of three groups of northern and central California Miwok—was decimated by one horror after another;

Spanish missionaries captured and enslaved them, smallpox killed them, John Sutter enslaved them (Wikipedia says Sutter "employed" them), and after gold was found near Sutter's mill, gold rush immigrants occupied what was left of Miwok land. The Ione Web site (http://www.ionemiwok.org) states, "Though our Tribe's federal recognition was reaffirmed in 1994, we remain landless to this day."

2. In *Dances with Wolves*, her family is killed by Pawnee warriors. She is rescued by Comanche warriors, who make her one of their own. Lt. John Dunbar, later Dances with Wolves (later still, Kevin Costner), rescues her from attempted suicide after her husband dies.

CHAPTER 15 — RELEARNING FOR LIFE

1. Christopher Wilson, telephone interview with the author, July 2007.

2. The program was begun in 1977 by California's Department of Corrections Resources' Development Division, with programs in four prison facilities, including San Quentin.

3. The path that led me to Henry Frank began with Insight Prison Project (http://www.InsightPrisonProject.org) based in San Rafael, California, and its executive director, Jacques Verduin. The Web site says the IPP "is dedicated to reducing recidivism, preventing re-victimization and serving public safety."

4. In an essay for an Ancient World History class, Henry critiqued Yurok author Lucy Thompson for using Christian terminology (such as "our Christ") for Yurok leaders in her book *To the American Indian: Reminiscences of a Yurok Woman* (1916; reprint, Berkeley: Heydey Books, 1991). He wondered if such usage were intended to make Native people more acceptable to white people.

CHAPTER 16 — ESKIMO ICE CREAM

1. The job was for the *America/24–7* series of state books.

2. The link is http://www.city-data.com/so/so-Kwethluk-Alaska.html.

CHAPTER 17 — ALOHA FROM HAWAI'I

1. See "1897 Petition against the Annexation of Hawaii," http://www.archives.gov/education/lessons/hawaii-petition.

Acknowledgments

The major challenge of this project was finding people of many backgrounds who were willing to talk to me. To those who were, and did, I thank them most of all for their time, their frankness, and their trust.

Although I located a number of interviewees on my own, the majority I met because of softening intermediaries, sometimes a row of them, and some not in person. My gratitude, as I picture the east-to-west arc of interviews, goes to Theda Perdue, Linda Oxendine, Laura Harris, Helen Robbins, Donald Fixico, Heather Ahtone, Cecilia Fire Thunder, Susan Masten, Kalyn Free, Randella Bluehouse, the late Carol Monpere, Cyn Rivera, Scott Ridgway, Kristi Denton Cohen, Aurolyn Stwyer, Jacques Verduin, Steve Emrick, Ruth Felt, Judy Harding, Melanie Mociun, Lorraine Thompson, and Manulele Clarke. Many thanks as well to everyone who made attempts that never bore fruit.

As a miserable fund-raiser (I still yearn for a foundation category called "de facto nonprofit for individuals"), I am especially grateful to Barbara Bencini, Mary Turnbull, the Marin Arts Council, and my beloved late cousin, Nancy Ann Owings.

To those who generously offered me a place to lay my head while away from home, I thank, in a roughly east to west line of pillows, in addition to some named above, Kathy Wahl, Carol Sibley, Pam Sweeney, LuAnn Jamieson, Marwin Begay, Jean Nahomni Mani, Karen Artichoker, Marg Elliston and Fred Harris, Emma George, Stella and Freddie Goldtooth, Ruth and Don Perdue, and Christine and Bobby Guy.

345

In the years-long course from inception to completion of this book, countless people offered advice, warnings, recommended readings, road tours, and more. Of them all, I am especially indebted (again, some sight unseen) to Paul Apodaca, Deborah Booker, Connie and Michael Brown, Beth Castle, Roxanne Dunbar-Ortiz, Luke Esty-Kendall, Malcolm Margolin, Peter Nabokov, Susanne and Jake Page, Edwin Schupman, Cris Stainbrook, and always helpful Indian-Americana librarians—John Berry of the University of California at Berkeley and Mario Klimiades of the Heard Museum. For unexpected gifts of unexpectedly helpful books, thank you John Dietz, Leah Garchik, Lindsay Miller, and John Peterson.

Undaunted transcribers Sheri Prager and Amy Smith rendered every audible word legible—no easy task considering the sometimes challenging background seasonings (powwow, restaurant, prison, car/van/truck engine) and the sometimes less than professional microphone placement and volume-level adjustment by interviewer. Sheri and Amy also both went well beyond their job description, offering such add-ons as Navajo spellings and relevant Web sites. A finicky quoter, I replayed every bit of audio as I went over every line of transcript, but with Sheri and Amy at the controls, there was rarely anything to correct. I always felt I owed them more than their invoices.

My writing group yet again listened to many chapters and improved them. Thank you Whitney Chadwick, Mary Felstiner, Carol Field, Diana Ketcham, Jean McMann, B. K. Moran, Annegret Ogden, Diana O'Hehir, and, most especially, Cyra McFadden, whom I leaned on in the final throes of wrestling my manuscript down to contractual size. Her suggested winnowings, parings, and trimmings were precisely, so to speak, what I needed. Thanks too to copyeditor Kathryn Gohl for extra finickiness.

To Ellen Levine and Leslie Mitchner, thank you for every detail.

Finally, throughout every moment, in every way, my husband, Jonathan Perdue, provided whatever was humanly possible. I thank him most of all.

Index

Abramoff, Jack, 25, 185

addictions: counselors and training in, 272, 282, 284–288; Dwanna Oldson's story about, 162–167; gambling, 24; self-awareness of, 134, 158; violence against Native women linked to, 156, 259, 320. *See also* alcohol; alcoholism; drug use

Afghanistan War, 213, 245, 304, 328

African Americans: judging based on features of, 104–105; in Lumbee ancestry, 44, 47, 55–56; music of, 131; racism against black Indians, 174–175

agriculture: child labor laws and, 2; effects of erosion on crops, 31–32; heritage of farming and sharecropping, 48, 49–50; organic debate about, 3–4; potato crops, 238, 246. *See also* blueberry harvest; corn; food

"A-ho," meaning of, 271, 275, 288

AIC. *See* American Indian Center (AIC)

AIM (American Indian Movement), 74, 147

AIO (Americans for Indian Opportunity), xxv, 337n1

Alaska: travel in, 309, 310–311, 318–319; violence against Native women in, 153. *See also* Kwethluk (Alaska); Yup'iks

Albuquerque Journal, 198, 202–203, 204

Alcatraz Island takeover (1969), xii, xxv, 284, 299

alcohol: avoidance of, 182–183, 195, 283; banned, 189, 310; child's fear of, 151; fetal alcohol effects, 156; military service and, 50; moderate approach to, 107; selling ancestral objects linked to, 113; as weapon in genocidal war, 155–156

alcoholism: in Alaska, 313–314, 320; birth mother's, 10; epidemiology of, 341n4; families' struggles with, 120–121, 133–134, 151–152, 162–164, 239–240, 278; high rate of, 53; paradox of dealing with, 207; reservations associated with, 60; violence against Native women linked to, 156, 259, 320. *See also* addictions; alcohol

Alexie, Sherman (Spokane/Coeur d'Alene), xiv

American Indian, use of term, xvii, 7. *See also* Native Americans

American Indian Center (AIC): Ansel Deon's role at, 102–103, 106; cultural outreach of, 92–99, 103–104; finances of, 106; founding of, 94

American Indian Movement (AIM), 74, 147

American Indians and Alaska Natives (AI/ANs), use of phrase, 321. *See also* Hawai'ians; Native Americans; Yup'iks; *specific tribes*

American Museum of Natural History, 115. *See also* National Museum of the American Indian

Americans for Indian Opportunity (AIO), xxv, 337n1

Amnesty International, 340n2

Apachería, use of term, 192

Apaches: bands of, 191–192, 341n3; flight from southern territory, 189; legislature's resolution to kill, 193; mourning among, 199; stereotypes of, 196. *See also* Jicarilla Apache Indian Reservation; San Carlos Apache Reservation

347

About the Author

ALISON OWINGS is the author of *Frauen: German Women Recall the Third Reich* and *Hey, Waitress! The USA from the Other Side of the Tray.* She lives in California.